T0293658

Financial Economics and Econometrics

Financial Economics and Econometrics

Editor: Douglas Walsh

MURPHY & MOORE
www.murphy-moorepublishing.com

www.murphy-moorepublishing.com

ⓂMURPHY & MOORE

Cataloging-in-Publication Data

Financial economics and econometrics / edited by Douglas Walsh.
    p. cm.
Includes bibliographical references and index.
ISBN 978-1-63987-740-9
1. Finance. 2. Economics. I. Walsh, Douglas.
HG173 .F56 2023
332--dc23

Murphy & Moore Publishing
1 Rockefeller Plaza,
New York City,
NY 10020, USA

ISBN 978-1-63987-740-9

Contents

Preface

Financial economics refers to a subfield of economics that studies the allocation and utilization of resources in markets. It typically entails the development of sophisticated models to test the variables influencing a specific decision. Financial economics is crucial in recognizing risks, making investment decisions, and determining the value of assets or securities. It has two basic aspects which include risk management and diversification, and the current value. Econometrics is a branch of economics that involves the study of economic data using mathematical and statistical techniques. There are two types of econometrics, namely, applied econometrics and theoretical econometrics. Null hypothesis testing, regression models, R-squared, t-tests, p-values, etc. are the some of the major techniques used in econometrics. It can also be utilized to make predictions about future financial or economic trends. This book elucidates the concepts and innovative models around prospective developments with respect to financial economics and econometrics. With its detailed analyses and data, it will prove immensely beneficial to professionals and students involved in these areas at various levels.

This book is the end result of constructive efforts and intensive research done by experts in this field. The aim of this book is to enlighten the readers with recent information in this area of research. The information provided in this profound book would serve as a valuable reference to students and researchers in this field.

At the end, I would like to thank all the authors for devoting their precious time and providing their valuable contribution to this book. I would also like to express my gratitude to my fellow colleagues who encouraged me throughout the process.

Editor

Financial Stress Index and Economic Activity in South Africa: New Evidence

Kehinde Damilola Ilesanmi *[iD] **and Devi Datt Tewari**

Department of Economics, Faculty of Commerce, Administration and Law, University of Zululand,
Private Bag X1001, KwaDlangezwa 3886, South Africa; TewariD@unizulu.ac.za
* Correspondence: ilesanmi.kd@gmail.com or IlesanmiK@unizulu.ac.za

Abstract: The importance of a sound and stable financial system and by extension economic stability was brought to the fore by the global financial crisis (GFC). The economic and social costs of the GFC have renewed the commitment of stakeholders in the financial sector including central banks to develop instruments and methodologies that will be useful in monitoring financial stress within the financial system and the real economy. This study contributes to the growing literature by developing a financial stress indicator for the South African financial market. The financial stress indicator (FSI) is a single aggregate indicator that is constructed to reflect the systemic nature of financial instability and also to measure the vulnerability of the financial system to both internal and external shocks. Using the principal component analysis (PCA), the results show that financial stress can be identified by the financial stress indicator. Furthermore, using a recursive Vector Autoregression (VAR) model to estimate the impact of financial stress on output and investment, the result shows that financial stress has a negative impact on economic growth and investment, though not immediately. FSI is very useful for gauging the effectiveness of government measures to mitigate the impact of financial stress. Concerted effort to stimulate investment and domestic production by relevant stakeholders is necessary to mitigate the impact of financial stress. This will go a long way to alleviating the impact of the financial stress on industrial production, employment and the economy at large.

Keywords: GFC; investment; PCA; South Africa; systemic risk

JEL Classification: E44; G1; G2; G15

1. Introduction

The importance of a sound and stable financial system and by extension economic stability was brought to the fore by the global financial crisis (GFC). The aftermath of the GFC on the financial system has led most central banks across the world to rethink and develop instruments and methodologies that will be useful in identifying, assessing and monitoring potential threats to the stability of the financial system and the economy as a whole (Ilesanmi and Tewari 2019a). The GFC has also shown that correlations across assets and banks' balance can abruptly rise, thereby causing systemic failure within the financial system (Alberola et al. 2011). According to Liao et al. (2015), systemic risk is endogenously created within the financial system due to exposure of banks to common macroeconomic factors and contagion through interbank linkages. However, it must be noted that, though individual banks' financial risks may be forecasted and curtailed, financial shocks to a single bank can quickly spread across a large number of institutions and markets, thereby threatening the whole system (Kama et al. 2013; Manizha 2014; Ilesanmi and Tewari 2019b). Early identification of a potential threat is important to put in place measures to mitigate its impact (Ilesanmi and Tewari 2019a).

Although several studies (Illing and Liu 2006; Hakkio and Keeton 2009; Holló et al. 2012; Huotari 2015; Iachini and Nobili 2016; Ilesanmi and Tewari 2019a) have been conducted to develop a simple composite index to measure stress within the financial system, there is no consensus as most of the studies differs either in terms of the number of the market segment to be included, variables to be used in each market segment, data frequency or methodologies. The financial stress indicator (FSI) is a single aggregate indicator that is constructed to reflect the systemic nature of financial instability and as well to measure the vulnerability of the financial system to both internal and external shocks. The financial stability index aims to reveal the functionality of the financial system due to uncertainty or stress and provides an aggregate measure of financial stress in the financial system and by extension the real economy. The financial system includes the money market, bond market, foreign exchange market and equity market. This study contributes to the growing literature by developing a financial stress indicator to measure financial stress in the South African financial market. This study further examined the impact of financial stress on real economic activities. The feedback effect on the real economy was also examined using the standard vector autoregression model. According to Mundra and Bicchal (2020), financial stress harms economic activities through investment and output contraction.

The remainder of this article is as follows: a literature review is provided in Section 2 while methodologies and data are dealt with in Section 3. Results and conclusions are presented in Sections 4 and 5, respectively.

2. Review of Literature

2.1. A Brief History of FSI

The financial stress index (FSI) aims to reveal the functionality of the financial system due to uncertainty or stress and to provide an aggregate measure of financial stress in the financial system as a whole which includes the money market, bond market, foreign exchange market etc. (Huotari 2015). In order words, developing FSI will enable regulatory authorities, government, policymakers and other stakeholders to understand the general condition of the financial sector. The FSI is a composite index that aggregates information from these markets to provide a single measure of stress for the whole financial system (Huotari 2015). This makes it easier to monitor the financial system and determine the likelihood of the occurrence of any financial crises. The FSI is a highly useful and appropriate dependent variable in an early signal warning model. It is also useful by macroprudential authorities during their macroprudential decision making process. Generally, FSIs are mostly calculated on a monthly basis for developed countries like the USA.

There have been numerous indicators that have been developed since the 1980s, such as the slope of the yield curve, which is based on the difference between long-term and short-term interest rates, credit risk as measured by commercial paper-Treasury bill spread and stock market trends (Ekinci 2013). The first broader financial condition, measure introduced by the Bank of Canada in the mid-1990s was named the monetary condition index (MCI), which is the weighted average changes in interest rates and exchange rates relative to their value during the base period (Ekinci 2013). MCIs are now used by policymakers as measures of monetary conditions in the economy. Soon after that, several similar indexes began to be used for monetary policy decisions by several central banks such as that of Canada, New Zealand and Sweden (Ekinci 2013). Several other indicators such as stock prices and real estate prices were also incorporated into the MCI, which made it broader; this new index became referred to as the FSI.

In 2009, the Bloomberg FCI was calculated using ten variables covering the money market, bond market as well as the equity market; it is believed to be a suitable indicator for monitoring financial conditions since it is accessible to many financial markets and has been updated daily from 1991 (Rosenberg 2009). In contrast to the Bloomberg FCI, the Citi FCI developed in 2008, which has been available from 1983, was calculated using six (6) variables. These variables include corporate spreads, money supply, equity values, mortgage rates, the trade-weighted dollar and energy prices (D'Antonio 2008). Similarly, the Deutsche Bank FCI also starts in 1983, although it differs with respect to the number of variables and methodology used. The index is made up of seven (7) variables which include the exchange rate as well as bond, stock and housing market indicators, and is calculated using principal component analysis (Hooper et al. 2010). In 2008, the OECD developed its own FCI which starts from 1995 by aggregating six financial variables. The weights were calculated based on the effects of each variable on GDP and this was done by regressing the output gap on a distributed lag of the financial indicators (Ekinci 2013). The FCI developed by the OECD differs from other FCIs in that it included variables for tightening of credit standards. In May 2009, a FSI was constructed for Turkey comprising five sub-market indexes which are the "foreign exchange market pressure index, the riskiness of the banking sector, equity markets and perceptions of uncertainty towards this market" (CBRT 2009, pp. 76–78).

Several other attempts (Illing and Liu 2006; Hakkio and Keeton 2009; Holló et al. 2012; Islami and Kurz-Kim 2014) have been made to develop a composite index for measuring financial stress. Researchers developed FSIs for the Canadian financial system, Kansas City and the Euro area. The construction of a FSI is based on the aggregation of market-specific sub-indexes which reflect the stress within a market segment though varying aggregation techniques and the number of variables used. Market segments include the equity markets, bond markets, foreign exchange markets as well as the banking sector. Major findings of these studies include the fact that FSIs can predict developments in the real economy and select risk variables based on their correlation with economic activities. More specifically, the findings of Illing and Liu (2006) captured previous stress events such as the 1992 credit losses as well as the 1998 Long-Term Capital Management (LTCM) among others.

In the same vein, Cardarelli et al. (2011) and Balakrishnan et al. (2011) developed a FSI to identify periods of financial turmoil and suggested a framework to investigate the impact of financial stress on the real economy for 17 advanced economies and emerging economies, respectively. They show that stress in the banking sector has greater effects on creating financial stress compared to the two other market segments (securities and foreign exchange) considered in the study. Also, Oet et al. (2011) developed a FSI for the United States called the Cleveland Financial Stress Index (CFSI). The CFSI was developed using daily data from 11 components reflecting four financial sectors: credit markets, equity markets, foreign exchange markets, and interbank markets. Most of the CFSI components are spreads (i.e., the interbank liquidity spread, corporate bond spread and liquidity spread) and two of the remaining CFSI components are ratios, and one is a measure of stock market volatility.

Iachini and Nobili (2016) introduced an indicator for measuring systemic risk in the Italian financial market using the portfolio aggregation theory method. This portfolio aggregation was used to capture the systemic dimension of liquidity stress. The result shows that the systemic liquidity risk indicator adequately captured extreme events that were characterized by high systemic risk.

In the case of emerging markets, Stolbov and Shchepeleva (2016) employed the PCA approach to calculate the FSI for emerging markets including Russia, China, India, Brazil, South Africa, Indonesia, Turkey, Mexico, Malaysia, Thailand, Philippines, Chile, Columbia as well as Peru. Using six variables, the results of the study show that the FSI for most emerging markets exhibited a surge around September—October 2008 and this is assumed to have been caused by the emergence of the GFC (Stolbov and Shchepeleva 2016). In this study, following the studies of Holló et al. (2012), Huotari (2015) and Ilesanmi and Tewari (2019a), a financial stress index for South Africa was developed by aggregating individual stress indicators from four different markets: the money market, bond market, equity market, and the foreign exchange market. Different aggregation methods have been used in literature such as the equal weighting method; correlation-based weighing method, principal component analysis, market size weight etc. This study employed the equal-variance and principal component analysis methods to develop a composite index for monitoring the financial system.

2.2. Financial Stress and Systemic Risk Indicators

Although it might be difficult to identify what systemic risk is since it is difficult to define and quantify, several attempts have been made to define it. According to De Bandt and Hartmann (2000) "systemic risk is defined as the systemic event that causes a particularly strong propagation of failures from one institution, market or system to another." In the words of Illing and Liu (2006), it can be referred to as shocks with negative effects on the real economy.

It is also defined as the disruption or obstruction of the financial system's ability to provide credit to all stakeholders within the economic system (Brockmeijer et al. 2011; Yellen 2010).

Although there is no consensus on the definition of financial stress, it is commonly accepted as referring to the disruption of the functioning of the financial market (Aklan et al. 2015). In order words, it is the emergence of an event or events that impair the smooth functioning of the financial system's ability to provide financial services, with attendant negative effects on the overall functioning of the entire economy. One common characteristic of financial stress is the increasing uncertainty of creditors and investors about the real value of financial assets, which in turn leads to increased volatility of asset prices. The computation of the FSI is important not only for evaluating macroeconomic conditions, but also to determine the source(s) of fragility in the financial sector.

As noted earlier, there is an increasing number of studies on FSI; however, these studies differ based on methodologies, frequency and countries. For example, Huotari (2015) in his study proposed a FSI for the Finnish financial system using the variance-equal weight (VEW), principal component analysis (PCA) and portfolio theory aggregation methods (PAM). The study utilized a formation which included the country's money market, bond market, equity market and foreign exchange markets and the banking sector. This FSI developed using the PCA and PAM captured previously known stress periods, although an FSI index produced by the VEW methods differs from the PCA and PAM by only showing stress events at the end of the sample. Kabundi and Mbelu (2020) developed a financial condition index (FCI) for the South African economy using 41 indicators, and their result revealed the strength of the FCI in signaling both domestic and foreign risk. However, as noted by Huotari (2015) using too many indicators that could constitute adding noise in the index.

Siņenko et al. (2013) developed a methodology for measuring the Latvian financial stress index and also analyzed the nature of financial stress. These results captured the changes in the Latvian financial system, as well as signaling periods of elevated stress and periods of excessively vigorous and imbalanced development of the financial system. Similar to the study of Siņenko et al. (2013), Kondratovs (2014) examined the fragility of the financial system of Latvia in comparison to the fluctuations in the global economy and changes in direction of international capital flows by creating a complex financial system stability index. The findings of the study revealed that a fall in the stability level of the Latvian financial system started in 2002 and became worse in 2005, which informed the need for policymakers to be more actively involved in preventing growing risks to the economy.

2.3. Financial Stress and Real Economy

Financial stress as explained above is the impairment of the financial system's ability to provide credit to the economy. One common characteristic of financial stress is increasing uncertainty of creditors and investors about the real value of financial assets, which in turn leads to increased volatility of asset prices (Huotari 2015). Increased volatility of asset prices makes firms more cautious in their investment decisions, while households cut back on their spending. This ultimately leads to decreased economic activity. Calculating the financial stress index is important not only for evaluating macroeconomic conditions, but also to determine the source(s) of fragility in the financial sector. Although the relationship that exists between the financial stress and the real economy is complex and may not be properly understood, it is clear that financial stress constitutes a threat to the economy due to its negative impact on households and businesses. During periods of financial stress, households and businesses tend to lower their investment and purchases due to uncertainty and tighter credit conditions (Davig and Hakkio 2010; Huotari 2015).

According to the study conducted by Hakkio and Keeton (2009), financial stress has slowed down economic activities in the United States. This is because financial stress makes credit institutions more cautious in granting loans. This has resulted in a decline in total loans granted and consequently slowed down economic activities. In the case of the Czech Republic, Malega and Horváth (2017) found that financial stress contributed to an increase in the unemployment rate.

3. Methodology and Data

3.1. Estimating Technique

There are a number of aggregation methods, including the equal weighing method (EWM), principal component analysis (PCA), regression-based weighing method, goal programming and portfolio aggregation method, among others. For the VEW method, the indicators (sub-indexes) are averaged together to produce a final measure (Cardarelli et al. 2011). With respect to the PCA, a common component which is assumed to capture the stress is extracted into many variables (Huotari 2015). In order words, the PCA assumes that each of the variables used to construct the FSI captures some aspect of financial stress. This factor, which is the first PC, becomes the FSI. The FSI also provides information on systemic stress which is not captured by the individual market stress measures, as well as making a decision about the release of the counter-cyclical capital buffer (Huotari 2015). That is to say, the FSI provides the information needed by policy makers and central banks to develop counter-cyclical buffer to cushion the effect of a financial crisis. Although the VEW method is the most commonly used aggregation method (Illing and Liu 2006, Cevik et al. 2013; Park and Mercado 2014; Malega and Horváth 2017), it does not capture the systemic nature of a stress event compared to the PCA (Hakkio and Keeton 2009). Also, the VEW method does not incorporate the correlation/co-movement between different stress indicators (Huotari 2015). This accounts for the use of PCA in addition to the VEW in this study. Another major advantage of using the PCA is that it helps in separating variables with minimal information loss. For PCA to be used, there must be sufficient correlation among the variables. This was assessed using the Kaiser-Meyer-Olkin (KMO) test statistics. It must however be noted that other aggregation techniques will be considered in future studies. The FSI is very useful for capturing the co-movement of risk from a broad array of data across different sectors. The variance-equal weight (VEW) and the principal component analysis aggregation methods were used in this study. They are explained briefly as follows:

3.1.1. Variance-Equal Weighting (VEW) Method

The variance-equal weight (VEW) is the most frequently used stress index aggregation method (Illing and Liu 2006, Cevik et al. 2013; Park and Mercado 2014; Malega and Horváth 2017). The method is the most straight forward and perhaps the most intuitive weighing method (Huotari 2015). The distance of each index from its mean is calculated. This ensures that each component in the index is given equal importance:

$$FSI_t = \sum_{i=1}^{k} \frac{X_{i,t} - \overline{X}_i}{\sigma_i} \qquad (1)$$

where k is the number of variables combined in the index, X_i is the sample mean of the variable X_i and σ_i is the sample standard deviation of the variable X_i. These variables are assumed to be normally distributed. However, the main limitation of this method is that it fails to incorporate the correlation/co-movement between different stress indicators (Huotari 2015). Therefore, the principal component analysis (PCA) was also used.

3.1.2. Principal Component Analysis (PCA)

The PCA which was developed by Pearson (1901) and Hotelling (1933) is a statistical technique which is widely used to generate a small number of artificial uncorrelated variables accounting for most of the variance of the initial multidimensional dataset, thereby arriving at condensed data representation with minimal loss of information (Sinenko et al. 2013). Each component is a linear combination of the original data and is ordered in such a way that the first component accounts for the largest share of the variance possible (see Cambón and Estévez 2016) for detailed mathematical notation). The PCA places more emphasis on variables with higher variances than on those with a low variance. Accordingly, a common component which is assumed to capture the stress is extracted from among many variables. That is, each of the indicators is believed to capture a proportion of financial stress. This factor, which is the first principal component (PC) becomes the FSI. The results will, therefore, depend on the unit of measure measurement for each variable. This implies that the PCA is best used when the variables of interest are of the same unit of measurement. The main aim is to capture the structural movements in a group of financial indicators. The forecasting ability of the FSI is tested using the Root Mean Square Error (RMSE), Mean Absolute Error (MAE), Theils Inequality Coefficient (TIC), Thiel U2 Coefficient and Symmetric MAPE.

In constructing FSIs, the first step is the selection of markets and market-specific indicators, which is followed by the transformation of the market-specific stress indicators. The second step is the selection of market-specific stress indicators to be included. Following Huotari (2015) and South African Reserve Bank (2015), four market categories (Money, bond, equity and foreign exchange) were selected.

The third step is to select variables that reflect stress in the selected market segments. After collecting the data for FSI, the variables can be grouped into sub-indexes based on volatility or co-movement of related variables. The 13 indicators used in this study were grouped into the four market segments: money, bond, equity and foreign exchange. Each of the raw indicators captures information about the stress level within each market segment. The market segment sub-indices were calculated based on a simple arithmetic average. This implies that each of the raw risk indicators is given equal weight in the sub-index.

The fourth stage is to aggregate the collected data based on the market segment into one measure. The sub-indexes were then aggregated into the final index referred to as the FSI. While aggregating the data into one measure, it is important to convert the data into a common unit of measurement for better comparisons (normalization). This helps to normalize fluctuations across variables and ensure that they are on the same scale. The methods include standardization (studying the difference in a variable level relative to an average from a reference period.), the cumulative density function (CDF) and mean/variance method (Nelson and Perli 2007; Cardarelli et al. 2011). The mean/variance method is carried out by subtracting each data point's historical (sample) mean and dividing the initial result by its standard deviation. Transformation of market-specific stress indicators was carried out using empirical normalization (Kočišová and Stavarek 2015). Through this process, all indicators were placed onto the same scale of between zero and one (0, 1). The formulae are presented below:

$$z_{ij} = \frac{x_{ij} - min_j[x_{ij}]}{max_j[x_{ij}] - min_j[x_{ij}]]} \tag{2}$$

where x_{ij} is the *jth* value of the *ith* component of FSI. This was done by subtracting the minimum value of the sample variable from each variable i and then dividing it by its range. The final step was the aggregation of these indicators into the final FSI.

Monthly data that capture financial stress in the system were utilized in this study. The data were obtained from the South Africa Reserve Bank (SARB), IMF-IFS, Bloomberg and investing.com. It must be noted that although the researcher intended to start the analysis from 2000 and continue on a daily or at most weekly basis, some of the data from that period and frequency were found to be unavailable. Monthly data from January 2006 (M1) until December 2017 (M12) were utilized. The data include 10-year government bonds (Govt. and Non-Govt), interbank rates (JIBAR), three-month Treasury bill (3MTB), interest rates (Repo rate), JSE all-share index, South African exchange rates (ZAR) against the US dollar, British pounds (GBP), and Euros (EUR) and the US 10-year bond yield. For better comparison, the unit of measurement was the US dollar.

3.2. Selection of Specific Market Stress Indicators

3.2.1. Money Market

The selection of indicators for the money market must reflect liquidity and counterparty risk in the interbank market. The variables capture some features like flight-to-quality and flight-to-liquidity effects as well as the effects of adverse selection problem on banks during stress periods, which include:

- Realized volatility of the 3-month interbank rate

Realised volatility of the 3-month interbank (JIBAR) rate (VIR) is calculated as the monthly average of the absolute daily rate of change. It is therefore calculated as the square root of the monthly sum of squared daily log returns using the formulae:

$$VIR = \sqrt{\sum_{t=1}^{n} R_t^2} \qquad (3)$$

where R is the monthly log-returns of the interbank rate, t is the trading month and n is the number of trading months. This is also used by Holló et al. 2012; Huotari 2015.

- Interbank liquidity spread

This involves the interest rate spread between the 3-month JIBAR rate and 3-month Treasury bills. This represents a measure of liquidity and counterparty risk and the convenience premium on short term Treasury papers.

$$\text{Interbank liquidity spread (ILS)} = 3\text{MJibar} - 3\text{MTB} \qquad (4)$$

where 3MJibar is the 3-month JIBAR rate and 3MTB is the 90-day Treasury bill market rate.

- Interbank cost of borrowing

To capture banking stress and as well as to measure the anxiety with which bank lend to one another, the 3-month JIBAR—Repo rate was used. This can be referred to as the interbank cost of borrowing. This indicates the risk premium that banks place on short term funds to lend to one another.

$$\text{Interbank cos}\,t\,\text{of borrowing (ICB)} = 3\text{MJibar} - \text{Repo} \qquad (5)$$

where 3MJibar is the 3-month JIBAR rate and Repo is the policy rate.

The 3-month JIBAR—Repo rate can also be used as an indicator of counterparty risk which is conceptually measured as the spread between 3-month JIBAR and Rand Overnight Deposit Swaps (RODS).

3.2.2. Bond Market

Selecting indicator indicators for the bond market must reflect the solvency and liquidity conditions in the bond market. This could include a result of increased uncertainty or the risk aversion of investors.

- The realized volatility of the 10-year government bond index

The realized volatility of the 10-year government bond index measures stress in the bond market yield spread between the 10-year government bond index and the US 10-year government index, with the same applying for the UK and the Euro. The procedure for calculating the realized volatility follows that of Equation 3. This also reflects the risks spread that investors require for investing in the South African government bond.

- Sovereign bond spread

The sovereign bond spread is measured by the difference between the South African bond yield (SABY) and that of the US (USBY).

$$\text{Sovereign bond spread (SBS)} = \text{SABY} - \text{USBY} \tag{6}$$

3.2.3. Foreign Exchange Market

The foreign exchange market is very important because of its ability to reflect fluctuations in the financial market through the exchange rate, as well as its impact of trade (both imports and exports). The indicators selected in this segment reflect movement in the foreign exchange markets.

- Realized volatility of the foreign exchange markets

Stress in the foreign exchange markets was measured by the volatility between South African Rands (ZAR) and three other major currencies, namely US dollars (USD) (VUZ), British Pounds (GBP) (VGZ) and the Euro (EUR) (VEZ). This was estimated using monthly averages of daily log returns and transformed using empirical normalization (Kočišová and Stavarek 2015). It must be noted that increased volatility reflects uncertainty in the foreign exchange markets.

- Maximum cumulative loss (CMAX)

The maximum cumulative loss (CMAX) for USD (MUZ), GBP (MGZ) and EUR (MEZ) to ZAR was used to measure the cumulative loss over the specific time frame:

$$CMAX_t = \frac{x_t}{Max\left[x \in \left(x_{t-j}\right)j = 0, 1, 2, \ldots, T\right]} \tag{7}$$

where x is the stock market index and the moving time window is determined by T (24 months). It must be noted that the CMAX compares the current value of the variable with its minimum values over sample T. This is advantageous because it makes any sharp decline in price more visible. The rolling maximum in the denominator was defined over a twenty-four (24) month period.

3.2.4. Equity Market

- Realized volatility of the equity market

The realised volatility of the total market equity (VAI) was used to capture stress in the equity market. It is calculated as the log-returns monthly sum of the all-share index:

$$VAI = \sqrt{\sum_{t=1}^{n} R_t^2} \tag{8}$$

where $RALSI$ is the monthly log returns for the all-share index.

- Maximum cumulative loss (CMAX)

The CMAX as explained earlier in Equation (7) for the all-share index (MAI). This helps in measuring the maximum cumulated loss over the time period.

$$CMAX\ (ALSI)_t = \frac{x_t}{Max\left[x \in \left(x_{t-j}\right)j = 0, 1, 2, \ldots, T\right]} \tag{9}$$

3.3. FSI and the Real Economy

It has been established in previous literature (Havránek et al. 2012; Hakkio and Keeton 2009; Cardarelli et al. 2011) that financial stress has a major impact on the real economy. Employing our newly developed FSI for South Africa, a Vector Autoregressive Model was estimated to check the impact of financial stress on the macroeconomic indicators. In this study, we employed the standard

Vector Autoregression (VAR) with a multi-variable time series. The standard VAR[1] model of order p can be written as

$$y_t = A_1 y_{t-1} + A_2 y_{t-2} + \ldots + A_p y_{t-p} + u_t. \tag{10}$$

Given K time series endogenous variable $y_t = (y_{1t}, y_{2t}, \ldots, y_{kt})'$, the VAR model can capture the dynamic interactions among the variables. $A_1, A_2 \ldots, A_p$ represents the $K \times K$ coefficient matrices to be estimated, while $u_t = (u_{1t}, u_{2t} \ldots, u_{Kt})'$ is the $Kx1$ white noise innovation process with a time-invariant, positive definite covariance matrix $E(u_t u_t') = \sum_u$. Accordingly, the u_t are independent stochastic vectors with $u_t \sim (0, \sum_u)$. The VAR model does not distinguish between the dependent and independent variables.

4. Results and Discussion

The FSIs constructed for the South African financial system using the VEW method as well as the PCA and the results are presented in this sub-section. FSIs were tested based on their capacity to reveal previously well-known periods of stress within the economy.

4.1. Descriptive Statistics

The descriptive statistics are presented in Table 1. All the indicators were standardized to values between 0 and 1 using the empirical normalization method. (Data: Supplementary Materials)

Table 1. Descriptive Statistics for the South Africa Financial Sector

Variable N	Nos of Observation	Mean	Std. Dev.	Min	Max
VIR	144	0.665735	0.143452	0	1
ILS	144	0.180793	0.137266	0	1
ICB	144	0.738199	0.101617	0	1
VBY	144	0.369467	0.129358	0	1
SBS	144	0.583882	0.210692	0	1
VUZ	144	0.44274	0.160191	0	1
VGZ	144	0.530947	0.15324	0	1
VEZ	144	0.510652	0.159521	0	1
MUZ	144	0.493765	0.293897	0	1
MGZ	144	0.577762	0.263284	0	1
MEZ	144	0.591845	0.240057	0	1
VAI	144	0.592538	0.157898	0	1
MAI	144	0.582082	0.239655	0	1
**MMS	144	-4.04×10^{-9}	1.000002	−7.26451	2.576354
**BMS	144	-4.90×10^{-9}	1	−2.77126	1.975004
**FXM	144	-1.55×10^{-9}	1.000002	−2.46544	1.700248
**EMS	144	2.06×10^{-9}	1	−2.42883	1.743836
FSI_S_KD	144	-2.99×10^{-9}	1.000003	−2.42884	1.743845

** MMS is the money market sub-index; BMS is the bond market sub-index; FXM is the foreign exchange market sub-index and EMS is the equity market sub-index.

[1] The descriptive statistics of the variables are given in Table 1. In general, the variables were selected based on international literature, previous study, systemic relevance of the variables in the South African financial system and availability.

See Lütkepohl (2006) for more details.

4.2. Construction of Sub-Indices

These indicators were grouped into four market segments (Money, bond, equity, and foreign exchange). Each of the raw indicators captures information about the stress level within each market segment. The market segment sub-indices were calculated based on a simple arithmetic average (Figure 1). This implies that each of the raw risk indicators was given equal weight in the sub-index. The indicators for each sub-index captures information about the level of stress in the specific market segment. This also implies that each of the raw liquidity risk indicators was given equal weight in the sub-index.

The sub-index for foreign exchange reached the maximum level during the 2008 global financial crisis.

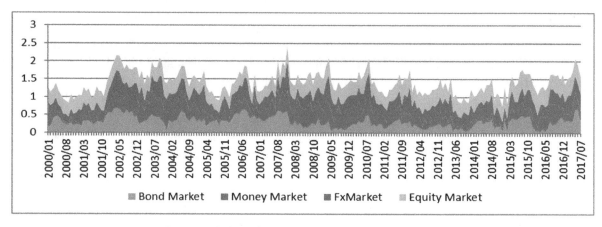

Figure 1. Sub-indices for the four market indices.

4.3. Aggregation of Sub-Indices into a Single Composite Index

4.3.1. Variance-Equal Weighting (VEW) Method

The result of the FSI using the VEW method is presented in Figure 2. This is the most common method used for estimating FSI in previous studies. It is easy to construct and interpret this method compared to other weighing methods. As noted earlier, all the indicators in each market segment were transformed using the empirical standardization method after they are aggregated using the arithmetic mean to derive each market segment sub-indices. The final FSI was then constructed using the arithmetic average of the four sub-indexes. Thus, the index values can be interpreted as the number of standard deviations from the sample mean.

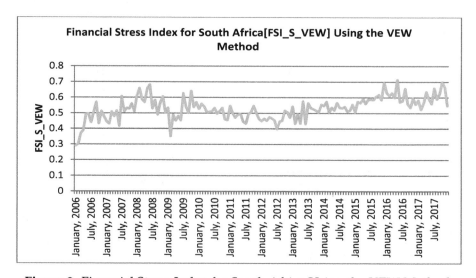

Figure 2. Financial Stress Index for South Africa Using the VEW Method.

The result as presented in Figure 2 revealed the extreme stress events caused by a global financial crisis and more of domestic crises ranging from a labor crisis, energy crisis and political uncertainty, which started in late 2015 and extended into 2016.

4.3.2. Principal Component Analysis (PCA) Method

Due to the limitation in the VEW method noted earlier, the FSI was also constructed using the PCA and is presented in Figure 3. Several other studies (Illing and Liu 2006; Hakkio and Keeton 2009; Sinenko et al. 2013; Huotari 2015) have also employed this method for the construction of FSI. For each market category, sub-indexes were then calculated by using the PCA. The PCA takes into account co-movement between stress indicators in each market segment. As noted earlier, the prerequisite for applying PCA is to assess the Kaiser-Meyer-Olkin (KMO) test statistics. In this study, the estimated KMO test statistics of 0.52 was greater than 0.5, this means we could carry out PCA to develop a FSI (See Appendix A). Table 2 presents the eigenvalue and the proportion of the four principal components captured within the market segment sub-indices. However, the first two principal components were used since their eigenvalues were greater than one (1). The Orthogonal rotation is presented in Appendix B. The first principal component (PC) captures the larger proportion of the total variation within the stress indicators. As presented in Table 2, the first PC captures 48 percent of the total variation within the indicators. Logically, the more PC is used for the FSI, the more the total variation that can be captured in the index. Nevertheless, adding more PC to the index also adds noise, which makes it difficult to identify crisis periods. Therefore, the first PC was used to estimate the FSI_S_PCA in line with the study of Levanon et al. (2015).

Table 2. Eigenvalue and Proportion of each Component in the PCA.

Components	Eigenvalue	Proportion	Cumulative
Component 1	1.91296	0.4782	0.4782
Component 2	1.23195	0.3080	0.7862
Component 3	0.500228	0.1251	0.9113
Component 4	0.354856	0.0887	1.0000

Source: Estimation.

The principal component (eigenvectors) for the first two components are presented in Table 3. The results show that the coefficient for all the market segment indicators are positive and they represent a one standard deviation change in the respective market segments from the final FSI, since all the indicators are standardized. The coefficients range from a low of 0.43 for the equity market segment to 0.53 for the foreign exchange market segment. The margin is quite small and this implies that all the markets affect the FSI_S_PCA by almost the same proportion, although the foreign exchange market contributes more to the final FSI (Table 3).

Table 3. Principal components (eigenvectors) for the first two component.

Market Segment	Component 1	Component 2	Unexplained
Money market	0.5044	−0.5148	0.1868
Bond market	0.5163	0.4458	0.2452
Equity market	0.4350	−0.4264	0.2218
Foreign exchange market	0.5383	0.5953	0.2013

Source: Estimation.

4.3.3. Identification of Stress Events

The FSI_S_PCA reflect dynamics in the surge that cause tension within the financial system. As noted earlier, the stress indicators were standardized to values between 0 and 1. This implies that a value of 0, which is the mean of the FSI_S_PCA, would mean that the financial system is experiencing an average risk level. This is therefore adopted as the threshold level above which would suggest extreme conditions or a signal of an impending crisis. The results as presented in Figure 3 revealed previous well-known financial crises. The well-known global financial crisis which began in 2007 as well as the sovereign debt crisis had some impacts on the South African financial system.

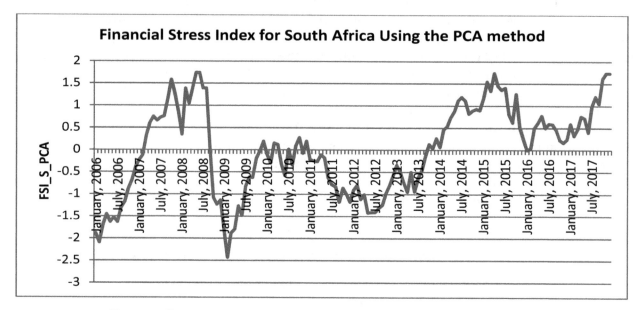

Figure 3. Financial Stress Index for South Africa Using the PCA Method.

The impact of the sub-prime mortgage crisis was then quickly shown to have implications beyond the US. The FSI_S_PCA first signaled an extreme level of stress around August 2007; this was the time when BNP Paribas suspended three investment funds that invested in asset-backed securities linked to the subprime mortgage debts which had become illiquid. Other events happened which led to a rise in the FSI_S_PCA and which reached its maximum level (1.74) around May/June 2008. At this time, global exports were down by 22 percent and Bear Stearns in the US had collapsed (Tooze 2018). By April 2008, the US Treasury and US Federal Reserve Bank had to bail out two financial institutions as the 'credit freeze' gripped the country's financial system. Like a pack of dominoes, most banks with large sub-prime exposures joined the solvency and liquidity scuffle.

As the liquidity situation became more challenging, investors began to withdraw funds from emerging markets in a so-called flight to quality as risk aversion set in. In South Africa, the Johannesburg Securities Exchange all-share index fell from a high of 32,542 on 23 May 2008 to a low of 18,066 on 21 November 2008, but volatility and uncertainty in the market were as worrying as the absolute fall in the index. New listings remained subdued throughout 2009. However, the all-share index then picked up, and it stood at 27,895 at 5 January 2010 (Padayachee 2012). The index increased above the threshold level almost during the entirety of 2008, after which there was a steady decline around February 2009. We also observed a mild increase in stress that was above the threshold of 0 in late 2010 (m4). It later rose in 2014 and reached another peak in 2015 (m4), as well as towards the end of the sample. For the latter part of the FSI_S, domestic factors such as political uncertainty played a role in this trend (Ousting of the former president Jacob Zuma in December 2017).

4.3.4. Forecast Accuracy Evaluation

In this section, the forecasting ability of the FSI_PCA was tested. The Root Mean Square Error (RMSE), Mean Absolute Error (MAE), Theils Inequality Coefficient (TIC), Thiel U^2 Coefficient and Symmetric MAPE among others were used and the results are presented in Table 4. For the models forecasting, the in-sample estimation was from 2006m1 to 2008m4, while the out-of-sample forecast was from 2008m5 to 2017m12. All the variables passed the necessary diagnostic test. The forecast was made using the dynamic model.

Table 4. Forecast model evaluation.

	RMSE	MAE	MAPE	Theil	Theil U^2	Bias	Variance	Covariance	SMAPE
FSI_F_PCA	5.0166	4.5585	4161.045	0.8659	77.4602	0.8257	0.0301	0.1442	172.5047

RMSE: Root Mean Square Error; MAE: Mean Absolute Error; MAPE: Mean Absolute Percentage Error; Theil: Theil inequality coefficient; Theil U^2 Coefficient; Bias, variance and covariance are the decomposed proportions of the Theil's Inequality coefficient.

From the results as presented in Table 4, it is clear that the FSI performs very well with regards to its forecasting ability. This is because of the RMSE (5.0166), MAE (4.5585), Theil's U coefficient (0.8659), U^2 (77.4602) and SMAPE (172.5047) of the FSI model. The same goes for the bias, variance and covariance decomposition of the Theil's coefficient. In Figure 4, the FSI for South Africa using the PCA aggregation method is plotted against the growth rate of industrial production (IPG). It can be seen that periods of high financial stress (2008m5 2015m4) are characterized by low industrial production, though with some time lag as it takes a while for stress to affect industrial output. Also, in the forecasted FSI values plotted in Figure 5, it can be seen that the 2008/09 GFC was picked as well as the domestic crises towards the end of the sample period.

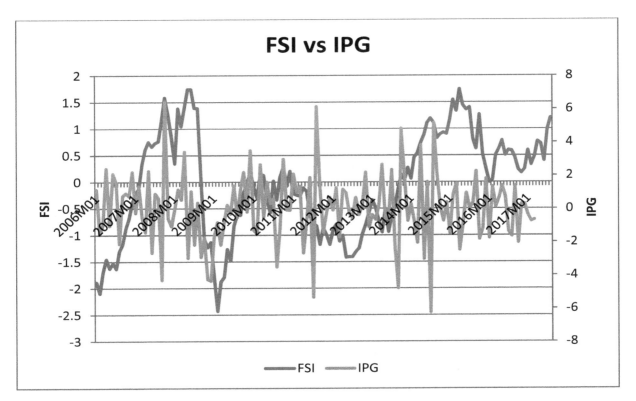

Figure 4. FSI for South Africa using the PCA and the growth rate of industrial production (IPG).

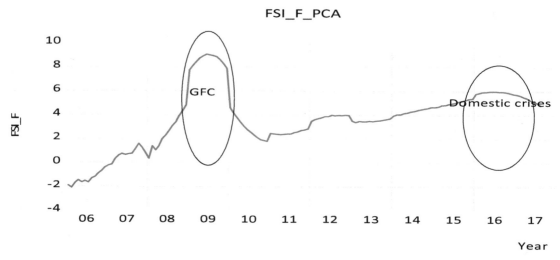

Figure 5. FSI forecast (FSI_F) for South Africa using the PCA.

The results as presented in Figure 5 show that both domestic and international shock created uncertainty in the South African financial system. On the international scene, we have the financial crisis while on the domestic scene we have slow growth, a labor crisis and an energy crisis, coupled with political uncertainty.

4.4. FSI and the Real Economy

To avoid spurious regression results, one of the major requirements of time series analysis is to test for stationarity. This study employed the Augmented Dickey-Fuller (ADF) method to test the stationarity of the variables and the result is presented in Table 5. It must be noted that the variables investment (INV) proxied by the gross fixed capital formation and industrial production (IDP) which is the proxy for economic output are in logged form, except for the FSI which is in index form.

Table 5. ADF Stationarity Test Result.

Variables	T Statistic	Critical Value (5%)	Lag Length (Automatic—Based on SIC)	Integrated Order	Restriction
FSI	−2.388850	−2.881685	0	I(0)	Constant
D(FSI)	−11.73655	−2.881830	0	I(1) *	Constant
INV	−2.092949	−2.882748	0	I(0)	Constant
D(INV)	−3.717822	−2.883930	13	I(1) *	Constant
IDP	−2.104219	−2.881830	1	I(0)	Constant
D(IDP)	−15.46115	−2.881830	0	I(1) *	Constant

Source: Estimation * means significant at a 5 percent level.

The ADF test as presented in Table 5 indicates that the variables FSI, INV and IDP exhibit a unit root problem, which means that they are not stationary at levels. This is because their estimated test statistic values are not more negative than their critical values at the 5 percent level. For stationary of the series to be accomplished, the test for the series was carried out at first difference. The result of the test at first difference shows that all the series are stationary, that is, they are integrated of order one I(1). Having established the order of the integration of the variables of interest, it is important to identify the appropriate lag length for the estimation. To select the lag order of the VAR, the information criteria approach was applied. The sequential modified LR test statistic (each test at 5% level) (LR), Final prediction error (FPE), Akaike information criterion (AIC), Schwarz information criterion (SIC) and Hannan-Quinn information criterion (HQ) lag lengths information criterion was employed to determine the lag length, and we chose 3 lag length for the estimated VAR (See Appendix C).

   Furthermore, the study employed the Cholesky impulse response to the impact of financial stress on investment and output proxied by industrial production. It must be noted that the impulse response function indicates the effect of one standard deviation shocks to one of the innovations on the adjustment path of the variables. The impulse response function reflecting the direction and magnitude of the linkages between the FSI based on the principal components as the aggregation method and the real economy is presented in Figure 6A,B.

Response to Cholesky One S.D. (d.f. adjusted) Innovations ± 2 S.E.

Response of IDP to FSI

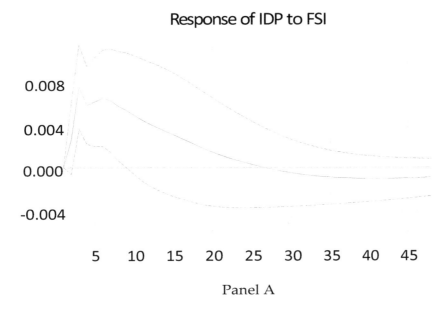

Panel A

Response to Cholesky One S.D. (d.f. adjusted) Innovations ± 2 S.E.

Response of IDP to INV

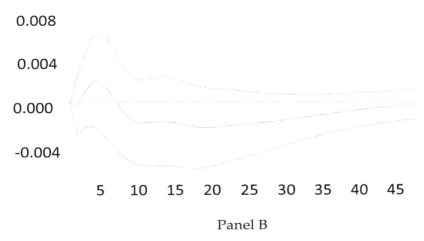

Panel B

Figure 6. (A,B) Impulse Response between Financial stress index and the real economy[2].

---

[2]   Note: FSI stands for South African financial stress index using the PCA method; IDP for industrial production which was proxied by manufacturing output; INV for investment rate which is proxied by gross fixed capital formation.

The result of the IRF as shown in panel a of Figure 6 indicates that with a one-unit shock in FSI, IDP first responds positively and thereafter began to fall after 3 months until it becomes negative. It must be noted that the point where the IRF becomes negative corresponds to the peak of the FSI.

This corresponds to the study of Stolbov and Shchepeleva (2016). During this period, domestic output fell significantly. Specifically, the manufacturing sector contracted by 20 percent during the period of the crisis, with the majority of job losses coming from the sector (Coleman 2009). The result, therefore, indicates that though the immediate impact of financial stress is not pronounced, it does have a negative future impact of output. This is similar to the study of Sahoo (2020) in the case of India. In this study, it was revealed that financial stress does harm growth but with a certain time lag. Furthermore, the results indicated in panel b of Figure 6 show that investment falls during financial stress periods but only after about 7 months. The highest decline in investment due to financial shock seems to occur approximately a year into the shock. The result is similar to the study of Malega and Horváth (2017). This, therefore, implies that there should be a concerted effort to stimulate investment and domestic production by relevant stakeholders to mitigate the impact of financial stress.

5. Conclusions

This study contributes to the existing body of knowledge by constructing a financial stress index for South Africa, as well as by examining its effects on the real economy. The construction of the financial stress index is important, as it combines the underlying factors in the various segments of the economy at any given point in time. The FSI is also useful and appropriate as the dependent variable in an early signal warning model. It can further be used to gauge the effectiveness of government measures to mitigate the impact of financial stress. A Financial stress index was constructed for the South African financial system using monthly series for 13 indicators, which were grouped into four (4) sub-indices: the money market, bond market, foreign exchange market, and the real estate market and equity market. The VEW and PCA methods were used in the aggregation of the indicators.

The result indicates that extreme values of FSIs are associated with well-known financial stress cases. It must be noted that the FSI constructed based on PCA provides importance to indicators with higher volatility. The result shows that both the domestic and international shocks created uncertainty in the South African financial system. On the international scene, we have the financial crisis while on the domestic scene we have slow growth, a labor crisis and political uncertainly. Furthermore, it was revealed that financial stress also affected domestic production and investment negatively, though not immediately. A concerted effort to stimulate investment and domestic production by relevant stakeholders is necessary to mitigate the impact of financial stress. This will go a long way to alleviating the impact of the financial stress on industrial production, employment and the economy at large.

Author Contributions: Conceptualization, methodology, software, formal analysis, writing—original draft preparation, writing—review and editing, K.D.I.; writing—review and editing, supervision, D.D.T. All authors have read and agreed to the published version of the manuscript.

Appendix A. Kaiser-Meyer-Olkin Measure of Sampling Adequacy

Variable	Kmo
Money market	0.5025
Bond market	0.5482
Equity market	0.5448
Foreign exchange market	0.4895
Overall	0.5219

Appendix B. Orthogonal Rotation

Principal components/correlation Number of obs				144
Number of comp.				2
Trace				4
Rotation: orthogonal varimax (Kaiser off) Rho				0.7862
Component	Variance	Difference	Proportion	Cumulative
Comp1	1.60838	0.071834	0.4021	0.4021
Comp2	1.53654		0.3841	0.7862
Rotated components				
Variable	Comp1	Comp2	Unexplained	
Money market	0.7193	−0.0454	0.1868	
Bond market	0.0857	0.6767	0.2452	
Equity market	0.6853	0.043	0.2218	
Foreign exchange market	−0.0747	0.7336	0.2013	
Component rotation matrix				
	Comp1	Comp2		
Comp1	0.7435	0.6688		
Comp2	−0.6688	0.7435		

Appendix C. VAR Lag Order Selection Criteria

VAR Lag Order Selection Criteria
Endogenous variables: IDP FSI INV
Exogenous variables: C
Date: 07/14/20 Time: 15:35
Sample: 2006M01 2017M12
Included observations: 139

Lag	LogL	LR	FPE	AIC	SC	HQ
0	231.5556	NA	7.49×10^{-9}	−3.288570	−3.225236	−3.262832
1	734.8705	977.6620	6.10×10^{-9}	−10.40101	−10.14768	−10.29807
2	807.1346	137.2499	2.46×10^{-9}	−11.31129	−10.86795	−11.13113
3	850.8368	81.11628 *	1.49×10^{-9} *	−11.81060 *	−11.17726 *	−11.55323 *
4	855.5381	8.523214	1.59×10^{-9}	−11.74875	−10.92541	−11.41417
5	863.6863	14.42053	1.61×10^{-9}	−11.73649	−10.72315	−11.32470

* indicates lag order selected by the criterion; LR: sequential modified LR test statistic (each test at 5% level); FPE: Final prediction error; AIC: Akaike information criterion; SC: Schwarz information criterion; HQ: Hannan-Quinn information criterion.

References

1. Aklan, Nejla, Mehmet Çinar, and Akay Hülya. 2015. Financial Stress and Economic Activity Relationship in Turkey: Post-2002 Period. *Yonetim Ve Ekonomi* 22: 567–80.
2. Alberola, Enrique, Carlos Trucharte, and Juan Luis Vega. 2011. Central Banks And Macroprudential Policy—Some Reflections from the Spanish Experience. *Documentos Ocasionales-Banco de España* 5: 5–26. [CrossRef]
3. Balakrishnan, Ravi, Stephan Danninger, Selim Elekdag, and Irina Tytell. 2011. The Transmission Of Financial Stress From Advanced To Emerging Economies. *Emerging Markets Finance And Trade* 47: 40–68.
4. Brockmeijer, Jan, Moretti Marina, Osinski Jacek, Blancher Nicholas, Gobat Jeanne, Jassaud Nadege, Lim Cheng Hoon, Loukoianova Elena, Mitra Srobona, Nier Erlend, and et al. 2011. Macro Prudential Policy: An Organizing Framework. *IMF*, March 14.
5. Cambón, Mª Isabel, and Leticia Estévez. 2016. A Spanish Financial Market Stress Index (Fmsi). *The Spanish Review of Financial Economics* 14: 23–41.
6. Cardarelli, Roberto, Selim Elekdag, and Subir Lall. 2011. Financial Stress And Economic Contractions. *Journal of Financial Stability* 7: 78–97. [CrossRef]
7. Central Bank of the Republic of Turkey. 2009. *Financial Stability Report*; Central Bank of the Republic of Turkey:

Novermber 2006. vol. 9. Available online: https://www.tcmb.gov.tr/wps/wcm/connect/726264e3-e640-47f5- 9aac-e4c237923b23/fulltext9.pdf?MOD=AJPERES&CACHEID=ROOTWORKSPACE-726264e3-e640-47f5-   9aac-e4c237923b23-m3fw7hd (accessed on 10 January 2017).

8.   Cevik, Emrah Ismail, Sel Dibooglu, and Ali M. Kutan. 2013. Measuring Financial Stress in Transition Economies. *Journal of Financial Stability* 9: 597–611. [CrossRef]

9.   Coleman, E. 2009. South Africa's Response to the Global Economic Crisis: Ministerial Briefing. Available online: https://pmg.org.za/committee-meeting/10717/ (accessed on 9 November 2020).

10. D'Antonio, Peter. 2008. *A View of the U.S. Subprime Crisis. Ema Special Report.* Edited by Robert Diclemente and Kermit Schoenholtz. New York: Citigroup Global Markets Inc., pp. 26–28.

11. Davig, Troy, and Craig Hakkio. 2010. *What Is the Effect Of Financial Stress on Economic Activity.* Economic Review. Kansas City: Federal Reserve Bank of Kansas City, vol. 95, pp. 35–62.

12. De Bandt, Olivier, and Philipp Hartmann. 2000. Systemic Risk: A Survey. CEPR Discussion Papers. p. 2634. Availableonline: https://papers.ssrn.com/sol3/papers.cfm?abstract_id=258430 (accessed on 10 January 2016).

13. Ekinci, Aykut. 2013. Financial Stress Index For Turkey. *Doğuş Üniversitesi Dergisi* 14: 213–29. [CrossRef]

14. Hakkio, Craig S., and William R. Keeton. 2009. Financial Stress: What Is It, How can It Be Measured, and Why Does It Matter? *Economic Review* 94: 5–50.

15. Havránek, Tomáš, Roman Horváth, and Jakub Matějů. 2012. Monetary Transmission and the Financial Sector in the Czech Republic. *Economic Change and Restructuring* 45: 135–55. [CrossRef]

16. Holló, Daniel, Manfred Kremer, and Marco Lo Duca. 2012. CISS—A Composite Indicator of Systemic Stress in The Financial System. Available online: https://papers.ssrn.com/sol3/papers.cfm?abstract_id=2018792 (accessed on 10 January 2017).

17. Hooper, Peter, Slok Torsten, and Dobridge Christine. 2010. *Improving Financial Conditions Bode Well For Growth.* Global Economic Perspectives. Frankfurt: Deutsche Bank.

18. Hotelling, Harold. 1933. Analysis of a Complex of Statistical Variables into Principal Components. *Journal of Educational Psychology* 24: 417. [CrossRef]

19. Huotari, Jarkko. 2015. Measuring Financial Stress—A Country Specific Stress Index for Finland. Available online: https://papers.ssrn.com/sol3/papers.cfm?abstract_id=2584378 (accessed on 10 January 2017).

20. Iachini, Eleonora, and Stefano Nobili. 2016. Systemic Liquidity Risk And Portfolio Theory: An Application To The Italian Financial Markets. *The Spanish Review of Financial Economics* 14: 5–14. [CrossRef]

21. Ilesanmi, Kehinde Damilola, and Devi Datt Tewari. 2019a. Developing a Financial Stress Index for the Nigerian Financial System. *African Journal of Business And Economic Research* 14: 135–57. [CrossRef]

22. Ilesanmi, Kehinde Damilola, and Devi Datt Tewari. 2019b. Management of shadow banks for economic and financial stability in South Africa. *Cogent Economics & Finance* 7: 1–13. [CrossRef]

23. Illing, Mark, and Ying Liu. 2006. Measuring Financial Stress in a Developed Country: An Application to Canada. *Journal of Financial Stability* 2: 243–65. [CrossRef]

24. Islami, Mevlud, and Jeong-Ryeol Kurz-Kim. 2014. A Single Composite Financial Stress Indicator and Its Real Impact in the Euro Area. *International Journal of Finance & Economics* 19: 204–11.

25. Kabundi, Alain, and Asithandile Mbelu. 2020. Estimating A Time-Varying Financial Conditions Index for South Africa. *Empirical Economics*, 1–28. [CrossRef]

26. Kama, Ukpai, M. Adigun, and Olubukola Adegbe. 2013. *Issues and Challenges for the Design and Implementation of Macro-Prudential Policy in Nigeria.* Occasional Paper No. 46. Abuja: Central Bank of Nigeria.

27. Kočišová, Kristína, and Daniel Stavarek. 2015. Banking Stability Index: New Eu Countries after Ten Years of Membership (No. 0024). Available online: http://www.iivopf.cz/images/Working_papers/WPIEBRS_24_ Kocisova_ Stavarek.pdf (accessed on 10 January 2018).

28. Kondratovs, Kirils. 2014. Modelling Financial Stability Index for Latvian Financial System. *Regional Formation and Development Studies* 3: 118–30.

29. Levanon, Gad, Jean-Claude Manini, Ataman Ozyildirim, Brian Schaitkin, and Jennelyn Tanchua. 2015. Using Financial Indicators to Predict Turning Points in the Business Cycle: The Case of the Leading Economic Index for the United States. *International Journal of Forecasting* 31: 426–45. [CrossRef]

30. Liao, Shuyu, Elvira Sojli, and Wing Wah Tham. 2015. Managing Systemic Risk in The Netherlands. *International Review of Economics and Finance* 40: 231–45. [CrossRef]

31. Lütkepohl, H. 2006. Structural vector autoregressive analysis for cointegrated variables. *Allgemeines Statistisches Archiv* 90: 75–88.

32. Malega, Ján, and Roman Horváth. 2017. Financial Stress in the Czech Republic: Measurement and Effects on the Real Economy. *Prague Economic Papers* 26: 257–68. [CrossRef]

33. Manizha, Sharifova. 2014. *Essays on Measuring Systemic Risk*. Santa Cruz: University of Califonia Santa Cruz, Available online: http://Scholar.Google.Com/Scholar?Hl=En&Btng=Search&Q=Intitle:Electronic+Theses+And+Dissertations+Uc+Santa+Cruz#0 (accessed on 10 January 2017).

34. Mundra, Sruti, and Motilal Bicchal. 2020. Evaluating Financial Stress Indicators: Evidence From Indian Data. *Journal of Financial Economic Policy*. [CrossRef]

35. Nelson, William R., and Roberto Perli. 2007. Selected Indicators of Financial Stability. *Risk Measurement And Systemic Risk* 4: 343–72.

36. Oet, Mikhail V., Ryan Eiben, Timothy Bianco, Dieter Gramlich, and Stephen J. Ong. 2011. The Financial Stress Index: Identification of Systemic Risk Conditions. Working Papers of the Federal Reserve Bank of Cleveland. pp. 11–30. Available online: https://papers.ssrn.com/sol3/papers.cfm?abstract_id=1917727 (accessed on 10 January 2020).

37. Padayachee, Vishnu. 2012. Global economic recession: Effects an implications for South Africa at a time of political challenges. Paper presented at the 20th anniversary LSE Department of International Development Conference, September 2011, viewed 23 May 2013. Available online: http://www. lse.ac.uk/internationalDevelopment/20thAnniversaryConference/ImpactoftheGlobalFC.pdf (accessed on 10 November 2020).

38. Park, Cyn-Young, and Rogelio V. Mercado Jr. 2014. Determinants of Financial Stress in Emerging Market Economies. *Journal of Banking & Finance* 45: 199–224.

39. Pearson, Karl. 1901. Principal Components Analysis. *The London, Edinburgh, and Dublin Philosophical Magazine and Journal of Science* 6: 559. [CrossRef]

40. Rosenberg, Michael. 2009. Financial Conditions Watch. *Bloomberg*, December 3.

41. Sahoo, Jayantee. 2020. Financial Stress Index, Growth And Price Stability in India: Some Recent Evidence. *Transnational Corporations Review*, 1–15. [CrossRef]

42. South African Reserve Bank. 2015. *Financial Stability Review*, 2nd ed. Pretoria: SARB.

43. Siņenko, Nadežda, Deniss Titarenko, and Mikus Āriņš. 2013. The Latvian Financial Stress Index As an Important Element of the Financial System Stability Monitoring Framework. *Baltic Journal of Economics* 13: 87–113. [CrossRef]

44. Stolbov, Mikhail, and Maria Shchepeleva. 2016. Financial Stress in Emerging Markets: Patterns, Real Effects, and Cross Country Spillovers. *Review of Development Finance* 6: 71–81. [CrossRef]

45. Tooze, Adam. 2018. The Forgotten History of the Financial Crisis: What the World Should Have Learned in 2008. Available online: https://www.foreignaffairs.com/articles/world/2018-08-13/forgotten-history-financial-crisis (accessed on 10 March 2019).

46. Yellen, Janet L. 2010. Macroprudential Supervision and Monetary Policy in the Post-Crisis World. *Business Economics* 46: 3–12. [CrossRef]

2

Portfolio Optimization-Based Stock Prediction using Long-Short Term Memory Network in Quantitative Trading

Van-Dai Ta⬤, Chuan-Ming Liu *⬤ and Direselign Addis Tadesse⬤

Department of Computer Science and Information Engineering, National Taipei University of Technology, Taipei 106, Taiwan; t104999002@ntut.edu.tw (V.-D.T.); t106999405@ntut.edu.tw (D.A.T.)
* Correspondence: cmliu@ntut.edu.tw

Abstract: In quantitative trading, stock prediction plays an important role in developing an effective trading strategy to achieve a substantial return. Prediction outcomes also are the prerequisites for active portfolio construction and optimization. However, the stock prediction is a challenging task because of the diversified factors involved such as uncertainty and instability. Most of the previous research focuses on analyzing financial historical data based on statistical techniques, which is known as a type of time series analysis with limited achievements. Recently, deep learning techniques, specifically recurrent neural network (RNN), has been designed to work with sequence prediction. In this paper, a long short-term memory (LSTM) network, which is a special kind of RNN, is proposed to predict stock movement based on historical data. In order to construct an efficient portfolio, multiple portfolio optimization techniques, including equal-weighted modeling (EQ), simulation modeling Monte Carlo simulation (MCS), and optimization modeling mean variant optimization (MVO), are used to improve the portfolio performance. The results showed that our proposed LSTM prediction model works efficiently by obtaining high accuracy from stock prediction. The constructed portfolios based on the LSTM prediction model outperformed other constructed portfolios-based prediction models such as linear regression and support vector machine. In addition, optimization techniques showed a significant improvement in the return and Sharpe ratio of the constructed portfolios. Furthermore, our constructed portfolios beat the benchmark Standard and Poor 500 (S&P 500) index in both active returns and Sharpe ratios.

Keywords: stock prediction; LSTM; portfolio optimization; quantitative trading

1. Introduction

A portfolio is defined as a collection of investment assets. Portfolio management refers to the process of investment decision making based on customized tactical investment strategies to match maximize the return for each investing time horizon. There are two popular approaches to manage the investment portfolio: traditional and quantitative. Both approaches share some common characteristics such as investigating a small set of key-driving factors of equity values, analyzing historical data to estimate these key drivers, adopting eligibility criteria for stock-selection decisions, and evaluating the performance over time. However, while traditional portfolio management relies heavily on the judgment depth analysis, regime shifts, key characteristics, and qualitative factors, quantitative portfolio management focuses on universe exploration, discipline, verification, risk management, and lower fees. Not only can it uncover mode opportunities, but it can also do a better job of controlling unintended risks [1].

Quantitative trading consists of trading strategies based on quantitative investment analysis, which relies on mathematical models to design an automated trading system. In quantitative trading, portfolio construction is the process of selecting and allocating investment on multiple stocks, which can be understood as diversification in quantitative trading in order to minimize the risk in trading. Market trend, entry and exit trade, price history, and volume are the key factors for each quantitative trading strategy. Developing an accurate forecasting model is considered as the most critical process to construct an efficient portfolio in the quantitative approach. In quantitative trading, stock prediction plays an important role in forecasting the movement of the market in general or a particular stock. Forecasting the stock price has been considered as one of the most challenging tasks in the financial market owing to the complexity of multivariate time series attributes as well as the amount of involved financial data. Numerous studies have been carried out to enhance prediction accuracy such as statistical and machine learning approaches [2]. Recently, artificial intelligence (AI) and deep learning algorithms offer a number of potential advantages over existing traditional prediction models on both accuracy and decision-making support. Deep learning algorithms allow for designing multiple trading strategies that are implemented consistently and are able to adapt to a real-time market [3,4]. Although deep learning has been extensively studied for its potentials in stock prediction, little attention has been paid to take advantage of the stock prediction phase to construct efficient quantitative portfolios. In this paper, a special variation of recurrent neural network (RNN), long short-term memory (LSTM), is proposed to build a prediction model for the stock price prediction, and then portfolio optimization techniques are applied to leverage the prediction results. Multiple quantitative portfolios are constructed based on a strategic asset allocation trading strategy. For each experiment, the prediction model achieves high accuracy in prediction, and our constructed portfolios have a considerable return in multiple predicted time periods compared with actual trading. The constructed portfolios outperform to the benchmark Standard and Poor 500 (S&P 500) index in terms of active return and risk control. The main contributions of this paper are summarized as follows:

- The LSTM prediction model was proposed to predict stock price in order to construct and optimize portfolios in quantitative trading.
- Presenting a comparison between LSTM prediction model performance to gated recurrent units (GRUs) and other conventional machine learning models such as linear regression (LR) and support vector regression (SVR) for stock prediction.
- Simulation modeling and optimization modeling approaches were used to optimize portfolios in quantitative trading.
- Finally, portfolio performance evaluation for the constructed portfolios was conducted in which our constructed portfolios outperform the benchmark on both active return and risk control.

The remaining part of the paper is structured as follows. The basic concepts in quantitative trading and related work are presented in Section 2. The proposed LSTM prediction models for stock prediction and portfolio optimization techniques are discussed in Section 3. The experiment and results are presented in Section 4. Finally, conclusions and discussions are summarized in Section 5.

2. Background and Literature Review

2.1. Fundamentals of Quantitative Trading

A typical system for quantitative investment management is outlined in Figure 1. The first fundamental piece of the system is the data collection process, in which data can be gathered from external sources, from a data vendor, or from proprietary research. Generally, there are two types of financial data structures: time-series data and cross-sectional data [5]. Data cleaning and preprocessing are the main tasks in order to get reliable data sources stored in the data warehouse. The role of the modeling process mainly focuses on building accurate prediction, statistical analysis, and optimization models. Finally, the results of the analysis are visualized and become the criteria for investment decision-making. The last two stages: modeling and analytics, are often employed in an iterative process of evaluating trends, determining strategies, backtesting, and assessing portfolio performance.

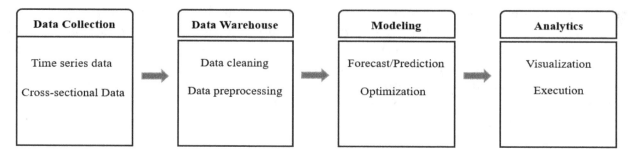

Figure 1. A type of quantitative investment management system.

Quantitative trading is an automated trading system in which the trading strategies and decisions are conducted by a set of mathematical models. The idea of quantitative trading is designed to leverage statistical mathematics, computer algorithms, and computational resources for high-frequency trading systems, which aims to minimize risk and maximize return based on the historical performance of the encode strategies tested against historical financial data. In quantitative portfolio management, quantitative trading is considered as the new era of trading that provides investors a variety of benefits from efficient execution to less transaction costs, as well as take advantage of technical tactics to improve portfolio performance. As the advance of computational resources, trading systems are required to digest massive financial data under various formats and quickly reacted to the changing of market conditions. Quantitative trading is extremely well suited for a high-frequency trading system. It became popular in the early 2000s. By 2005, it accounted for about 25% of the total volume. The industry faced an acceleration of quantitative trading, where volumes increased threefold to 75% in 2009. Quantitative trading also provides investors with many benefits such as lower commissions, anonymity, control, discipline, transparency, access, competition, and reduced transaction costs [6]. A typical quantitative trading system has five modules: alpha model, risk model, transaction model, portfolio construction model, and execution model. Quantitative trading strategy workflow consists of six stages: data collection, data preprocessing, trade analysis, portfolio construction, back-testing, and execution [7].

2.2. Quantitative Portfolio Management

2.2.1. Portfolio Construction

Portfolio construction attempts to construct an efficient portfolio that maximizes expected return for a given level of risk, or equivalently, minimizes the risk for a given expected return on a specific investment time horizon. In general, portfolio construction is the decision making about asset allocation and security selection. Asset allocation is often used to describe the money management strategy that designates how capital should be distributed into various asset classes, or broad types of investments such as stocks, bonds, commodities, and cash within an investment portfolio. Most asset allocation techniques fall within six distinct strategies: strategic asset allocation, tactical asset allocation, dynamic asset allocation, constant-weight asset allocation, insured asset allocation, and integrated asset allocation [8]. On the basis of investment strategy, risk tolerance, and liability utilization, the portfolio construction strategy can be classified as either active or passive portfolio. Security selection is the process of identifying individual securities within a certain asset class that will make up the portfolio. Security selection comes after the asset allocation has been set. After the asset allocation strategy has been developed, securities must be selected to construct the portfolio and populate the allocation targets according to the strategy. While asset allocation is based on investing strategies, security selection heavily relies on a prediction or forecast. Hence, a precise investing strategy making sure a portfolio has the right mix of assets to suit individual circumstances, investment objectives, and attitude to risk with the highly accurate prediction model is the key to determine the expected portfolio return. There are three key inputs for portfolio construction: expected return, variance of asset returns (volatility), and correlation (or covariance) of asset returns. The expected return of a portfolio provides an estimate of how much return one can get from a portfolio. The variance gives an estimate of the risk that an investor is taking while holding that portfolio. The returns and the risk of the portfolio depend on the returns and risks of the individual stocks and their corresponding shares in the portfolio.

Quantitative portfolio risk management often relies on statistical measures related to the spread or the tails or distribution of portfolio returns. Such measures include variance and standard deviation (spread), coefficient of variation (risk relative to mean), and percentiles of the distribution (tails). The concept of risk in finance investment is captured in many ways. However, the basic and most widely used one is concerned with risk as an uncertain variable that will fall from what one expects. Therefore, a natural way to define a measure of uncertainty is as the average spread or dispersion of a distribution. There are two aspects of risk: the distances between possible values and the expectation, and the probabilities of attaining the various possible values. Two measures that describe the spread of the distribution are variance and standard deviation, in which the standard deviation is the square root of the variance. The higher spread or dispersion indicates a higher variance/standard deviation that could be considered a higher risk.

The idea behind covariance is to measure simultaneous deviations from the means for two random variables. The problem with covariance is that its units are products of the original units or the two random variables, so the value for covariance is difficult to interpret. The correlation coefficient divides the covariance by the product of the standard deviations of the two random variables.

2.2.2. Portfolio Optimization

In general, portfolio optimization techniques are proposed to optimal asset allocation in order to maximize a portfolio return and minimize its risk. Modern portfolio theory was a theory on how risk-averse investors can construct portfolios to optimize or maximize expected return based on a given level of risk, emphasizing that risk is always an inherent part of higher reward [9]. Sharpe further introduced the industry to the capital asset pricing model (CAPM), which in the simplest forms, was a technique to combine the market portfolio with a risk-free asset to further improve the set of risk-return above the efficient frontier [10]. Modern portfolio theory and capital market theory provide a framework to specify and measure investment risk and to develop relationships between expected return and risk. These relationships are called asset pricing models. The arbitrage pricing theory (APT) as an alternative to the CAPM was developed in the work of [11]. Unlike in the CAPM, markets were assumed as perfectly efficient; APT was a multi-factor asset pricing model based on the idea that an asset's returns can be predicted using the linear relationship between the asset's expected return and a number of macroeconomic variables that capture systematic risk. The Fama French three-factor model was an asset pricing model that expands on the CAPM by adding size risk and value risk factors to the market risk factors. This model considers the fact that value and small-cap stocks outperform markets on a regular basis. By including these two additional factors, the model adjusts for this outperforming tendency, which is thought to make it a better tool for evaluating manager performance [12]. The Black–Litterman model was essentially a combination of two main portfolio theories: the CAPM and the modern portfolio theory [13]. The main benefit of the Black–Litterman model is that it allows the portfolio manager to use it as a tool for producing a set of expected returns within the mean-variance optimization framework. In addition to developing portfolio theories as the principle of portfolio management, multiple optimization techniques have been proposed to extend the impact of modern portfolio theory. A 60-year review of different approaches developed to address the challenges encountered when using portfolio optimization in practice, such as the transaction costs, portfolio constraints, and estimates errors was provided in [14]. Mathematical optimization has also attracted widespread interest in multi-objective optimization. There exist a whole series of optimization algorithms such as convex programming, integer programming, linear programming, and stochastic programming developed to solve optimization problems not only for linear constraints but also for random constraints [15,16]. Metaheuristic is a subfield of computational intelligence that represents an efficient way to deal with complex optimization problems and is applicable to both continuous and combinatorial optimization problems. Evolutionary algorithms such as genetic algorithms have shown an effective impact on complex objectives and constraint optimization tasks [17]. Much research in recent years has focused on uncertainty in financial investment. Probabilistic programming techniques have also been applied to handle the uncertainty of the financial markets to support portfolio selection. The fuzzy set theory has been widely used to solve many practical problems, including financial risk management. Using fuzzy approaches, quantitative analysis, qualitative analysis, experts' knowledge, and investors' subjective strategies can be better integrated into a portfolio selection model [18]. One significant difference between the discussed approaches and this work is that the input values such as expected returns and risk for optimization models, which either are calculated by a mathematical or statistical model, are based on historical data. In quantitative trading, the expected return and risk are calculated by the alpha and risk models, respectively. In other words, input values for the optimization model are calculated based on the prediction model. Optimization is performed on predicted data, which is an important requirement for active portfolio management in quantitative trading, where dynamic and large-scale portfolio optimization is the top priority.

2.2.3. Portfolio Performance Evaluation

Portfolio performance evaluation is taken to test the notion of market efficiency. The evaluation process is conducted for three important benefits: increase efficiency, monitor risk, and analyze returns. There are a variety of different measures that can be used to evaluate portfolio performance. The ability to derive above-average returns for a given risk class and the ability to diversify the portfolio completely to eliminate all unsystematic risk, relative to the portfolio's benchmark, are two desirable attributes for an efficient portfolio. The performance evaluation methods generally fall into two categories, namely conventional and risk-adjusted methods [19]. The most widely used conventional methods include benchmark comparison and style comparison. The risk-adjusted methods adjust returns in order to take account of differences in risk levels between the managed portfolio and the benchmark portfolio. The risk-adjusted methods are preferred to conventional methods. Some of the most common metrics of portfolio performance are listed in the work of [20].

2.3. Deep Learning in Stock Prediction

With the enormous growth of financial data in volume and complexity, machine-learning algorithms provide powerful tools to extract patterns from data processed all across the global. For many years, stock prediction always has drawn attention to the development of intelligent trading systems. There are substantial benefits to be gained from stock prediction for security selection and quantitative investment analysis.

In practice, stock prediction can be conducted by fundamental analysis, technical analysis, and sentiment analysis. Fundamental analysis is the most conventional use, which tries to determine a stock's value or price based on financial statements such as income statement, balance sheet, and cash-flow statement. In other words, the main objective of fundamental analysis is to estimate a company's intrinsic value. Fundamental signals have a positive and significant correlation with future earnings performance [21]. Fundamental analysis is the prerequisite investigation for value investing as known as long-term investing. In contrast, technical analysis typically begins with charts and technical indicators based on historical data. Technical analysis is usually used to predict short- to medium-term time horizons. An artificial neural network-based stock trading system using technical analysis and big data framework has been proposed in the work of [22]. The results have shown that, by choosing the most appropriate technical indicators, the neural network model can obtain comparable results against the buy and hold strategy in most of the cases. Furthermore, fine-tuning the technical indicators and/or optimization strategy can enhance the overall trading performance.

In the short-term, the stock market is irrational movement by the effect of emotion trading. Sentiment analysis is the new trend for stock prediction based on finding the correlation between public sentiment and market sentiment. The results show that social media content can give an impact on stock price via sentiment analysis [23,24]. On the effort of improving the prediction accuracy, many studies have been conducted by combining multiple analysis approaches [25,26].

Recently, there is considerable interest in stock prediction using deep learning methods. Deep learning techniques have been receiving a lot of attention lately, with breakthroughs in image processing and natural language processing. However, its application to finance does not yet seem to be commonplace. It has been used for limit order book modeling, financial sentiment analysis, volatility prediction, and portfolio optimization [27–30]. With the effort to decompose and eliminate the noise of the stock price time-series data, the wavelet transform was used. Features are extracted from the decomposed data using stacked autoencoders, and then the high-level de-noising features are fed into long short-term memory (LSTM) to build the model and forecast the next day's closing price [31]. Stock price exchange rates are forecasted by improving the deep belief network (DBN). The structure of the DBN is optimally determined through experiments and, to accelerate the speed of learning rate, conjugate gradient methods are applied. The model shows more efficiency at foreign exchange rate prediction compared with the feedforward network (FFNN) [32]. In the work of [33], the recurrent neural network was introduced and used, however, it suffers from the vanishing gradient problem. The vanishing gradient problem was improved in the LSTM and GRU model. The LSTM model has update, input, forget, and output gates, and maintains the internal memory state and applies a non-linearity(sigmoid) before the output gate, whereas GRU has only update and reset gates.

3. Methodology

Our proposed methodology architecture is developed based on the typical quantitative investment management system mentioned in Section 1. Historical data and cross-sectional data were collected from multiple resources in various formats. It could be technical, fundamental, macro-economics, and sentiment data. Multiple prediction models were conducted to predict stock prices such as LR, SVR, and LSTM. On the basis of the predicted results for each period, the expected return and volatility were calculated by the alpha model and risk model, respectively. The portfolio was constructed by selecting the outperform stocks from the predicted result in terms of the highest expected return and lowest risk. Optimal stock allocation for the constructed portfolio was evaluated by simulation and optimization modeling. Equal-weights allocation (EQ), simulation modeling Monte Carlo simulation (MCS), and mean-variance optimization (MVO) were used to evaluate the optimal stock allocation weights. The overview of the architecture is presented in Figure 2.

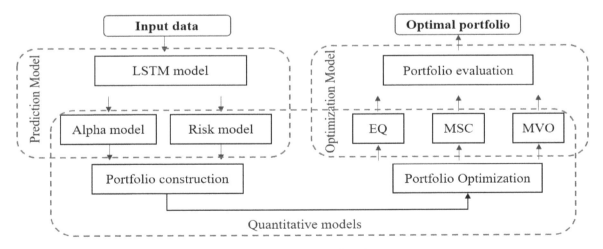

Figure 2. The overview of architecture.

3.1. Prediction Model

In this section, we proposed LSTM network to predict the stock price and construct the portfolio based on the prediction outputs.

LSTM network is a variant of RNN, which has memory blocks (cells) in the hidden layer that are recurrently connected. There are two states that are being transferred to the next cell: the cell state and the hidden state. The memory blocks are responsible for remembering things and manipulations to this memory are done through three major mechanisms, called gates. A forget gate is responsible for removing information from the cell state. The input gate is responsible for the addition of information to the cell state. The output gate decides which next hidden state should be selected. Operations performed on LSTM network units are explained in (1–6), where x_t is the input at time t and f_t is the forget gate at time t, which clears information from the memory cell when needed and keeps a record of the previous frame whose information needs to be cleared from the memory. The output gate o_t keeps the information about the upcoming step, where g is the recurrent unit, having activation function "$tanh$", and is computed from the input of the current frame and state of the previous frame h_{t-1}. In all input (I_t), forget (f_t), and output (O_t) gates, as well as the recurrent unit (g_t), we use $\left(W_i, W_f, W_o, W_g\right)$ and $\left(b_i, b_f, b_o, b_g\right)$ as weights and bias, respectively. The input gate determines what parts of the transformed input g_t need to be added to the long-term state c_t. This process updates the long-term state c_t, which is directly transmitted to the next cell. Finally, the output gate transforms the updated long-term state c_t through $tanh(.)$; filters it by o_t; and produces the output y_t, which is also sent to the next cell as the short-term state h_t.

The equations for LSTM computations are given by the following:

$$i_t = \sigma\left(W_{x_i}^T x_t + W_{h_i}^T h_{t-1} + b_i\right), \tag{1}$$

$$f_t = \sigma\left(W_{x_f}^T x_t + W_{h_f}^T h_{t-1} + b_f\right), \tag{2}$$

$$o_t = \sigma\left(W_{x_O}^T x_t + W_{h_O}^T h_{t-1} + b_O\right), \tag{3}$$

$$g_t = tanh\left(W_{x_g}^T x_t + W_{h_g}^T h_{t-1} + b_g\right), \tag{4}$$

$$c_t = f_t c_{t-1} + i_t g_t, \tag{5}$$

$$y_t = h_t = o_t tanh c_t, \tag{6}$$

where $\sigma(.)$ is the logistic function, and $tanh(.)$ is the hyperbolic tangent function. The three gates open and close according to the value of the gate controllers f_t, i_t, and o_t, all of which are fully connected layers of neurons. The range of their outputs is $[0, 1]$, as they use the logistic function for activation. In each gate, their outputs are fed into element-wise multiplication operations, so, if the output is close to 0, the gate is narrowed and less memory is stored in c_t, while if the output is close to 1, the gate is more widely open, letting more memory flow through the gate. Given LSTM cells, it is common to stack multiple layers of the cells to make the model deeper to be able to capture the nonlinearity of the data. Figure 3 illustrates how computation is carried out in an LSTM cell. To keep the wealth of a stock market, we have to have an efficient prediction model that can predict based on the previous data generated from the stock market. In this paper, we used LSTM networks to build a model that can predict the stock price [34,35]. On the basis of the output of the forecasted price, a portfolio is constructed.

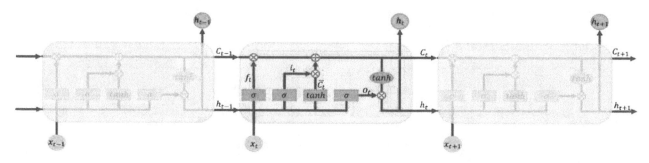

Figure 3. A recurrent neural network with LSTM network architecture.

3.2. Quantitative Models

3.2.1. Multiple Assets Portfolio Construction

Suppose that a portfolio consists of N stocks, and S_0 is the set of initial value for each stock in the portfolio, denoted as $S_0 = \left(s_1^0, \ldots, s_N^0\right)$. The number of each stock in the portfolio is denoted as $X = (x_1, \ldots, x_N)$. The initial value of the portfolio V_0 is calculated as follows:

$$V_0 = x_1 s_1^0 + \cdots + x_N s_N^0 = \sum_{i=1}^{N} x_i s_i^0 \tag{7}$$

The decision on the number of shares in each asset will follow the decision on the division of our capital, which is our primary concern, and is expressed as the weights $W = (w_1, \ldots, w_N)$ with the constraint $\sum_{i=1}^{N} w_i = 1$, defined by $w_i = \frac{x_i s_i^0}{V_0}$ with $i = 1, .., N$.

At the end of the period t, the values of the stocks change $S_t = \left(s_1^t, \ldots, s_N^t\right)$, which gives the final value of the portfolio V_t as a random variable,

$$V_t = x_1 s_1^t + \cdots + x_N s_N^t = \sum_{i=1}^{N} x_i s_i^t \tag{8}$$

The actual return of a portfolio $R_P = (r_1, \ldots, r_N)$ is the set of random returns on each stock of the portfolio, and the vector of expected return by $\mu = (\mu_1, \mu_2, \ldots, \mu_N)$ with $\mu_i = E(r_i)$ for $i = 1, 2, \ldots, N$. The actual return on the portfolio of multiple assets over some specific time period is straightforwardly calculated as follows:

$$R_P = w_1 r_1 + w_2 r_2 + \cdots + w_N r_N \tag{9}$$

The expected portfolio return is the weighted average of the expected return of each asset in the portfolio. The weight assigned to the expected return of each asset is the percentage of the market value of the asset to the total market value of the portfolio. Therefore, the expected return $E(R_P) = \mu_P$ of the portfolio at the end of the period t is calculated as follows:

$$E(R_P) = w_1 E(r_1) + w_2 E(r_2) + \cdots + w_N E(r_N) = \sum_{i=1}^{N} w_i \mu_i \tag{10}$$

Variance of return for the portfolio used above part as follows:

$$Var(R_P) = E(R_P - \mu_P)^2 = E\left(R_P{}^2\right) - \mu_P^2 \tag{11}$$

The variance of the return can be computed from the variance of S_t,

$$Var(R_P) = Var\left(\frac{S_t - S_0}{S_0}\right) = \frac{1}{S_0{}^2} Var(S_t - S_0) = \frac{1}{S_0{}^2} Var(S_t) \tag{12}$$

The standard deviations of various random returns is $\sigma_P = \sqrt{Var(R_P)}$. The covariance between asset returns will be denoted by $\sigma_{ij} = Cov\left(r_i, r_j\right)$, in particular $\sigma_{ii} = \sigma_i^2 = Var(r_i)$. These are the entries of the $N \times N$ covariance matrix Cov.

$$Cov\left(r_i, r_j\right) = E\left[(r_i - \mu_i)(r_j - \mu_j)\right] \tag{13}$$

$$Cov = \begin{bmatrix} \sigma_{11} & \sigma_{12} & \cdots & \sigma_{1N} \\ \sigma_{21} & \sigma_{22} & \cdots & \sigma_{2N} \\ \vdots & \vdots & \ddots & \vdots \\ \sigma_{N1} & \sigma_{N2} & \cdots & \sigma_{NN} \end{bmatrix} \tag{14}$$

3.2.2. Portfolio Optimization

The objective of portfolio optimization is to try to find the optimal asset allocation based on the stock price prediction phrase. Portfolio construction top-down investing was adapted to pick up the top-performing stock based on the prediction model to construct a multiple asset portfolio, as shown in Figure 4. On the basis of stock prediction results, the expected return and standard deviation for each stock are calculated. For each time period, the top predicted performance stocks with the highest predicted expected returns will be selected to construct a portfolio with initial weights, in which EQ is most commonly assigned. As the number of stocks and the correlated weights are determined, the portfolio cumulative return is calculated by (9). The optimal set is a set of current allocation weights for the selected stocks in the constructed portfolio. By adjusting the model parameters of the portfolio optimizers, we can figure out the optimal weights for the selected stocks in the constructed portfolio. Simulation and optimization techniques were used to seek the optimal weights for the constructed portfolio, instead of using the conventional EQ method.

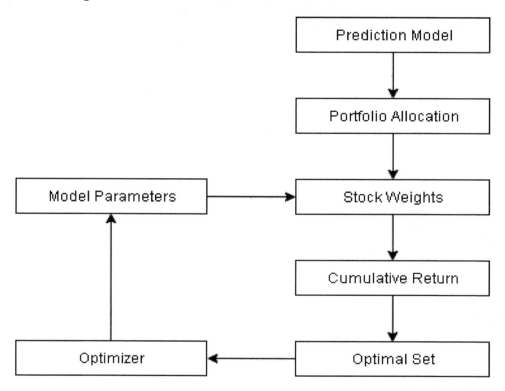

Figure 4. Portfolio optimization model.

1.   Simulation Modeling: Monte Carlo Simulation (MCS)

Simulation is a widely used technique for portfolio risk assessment and optimization. Portfolio exposure to different factors is often evaluated over multiple scenarios, and portfolio risk measures such as value-at-risk are estimated. Generating meaningful scenarios is an art as much as science, and presents a number of modeling and computational challenges. Monte Carlo simulation (MCS) is a valuable tool for evaluating functional relationships between variables, visualizing the effect of multiple correlated variables, and testing strategies. MCS solves a deterministic problem based on probabilistic analog by creating scenarios for output variables of interest. First, it generates random portfolio weights and calculates the corresponding portfolio measurements such as expected returns, volatility, and Sharpe ratio. The random weights are adjusted until reaching the highest Sharpe ratio value. All possible generated portfolio scenarios can be seen as a color map as the distribution of random weights in Figure 5a, where an efficient portfolio was found as a red dot sign with the highest Sharpe ratio value. The efficient frontier line is also presented in Figure 5b.

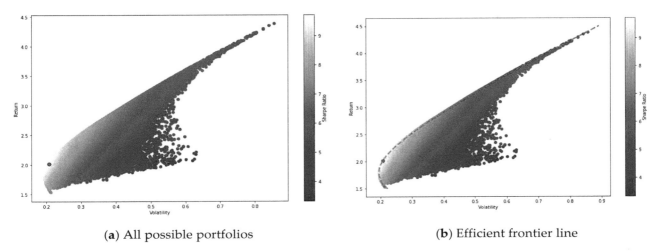

(**a**) All possible portfolios   (**b**) Efficient frontier line

Figure 5. Portfolio efficient frontier.

Algorithm 1: Pseudocode of the Monte Carlo Simulation

Input

- Number of iteration: n
- Number of assets for each portfolio: N
- Initial weight array: $W_0 = [w_1, \ldots, w_N]$ with $\sum_{i=1}^{N} w_i = 1$ and $i = 1, .., N$

Output

- Maximum of Sharpe ratio
- Optimal weight array $W = [w_1, \ldots, w_N]$ with $\sum_{i=1}^{N} w_i = 1$

for i **in** *range(n)*:

- Initial random weights: W_i
- Save the temporary weights: W_i
- Calculate expected portfolio return *exp_ret[i]*
- Calculate expected volatility *exp_vol[i]*
- Calculate Sharpe ratio: *SR[i] = exp_ret[i]/exp_vol[i]*

end

---

2.   Optimization Modeling: Mean-variance Optimization (MVO)

A portfolio constructed from N different assets can be described by means of the vector of weights $w = (w_1, w_2, \ldots w_N)$, with the constraint given $\sum_{i=1}^{N} w_i = 1$. The N-dimensional vector $I = (1, 1, \ldots, 1)$ is denoted by I. Therefore, the constraint can conveniently be written as $w^T I = 1$. Denote the random returns on the stocks by $r_1, \ldots, r_N$, and the vector of expected return by $\mu = (\mu_1, \mu_2, \ldots, \mu_N)$ with $\mu_i = E(r_i)$ for $i = 1, 2, \ldots, N$. The covariances between returns will be denoted by $\sigma_{ij} = Cov(r_i, r_j)$, in particular $\sigma_{ii} = \sigma_i^2 = \text{Var}(r_i)$. These are the entries of the $N \times N$ covariance matrix $\mathbf{\Phi}$.

$$\mathbf{\Phi} = \begin{bmatrix} \sigma_{11} & \sigma_{12} & \cdots & \sigma_{1N} \\ \sigma_{21} & \sigma_{22} & \cdots & \sigma_{2N} \\ \vdots & \vdots & \ddots & \vdots \\ \sigma_{N1} & \sigma_{N2} & \cdots & \sigma_{NN} \end{bmatrix} \tag{15}$$

The expected return $\mu_P = E(R_P)$ and variance $\sigma_P^2 = \text{Var}(R_P)$ of a portfolio with weights w are given by

$$\mu_P = \sum_{i=1}^{N} w_i \mu_i = w^T \mu, \tag{16}$$

$$\sigma_P^2 = Var(R_P) = \sum_{i,j=1}^{N} w_i w_j \sigma_{ij} = w^T \mathbf{\Phi} w. \tag{17}$$

The classical mean-variance portfolio allocation problem is formulated as follows:

$$\begin{aligned}
\text{Minimize } (w) \quad & w^T \mathbf{\Phi} w, \\
\text{s.t} \quad & w^T \mu = r_{target}, \\
& w^T I = 1.
\end{aligned}$$

4. Experiment and Results

4.1. Data Collection and Experiment Design

In this section, 10-year daily historical stock prices of 500 large-cap stocks listed on the America Stock Exchange Standard & Poor's 500 (S&P 500), which covers nearly 80 percent of the American equity capitalization, was collected by Quandl API from 1 January 2008 till 1 January 2018, with 2516 total trading days. For each stock, daily *Open-High-Low-Close* and *trading volume* was used as the main input values of the dataset. The experiments were conducted on the Ubuntu OS machine containing Intel Core i7-7700 (3.60 GHz) CPU with 64 GB RAM and GeForce GTX 1080 Ti 11176 MB GPU. For model configuration, we used Python 3.6 and Keras library with TensorFlow backend.

In order to set up the hyperparameters for the LSTM prediction model, we first randomly selected one stock from the S&P500 dataset and then performed different measurements. There are two important hyperparameters that might have a high impact on neural network performance, including the number of hidden layers and the number of neurons. We iteratively tuned the number of hidden layers from 2 to 10, and the number of neurons from 1 to 600, to select the optimal model parameters. Prediction loss values were calculated using mean square error (MSE) by adjusting the values of epochs between 5 and 8000; the least loss error was obtained at 4000 epochs. As evident from Figure 6, the minimum prediction loss error was found at 256 and 512 neurons, respectively. A stacked LSTM architecture comprised of 2 LSTM hidden layers was used. As reported in the work of [33], Adam optimization is more suitable for deep learning problems with larger datasets. Therefore, Adam optimizer with default parameters provided by Keras was employed in our experiments. The train–test split ratio used for the LSTM prediction model is 80:20. The detail selected hyperparameters are summarized in Table 1. For machine learning models, the scikit-learn library was used for training prediction models.

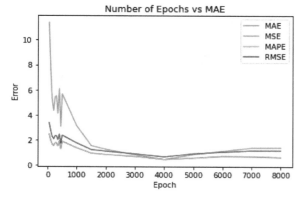
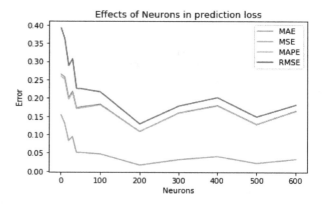

Figure 6. Model parameters selection. MAE-mean absolute error, MSE-mean square error, MAPE-mean absolute percentage error, RMSE-root mean square error.

Table 1. Experiment hyperparameters setup.

Categories	Hyperparameters
Optimizer	Adam
The number of hidden layers	2
The number of neurons	512 and 256
Number of epochs	4000

4.2. Performance Evaluation

4.2.1. Stock Prediction Evaluation

To evaluate the prediction error rates and model performance, the mean absolute error (MAE) and mean squared error (MSE) were used to measure the difference between the predicted and practical data. MAE and MSE was calculated as follows:

$$MAE = \frac{\sum_{i=1}^{T} |y_i - y_i'|}{T}, \tag{18}$$

$$MSE = \frac{\sum_{i=1}^{T} (y_i - y_i')^2}{T}, \tag{19}$$

where $Y = (y_1, y_2, \ldots, y_T)$ is a vector of actual observations, $Y' = \left(y_1', y_2', \ldots, y_T'\right)$ is a vector of predicted values, and T is the number of prediction time horizons.

At first, we conducted two variant types of RNN LSTM and GRU models to predict the stock price. Machine learning models such as LR and SVR were also employed to compare the effectiveness of the LSTM prediction model.

4.2.2. Portfolio Performance Evaluation

On the basis of the prediction results for each time horizon from 1% to 10% of total trading days, as shown in Table 2, a portfolio was constructed P_i $(i = 1, 2, \ldots, 10)$ by selecting the top four stocks with the highest predicted returns. For the purpose of optimizing those constructed portfolio performances, simulation modeling and optimization modeling were adopted to select ten efficient portfolios, as represented by $P_{1,\ldots 10}$, at the final stage by allocating optimal weights. A statistical model for each portfolio was conducted to calculate key factors such as daily return, cumulative return, average daily return, and standard daily return. The cumulative return was used as an identical investment reward to evaluate the performance of each portfolio. However, a high return may come with high volatility or risk in investment. Sharpe ratio (SR) was used for calculating risk-adjusted return, which has used as the industry-standard measurement. Furthermore, active returns of optimal portfolios represented as the difference between the portfolio's actual return on a benchmark were calculated. In our work, the S&P 500 market index was selected as the benchmark. In order to optimize asset allocation for the constructed portfolios, we carried out three different techniques for portfolio optimization:

- Equal-weighted portfolio (EQ) is a type of weighting that gives the same weight to each stock in a portfolio. In our work, we chose initial weight $w = [.25, .25, .25, .25]$.

- Monte Carlo simulation (MCS) was used to find the optimal weights of thousands of scenarios or iterations. The number of iterations is n = 50,000.

- Mean-variance optimization (MVO) was used to find an adaptive weights portfolio that adapted the stock weights using the prediction models.

Table 2. Prediction time horizon.

Period	Start	End	Days
1	2017/11/22	2017/12/29	26
2	2017/10/17	2017/12/29	51
3	2017/09/12	2017/12/29	76
4	2017/08/07	2017/12/29	100
5	2017/06/30	2017/12/29	126
6	2017/05/25	2017/12/29	151
7	2017/04/19	2017/12/29	177
8	2017/03/14	2017/12/29	202
9	2017/02/06	2017/12/29	227
10	2016/12/29	2017/12/29	252

4.3. Experiment Results

4.3.1. Stock Prediction Results

At the beginning, portfolios $P_i(i = 1, \ldots, 10)$ were constructed based on the stock prediction models. We evaluated LSTM and GRU prediction models as both are variations of RNN and able to prevent vanishing gradient problems. Table 3 summarized the detailed portfolio as well as the loss of error values for each stock in the constructed portfolios.

Table 3. Summarized prediction loss of error. LSTM, long short-term memory; GRU, gated recurrent unit; MAE, mean absolute error; MSE, mean square error.

P	LSTM			GRU		
	Stock	**MAE**	**MSE**	**Stock**	**MAE**	**MSE**
1	DVA	0.05965	0.00413	DVA	0.04731	0.00258
	FCX	0.01899	0.00064	FCX	0.02019	0.00067
	KSS	0.01364	0.00038	M	0.03484	0.00164
	LB	0.03459	0.00195	LB	0.02525	0.00092
2	FL	0.04111	0.00279	FL	0.02515	0.00089
	NKTR	0.01227	0.00024	NKTR	0.01232	0.00028
	KSS	0.01403	0.00035	KR	0.04080	0.00197
	LB	0.02482	0.00105	LB	0.02604	0.00105
3	MRO	0.04735	0.00376	MRO	0.01433	0.00035
	NKTR	0.04052	0.00236	NKTR	0.01565	0.00033
	NATP	0.02651	0.00124	SIVB	0.01357	0.00034
	LB	0.00850	0.00016	LB	0.04476	0.00302
4	GPS	0.00321	0.00003	GPS	0.01324	0.00028
	NKTR	0.00205	0.00001	NKTR	0.01554	0.00032
	MU	0.00230	0.00001	MU	0.01201	0.00025
	URI	0.00360	0.00002	URI	0.01473	0.01554
5	GPS	0.01071	0.00019	GPS	0.01130	0.00021
	NKTR	0.01347	0.00028	NKTR	0.01567	0.00035
	NRG	0.01485	0.00048	NRG	0.01461	0.00047
	URI	0.01726	0.00047	URI	0.01658	0.00046
6	ALGN	0.01432	0.00043	ALGN	0.01034	0.00026
	NKTR	0.00267	0.00002	NKTR	0.00114	0.00000
	NRG	0.01930	0.00044	NRG	0.00597	0.00005
	TROW	0.01360	0.00027	URI	0.01389	0.00029
7	ALGN	0.00514	0.00004	ALGN	0.00892	0.00019
	NKTR	0.00426	0.00004	NKTR	0.00367	0.00003
	IPGP	0.00294	0.00002	NDVA	0.01476	0.00037
	NDVA	0.00261	0.00002	TTWO	0.01806	0.00053

Table 3. *Cont.*

P	Stock	LSTM MAE	MSE	Stock	GRU MAE	MSE
8	ABMD	0.00813	0.00014	ALGN	0.01011	0.00021
	ADBE	0.00756	0.00010	IPGP	0.00662	0.00008
	ALGN	0.00161	0.00000	NKTR	0.00186	0.00001
	AMZN	0.01258	0.00027	NDVA	0.01095	0.00021
9	ALGN	0.00522	0.00006	ABMD	0.00847	0.00016
	IPGP	0.01104	0.00030	ADBE	0.01157	0.00025
	NKTR	0.01319	0.00027	ALGN	0.00919	0.00012
	TTWO	0.02046	0.00063	ATVI	0.01863	0.00055
10	ALGN	0.00751	0.00013	ALGN	0.00672	0.00010
	IPGP	0.01134	0.00014	IPGP	0.00469	0.00005
	NKTR	0.00273	0.00002	NKTR	0.00505	0.00004
	TTWO	0.00969	0.00015	TTWO	0.01234	0.00027

In general, both the LSTM and GRU models had low error values. The LSTM model was found more efficient than the GRU model by obtaining lower error rates. LSTM controls the exposure of memory content (cell state), while GRU exposes the entire cell state to other units in the network. The LSTM unit has separate input and forget gates, while the GRU performs both of these operations together via its reset gate.

4.3.2. Portfolio Performance Evaluation

Secondly, we evaluated the constructed portfolios based on prediction models, including SVR, LR, and LSTM models. In order to optimize the performance of the constructed portfolio, MCS and MVO were employed to evaluate the impact of optimization on portfolio performances. In the majority of cases, expected returns showed a tendency to increase, while SRs tended to decline gradually over time, except in the SVR model, where they fluctuated significantly. It can be observed in Figures 7–9 that MCS and MVO techniques perform approximately the same in all built prediction models. As predicted by the SVR prediction model in Figure 7, expected returns fluctuated. Although SRs obtained by MCS and MVO methods were considerably higher than EQ, the performance of constructed portfolios showed poorer performance compared with the LR and LSTM models in both expected returns and SRs. For example, the highest expected return and SR were only 55% and 0.05 at P_8 and P_{10}, respectively.

As shown in Figure 8, portfolios constructed by the LR model obtained the highest expected returns using the EQ method compared with MCS and MVO over periods. However, the constructed portfolios obtained higher SRs using MCS and MVO compared with the EQ method. This suggests that optimization methods can improve the performance of constructed portfolios by increasing the SR values; in other words, optimization techniques are not inevitably guaranteed to improve the return but can reduce the risk in trading. As reported in Figure 9, our constructed portfolios based on the LSTM prediction model obtained the highest expected returns as well as SRs in most of the predicted periods. EQ showed the effectiveness of returns, however, the gap between MCS and MVO was smaller than EQ, as shown in Figure 9. Therefore, the LSTM prediction model is more efficient than the SVR and LR models.

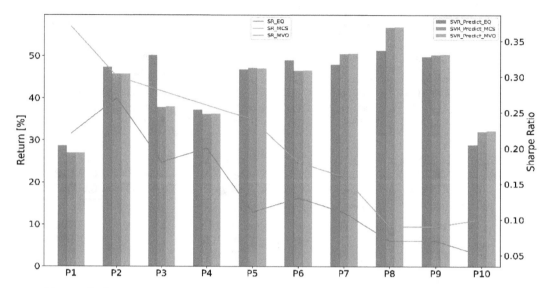

Figure 7. Support vector regression (SVR) constructed portfolios' performance.

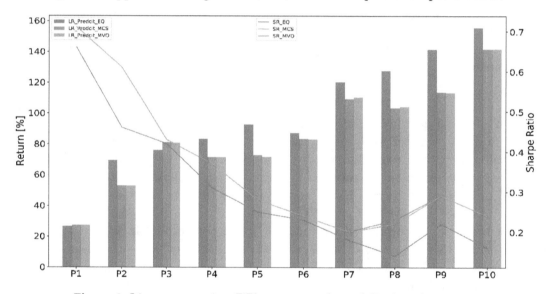

Figure 8. Linear regression (LR) constructed portfolios' performance.

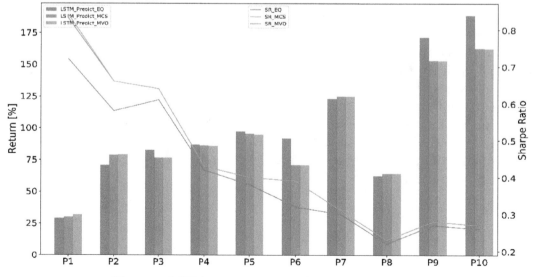

Figure 9. LSTM constructed portfolios' performance.

Third, the constructed portfolios and weights for each portfolio in the prediction phase were tested in actual trading. The constructed portfolios' performance based on prediction models is presented in Figures 10–12. Actual returns and SRs based on the SVR prediction model fluctuated significantly on time periods. MCS and MVO weights showed effective improvements in the returns but showed less impact on SRs. Especially, the actual return and SR suddenly drop to negative in P_8, as shown in Figure 10. The fluctuation can be the cause of low predicted accuracy. Therefore, predicted stocks and adjusted weights were ineffective. Constructed portfolios based on the LR prediction model performed better than those based on the SVR prediction model in practical trading, as shown in Figure 11, and EQ weights obtained higher returns compared with MCS and MVO. Unfortunately, SRs produced by MCS and MVO weights gradually decreased, even lower than EQ weights. The results seem to indicate that the predicted accuracy contributed a considerable impact on the optimization phase. In this phase, constructed portfolios based on the LSTM model outperformed, as shown in Figure 12, with the highest returns and SRs. On one hand, the returns from EQ, MCS, and MVO were pretty much the same in almost cases. On the other hand, SRs obtained by MCS and MVO were higher compared with EQ weights. It is apparent that the constructed portfolio based on the LSTM prediction model outperformed the proposed prediction models. The higher the accuracy obtained, the higher the return and reliable risk control we can construct.

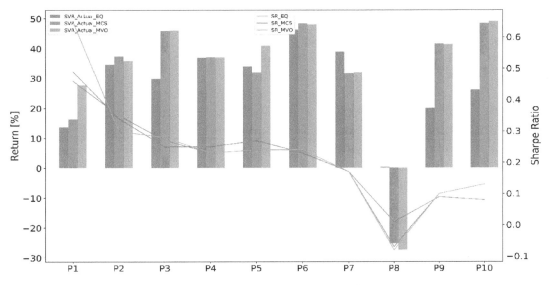

Figure 10. SVR actual portfolios' performance.

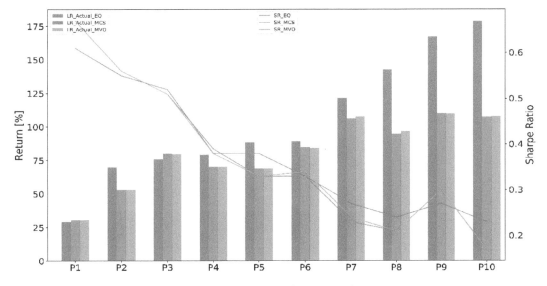

Figure 11. LR actual portfolios' performance.

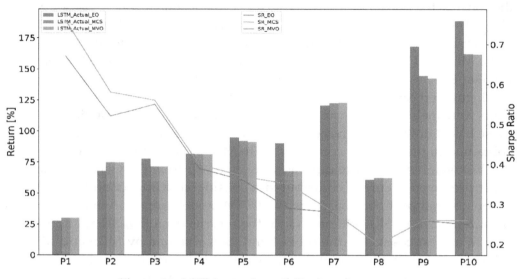

Figure 12. LSTM actual portfolios' performance.

After evaluating the efficiency of the proposed prediction models in both prediction and practical trading. The results showed that the LSTM prediction model outperformed the proposed prediction models. The efficient prediction is not only for prediction but also support for the optimization phase. These constructed portfolios were selected as efficient portfolios for quantitative trading. As we can see from the results, MCS and MVO weights were slightly different, however, as the number of iterations (scenarios) increases, more computational resources are required. Therefore, MVO weights were selected as the optimal weights for efficient portfolios. The comparison of efficient portfolio performance is given in Figure 13. Returns were gradually increased in both prediction and practical trading. In addition, returns obtained in practical trading are correlated with predicted results. Although SRs showed a tendency to decline, there was only a slight difference between prediction and practical trading. This is evidence that efficient portfolios beat the benchmark S&P 500 in both returns and SRs. Figure 14 shows a summary of the optimal portfolio allocation based on the LSTM prediction model. It showed that the optimal weights of stocks in the portfolio lead to higher active returns and lower volatility relative to the benchmark index. All these differences were statistically significant at approximately 86 and 48 percent higher than the benchmark in terms of return and SR, respectively. Table 4 summarizes the comparison between the efficient portfolios and the benchmark on active returns for each time period. Our constructed portfolios outperformed the benchmark the S&P 500 index.

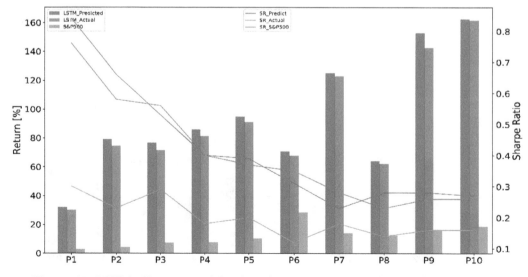

Figure 13. LSTM efficient portfolios' performances versus the benchmark index.

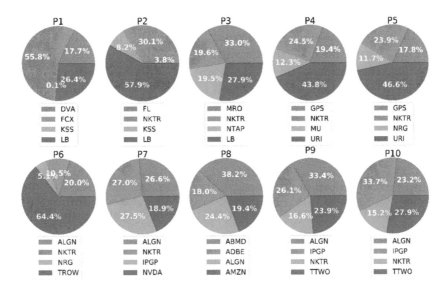

Figure 14. The detailed LSTM optimal allocation for each efficient portfolio.

Table 4. Optimal portfolio returns.

P	Portfolio [%]	Benchmark [%]	Active Return [%]
1	30.09	2.95	24.71
2	74.77	4.53	70.23
3	71.51	7.46	64.06
4	81.36	7.77	73.59
5	91.31	10.49	80.82
6	67.89	28.78	39.11
7	122.94	14.15	108.79
8	62.40	12.65	49.75
9	142.59	16.73	126.22
10	161.84	18.83	143.01

5. Conclusions and Discussions

Stock prediction plays a significant role in constructing an investment portfolio in terms of two important aspects stock selection and allocation. This paper presented the LSTM network, a type of recurrent neural network, to predict the stock price in order to demonstrate a typical quantitative trading strategy. The proposed model works efficiently by achieving high accuracy compared with other machine learning such as LR and SVM. As a result, we can take advantage of the prediction results to construct a quantitative portfolio for each predicted time horizon. On the basis of the optimization techniques, our constructed portfolios performed effectively by obtaining high returns in both prediction and actual trading, as well as compared with the S&P 500 index. According to the performance of constructed portfolios, the active returns are in inverse proportion to Sharpe ratio values, which can be understood as a fact of risk-return trade-offs in existence in our work. A prediction model that combines a strategic prediction based on historical data with a dynamic prediction, based on valuation, momentum, and spillover, should be extensively investigated in order to minimize the risk-return trade-offs. Furthermore, dynamic portfolio optimization and diversification are also considered as the target for further research that allows designing multiple tactical, flexible trading strategies in order to maximize trading profits.

There are several challenges for building effective quantitative trading strategies through deep learning. First, market data exhibit a high noise to signal ratio. The prediction models can perform well on the historical data set. However, the stock market always fluctuates as a result of factors such as market psychology, macroeconomics, and even political issues. Therefore, high performance on the historical dataset does not guarantee earning a desirable profit in practical trading. Second, backtesting is not only a tool to evaluate the discovered strategy but also helps to avoid false positives. Finally, developing a flexible, efficient trading strategy is critically important for quantitative trading. It is one of the most challenging tasks in the quantitative trading system. Diverse data sources and formats, as well as different characteristics of data, are causing the prediction task to become more complex. In summary, the deep learning approach shows a remarkable effect on stock prediction performance, which can be an essential condition for portfolio construction and optimization process in quantitative trading.

Author Contributions: Conceptualization, V.-D.T. and C.-M.L.; methodology, V.-D.T. and D.A.T.; software, V.-D.T. and D.A.T.; validation, V.-D.T.; formal analysis, V.-D.T. and C.-M.L.; investigation, V.-D.T.; resources, C.-M.L.; data curation, V.-D.T.; writing—original draft preparation, V.-D.T. and D.A.T.; writing—review and editing, V.-D.T. and C.-M.L.; visualization, V.-D.T. and D.A.T.; supervision, C.-M.L.; project administration, C.-M.L.; funding acquisition, C.-M.L. All authors have read and agreed to the published version of the manuscript.

References

1.   Fabozzi, F.J.; Markowitz, H.M. *The Theory and Practice of Investment Management: Asset Allocation, Valuation, Portfolio Construction, and Strategies*, 2nd ed.; John Wiley and Sons: Hoboken, NJ, USA, 2011; Volume 198, pp. 289–290.

2.   Adebiyi, A.A.; Adewumi, A.O.; Ayo, C.K. Comparison of ARIMA and artificial neural networks models for stock price prediction. *J. Appl. Math.* **2014**. [CrossRef]

3.   Cumming, J.; Alrajeh, D.D.; Dickens, L. An Investigation into the Use of Reinforcement Learning Techniques Within the Algorithmic Trading Domain. Master's Thesis, Imperial College London, London, UK, 2015.

4.   Chong, E.; Han, C.; Park, F.C. Deep learning networks for stock market analysis and prediction: Methodology, data representations, and case studies. *Expert Syst. Appl.* **2017**, *83*, 187–205. [CrossRef]

5.   Fabozzi, F.J.; Pachamanova, D.A. *Portfolio Construction, and Analytics*; John Wiley & Sons: Hoboken, NJ, USA, 2016; pp. 111–112.

6.   Kissell, R.L. *The Science of Algorithmic Trading and Portfolio Management*; Academic Press: Cambridge, MA, USA, 2013; pp. 111–112.

7.   Ta, V.D.; Liu, C.M.; Addis, D. Prediction and Portfolio Optimization in Quantitative Trading Using Machine Learning Techniques. In Proceedings of the Ninth International Symposium on Information and Communication Technology, Da Nang, Vietnam, 6–7 December 2018; pp. 98–105.

8.   Six Asset Allocation Strategies that Work. Available online: https://www.investopedia.com/investing/6-asset-allocation-strategies-work/ (accessed on 4 October 2019).

9.   Markowitz, H. Portfolio selection. *J. Financ.* **1952**, *7*, 779–781.

10.   Sharpe, W.F.; Sharpe, W.F. *Portfolio Theory and Capital Markets*; McGraw-Hill: New York, NY, USA, 1970; Volume 217.

11.   Roll, R.; Ross, S.A. An empirical investigation of the arbitrage pricing theory. *J. Financ.* **1980**, *35*, 1073–1103. [CrossRef]

12.   Fama, E.F.; French, K.R. Common risk factors in the returns on stocks and bonds. *J. Financ. Econ.* **1993**, *33*, 35–36. [CrossRef]

13.   He, G.; Litterman, R. *The Intuition Behind Black-Litterman Model Portfolios*; Goldman Sachs Investment Management Research: New York, NY, USA, 1999.

14.   Kolm, P.N.; Tutuncu, R.; Fabozzi, F.J. 60 Years of portfolio optimization: Practical challenges and current trends. *Eur. J. Oper. Res.* **2014**, *234*, 356–371. [CrossRef]

15.   Ahmadi-Javid, A.; Fallah-Tafti, M. Portfolio optimization with entropic value-at-risk. *Eur. J. Oper. Res.* **2019**, *279*, 225–241. [CrossRef]

16.   Lejeune, M.A.; Shen, S. Multi-objective probabilistically constrained programs with variable risk: Models for multi-portfolio financial optimization. *Eur. J. Oper. Res.* **2016**, *252*, 522–539. [CrossRef]

17.   Lwin, K.T.; Qu, R.; Mac Carthy, B.L. Mean-VaR portfolio optimization: A nonparametric approach. *Eur. J. Oper. Res.* **2017**, *260*, 751–766. [CrossRef]

18.   Qin, Z. Mean-variance model for portfolio optimization problem in the simultaneous presence of random and uncertain returns. *Eur. J. Oper. Res.* **2015**, *245*, 480–488. [CrossRef]

19.   Samarakoon, L.P.; Hasan, T. *Portfolio performance evaluation*. *Encyclopedia of Finance*, 2nd ed.; Springer: New York, NY, USA, 2006; pp. 617–622.

20. Aragon, G.O.; Ferson, W.E. Portfolio performance evaluation. *Found. Trends Financ.* **2007**, *2*, 831–890. [CrossRef]

21. Elleuch, J.; Trabelsi, L. Fundamental analysis strategy and the prediction of stock returns. *Int. Res. J. Financ. Econ.* **2009**, *30*, 95–107.

22. Sezer, O.B.; Ozbayoglu, A.M.; Dogdu, E. An artificial neural network-based stock trading system using technical analysis and big data framework. In Proceedings of the South East Conference, Haines, AK, USA, 4–12 April 2017; pp. 223–226.

23. Fang, L.; Yu, H.; Huang, Y. The role of investor sentiment in the long-term correlation between US stock and bond markets. *Int. Rev. Econ. Financ.* **2018**, *58*, 127–139. [CrossRef]

24. Nguyen, T.H.; Shirai, K.; Velcin, J. Sentiment analysis on social media for stock movement prediction. *Expert Syst. Appl.* **2015**, *42*, 9603–9611. [CrossRef]

25. Lam, M. Neural network techniques for financial performance prediction: Integrating fundamental and technical analysis. *Decis. Support Syst.* **2004**, *37*, 567–581. [CrossRef]

26. Deng, S.; Mitsubuchi, T.; Shioda, K.; Shimada, T.; Sakurai, A. Combining technical analysis with sentiment analysis for stock price prediction. In Proceedings of the 2011 IEEE Ninth International Conference on Dependable, Autonomic and Secure Computing, Sydney, Australia, 12–14 December 2011; pp. 800–807.

27. Sirignano, J.A. Deep learning for limit order books. *Quant. Financ.* **2019**, *19*, 549–570. [CrossRef]

28. Sohangir, S.; Wang, D.; Pomeranets, A.; Khoshgoftaar, T.M. Big Data: Deep Learning for financial sentiment analysis. *J. Big Data* **2018**, *5*, 3. [CrossRef]

29. Xiong, R.; Nichols, E.P.; Shen, Y. Deep Learning Stock Volatility with Google Domestic Trends. *arXiv* **2015**, arXiv:1512.04916.

30. Heaton, J.B.; Polson, N.G.; Witte, J.H. Deep learning for finance: Deep portfolios. *Appl. Stoch. Models Bus. Ind.* **2017**, *33*, 3–12. [CrossRef]

31. Bao, W.; Yue, J.; Rao, Y. A deep learning framework for financial time series using stacked autoencoders and long-short term memory. *PLoS ONE* **2017**, *12*, e0180944. [CrossRef]

32. Shen, F.; Chao, J.; Zhao, J. Forecasting exchange rate using deep belief networks and conjugate gradient method. *Neurocomputing* **2015**, *167*, 243–253. [CrossRef]

33. Chung, J.; Gulcehre, C.; Cho, K.; Bengio, Y. Empirical Evaluation of Gated Recurrent Neural Networks on Sequence Modeling. *arXiv* **2014**, arXiv:1412.3555.

34. Fischer, T.; Krauss, C. Deep learning with long short-term memory networks for financial market predictions. *Eur. J. Oper. Res.* **2018**, *270*, 654–669. [CrossRef]

35. Nguyen, T.T.; Yoon, S. A Novel Approach to Short-Term Stock Price Movement Prediction using Transfer Learning. *Appl. Sci.* **2019**, *9*, 4745. [CrossRef]

3

Predicting Primary Energy Consumption using Hybrid ARIMA and GA-SVR Based on EEMD Decomposition

Yu-Sheng Kao [1], Kazumitsu Nawata [1] and Chi-Yo Huang [2,*]

[1] Department of Technology Management for Innovation, The University of Tokyo, 7-3-1 Hongo, Bunkyo-ku, Tokyo 113-8656, Japan; sunkao1035@gmail.com (Y.-S.K.); nawata@tmi.t.u-tokyo.ac.jp (K.N.)

[2] Department of Industrial Education, National Taiwan Normal University, Taipei 106, Taiwan

* Correspondence: cyhuang66@ntnu.edu.tw

Abstract: Forecasting energy consumption is not easy because of the nonlinear nature of the time series for energy consumptions, which cannot be accurately predicted by traditional forecasting methods. Therefore, a novel hybrid forecasting framework based on the ensemble empirical mode decomposition (EEMD) approach and a combination of individual forecasting models is proposed. The hybrid models include the autoregressive integrated moving average (ARIMA), the support vector regression (SVR), and the genetic algorithm (GA). The integrated framework, the so-called EEMD-ARIMA-GA-SVR, will be used to predict the primary energy consumption of an economy. An empirical study case based on the Taiwanese consumption of energy will be used to verify the feasibility of the proposed forecast framework. According to the empirical study results, the proposed hybrid framework is feasible. Compared with prediction results derived from other forecasting mechanisms, the proposed framework demonstrates better precisions, but such a hybrid system can also be seen as a basis for energy management and policy definition.

Keywords: ensemble empirical mode decomposition (EEMD); autoregressive integrated moving average (ARIMA); support vector regression (SVR); genetic algorithm (GA); energy consumption; forecasting

1. Introduction

Research on energy supply and demand has become critical since the 1973 oil crisis. In the past decades, the average annual worldwide energy consumption grew due to the rapid economic growth of major economies. Based on the forecast by BP [1], the worldwide energy consumption will increase by 34% between 2014 and 2035. Over 90% of the world's energy consumption comes from coal, oil, natural gas, and nuclear sources [1]. Furthermore, energy consumption always plays a dominant role in countries' long-term sustainability. For most industries, e.g., heavy industries, much more energy will be required for sustainable growth. Therefore, the understanding and prediction of energy consumption in general, and of a specific economy in particular, are critical from an economic perspective.

Recently, scholars have started to forecast the demand and supply of energy by integrating various models into a hybrid one [2–4]. In general, such hybrid forecasting methods can be divided into two: causal models and time series models. On the one hand, causal models are mainly constructed based on one or more independent variables. Then the dependent variables can be predicted. Strict assumptions and theoretical bases are required for constructing such causal models. On the other hand, time series models are based on historical data. Whether linear or nonlinear, such models are used for estimating future values. These approaches are always regarded as the most feasible ways to predict energy consumption. The fundamental purpose of time series is to derive trends or patterns that can be modeled by econometric methods such as the autoregressive integrated moving average (ARIMA).

However, the models for nonlinear time series predictions are always difficult to realize due to the uncertainty and volatility of the time series. Since the linear models cannot be used to predict complex time series, nonlinear approaches are more suitable for such purpose. Thus, this study aims to predict energy consumption by using integrated methods that incorporate linear and nonlinear methods. Due to issues that arise in time series forecasting, accurate predictions are essential. Conventional linear approaches are effective in the event of forecasting issues. However, more studies are finding that, compared to nonlinear methods, such as support vector machines (SVMs) and tree-based algorithms, linear methods do not perform well in the event of various time series problems, especially complex time sequences. This is because linear methods cannot be used to detect the complex implicit patterns in time series. This study adopts a hybrid model by incorporating linear and nonlinear methods to predict energy consumption and overcome this problem.

However, in accordance with previous studies, no single prediction model is applicable to all scenarios. Therefore, many researchers have introduced hybrid models for predicting time series; such models incorporate both linear and nonlinear models or combine two linear models [5]. Earlier works have also revealed that such hybridization of prediction frameworks not only shows the complementary nature of the frameworks with respect to predictions but also enhances the accuracy of predictions. Thus, models in hybrid forms have become a common practice in forecasting. However, noise and unknown factors exist in time series. These factors influence the volatility of time series and cannot be easily solved by hybridizing linear and nonlinear patterns only. Such hybridization probably produces an overfitting problem; thus, the optimal parameters required to model a prediction framework cannot be derived. Fortunately, such difficulties can be partially solved by leveraging the ensemble empirical mode decomposition (EEMD) proposed by Wu and Huang [6] because the EEMD can solve the noise problems and enhance the prediction performance. Noises, such as trend, seasonality, and unknown factors, which often exist in time series, influence forecasting performance. To make the prediction more precise, noise problems should be carefully dealt with. There are several ways to approach noise problems and enhance forecasting performance. One way is to tune the hyperparameter for algorithms (such as the support vector regression, SVR). As a result, the prediction's performance will improve. Another way is to first deal with the time sequence using a decomposition method, such as the EEMD method. If a decomposition approach is used, the time series can be split into several stable sequences for prediction. The more stable the sequences, the better the model's prediction performance. The feasibility of EEMD has been verified by various works (e.g., [7,8]) in solving nonstationary time series and complex signals.

Given the abovementioned advantages regarding the advantages of the hybrid prediction system as well as the EEMD for time series, this research proposes a novel hybrid framework integrating the EEMD, ARIMA, genetic algorithm (GA), and the SVR to predict primary energy consumption. The concept of the proposed model comes from several sources. First, in conventional time series methods, ARIMA is popular and powerful. It has been extensively used to deal with various forecasting issues. Therefore, the ARIMA method is suitable for this study. Second, based on past research, univariate or single methods used to deal with forecasting problems cannot yield a high forecasting performance when compared to hybrid methods. Therefore, this study simultaneously uses another nonlinear method, SVR, to enhance the prediction performance. In past decades, SVR has been useful in a wide variety of prediction domains. Therefore, SVR is suitable for this study. Although SVR has obtained several important prediction records, it has a significant problem: hyperparameter tuning. Hyperparameter tuning will affect forecasting performance. It is thus necessary to find a way to select the ideal hyperparameter for SVR. Due to computing speed, the authors cannot spend much time searching for the ideal hyperparameters. Consequently, the greedy algorithm (grid search) will be abandoned. Instead, the authors intend to adopt a heuristic algorithm, such as the GA approach, to find the best hyperparameters in SVR. Finally, decomposition methods' effectiveness in enhancing models' forecasting performance has been verified by past literature. The EEMD, Wavelet, and other methods have been hugely successful in the signal processing field. Due to the innovativeness and power of EEMD, recent studies have widely adopted the method in signal processing research.

Based on above-mentioned reasons, the authors attempt to combine the EEMD, ARIMA, GA, and SVR into a prediction model for energy consumption. First, the time series of energy consumption is divided into several intrinsic mode functions (IMFs) and a residual term. Here, IMFs stand for different frequency bands of time series, which range from high to low, while each IMF represents a series of oscillatory functions [9,10]. That way, each time series component can be identified and modeled accordingly. The characteristics of the time series can also be captured in detail. The ARIMA is then introduced to predict the future values of all extracted IMFs and the residue independently. Since the accuracy of the nonlinear time series derived using the ARIMA may be unacceptable, the SVR is utilized based on the nonlinear pattern to further improve prediction performance. In addition, the accuracy of the SVR-based prediction models completely depends on the control parameters, and the parameters should be optimized. Therefore, the GA is leveraged to derive the optimal parameters. In general, the prediction model fuses EEMD, ARIMA, SVR, and GA into a hybrid prediction framework. The predicted IMFs and the residue will be split into a final ensemble result. The proposed hybrid framework will be verified by a prediction of Taiwanese primary energy consumption for the next four years. Meanwhile, the accuracy of the prediction results will be compared with the ones derived by other forecast methods, which include ARIMA, ARIMA-SVR, ARIMA-GA-SVR, EEMD-ARIMA, EEMD-ARIMA-SVR, and EEMD-ARIMA-GA-SVR. Based on the empirical study results, the effectiveness of the prediction framework can be verified.

The remaining part of this work is structured as follows. Section 2 reviews the related literature regarding the consumption and forecasting methods of energy. Section 3 introduces the methods used in this paper, which include ARIMA, SVR, and GA. Section 4 describes the background of the empirical study case, the dataset, and the empirical study process. Section 5 concludes the whole work, with major findings and opportunities for future studies.

2. Literature Review

For decision-makers to effectively understand the trend of energy fluctuation, which may generate far-reaching implications, the precise forecasting of primary energy consumption is indispensable. On the one hand, with an accurate forecasting of energy consumption, the government can establish energy plans for fluctuations in oil supply. On the other hand, energy predictions can be useful for the investment of firms. Albeit important, predicting energy consumption is not always simple. Therefore, a robust forecasting model will be necessary.

In the literature on energy prediction, several researchers have completed accurate predictions [2–4,11,12]. Some researchers adopted economic indicators by mixing various energy indicators for predicting energy consumption. Other researchers used only time series data for forecasting. While these forecast methods are different, the prediction results of the two categories of models can serve as solid foundations for further investigations on energy consumption.

Furthermore, to enhance the accuracy of predictions, some authors employed hybrid models. Of such models, linear and nonlinear ones were integrated. The fusion of linear and nonlinear models can overcome the shortage of adopting only one kind of method and provide more accurate results [3,5,13]. In addition to the hybrid methods involving both linear and nonlinear models, some studies have attempted to transform the data by integrating data preprocessing and post-processing procedures [14,15]. By doing so, the forecasting capabilities of the hybrid models with data preprocessing and postprocessing procedures can show superior performance in energy predictions.

Further, several studies have proposed machine learning methods for predicting energy consumption. Al-Garni, Zubair, and Nizami [16] used weather factors as explanatory variables of a regression model for predicting the consumption of electric energy in eastern Saudi Arabia. Azadehet al. [12] modeled Turkey's electricity consumption on the sector basis by utilizing the artificial neural network (ANN). Wong, Wan, and Lam [17] developed an ANN-based model for analyzing the energy consumption of office buildings. Fumo and Biswas [11] employed simple and multiple regression models as well as the quadratic regression model to predict residential energy consumption. Ahmadet al. [13] attempted to review the applications of ANN and the SVM for energy consumption prediction and found that both seem to show better performance in energy forecasting [13]. Ardakani and Ardehali [3] applied regressive methods consisting of linear, quadratic, and ANN models by incorporating an optimization algorithm into the model to achieve better performance in predicting long-term energy consumption.

Although many scholars have empirically verified the effectiveness of machine learning methods for dealing with time series problems, no single prediction model seems applicable to all scenarios. That is, even if the machine learning model outperforms other traditional linear methods, using a single machine learning model to address all time series issues would be problematic and unrealistic.

Many researchers have thus employed hybrid time series forecasting models, which incorporate linear with nonlinear models or combine two kinds of linear models [5]. Previous studies have also revealed that such hybrid frameworks not only complement each other in prediction but also enhance prediction accuracy. Thus, models in hybrid forms have become a common practice in forecasting.

For example, Yuan and Liu [2] proposed a composite model that combined ARIMA and the grey forecasting model, GM (1,1), to predict the consumption of primary energy in China. Based on their findings, the results obtained when using the hybrid model were far superior to those obtained when only using the ARIMA or GM (1,1) models. Zhang [18] developed a hybrid prediction model consisting of both ARIMA and ANN. Zhu et al. [4] developed a hybrid prediction model of energy demands in China, which employed the moving average approach by integrating the modified particle swarm optimization (PSO) method for enhancing prediction performance. Wang, Wang, Zhao, and Dong [19] combined the PSO with the seasonal ARIMA method to forecast the electricity demand in mainland China and obtain a more accurate prediction. Azadeh, Ghaderi, Tarverdian, and Saberi [20] also adopted the GA and ANN models to predict energy consumption based on the price, value-add, number of customers, and energy consumption. Lee and Tong [21] proposed a model that combined ARIMA and genetic programming (GP) to improve prediction efficiency by adopting the ANN and ARIMA models.

Further, Yolcuet et al. [5] developed a linear and nonlinear ANN model with the modified PSO approach for time series forecasting. They achieved prediction results superior to those of conventional forecasting models. According to the analytical results, the hybrid model is more effective because it adopts a single prediction method and can thus improve the prediction accuracy.

Though hybrid models based on ARIMA and ANN have achieved great success in various fields, they have several limitations. First, this hybrid approach requires sufficient data to build a robust model. Second, the parameter control, uncertainties in weight derivations, and the possibility of overfitting must often be discussed when using ANN models. Because of these limitations, more researchers started to adopt SVR in forecasting since it can mitigate the disadvantages of ANN models. SVR is suitable for forecasts based on small datasets.

Pai and Lin's [22] work is a representative example of adopting SVR methods in hybrid models for forecasting. They integrated ARIMA and SVR models for stock price predictions. Patel, Chaudhary, and Garg [23] also adopted the ARIMA-SVR for predictions and derived optimal results based on historical data. Alwee, Hj Shamsuddin, and Sallehuddin [24] optimized an ARIMA-SVR-based model, using the PSO for crime rate predictions. Fan, Pan, Li, and Li [25] employed independent component analysis (ICA) to examine crude oil prices and then used an ARIMA-SVR-based model to predict them.

Based on the results of the literature review, hybrid models, including both the SVR and the ANN, have achieved higher prediction accuracies than traditional prediction techniques. However, the invisible and unknown factors which can influence the volatility of time series cannot be addressed easily by hybridizing linear and nonlinear patterns. The problem of overfitting can emerge; thus, the optimal parameters cannot be derived.

Fortunately, such difficulties can be partially resolved by leveraging the EEMD proposed by Wu and Huang [6]. The method has been feasible and effective in solving problems consisting of nonstationary time series and complex signals [7,8]. Wang et al. [7] integrated the EEMD method with the least square SVR (LSSVR) and successfully predicted the time series of nuclear energy consumption. Prediction performance has increased significantly and outperformed some well-recognized approaches based on level forecasting and directional prediction. Zhang, Zhang, and Zhang [26] predicted the prices of crude oil by hybridizing PSO-LSSVM and EEMD decomposition. The work demonstrated that the EEMD technique can decompose the nonstationary and time-varying components of times series of crude oil prices. The hybrid model can be beneficial to model the different components of crude oil prices and enhance prediction performance.

The previous studies in the literature review section aimed to develop a model that could effectively and accurately predict energy consumption and demand. In their methodologies, these works being reviewed attempted to use linear or nonlinear methods to predict energy consumption. Furthermore, they tried to use the parameter search algorithm in their model to enhance its prediction accuracy. Based on the review results, complex time series can be split by the EEMD into several relatively simple subsystems. The hidden information behind such complex time series can be explored more easily. Thus, in the following section, a hybrid analytical framework consisting of ARIMA, SVR, and GA will be proposed. The framework will be adopted to predict primary energy consumption.

3. Research Methods

This section first introduces the data processing method. Next, the individual models including ARIMA and SVR will be introduced. Afterward, the optimization approach based on GA will be introduced. Finally, the analytical process of the proposed hybrid model will be described.

3.1. EEMD

Empirical mode decomposition (EMD), an adaptive approach based on the Hilbert–Huang transformation (HHT), is often used to deal with time series data including ones with nonlinear and nonstationary forms [8]. Since such time series are complicated, various fluctuation modes may coexist. The EMD technique can be used to decompose the original time series into several simple IMFs, which correspond to different frequency bands of the time series and range from high to low; each IMF stands for a series of oscillatory functions [9,10]. Moreover, the IMFs must satisfy two conditions [6]: (1) in the whole data series, the number of extrema and zero crossings must either be equal or differ at most by 1; and (2) at any point, the mean value of the envelope (envelope, in mathematics, is a curve that is tangential to each one of a family of curves in a plane) defined by the local minima is 0.

Based on the above definitions, IMFs can be extracted from the time series $y(t)$ according to the following shifting procedures [27]: (1) identify the local maxima and the minima; (2) connect all local extrema points to generate an upper envelope $e_{max}(t)$ and connect all minima points to generate a lower envelope $e_{min}(t)$ with the spline interpolation, respectively; (3) compute the mean of the envelope, $a(t)$, from the upper and lower envelopes, where $a(t) = (e_{max}(t) + e_{min}(t))/2$; (4) extract the mean from the time series and define the difference between $y(t)$ and $a(t)$ as $c(t)$, where $c(t) = y(t) - a(t)$; (5) check the properties of $c(t)$: (i) if $c(t)$ satisfies the two conditions illustrated above, an IMF will be extracted and replace $y(t)$ with the residual, $r(t) = y(t) - c(t)$; (ii) if $c(t)$ is not an IMF, then $y(t)$ will be replaced by $c(t)$; and (6) the residue $r_1(t) = y(t) - c_1(t)$ is regarded as the new data subjected to the same shifting process, which was described above for the next IMF from $r_1(t)$. When the residue $r(t)$ becomes a monotonic function or at most has one local extrema point from which no more IMF can be extracted [27], the shifting processes can be terminated.

Through the abovementioned shifting process, the original data series $y(t)$ can be expressed as a sum of IMFs and a residue, $y(t) = \sum_{i=1}^{m} c_i(t) + r_m(t)$, where m is the number of IMFs, $r_m(t)$ is the final residue, and $c_i(t)$ is the ith IMF. All the IMFs are nearly orthogonal to each other, and all have nearly zero means.

Although the EMD has been widely adopted in handling data series, the mode-mixing problem still exists. The problem can be defined as either a single IMF consisting of components of widely disparate scales or a component of a similar scale residing in different IMFs. To overcome this problem, Wu and Huang [6] proposed the ensemble EMD (EEMD), which adds white noise to the original data, and thus the data series of different scales can be automatically assigned to proper scales of reference built by the white noise [7]. The core concept of the EEMD method is to add the white noise into the data processing. White noise can be viewed as a sequence with zero mean value; this sequence does not fall under any distribution. Based on different algorithms, the white noise can be assigned to specific distributions for calculation. In EEMD, the purpose of this method is to make the original sequence the stable sequence. Hence, this method employs simulation, using the original sequence to generate various sequences of normal distributions—this is the white noise concept. With this method, the original sequence can be split into several different sequences. Meanwhile, the sum of the decomposed sequences equals the original sequence. These decomposed sequences are called IMFs. This way, the mode-mixing problem can be easily solved. The EEMD procedure is developed as follows [6]: (1) add a white noise series to the original data; (2) decompose the data with added white noise into IMFs; (3) repeat steps 1 and 2 iteratively, but with different white noise each time; and (4) obtain ensemble means of corresponding IMFs as the final results.

In addition, Wu and Huang [6] established a statistical rule to control the effect of added white noise: $e_n = \varepsilon / \sqrt{n}$, where n is the number of ensemble members, ε represents the amplitude of the added noise, and e_n is the final standard deviation of error, which is defined as the difference between the input signal and the corresponding IMFs. Based on previous studies, the number of ensemble members is often set to 100, and the standard deviation of white noise is set to 0.2.

3.2. The ARIMA Model

The ARIMA model for forecasting time series was proposed by Box, Jenkins, and Reinsel [28]. The model consists of the autoregressive (AR) and the moving average (MA) models. The AR and MA models were merged into the ARMA model, which has already become matured in predictions. The future value of a variable is a linear function of past observations and random errors. Thus, the ARMA can be defined as

$$y_t = \phi_1 y_{t-1} + \phi_2 y_{t-2} + \cdots + \phi_p y_{t-p} + \varepsilon_t - \theta_1 \varepsilon_{t-1} - \theta_2 \varepsilon_{t-2} - \cdots - \theta_q \varepsilon_{t-q} \qquad (1)$$

where y_t is the forecasting value; ϕ_i is the coefficient of the ith observation; y_{t-i} is the ith observation; θ_i is the parameter associated with the ith white noise; ε_t is the white noise, whose mean is zero; and ε_{t-i} is the noise terms.

The ARMA model can satisfactorily fit the original data when the time series data is stationary. However, if the time series are nonstationary, the series will be transformed into a stationary time series using the dth difference process, where d is usually set as 0, 1, or 2. ARIMA is used to model the differenced series. The process is called ARIMA (p, d, q), which can be expressed as

$$w_t = \phi_1 w_{t-1} + \phi_2 w_{t-2} + \cdots + \phi_p w_{t-p} + \varepsilon_t - \theta_1 \varepsilon_{t-1} - \theta_2 \varepsilon_{t-2} - \cdots - \theta_q \varepsilon_{t-q} \qquad (2)$$

where w_t is denoted as $\nabla^d y_t$. When d equals zero, the model is the same as Equation (1) of ARMA.

The ARIMA model was developed by using the Box–Jenkins method. The procedure of the ARIMA involves three steps: (1) Model identification: Since the stationary series is indispensable for the ARIMA model, the data needs to be transformed from a nonstationary one to a stable one. For the stability of the series, the difference method is essential for removing the trends of the series. This way, the d parameter is determined. Based on the autocorrelation function (ACF) and the partial autocorrelation function (PACF), a feasible model can be established. Through the parameter estimation and diagnostic checking process, the proper model will be established from all the feasible models. (2) Parameter estimation: Once the feasible models have been identified, the parameters of the ARIMA model can be estimated. The suitable ARIMA model based on Akaike's information criterion (AIC) and Schwarz's Bayesian information criterion (BIC) can be further determined. (3) Diagnostic checking: After parameter estimation, the selected model should be tested for statistical significance. Meanwhile, hypothesis testing is conducted to examine whether the residual sequence of the model is a white noise. Based on the above procedures, the forecasting model will be determined. The derived model will be appropriate as the training model for predictions.

In this research, the ARIMA models will be built by feeding each decomposed data. The separated ARIMA models will then be integrated with an SVR model for further analysis. Fitting performance is expected to be enhanced further.

3.3. SVR

SVR was proposed by Vapnik [29], who thought that theoretically, a linear function f exists to define the nonlinear relationship between the input and output data in the high-dimensional-feature space. Such a method can be used to solve the function with respect to fitting problems. Based on the concepts of SVR, the basis function can be described as

$$f(x) = w^T \cdot \varphi(x) + b, \tag{3}$$

where $f(x)$ denotes the forecasting values, x is the input vector, w is the weight vector, b is the bias, and $\varphi(x)$ stands for a mapping function to transform the nonlinear inputs into a linear pattern in a high-dimensional-feature space.

Conventional regression methods take advantage of the square error minimization method for modeling the forecasting patterns. Such a process can be regarded as an empirical risk in accordance with the loss function [29]. Therefore, the $\varepsilon-$ insensitive loss function (T_ε) is adopted in the SVR and can be defined as

$$T_\varepsilon(f(x), y) = \left\{ \begin{matrix} |f(x) - y| - \varepsilon \\ 0 \end{matrix} \right\} \qquad \begin{matrix} \text{if} |f(x) - y| \geq \varepsilon \\ \text{otherwise} \end{matrix}, \tag{4}$$

where y is the target output and ε is expressed as the region of $\varepsilon-$ insensitive. When the predicted value falls into the band area, the loss is equal to the difference between the predicted value and the margin [30]. $T_\varepsilon(f(x), y)$ is leveraged to derive an optimum hyperplane on the high-feature space to maximize the distance which can divide the input data into two subsets. The weight vector (w) and constant (b) in Equations (4) can be estimated by minimizing the following regularized risk function:

$$P(c) = c\frac{1}{n}\sum_{i=1}^{n} T_\varepsilon(f(x_i), y_i) + \frac{1}{2}\|w\|^2, \tag{5}$$

where $T_\varepsilon(f(x_i), y_i)$ is the $\varepsilon-$ insensitive loss function in Equation (5). Here, $1/2\|w\|^2$ plays the regularizer role, which tackles the problem of trade-off between the complexity and approximation accuracy of the regression model.

Equation (5) above aims to ensure that the forecasting model has an improved generalized performance. In the regularization process, c is used to specify the trade-off between the empirical risk and the regularization terms. Both c and ε can be defined by hyper-parameter search algorithms and users. These parameters significantly determine the prediction performance of the SVR.

In addition, based on the concept of the tube regression, if the predicted value is within the $\varepsilon-$ tube, the error will be zero. However, if the predicted value is located outside the $\varepsilon-$ tube, the error will be produced. Such an error, the so-called $\varepsilon-$ insensitive error, is calculated in terms of the distance between the predicted value and the boundary of the tube. Since some predicted values exist outside the tube, the slack variables $(\xi + \xi_i^*)$ are introduced and defined as tuning parameters. These variables stand for the distance from actual values to the corresponding boundary values of the tube. Given the synchronous structural risk, Equation (5) is transformed into the following constrained form by using the slack variables:

Minimize $\frac{1}{2}\|w\|^2 + c\sum_{i=1}^{n}(\xi + \xi_i^*)$

Subject to

$$\left\{\begin{array}{c} y_i - (\mathbf{w}^T \cdot \varphi(x_i)) - b \le \varepsilon + \xi_i \\ (\mathbf{w}^T \cdot \varphi(x_i)) + b - y_i \le \varepsilon + \xi_i^* \\ \xi_i, \xi_i^* \ge 0, \qquad \text{for} \quad i = 1, \ldots, n \end{array}\right\} \tag{6}$$

The constant c determines the trade-off between the flatness of f and the amount up to which deviations larger than ε are tolerated. To solve the above problem, the Lagrange multiplier and the Karush–Kuhn–Tucker (KKT) conditions will be leveraged. After the derivation, the general form of the SVR function can be expressed as

$$f(\mathbf{x}, \mathbf{w}) = f(\mathbf{x}, \alpha_i, \alpha_i^*) = \sum_{i=1}^{n}(\alpha_i - \alpha_i^*) \times K(\mathbf{x}, x_i) + b \tag{7}$$

where α_i and α_i^* are the Lagrange multipliers, and $K(\mathbf{x}, x_i)$ is the inner product of two vectors in the feature space, $\varphi(x_i)$ and $\varphi(x_j)$. Here, $K(\mathbf{x}, x_i)$ is called the kernel function. In general, the most popular kernel function is the Gaussian radial basis function (RBF), which can be defined as $K(x_i, x_j) = \exp(-\|x_i - x_j\|^2/2\sigma^2)$ [29]. In this work, the RBF is employed for predictions. In addition, since σ is a free parameter, the RBF kernel can be described as $K(x_i, x_j) = \exp(-\gamma\|x_i - x_j\|^2)$, where γ is a parameter of the RBF kernel.

3.4. Optimization by GA

While defining a prediction model, the enhancement of prediction accuracy and the avoidance of overfitting are the most important tasks. By doing so, the training model can achieve far better performance in predictions when testing data are inputted. In the SVR-based models, the c, ε, and γ parameters play a dominant role in determining modeling performance. That is, if these parameters can be defined correctly and appropriately, the forecasting model will be efficient. To select the best parameters, the method for searching these parameters will be indispensable. In this work, GA will be adopted in selecting the optimal values for these three SVR parameters.

GA, a concept first proposed by Holland [31], is a stochastic search method based on the ideas of natural genetics and the principle of evolution [32,33]. GA works with a population of individual strings (chromosomes), each of which stands for a possible solution to a given problem. Each chromosome is assigned a fitness value based on the result of the fitness function [34]. GA allows more opportunities to fit chromosomes to reproduce the shared features originating from their parent generation. It has been regarded as a useful tool in many applications and has been extensively applied to derive global solutions to optimization problems. The algorithm is also applicable to large-scale and complicated nonlinear optimal problems [35]. The GA procedure is summarized below based on the work by [36]:

Step 1: Randomly generate an initial population of n agents; each agent is an $n-$bit genotype (chromosome).

Step 2: Evaluate the fitness of each agent.

Step 3: Repeat the following procedures until n offspring has been created.

(a) Select a pair of parents for mating: A proportion of the existing population is selected to create a new generation. Thus, the most appropriate members of the population survive in this process while the least appropriate ones are eliminated.

(b) Apply variation operators (crossover and mutation): Such operators are inspired by the crossover of the deoxyribonucleic acid (DNA) strands that occur in the reproduction of biological organisms. The subsequent generation is created by the crossover of the current population.

Step 4: Replace the current population with the new one.

Step 5: The whole process is finished when the stopping condition is satisfied. Then the best solution is returned to the current population. Otherwise, the process will go back to Step 2 until the terminating condition can be satisfied.

3.5. The Proposed Hybrid Model

The abovementioned prediction approaches including ARIMA and SVR deliver good performance in general since these methods deal with regression problems effectively. For linear models, ARIMA performs quite well in forecasting time series. However, its prediction performance is limited since it cannot appropriately predict highly nonlinear and nonstationary time series. Therefore, the data stabilization technique based on EEMD decomposition is introduced to handle nonlinear data; the nonstationary process is introduced as well. Complexities such as randomness and intermittence often exist in the time series. Even if the series have been proceeded by the EEMD, unknown factors that influence the series remain. To enhance the forecasting accuracy of the EEMD-ARIMA, the SVR method is integrated. SVR based on the nonlinear method is good at coping with small data and unstable data series. Thus, the EEMD-ARIMA, integrated with the SVR, will be useful in predicting nonlinear time series generally and energy consumption specifically. Meanwhile, GA is adopted to derive the best parameters for SVR, which can improve the performance of the hybrid model.

In general, the proposed EEMD-ARIMA-GA-SVR prediction framework (Figure 1) is composed of the following steps:

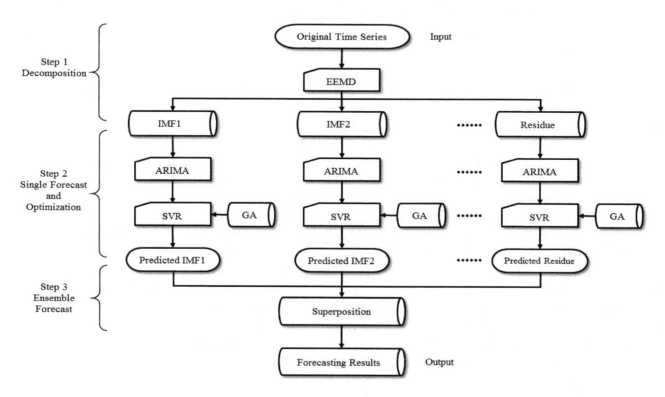

Figure 1. General procedure of the proposed ensemble empirical mode decomposition- autoregressive integrated moving average-genetic algorithm-support vector regression (EEMD)-(ARIMA)-(GA)-(SVR) modeling framework for primary energy consumption forecasting.

Step 1: The original time series of primary energy consumptions, y_t, $t = 1, 2, \ldots, n$, is decomposed into m IMF components $c_i(t)$, $i = 1, 2, \ldots, m$, and a residual component $r_m(t)$ using the EEMD method.

Step 2: ARIMA and SVR are introduced as stand-alone prediction methods to extract the IMFs and residual of the time series, respectively. Meanwhile, GA is introduced to optimize the parameters associated with SVR. Accordingly, the corresponding prediction results for all components can be obtained.

Step 3: The independent prediction results of all the IMFs and the residual are aggregated as an output, which can be regarded as the final prediction results of the original time series $y(t)$.

Thus, the fitted values can be accordingly derived from this proposed hybrid prediction framework. Further, to demonstrate the effectiveness of the proposed hybrid EEMD-ARIMA-GA-SVR framework, the time series of Taiwanese primary energy consumption will be adopted to verify the feasibility of the proposed framework. Meanwhile, the prediction results based on ARIMA, ARIMA-SVR, ARIMA-GA-SVR, EEMD-ARIMA, and EEMD-ARIMA-SVR will be introduced for comparison.

3.6. Performance Measures for Predictions

Different measures for prediction errors will be adopted to evaluate the accuracy of the prediction models. In this research, the mean absolute error (MAE), mean absolute percentage error (MAPE), mean square error (MSE), and root mean square error (RMSE) will be adopted. The four metrics are used here to evaluate the forecasting performance. The MAPE and RMSE metrics can be useful to explain the performance of predictions. To yield more accurate evaluation results, we further provide results being derived by MAE and MSE as references. These performance measures are defined below:

$$\text{MAE} = \frac{1}{n}\sum_{i=1}^{n}\left|y_t - \hat{y}_t\right| \tag{8}$$

$$\text{MAPE} = \frac{1}{n}\sum_{i=1}^{n}\left|\frac{y_t - \hat{y}_t}{y_t}\right| \times 100 \tag{9}$$

$$\text{MSE} = \frac{1}{n}\sum_{i=1}^{n}(y_t - \hat{y}_t)^2 \tag{10}$$

$$\text{RMSE} = \sqrt{\frac{1}{n}\sum_{i=1}^{n}(y_t - \hat{y}_t)^2} \tag{11}$$

where n stands for the size of the test data and y_t as well as $\hat{y}_t$ denote the actual value and the predicted value. Based on these measures, the lower values of all performance measures represent superior forecasting. The MAE reveals how similar the predicted values are to the observed values while the MSE and RMSE measure the overall deviations between the fitted and predicted values. Generally, the MAPE value should be less than 10%. To prove the effectiveness of the proposed hybrid EEMD-ARIMA-GA-SVR model in forecasting, alternative methodologies consisting of ARIMA, ARIMA-SVR, ARIMA-GA-SVR, EEMD-ARIMA, and EEMD-ARIMA-SVR will be used as benchmark models to compare with proposed model.

To test the differences of means between fitted and actual values, the paired-sample Wilcoxon signed-rank test is introduced in this research, where μ_1 stands for the mean of the actual data while μ_2 represents the mean of the fitted data. The null hypothesis is defined as H_0: $\mu_1 - \mu_2 = 0$ while the alternative hypothesis is defined as H_1: $\mu_1 - \mu_2 \neq 0$. The null hypothesis cannot be rejected while the result of the subtraction between the mean value of the actual data and the mean value of the fitted data is 0. Such a case means that there is no mean difference between the fitted data and the actual data. In other words, the training model is suitable as a prediction model since it is consistent with the real situation.

4. Forecasting Taiwan's Primary Energy Consumption

In this section, an empirical case based on Taiwanese primary energy consumption is presented to verify the feasibility and effectiveness of the proposed hybrid framework. Comparisons with other benchmark models will be provided to demonstrate the forecasting capabilities of the proposed framework. The background of the Taiwanese primary energy consumption will be presented first. Then the raw data and analytic process will be introduced in Section 4.2. Afterward, the time series will be decomposed by the EEMD for the predictions in Section 4.3. Modeling via ARIMA will be introduced in Section 4.4. The predictions of energy consumptions using the EEMD-ARIMA-SVR model optimized by the GA method will be discussed in Section 4.5. Finally, the evaluations of hybrid models and forecasting results will be described in Section 4.6.

4.1. Background

Because of its shortage of natural resources, Taiwan relies heavily on energy imports. In managing energy imports, energy consumption predictions are indispensable. Such energy predictions can help the government sector define relevant energy policies for sustainable development.

4.2. Raw Data and Modeling Method

In this study, the time series of the Taiwanese primary energy consumption (Figure 2) was adopted to verify the effectiveness of the prediction models. Annual primary energy consumption from 1965 to 2014 was provided by BP [1]. The time series was separated into two subsets where 90% (46 samples) of the dataset were chosen as the training set while the remaining 10% (4 samples) were selected as the test set for verifying the prediction efficiency.

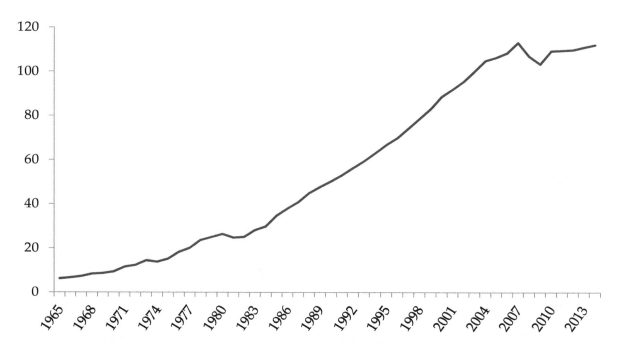

Figure 2. Taiwan's primary energy consumption (million barrels of oil equivalent). Source: BP Statistical Review of World Energy 2015.

For accurate predictions, the original dataset will be transformed by the EEMD method. After the decomposition of the time series, the results of decompositions can be further predicted by the ARIMA method. Then, the prediction results derived from the ARIMA method will be aggregated as the final prediction results for energy consumption.

Meanwhile, such procedures can be extended by adopting SVR. Moreover, to help build the training model and avoid overfitting risks, the k-fold cross-validation was introduced into model construction within the prediction process. The k-fold cross-validation is used in SVR prediction error examinations based on selected hyperparameters from GA. In this study, the authors adopt five-fold cross-validation. A five-fold validation entails that all samples are divided into five portions;

four of the five portions are used for training, and one of the five portions is for testing. The process is repeated five times. At first, the GA algorithm generates a set of hyperparameters. Through the five-fold cross-validation, we can obtain a performance. Next, the GA algorithm will continue to generate different hyperparameters based on cross-validation, thus obtaining a performance. Finally, we can select the best hyperparameters in terms of the best performances. The training data was randomly divided into k subsamples. Among the k samples, the $k-1$ subsamples were selected as the training data, and the remaining subsample was considered as validation data for testing the model. This research adopted 5-fold cross-validation into the model construction process.

4.3. Data Preprocessing Using EEMD Decomposition

Before conducting the prediction using the proposed hybrid framework, the time series of energy consumptions will be processed using the EEMD decomposition method, which separates the original time series into several IMFs and a residue. The results are depicted in Figure 3. The four independent IMF components correspond to different frequency bands of the time series, which range from high to low.

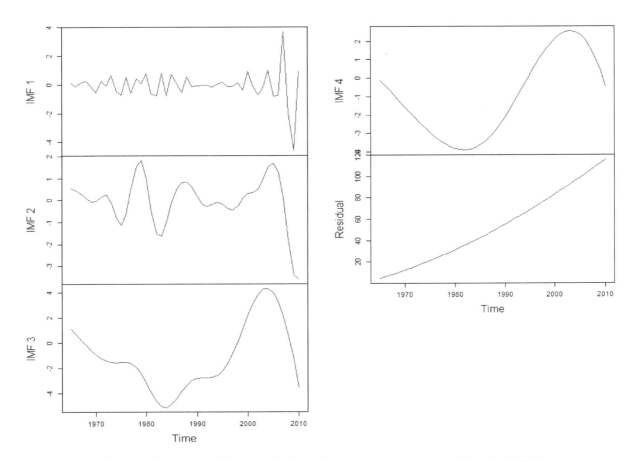

Figure 3. Decomposition results for primary energy consumption via EEMD.

In Figure 3, the IMFs stand for changing frequencies, amplitudes, and wavelengths. IMF_1 represents the highest frequency, maximum amplitude, and the shortest wavelength. The frequencies and amplitudes associated with the rest of the IMFs are lower while the wavelengths are longer. The residue represents a mode slowly varying around the long-term average.

4.4. Forecasting with the ARIMA Model

To establish the prediction model of primary energy consumption in terms of the historical time series dataset, the ARIMA method is introduced. Since the ARIMA model must be built into the series stationarity, the d times difference needs to be obtained to have an ARIMA (p, d, q) model with d as the order of differencing used. To test the stationarity of d times differencing, the augmented Dickey–Fuller (ADF) test is utilized.

The construction of the ARIMA model depends on model identification. Here, differencing will be important for solving non-stationarity. Moreover, the order of AR (p) and MA (q) needs to be identified. Through ACF and PACF, the order of AR (p) and MA (q) can further be determined [28]. However, the ACF and PACF method may not be useful when performing hybrid ARMA processes. Commonly, AIC or BIC measures can be used to easily inspect the appropriateness of the ARMA model. In this research, the best forecasting model is determined based on AIC measures and statistically significant results. Once the forecasting model has been selected, the nonlinear method based on the optimization approach will be integrated into this model.

First, the stationary test for the decomposed data series and the first difference of the original time series derived from the ADF test is implemented and shown in Table 1. According to the results of the ADF test, all the data series belonged to the stationary. That is, all the transformed data can be used to model constructions.

Table 1. Stationary analysis of primary energy consumption in Taiwan.

Difference and Decomposition	Specification	t-Value	Critical Value		
			1%	5%	10%
First difference of original values	Trend	−4.267	−4.150	−3.500	−3.180
	Drift	−2.869	−3.580	−2.930	−2.600
	None	−1.792	−2.620	−1.950	−1.610
IMF1	Trend	−10.045	−4.150	−3.500	−3.180
	Drift	−10.000	−3.580	−2.930	−2.600
	None	−10.022	−2.620	−1.950	−1.610
IMF2	Trend	−9.793	−4.150	−3.500	−3.180
	Drift	−9.954	−3.580	−2.930	−2.600
	None	−10.066	−2.620	−1.950	−1.610
IMF3	Trend	−4.431	−4.150	−3.500	−3.180
	Drift	−4.797	−3.580	−2.930	−2.600
	None	−4.801	−2.620	−1.950	−1.610
IMF4	Trend	−46.468	−4.150	−3.500	−3.180
	Drift	−20.728	−3.580	−2.930	−2.600
	None	−7.099	−2.620	−1.950	−1.610

To further determine the parameters of the ARIMA order, ACF and PACF will be utilized. Likewise, such a procedure can also be followed for the decomposed data set using EEMD. To simplify the analytical procedure of EEMD-ARIMA, the corresponding ACF and PACF diagrams are not presented here.

Through the AIC and the statistical significance test, the suitable ARIMA models can be derived for the first difference time series and decomposed time series via the EEMD. Then the optimal form is specified as ARIMA(1,1,1). Table 1 shows the test results in the first difference of the original sequence. The original sequence is not stationary. Based on the first difference in the original difference, the sequence shows a stable status. Therefore, the difference d will be set as 1. IMF1 ~ IMF4 and the residual are derived from the original sequence using the EEMD method. The sum of the IMFs and the residual is equal to the original sequence. The rationality has already been explained in the fourth paragraph of Section 3.1, where the original sequence was split into several different sequences. The sum of decomposed sequences equals to original sequence. Finally, after determining the proper parameters of the ARIMA models, whether the residual of the selected model possesses the autocorrelation problem should be confirmed. Therefore, the ACF and PACF tests were conducted to verify the selected model. Figure 4 demonstrates the estimated residuals using the ACF and PACF tests. According to the test results, no autocorrelation and partial autocorrelation exist within the residuals.

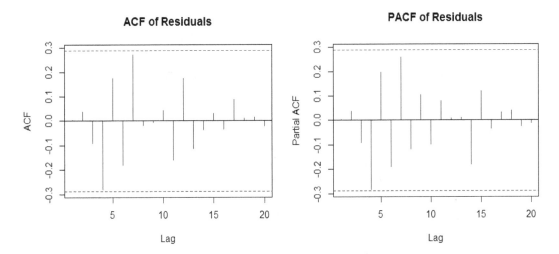

Figure 4. Residual error by autocorrelation function (ACF) and partial autocorrelation function (PACF) for ARIMA(1,1,1).

4.5. Forecasting with the EEMD-ARIMA-SVR Model Optimized by the GA Method

After building the EEMD-ARIMA model, the SVR method will be introduced to reduce the errors produced by ARIMA and enhance forecasting accuracy. According to earlier works, the prediction performance of the SVR method is outstanding; further, it can be fused with other nonlinear or linear methods successfully. Thus, after building the EEMD-ARIMA model, the SVR method will be introduced to reduce the errors produced by ARIMA and enhance forecasting accuracy.

Regarding the hybrid models in this research, the ARIMA initially served as a preprocessor to filter the linear pattern of the decomposed data series. Then, the error terms of the ARIMA model were fed into the SVR model to improve prediction accuracy. Generally, three parameters, c, ε, and γ, can influence the accuracy of the SVR model. Currently, no clear definition and standard procedure are available for determining the above three parameters [21]. However, the improper selection of the three parameters will cause either overfitting or underfitting. To prevent these, the GA method with cross-validation will be introduced to derive the best parameters for constructing the forecasting model. Meanwhile, some studies have pointed out that the utilization of the RBF can yield better prediction performance [21,22]. Thus, the RBF kernel with the 5-fold cross-validation based on the RMSE measure is adopted to help derive the best parameters of the SVR using GA. The above procedures will be applied to the ARIMA-SVR and EEMD-ARIMA-SVR models.

In GA, the number of iterations is set as 100, the population size is defined as 50, and the maximum number of iterations is defined as 50. The search boundaries for c, ε, and γ are within the intervals $[\ 10^{-4},\ 10^{2}\ ]$, $[\ 10^{-4},\ 2\ ]$, and $[\ 2^{-4},\ 2^{2}\ ]$, respectively. The optimal values for c, ε, and γ can thus be 0.441, 3.813, and 0.219, respectively. Further, the c, ε, and γ parameters of the decomposed time series belonging to the four independent IMFs and the residual (Figure 3) are summarized in Table 2. Once the parameters have been derived using GA, the optimal hybrid prediction model can be established.

Table 2. The parameter selection of forecasting model optimized by GA.

Models		c	γ	ε
ARIMA-GA-SVR		0.441	3.813	0.219
	IMF1	0.995	1.072	0.195
	IMF2	4.775	0.852	0.100
EEMD-ARIMA-GA-SVR	IMF3	0.751	1.134	0.461
	IMF4	0.304	3.308	0.470
	Residuals	0.022	1.501	0.352

4.6. Evaluations of Hybrid Models and Forecasting Results

After the construction of the hybrid models, the effectiveness of predictions will be compared further with those of different models including ARIMA, ARIMA-SVR, ARIMA-GA-SVR, EEMD-ARIMA, and EEMD-ARIMA-SVR. The superiority of the proposed EEMD-ARIMA-GA-SVR model of forecasting capability will be verified accordingly. The parameters derived using the GA with the fivefold cross-validation will be utilized to construct the SVR model. The parameters can yield better forecasting performances in related ARIMA-SVR models.

Based on the proposed hybrid framework and the five models for comparisons, the primary energy consumption in Taiwan for 2010–2014 is predicted and summarized in Table 3. According to the prediction results, EEMD-ARIMA-SVR and EEMD-ARIMA-GA-SVR outperformed the other four models. Meanwhile, the prediction results derived using ARIMA and ARIMA-SVR were unsatisfactory from the aspect of inconsistencies between predicted versus actual values. The four prediction performance measures, MAE, MAPE, MSE, and RMSE, derived from the six training models versus the actual values are illustrated in Figure 5 and summarized in Table 4. Based on the results of comparisons, the proposed model outperformed ARIMA. MAE and MSE decreased by 70.43% and 93.28% in the training stage, respectively; further, the two measures decreased by 71.89% and 88.51% in the testing stage, respectively. From the aspects of MAPE and RMSE, both measures improved by 64.68% and 74.07% in the training stage, respectively; they also improved by 71.85% and 66.10% in the testing stage, respectively.

Table 3. Data Test by four sample ranging from 2011 to 2014.

Year	2011	2012	2013	2014
Actual	109.542	109.797	110.959	112.019
ARIMA	111.896	114.527	117.200	119.914
ARIMA-SVR	110.579	113.137	115.735	118.372
ARIMA-GA-SVR	110.071	112.591	115.160	117.777
EEMD-ARIMA	113.174	110.733	111.934	115.542
EEMD-ARIMA-SVR	112.222	110.112	110.809	115.061
EEMD-ARIMA-GA-SVR	112.057	110.075	110.678	114.912

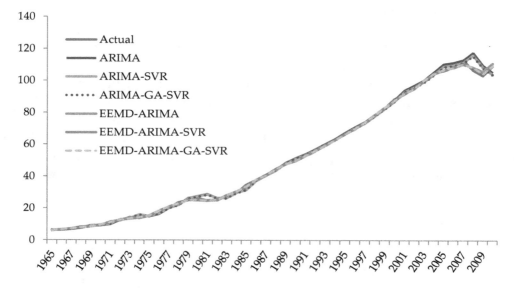

Figure 5. Fittings of the six models.

The proposed model outperformed ARIMA-SVR. MAE and MSE decreased by 67.85% and 91.59% in the training stage, respectively; further, the two measures decreased by 61.52% and 80.31% in the testing stage, respectively. Meanwhile, MAPE and RMSE improved by 62.26% and 71.01% in the training stage and by 61.44% and 55.63% in the testing stage, respectively.

Table 4. Comparison of forecasting indices.

Models	Training				Testing			
	MAE	MAPE [*]	MSE	RMSE	MAE	MAPE [*]	MSE	RMSE
ARIMA	1.397	3.704	5.669	2.381	5.305	4.782	32.301	5.683
ARIMA-SVR	1.285	3.467	4.535	2.130	3.877	3.491	18.851	4.342
ARIMA-GA-SVR	1.257	3.408	4.246	2.061	3.320	2.988	14.723	3.837
EEMD-ARIMA	0.499	1.429	0.611	0.781	2.266	2.048	6.856	2.618
EEMD-ARIMA-SVR	0.425	1.351	0.388	0.623	1.547	1.396	4.139	2.034
EEMD-ARIMA-GA-SVR	0.413	1.308	0.381	0.617	1.492	1.346	3.711	1.926

Remark: *: numbers in percentage.

Compared with ARIMA-GA-SVR, the proposed model performed better as well. MAE and MSE decreased by 67.14% and 91.02%, in the training stage and by 55.08% and 74.79% in the testing stage, respectively. Further, MAPE and RMSE improved by 61.61% and 70.04% in the training stage and by 54.96% and 49.79% in the testing stage, respectively. Based on the above comparison results, the hybrid model integrated with the EEMD method showed better forecasting performance than other models without the data decomposition process.

The proposed model also outperformed EEMD-ARIMA. MAE and MSE decreased by 17.17% and 37.57% in the training stage and by 34.19% and 45.87% in the testing stage, respectively. Meanwhile, MAPE and RMSE were enhanced by 8.41% and 20.98% in the training stage and by 34.27% and 26.43% in the testing stage, respectively.

Compared with EEMD-ARIMA-SVR, the proposed framework performed better. From the aspect of MAE and MSE, the proposed framework outperformed EEMD-ARIMA-SVR by reducing both measures by 2.76% and 1.80% in the training stage and by 3.57% and 10.33% in the testing stage, respectively. At the same time, MAPE and RMSE were enhanced by 3.19% and 0.91% in the training stage and by 3.58% and 5.30% in the testing stage, respectively.

More specifically, from the aspect of training models, the hybrid models including EEMD-ARIMA-SVR and EEMD-ARIMA-GA-SVR performed better, with relatively smaller residual errors in comparison with results derived from any stand-alone or hybrid models. The predictions based on the models without the EEMD decomposition show the limited forecasting capability of the training models. Similarly, from the perspective of the testing model, the proposed model achieved better performance in predicting primary energy consumption. In this study, the comparison results show that the hybrid models with EEMD decomposition can significantly reduce overall forecasting errors. That is, the EEMD method is useful in manipulating the nonstationary time series; thus, better prediction results can be derived by integrating other forecasting methods. Further, GA can reduce forecasting errors by ARIMA-SVR. Based on the analytical results, the proposed EEMD-ARIMA-GA-SVR is a powerful tool and model for energy consumption prediction.

Finally, to identify the significant differences between the prediction results of any two models adopted in this work, the Wilcoxon signed-rank test is performed. This test was adopted extensively in examining the prediction results of two different models and justifying whether these results are significantly different based on small samples [37,38]. The null and alternative hypotheses are described as follows:

$$H_0: \mu_1 - \mu_2 = 0 \text{ (null hypothesis) and}$$

$$H_1: \mu_1 - \mu_2 \neq 0 \text{ (alternative hypothesis)},$$

where μ_1 represents the mean of the actual data and μ_2 stands for the mean of the predicted data. The Wilcoxon test can easily determine whether the mean differences are significant or not. All the

p-values derived from the testing of the six pairs of methods were higher than 0.05. That is, no mean differences are observed between the test and predicted values derived from each method.

5. Conclusions

This study presented a hybrid prediction model consisting of ARIMA, SVR, EEMD, and GA. The empirical results have verified the feasibility of the proposed method. Such a hybrid model that combines linear and nonlinear patterns based on the ARIMA and the SVR models as well as adopts data preprocessing and parameter optimization for time series predictions can produce more precise prediction results. From the aspect of limitations and future research possibilities, different datasets on energy consumption can be used at the same time to evaluate whether the forecasting performance of the proposed model will be the best among all prediction models. The data post-processing procedure can be integrated; the differences of the prediction results derived from the proposed model and the framework consisting of the post-processing procedure can be compared. In the future, a dynamic procedure in terms of multiple-step-ahead forecasting can be adopted to replace the one-step-ahead forecasting techniques being used in this work. Much more meaningful and valuable information can be derived for decision-makers in energy predictions.

Author Contributions: Y.-S.K. designed, performed research, analyzed the data, and wrote the paper. K.N. advised on the research methods. C.-Y.H. advised on the research methods, re-wrote, and proof-read the whole article. All authors have read and agreed to the published version of the manuscript.

References

1. BP Statistical Review of World Energy. June 2015. Available online: http://www.bp.com/content/dam/bp/pdf/Energy-economics/statistical-review-2015/bpstatistical-review-of-world-energy-2015-full-report.pdf (accessed on 1 July 2017).
2. Yuan, C.; Liu, S.; Fang, Z. Comparison of china's primary energy consumption forecasting by using arima (the autoregressive integrated moving average) model and GM (1, 1) model. *Energy* **2016**, *100*, 384–390. [CrossRef]
3. Ardakani, F.; Ardehali, M. Long-term electrical energy consumption forecasting for developing and developed economies based on different optimized models and historical data types. *Energy* **2014**, *65*, 452–461. [CrossRef]
4. Zhu, S.; Wang, J.; Zhao, W.; Wang, J. A seasonal hybrid procedure for electricity demand forecasting in china. *Appl. Energy* **2011**, *88*, 3807–3815. [CrossRef]
5. Yolcu, U.; Egrioglu, E.; Aladag, C.H. A new linear & nonlinear artificial neural network model for time series forecasting. *Decis. Support Syst.* **2013**, *54*, 1340–1347.
6. Wu, Z.; Huang, N.E. Ensemble empirical mode decomposition: A noise-assisted data analysis method. *Adv. Adapt. Data Anal.* **2009**, *1*, 1–41. [CrossRef]
7. Wang, T.; Zhang, M.; Yu, Q.; Zhang, H. Comparing the applications of emd and eemd on time–frequency analysis of seismic signal. *J. Appl. Geophys.* **2012**, *83*, 29–34. [CrossRef]
8. Tang, L.; Yu, L.; Wang, S.; Li, J.; Wang, S. A novel hybrid ensemble learning paradigm for nuclear energy consumption forecasting. *Appl. Energy* **2012**, *93*, 432–443. [CrossRef]
9. Fei, S.-W. A hybrid model of emd and multiple-kernel rvr algorithm for wind speed prediction. *Int. J. Electr. Power Energy Syst.* **2016**, *78*, 910–915. [CrossRef]
10. Bagherzadeh, S.A.; Sabzehparvar, M. A local and online sifting process for the empirical mode decomposition and its application in aircraft damage detection. *Mech. Syst. Signal Process.* **2015**, *54*, 68–83. [CrossRef]
11. Fumo, N.; Biswas, M.R. Regression analysis for prediction of residential energy consumption. *Renew. Sustain. Energy Rev.* **2015**, *47*, 332–343. [CrossRef]
12. Azadeh, A.; Ghaderi, S.; Sohrabkhani, S. Annual electricity consumption forecasting by neural network in high energy consuming industrial sectors. *Energy Convers. Manag.* **2008**, *49*, 2272–2278. [CrossRef]
13. Ahmad, A.; Hassan, M.; Abdullah, M.; Rahman, H.; Hussin, F.; Abdullah, H.; Saidur, R. A review on applications of ann and svm for building electrical energy consumption forecasting. *Renew. Sustain. Energy Rev.* **2014**, *33*, 102–109. [CrossRef]
14. Xiong, T.; Bao, Y.; Hu, Z. Does restraining end effect matter in emd-based modeling framework for time series prediction? Some experimental evidences. *Neurocomputing* **2014**, *123*, 174–184. [CrossRef]

15. Lin, C.-S.; Chiu, S.-H.; Lin, T.-Y. Empirical mode decomposition–based least squares support vector regression for foreign exchange rate forecasting. *Econ. Model.* **2012**, *29*, 2583–2590. [CrossRef]

16. Al-Garni, A.Z.; Zubair, S.M.; Nizami, J.S. A regression model for electric-energy-consumption forecasting in eastern saudi arabia. *Energy* **1994**, *19*, 1043–1049. [CrossRef]

17. Wong, S.L.; Wan, K.K.; Lam, T.N. Artificial neural networks for energy analysis of office buildings with daylighting. Appl. *Energy* **2010**, *87*, 551–557.

18. Zhang, G.P. Time series forecasting using a hybrid arima and neural network model. *Neurocomputing* **2003**, *50*, 159–175. [CrossRef]

19. Wang, Y.; Wang, J.; Zhao, G.; Dong, Y. Application of residual modification approach in seasonal arima for electricity demand forecasting: A case study of china. *Energy Policy* **2012**, *48*, 284–294. [CrossRef]

20. Azadeh, A.; Ghaderi, S.; Tarverdian, S.; Saberi, M. Integration of artificial neural networks and genetic algorithm to predict electrical energy consumption. *Appl. Math. Comput.* **2007**, *186*, 1731–1741. [CrossRef]

21. Lee, Y.-S.; Tong, L.-I. Forecasting time series using a methodology based on autoregressive integrated moving average and genetic programming. *Knowl. Based Syst.* **2011**, *24*, 66–72. [CrossRef]

22. Pai, P.-F.; Lin, C.-S. A hybrid arima and support vector machines model in stock price forecasting. *Omega* **2005**, *33*, 497–505. [CrossRef]

23. Patel, M.; Chaudhary, S.; Garg, S. Machine learning based statistical prediction model for improving performance of live virtual machine migration. *J. Eng.* **2016**, *2016*, 3061674. [CrossRef]

24. Alwee, R.; Hj Shamsuddin, S.M.; Sallehuddin, R. Hybrid support vector regression and autoregressive integrated moving average models improved by particle swarm optimization for property crime rates forecasting with economic indicators. *Sci. World J.* **2013**, *2013*, 951475. [CrossRef]

25. Fan, L.; Pan, S.; Li, Z.; Li, H. An ica-based support vector regression scheme for forecasting crude oil prices. *Technol. Forecast. Soc. Chang.* **2016**, *112*, 245–253. [CrossRef]

26. Zhang, J.-L.; Zhang, Y.-J.; Zhang, L. A novel hybrid method for crude oil price forecasting. *Energy Econ.* **2015**, *49*, 649–659. [CrossRef]

27. Huang, N.E.; Shen, Z.; Long, S.R.; Wu, M.C.; Shih, H.H.; Zheng, Q.; Yen, N.-C.; Tung, C.C.; Liu, H.H. The empirical mode decomposition and the hilbert spectrum for nonlinear and non-stationary time series analysis. *Proc. R. Soc. Lond. Ser. A Math. Phys. Eng. Sci.* **1998**, *454*, 903–995. [CrossRef]

28. Box, G.E.; Jenkins, G.M.; Reinsel, G.C. *Time Series Analysis: Forecasting and Control*; Holdenday: San Francisco, CA, USA, 1976.

29. Vapnik, V. *The Nature of Statistical Learning Theory*; Springer: New York, NY, USA, 2000.

30. Kao, L.-J.; Chiu, C.-C.; Lu, C.-J.; Yang, J.-L. Integration of nonlinear independent component analysis and support vector regression for stock price forecasting. *Neurocomputing* **2013**, *99*, 534–542. [CrossRef]

31. Holland, J.H. *Adaptation in Natural and Artificial Systems: An Introductory Analysis with Applications to Biology, Control, and Artificial Intelligence*; University of Michigan Press: Ann Arbor, MI, USA, 1975.

32. Davis, L. *Handbook of Genetic Algorithms*; Van Nostrand Reinhold: New York, NY, USA, 1991.

33. Goldberg, D.E. *Genetic Algorithms in Search, Optimization, and Machine Learning*; Addison-Wesley Reading: Menlo Park, CA, USA, 1989.

34. Mitchell, M. *An Introduction to Genetic Algorithms*; MIT Press: Cambridge, MA, USA, 1998.

35. Jin, Y.; Branke, J. Evolutionary Optimization in Uncertain Environments-A Survey. *IEEE Trans. Evol. Comput.* **2005**, *9*, 303–317. [CrossRef]

36. Huang, C.-F. A hybrid stock selection model using genetic algorithms and support vector regression. *Appl. Soft Comput.* **2012**, *12*, 807–818. [CrossRef]

37. Wang, Y.; Gu, J.; Zhou, Z.; Wang, Z. Diarrhoea outpatient visits prediction based on time series decomposition and multi-local predictor fusion. *Knowl. Based Syst.* **2015**, *88*, 12–23. [CrossRef]

38. Yan, W. Toward automatic time-series forecasting using neural networks. *IEEE Trans. Neural Netw. Learn. Syst.* **2012**, *23*, 1028–1039. [PubMed]

4

Financial Distress Prediction and Feature Selection in Multiple Periods by Lassoing Unconstrained Distributed Lag Non-linear Models

Dawen Yan [1], Guotai Chi [2] and Kin Keung Lai [3],*

[1]   School of Mathematical Sciences, Dalian University of Technology, Dalian 116024, China;
       dawenyan@dlut.edu.cn
[2]   School of Economics and Management, Dalian University of Technology, Dalian 116024, China;
       Chigt@dlut.edu.cn
[3]   College of Economics, Shenzhen University, Shenzhen 518060, China
*   Correspondence: mskklai@outlook.com

Abstract: In this paper, we propose a new framework of a financial early warning system through combining the unconstrained distributed lag model (DLM) and widely used financial distress prediction models such as the logistic model and the support vector machine (SVM) for the purpose of improving the performance of an early warning system for listed companies in China. We introduce simultaneously the 3~5-period-lagged financial ratios and macroeconomic factors in the consecutive time windows $t-3$, $t-4$ and $t-5$ to the prediction models; thus, the influence of the early continued changes within and outside the company on its financial condition is detected. Further, by introducing lasso penalty into the logistic-distributed lag and SVM-distributed lag frameworks, we implement feature selection and exclude the potentially redundant factors, considering that an original long list of accounting ratios is used in the financial distress prediction context. We conduct a series of comparison analyses to test the predicting performance of the models proposed by this study. The results show that our models outperform logistic, SVM, decision tree and neural network (NN) models in a single time window, which implies that the models incorporating indicator data in multiple time windows convey more information in terms of financial distress prediction when compared with the existing singe time window models.

Keywords: financial distress prediction; unconstrained distributed lag model; multiple periods; Chinese listed companies

1. Introduction

Over the last four decades, models and methods for the prediction of corporate financial distress have attracted considerable interest among academics as well as practitioners. Financial distress prediction models can be used for many purposes including: monitoring of the solvency of regulated companies, assessment of loan default risk and the pricing of bonds, credit derivatives, and other securities exposed to credit risk (see [1–4]).

Different countries have different accounting procedures and rules; thus, the definition of financial distress put forward by different scholars is not always the same (see [4–7]). Bankruptcy is one of the most commonly used outcomes of financial distress of a company [5]. The nature of a bankrupt firm is that the owners can abandon the firm and transfer ownership to the debt holders, and bankruptcy occurs whenever the realized cash flow is less than the debt obligations [8]. It is generally agreed on that financial failure leads to substantive weakening of profitability of the company over time, but it is also feasible that a financially distressed firm may not change its formal status to bankrupt [9].

Therefore, in this paper, as done by [3] and [4], we identify a financially distressed company as the one at risk of failing, but which remains a viable entity at the present time. More specifically, "special treatment" (ST) is used to measure the financial distress status of a listed company. Further, in this paper, we provide a group of financial distress prediction models that incorporate the panel data of financial and macroeconomic indicators to implement early financial distress prediction.

In the existing studies, many classical statistical methods, such as discriminant analysis [1]; logistic regression and multinomial logit models (see [2–4,10]); heuristic algorithm methods such as the genetic algorithm and particle swarm optimization [11]; currently popular machine learning techniques, such as the support vector machine, decision tree and neural networks (see [7,12–16]), have been widely applied to develop financial distress prediction models. The relevant studies also realize that a set of indicators can be used to predict the financial distress, including financial indicators (e.g., see [7,17–20]) and macroeconomic indicators (e.g., see [4]). For example, accounting models such as Altman's 5-variable (Z-score) model (see [1]), 7-variable model (see [21]) etc. have gained popularity in both academic and industrial fields due to their discriminating ability and predictive power.

A few extant studies have predicted financial distress by using the accounting ratios from one or more years prior to its observation, given that early change in financial indicators may provide the warning sign of deterioration of financial conditions. The authors of [1] provide the evidence that bankruptcy can be predicted two years prior to the event, while those of [4] construct respectively two groups of financial distress prediction models for two periods: one year and two years before the observation of the financial distress event. They found that the models in the both time-windows have good predictive performance. Other similar examples can be found in [7,20,22].

In the relevant literatures, financial indicators in the different time windows have proven their contribution to the performance of the distress prediction models, in spite of the fact that the degree of their impact tends to change over time. However, the procedures are performed for all the different lag periods separately, i.e., only using information of one specific year prior to the date of the distress event. To the best of the authors' knowledge, no previous study, which solves the listed companies' financial distress prediction problem, takes into account the impacts of relevant indicators in the different and consecutive lag periods.

In this study, we take the form of the distributed lag model (DLM), in addition to classical classification techniques, into the financial distress prediction problem and propose a group of distress prediction models including the logistic-distributed lag model and the SVM-distributed lag model that can be treated as generalized distributed lag model. We construct the linkage between multiple lagged values of financial ratios and macroeconomic indicators and current financial status in order to capture the dynamic natures of the relevant data. Further, we propose to implement the penalized logistic-distributed lag financial distress model with the least absolute shrinkage and selection operator (lasso) penalty via the algorithm framework of the alternating direction method of multipliers (ADMM) that yields the global optimum for convex and the non-smooth optimization problem. Lasso-type penalty was applied for three purposes: to avoid the collinearity problem in applying the distributed lag models directly, to simultaneously select significant variables and estimate parameters, and to address the problem of over-fitting. We conduct a series of empirical studies to illustrate the application of our distributed lag financial distress models, including a comparison of predictive performances of the two distributed lag financial distress models proposed in this paper as well as the comparisons of predictive performances of our models with a group of widely used classification models in the different time windows. The results show that all distributed lag financial distress models aggregating the data in three consecutive time windows outperform the ones that incorporate the data in any single-period: 3 years, 4 years or 5 years before the observation year of financial distress, when the financial and macroeconomic factors are included. This paper may provide a means of improving the predictive performance of financial distress model by incorporating data of financial and macroeconomic indicators in consecutive and multiple periods before the observation of financial distress.

The rest of this paper is organized as follows. Section 2 briefly reviews the previous financial distress prediction literature and distributed lag modeling. Section 3 constructs a group of generalized distributed lag models composed of lagged explanatory variables and l_1 regularization, the logistic regression-distributed lag model and the lasso–SVM model with lags, and proposes the ADMM algorithm framework for coefficient estimations and variable selection at same time. Section 4 provides a description of the data. Section 5 presents the empirical results and compares the predictive performance of our models reflecting the extended lag effects of used indicators with the existing financial distress prediction models. Section 6 concludes the paper.

2. Background

2.1. Literature on Financial Distress Prediction

2.1.1. Financial Factors and Variable Selection

There is a large amount of theoretical and empirical microeconomic literature pointing to the importance of financial indicators on financial distress forecasting. The authors of [1] selected five financial indicators of strong predictive ability from the initial set of 22 financial indicators using stepwise discriminant analysis: earnings before interest and taxes/total assets, retained earnings/total assets, working capital/total assets, market value equity/book value of total debt and sales/total assets, which measures the productivity of assets of a firm. The other studies that concern the similar accounting ratios in financial distress prediction can also be found in [23,24]. Furthermore, the current-liabilities-to-current-assets ratio used to measure liquidity (see [22,25]) and the total-liabilities-to-total-assets ratio used to measure the degree of indebtedness of a firm (see [22,25,26]) and cash flow (see [18]) have been incorporated into the distress prediction models because of their predictive performance. The authors of [20] considered nine financial indicators and use them to predict the regulatory financial distress in Brazilian electricity distributors. The authors of [7] introduced 31 financial indicators and found that the most important financial indicators may be related to net profit, earnings before income tax, cash flow and net assets. Along this line, with machine learning methods developing, more diversified financial indicators have been considered in very recent studies of Hosaka [27], Korol et al. [28], and Gregova et al. [29].

Another very important recent research line in the area of financial distress prediction is the suitability problem of these financial ratios used as explanatory variables. For example, Kovacova et al. [30] discussed the dependence between explanatory variables and the Visegrad Group (V4) and found that enterprises of each country in V4 prefer different explanatory variables. Kliestik [31] chose eleven explanatory financial variables and proposed a bankruptcy prediction model based on local law in Slovakia and business aspects.

In this paper, we construct an original financial dataset including 43 financial ratios. The ratios are selected on the basis of their popularity in the previous literature (see [1,7,27]) and potential relevancy to this study. Then, like many relevant studies [32–34], we use the lasso method and conduct feature selection in order to exclude the potentially redundant factors.

2.1.2. Macroeconomic Conditions

Macroeconomic conditions are relevant for the business environment in which firms are operating; thus, the deterioration of macroeconomic conditions may induce the occurrence of the financial distress. Macroeconomic variables have been found to impact corporate default and bankruptcy risk significantly, and good examples can be found in [35–39]. In the aspect of financial distress of listed companies, [4] consider the macroeconomic indicators of the retail price index and the short-term bill rate adjusted for inflation in addition to the accounting variables. The results in their studies suggest that all macroeconomic indicators have significant impact on the likelihood of a firm's financial distress. In this paper, we control for macroeconomic conditions, GDP growth, inflation, unemployment rate in the urban area and consumption level growth over the sample period. GDP growth is widely understood to be an important variable to measure economic strength and prosperity, and the increase in GDP growth may decrease the likelihood of distress. The authors of [22,40] have pointed out that the decline in GDP is significantly linked to the tightening of a firm's financial conditions, especially during the financial crisis period. The unemployment rate and inflation are two broadly used measures of overall health of the economy. High unemployment and high inflation that reflect a weaker economy may increase the likelihood of financial distress. Their impacts on financial distress have been examined in [16,37].

Different from the existing relevant studies that consider the lagged effect of macroeconomic variables only in a fixed window, such as 3 years prior to financial distress [16], this paper imposes a distributed lag structure of macroeconomic data, in addition to financial ratio data, and considers the lagged effects of the factors in the multi-periods. Particular attention is devoted to the lag structure and whether the predicting performance can be improved after introducing a series of lagged macroeconomic variables. The theoretical and empirical investigations in this study may complement the literature on financial distress prediction concerned with applying dynamic macro and financial data.

2.1.3. Related Literature on Chinese Listed Companies

The Chinese stock market has grown to over 55 trillion in market capitalization as of February 2020, and the number of listed firms has surpassed 3200, becoming the world's second largest market. Its ongoing development and the parallel evolution of regulations have made China's stock market an important subject for mainstream research in financial economics [41]. In April 1998, the Shanghai and Shenzhen stock exchanges implemented a special treatment (ST) system for stock transactions of listed companies with abnormal financial conditions or other abnormal conditions. According to the regulations, there are three main reasons for designation of a *ST* company: (1) a listed company has negative net profits for two consecutive years; (2) the shareholders' equity of the company is lower than the registered capital; (3) a firm's operations have stopped and there is no hope of restoring operations in the next 3 months due to natural disasters, serious accidents, or lawsuits and arbitration [7]. *ST* status is then usually applied as a proxy of financial distress (e.g., [7,16,42–45]).

Researchers regard the topic of financial distress prediction of Chinese listed companies as data-mining tasks, and use data mining, machine learning or statistical methods to construct a series of prediction models incorporating financial data (see [7,42,43]) or financial plus macroeconomic data [16] in one-time-period, but not in multiple periods of time. In the very recent study of [45], the authors proposed a financial distress forecast model combined with multi-period forecast results. First, with the commonly used classifiers such as the support vector machine (SVM), decision tree (DT) etc., the two to five-year-ahead financial distress forecast models are established one by one and denoted as *T*-2 to *T*-5 models, respectively. Then, through combining the forecast results of these one-time-period models, the multi-period forecast results, as a weighted average over a fixed window, with exponentially declining weights, are provided. This is obviously different from our model, as we introduce the multi-period lagged explanatory variables and detect simultaneously the effects of the variables in different prior periods on financial distress in the process of modeling.

2.2. Distributed Lag Models

Sometimes the effect of an explanatory variable on a specific outcome, such as the changes in mortality risk, is not limited to the period when it is observed, but it is delayed in time [46,47]. This introduces the problem of modeling the relationship between a future outcome and a sequence of lags of explanatory variables, specifying the distribution of the effects at different times before the outcome. Among the various methods that have been proposed to deal with delayed effects, as a major econometric approach, distributed lag models (DLMs) have been used to diverse research fields including assessing the distributed lag effects of air pollutants on children's health [48], hospital admission scheduling [49], and economical and financial time series analysis [50,51].

DLMs model the response Y_t, observed at time t in terms of past values of the independent variable X, and have a general representation given by

$$g(Y_t) = \alpha_0 + \sum_{l=0}^{L} s_l(x_{t-l}; \alpha_l) + \varepsilon_t, t = L, +1, \ldots, T \tag{1a}$$

where Y_t is the response at time t and g is a monotonic link function; the functions s_l denote a smoothed relationship between the explanatory vector x_{t-l} and the parameter vector α_l; α_0 and ε_t denote the intercept term and error term with a zero mean and a constant variance σ^2; l, L are the lag number and the maximum lag. The form that link function g takes presents a distributed lag linear model or a non-linear model. For example, linear g plus the continuous variable Y_t present distributed lag linear models, while the logit function g plus the binary variable Y_t present a distributed lag non-linear model. In model (1a), the parametric function s_l is applied to model the shape of the lag structure, usually polynomials (see [49,52]) or less often regression splines [53] or more complicated smoothing techniques of penalized splines within generalized additive models [47,48]. In fact, the introduction of s_l is originally used to solve the problem that these successive past observations may regard as collinear. If L, the number of relevant values of X, is small, as may well be the case for some problems if annual data are involved, then model (1a) degrades to an unconstrained distributed lag model given by the following general representation

$$g(Y_t) = \alpha_0 + \sum_{l=0}^{L} \alpha_l^T x_{t-l} + \varepsilon_t, \ t = L, +1, \ldots, T \tag{1b}$$

In (1b), the definitions of variables are the same as those in (1). Correspondingly, the coefficients in model (1b) can be estimated directly by pooled least squares for the linear case or pooled maximum likelihood for the non-linear case, e.g., logit link function g under the assumption that x_{t-l} is strictly exogenous [54].

In this paper, logistic regression with an unconstrained distributed lag structure is used to identify the relationship between financial and macroeconomic indicators and future outcome of financial distress. The logistic regression may be the most frequently used technique in the financial distress prediction field ([4,20]) because logistic regression relies on fewer assumptions due to the absence of the need for multivariate normality and homogeneity in the variance–covariance matrices of the explanatory variables [23]. Further, a lasso penalty is introduced to conduct simultaneous parameter estimation and variable selection, considering that the lasso penalty method has good performance for solving the overfitting problem caused by the introduction of factors in adjacent windows and selecting the features and the corresponding exposures with relatively significant influence on the response. In fact, the lasso method has been applied for linear-distributed lag modelling (e.g., [55]).

3. Methodology

In this section, by combining the logistic regression method and unconstrained distributed lag model, we seek to estimate which indicators and in which period prior to the distress event best predicts financial distress. First, we construct Model 1 that represents the "accounting-only" model and incorporates the financial ratios. We introduce the 3-period-lagged financial ratios as independent variables into Model 1 and use the model to predict the financial distress event in year t by using the data of relevant indicator of the consecutive years, $t-3$, $t-4$, $t-5$, simultaneously. Note that t refers to the current year in this paper. Then, we construct Model 2, which represents the 'accounting plus macroeconomic indicators' model, and includes, in addition to the accounting variables, 3-period-lagged macroeconomic indicators. Then, we introduce lasso penalty to the models and implement the coefficient estimation and feature selection. Further, we provide the algorithm framework of alternating direction method of multipliers (ADMM) that yields the global optimum for convex and the non-smooth optimization problem to obtain the optimal estimation for the coefficients. Finally, we propose a support vector machine model that includes the lagged variables of the accounting ratios and macroeconomic factors. This model is used for comparison of the predictive performance of the logistic model with a distributed lag of variables.

3.1. Logistic Regression Framework with Distributed Lags

3.1.1. The Logistic Regression-Distributed Lag Model with Accounting Ratios Only

The logistic regression may be the most frequently used technique in the financial distress prediction field and has been widely recognized ([11,20]). We propose a logistic model composed of lagged explanatory variables. Similar to the distributed lag linear model, the model has the following general form:

$$P\left(Y_{i,t} = 1 \middle| X_{i,t-l}\right) = (1 + \exp(-(\alpha_0 + \sum_{l=0}^{L} \alpha_{t-l}^T X_{i,t-l})))^{-1}, \ t = t_0 + L, t_0 + L + 1, \ldots, t_0 + L + d \quad (2)$$

In (2), $Y_{i,t}$ is a binary variable, and if $Y_{i,t} = 1$, then it means that firm I at time t is a financially distressed company, otherwise, firm i ($i = 1, 2, \ldots, n$) is a financially healthy company, corresponding the case of $Y_{i,t} = 0$; α_0 is intercept, and $\alpha_{t-l} = (\alpha_{t-l,1}, \alpha_{t-l,2}, \ldots, \alpha_{t-l,p})^T$ is the coefficient vector for the explanatory variable vector $X_{i,t-l}$ at time $t-l$; $X_{i,t-l}$ is the p-dimension accounting ratio vector for firm i at time $t - l$, $l = 0, 1, 2, \ldots, L$; l, L are the lag number and the maximum lag; t_0 is the beginning of the observation period and d is the duration of observation. The idea in (2) is that the likelihood of occurrence of the financial distress at time t for a listed company may depend on X measured not only in the current time t, but also in the previous time windows $t - 1$ through $t - L$.

In Formula (2), we assume a five-year effect and set the maximum lag $L = 5$, given that (1) the effect of the explanatory variable on the response variable may decline to zero in the time series data scenario; (2) the considered length of lag is not more than 5 years in most of the previous studies of financial distress prediction (see [1,7,37]). Besides, we set directly the coefficient $\alpha_{t-0}, \alpha_{t-1}, \alpha_{t-2}$ for the variables in the current year and the previous two year before ST to be 0 vectors, because (1) the financial statement in the current year (year t) is not available for financial distressed companies labeled as in financial distress in year t, since the financial statement is published at the end of the year, but special treatment probably occurs before the publication; (2) designation of an ST company depends on the financial and operating situations of the previous year before the label of ST. Put simply, it is not meaningful to forecast ST risk 0, 1 or 2 years ahead (see [7,45]). Therefore, the logistic model containing the 3~5-period-lagged financial indicators, defined as Model 1, is presented as follows:

$$P(Y_{i,t} = 1) = (1 + \exp(-\alpha_0 - \alpha_{t-3}^{T} X_{i,t-3} - \alpha_{t-4}^{T} X_{i,t-4} - \alpha_{t-5}^{T} X_{i,t-5})^{-1} \quad (3)$$

In Equation (3), $Y_{i,t}$ is binary response and is defined the same in (2); $X_{i,t-3}$, $X_{i,t-4}$ and $X_{i,t-5}$ are the p-dimensional financial indicator vectors of firm i observed in year $t - 3$, $t - 4$ and $t - 5$; α_0, α_{t-3}, $\alpha_{t-4}, \alpha_{t-5}$ are intercept terms and the coefficient vectors for the explanatory vectors $X_{i,t-3}, X_{i,t-4}$ and $X_{i,t-5}$, respectively, and α_{t-l} ($l = 3, 4, 5$) stands for the average effect of increasing by one unit in $X_{i,t-l}$ on the log of the odd of the financial distress event holding others constants. Of course, in Model 1, we consider the effect of changes in financial ratios on financial distress probability during three consecutive years ($t - 3, t - 4, t - 5$).

3.1.2. The Logistic Regression-Distributed Lag Model with Accounting Plus Macroeconomic Variables

We further add the macro-economic factors into Equation (3) to detect the influence of macroeconomic conditions, in addition to financial indicators. Model 2, including both accounting variables and macroeconomic variables, takes the following form:

$$P(Y_{i,t} = 1) = (1 + \exp(-\alpha_0 - \alpha_{t-3}^{T} X_{i,t-3} - \alpha_{t-4}^{T} X_{i,t-4} - \alpha_{t-5}^{T} X_{i,t-5} - \eta_{t-3}^{T} Z_{i,t-3} - \eta_{t-4}^{T} Z_{i,t-4} - \eta_{t-5}^{T} Z_{i,t-5}))^{-1} \quad (4)$$

In Equation (4), Z_{t-l} ($l = 3, 4, 5$) represents the m-dimensional macroeconomic factor vector of year $t - l$; η_{t-l} ($l = 3, 4, 5$) is the coefficient vector for $Z_{i,t-l}$; the others are defined as in Equation (3). Similarly, $\eta_{j,t-3} + \eta_{j,t-4} + \eta_{j,t-4}$ represent the cumulative effects on log odd of the distress event of the j-th ($j = 1, 2, \ldots, m$) macroeconomic factor.

Models 1 and 2, marked as Equations (3) and (4), can reflect the continued influence of the financial statement and macroeconomic conditions for multi-periods on the response; however, a considerable amount of potentially helpful financial ratios, macroeconomic factors and their lags may bring redundant information, thus decreasing the models' forecast performances. In the following section, we implement feature selection by introducing lasso penalty into the financial distress forecast logistic models. Further, we provide an ADMM algorithm framework to obtain the optimal estimation for the coefficients.

3.2. The Lasso–Logistic Regression-Distributed Lag Model

There is currently much discussion about the lasso method. Lasso, as an l_1-norm penalization approach, has been actively studied. In particular, lasso has been used on the distributed lag linear model, and lasso estimators for coefficients are obtained through minimizing the residual sum of squares and the l_1-norm of coefficients simultaneously (e.g., [55]). For the logistic model with lagged financial variables (3), we can extend to logistic–lasso as follows in Equation (5):

$$(\hat{\alpha}_0, \hat{\alpha}) = \underset{\alpha_0, \alpha}{argmin} f(\alpha_0, \alpha | X_{i,t-3}, X_{i,t-4}, X_{i,t-5}, Y_{i,t}) + \lambda \|\alpha\|_1 \tag{5}$$

where

$$f(\alpha_0, \alpha | X_{it}, Y_{i,t}) = \sum_{t=t_0+5}^{t_0+d} \sum_{i=1}^{n} (-Y_{i,t}(\alpha_0 + \alpha^T X_{it}) + \ln(1 + \exp\{\alpha_0 + \alpha^T X_{it}\}))$$

and $\hat{\alpha}_0$ and $\hat{\alpha}$ denote the maximum likelihood estimations for intercept α_0 and coefficient vector α; f denotes the minus log-likelihood function of Model 1 and can be regarded as the loss function of the observations; $\alpha = (\alpha_{t-3}{}^T, \alpha_{t-4}{}^T, \alpha_{t-5}{}^T)^T$ are the unknown coefficients for explanatory variables; $X_{it} = (X_{i,t-3}{}^T, X_{i,t-4}{}^T, X_{i,t-5}{}^T)^T$, $Y_{i,t}$ are known training observations and defined as above; λ is the turning parameter; $\|\cdot\|_1$ denotes l_1-norm of a vector, i.e., the addition of absolute values of each element of a vector; t_0 and d are defined as before; n is the number of observed company samples.

Introducing the auxiliary variable $\beta \in \mathbf{R}^{3p}$, the lasso–logistic model (5) can be explicitly rewritten as follows:

$$\underset{\alpha_0, \alpha, \beta}{min} f(\alpha_0, \alpha | X_{i,t-3}, X_{i,t-4}, X_{i,t-5}, Y_{i,t}) + \lambda \|\beta\|_1 \; s.t. \alpha = \beta \tag{6}$$

In this paper, we solve the optimization problem (6) by using alternating direction method of multipliers (ADMM) algorithm that was first introduced by [56]. ADMM is a simple but powerful algorithm and can be viewed as an attempt to blend the benefits of dual decomposition [57] and augmented Lagrangian methods for constrained optimization [58]. Now, the ADMM algorithm becomes a benchmark first-order solver, especially for convex and non-smooth minimization models with separable objective functions (see [59,60]), thus, it is applicable for the problem (6).

The augmented Lagrangian function of the optimization problem (6) can be defined as

$$L_\rho(\alpha_0, \alpha, \beta, \theta) = f(\alpha_0, \alpha | X_{it}, Y_{i,t}) + \lambda \|\beta\|_1 - \theta^T(\alpha - \beta) + \frac{\rho}{2} \|\alpha - \beta\|_2^2 \tag{7}$$

where L_ρ is the Lagrange function; θ is a Lagrange multiplier vector and $\rho(>0)$ is an augmented Lagrange multiplier variable. In this paper, ρ is predetermined to be 1 for simplicity. Then, the iterative scheme of ADMM for the optimization problem (6) reads as

$$(\alpha_0^{k+1}, \alpha^{k+1}) = \underset{\alpha_0, \alpha}{argmin} L_\rho((\alpha_0, \alpha), \beta^k, \theta^k) \tag{8a}$$

$$\beta^{k+1} = \underset{\beta}{argmin} L_\rho\left(\alpha^{k+1}, \beta, \theta^k\right) \tag{8b}$$

$$\theta^{k+1} = \theta^k - \rho\left(\alpha^{k+1} - \beta^{k+1}\right) \tag{8c}$$

In (8a)–(8c), α_0^{k+1}, α^{k+1}, β^{k+1}, and θ^k are the values of α_0, α, β, and θ the k-th iterative step of the ADMM algorithm, respectively. Further, the ADMM scheme (8a)–(8c) can be specified as

$$\left(\alpha_0^{k+1}, \alpha^{k+1}\right) = \underset{\alpha_0, \alpha}{argmin} f(\alpha_0, \alpha) - (\theta^k)^T\left(\alpha - \beta^k\right) + \frac{\rho}{2}\|\alpha - \beta^k\|_2^2 \tag{9a}$$

$$\beta^{k+1} = \underset{\beta}{argmin} \lambda\|\beta\|_1 - (\theta^k)^T\left(\alpha^{k+1} - \beta\right) + \frac{\rho}{2}\|\alpha^{k+1} - \beta\|_2^2 \tag{9b}$$

$$\theta^{k+1} = \theta^k - \rho\left(\alpha^{k+1} - \beta^{k+1}\right) \tag{9c}$$

The sub-problem in (9a), that is, the convex and smooth optimization problem, can be fast solved by the Newton method [61], after setting the initial θ, β to be arbitrary constants. More specifically, let $\alpha_*^{k+1} = (\alpha_0^{k+1}; \alpha^{k+1})$ and α_*^{k+1} be calculated via the following process:

$$\alpha_*^{k+1} = \alpha_*^k - (\nabla^2 l)^{-1} \nabla l \tag{10}$$

where

$$l(\alpha_*) = l(\alpha_0; \alpha) = f(\alpha_0, \alpha) - (\theta^k)^T\left(\alpha - \beta^k\right) + \frac{\rho}{2}\|\alpha - \beta^k\|_2^2$$

and $\nabla^2 l \in R^{(3p+1)\times(3p+1)}$, $\nabla l \in R^{3p+1}$ are the hessian matrix and the derivative of differentiable function l with respect to α_*, respectively. For sub-problem (9b), its solution is analytically given by

$$\beta_r^{k+1} = \begin{cases} \alpha_r^{k+1} - \frac{\lambda+\theta_r^k}{\rho}, & \alpha_r^{k+1} > \frac{\lambda+\theta_r^k}{\rho} \\ 0, & \frac{-\lambda+\theta_r^k}{\rho} < \alpha_r^{k+1} \leq \frac{\lambda+\theta_r^k}{\rho} \\ -, & \alpha_r^{k+1} \leq \frac{-\lambda+\theta_r^k}{\rho} \end{cases} \tag{11}$$

where β_r^{k+1}, α_r^{k+1} and θ_r^k are the r-th components of β^{k+1}, α_r^{k+1} and θ^k, respectively, for the k-th iterative step and $r = 1, 2, \ldots, 3p$.

The choice of tuning parameters is important. In this study, we find an optimal tuning parameter λ by the 10-fold cross validation method. We then compare the forecast accuracy of each method based on the mean area under the curve ($MAUC$) given as follows:

$$MAUC(\lambda) = \sum_{j=1}^{10} AUC^j(\lambda)/10 \tag{12}$$

where $AUC^j(\lambda)$ denotes the area under the receiver operating characteristic (ROC) curve on j-th validation set for each tuning parameter λ.

So far, the lasso estimators for the logistic model (5) including 3~5-period-lagged financial ratios have been obtained by following the above procedures. For the convenience of readers, we summarize the whole optimization procedures in training the lasso–logistic with lagged variables and describe them in Algorithm 1.

Algorithm 1. An alternating direction method of multipliers (ADMM) algorithm framework for lasso–logistic
with lagged variables (5). [1]: Dual residual and prime residua denote $\|\beta^{k+1} - \beta^k\|_2$ and $\|\alpha^{k+1} - \beta^k + 1\|_2$ respectively.
[2]: N denotes the maximum iterative number of the ADMM algorithm.

Require:

1. Training data $\{X_{i,t-3}, X_{i,t-4}, X_{i,t-5}, Y_{i,t}\}$, where $X_{i,t-l} \in R^P, l = 3, 4, 5$ and $Y_{i,t} \in \{0,1\}, i = 1, 2, \ldots, n, t = t_0 + 5,$
    $t_0 + 6, \ldots, t_0 + d$

2. Turning parameter λ

3. Choose augmented Lagrange multiplier $\rho = 1$. Set initial $(\theta^0, \beta^0) \in R \times R^P, (\alpha_0^0, \alpha^0) \in R \times R^P$ and stopping
    criterion $\varepsilon = 10^{-6}$.

Ensure:

4. **While** not converging (i.e., dual residual and prime residual [1] are greater than stopping criterion of 10^{-6}) **do**
5. **For** $k = 0, 1, \ldots, N^2$ **do**
6.   Calculate α^{k+1} following the Newton algorithm (10)
7.   Calculate β^{k+1} following (11)
8.   Update $\theta^{k+1} \leftarrow \theta^k - \rho(\alpha^{k+1} - \beta^{k+1})$
9. **End for**
10. **End while.**

For the logistic model (4) with lag variables of the financial ratio and macroeconomic indicators,
we can also extend the lasso as follows in (13):

$$(\hat{\alpha}_0, \hat{\gamma}) = \underset{\alpha_0, \gamma}{argmin} f\left(\alpha_0, \gamma \middle| X_{i,t-3}, X_{i,t-4}, X_{i,t-5}, Z_{i,t-3}, Z_{i,t-4}, Z_{i,t-5}, Y_{i,t}\right) + \lambda\|\gamma\|_1 \tag{13}$$

where $\hat{\gamma} = (\hat{\alpha}, \hat{\eta})$ is the lasso estimator vector for coefficients of lagged financial ratios and
macroeconomic indicators; $\gamma = (\alpha^T, \eta^T)^T$ represents the unknown coefficients for explanatory variables;
$\alpha, \eta = (\eta_{t-3}{}^T, \eta_{t-4}{}^T, \eta_{t-5}{}^T)^T$ and the others are defined as in Equations (4) and (5). The lasso estimator
for model (13) can also be found by using the ADMM algorithm presented above.

3.3. The Lasso–SVM Model with Lags for Comparison

The support vector machine (SVM) is a widely used linear classifier with high interpretability.
In this sub-section, we construct a lasso–SVM model that includes the 3-period-lagged financial
indicators for comparison with the lasso–logistic-distributed lag model. The SVM formulation combing
the original soft-margin SVM model [62] and a 3~5–period-lagged financial ratio variable vector is
as follows:

$$\begin{cases} \underset{\alpha_0, \alpha, \xi}{min} \frac{1}{2}\|\alpha\|_2^2 + C \sum_{t=t_0+5}^{t_0+d} \sum_{i=1}^{n} \xi_{i,t} \\ s.t. \ Y_{i,t}\left(\alpha_0 + \alpha_{t-3}{}^T X_{i,t-3} + \alpha_{t-4}{}^T X_{i,t-4} + \alpha_{t-5}{}^T X_{i,t-5}\right) \geq 1 - \xi_{i,t}, \ \xi_{i,t} \geq 0, \\ \qquad\qquad i = 1, 2, \ldots, n, \ t = t_0 + 5, \ldots, Id \end{cases} \tag{14}$$

In (14), α_0 (intercept) and $\alpha = (\alpha_{t-3}; \alpha_{t-4}; \alpha_{t-5})$ (normal vector) are the unknown coefficients
of hyper-plane $f(X_{it}) = \alpha_0 + \alpha^T X_{it}$; $\|\cdot\|_2$ denotes l_2-norm of a vector; C is the penalty parameter and
a predetermined positive value; $\xi_{i,t}$ is the unknown slack variable; $Y_{i,t}$ is a binary variable and
$Y_{i,t} = 1$, when firm i is a financially disIressed company in year t, otherwise $Y_{i,t} = -1$; $X_{it} = (1; X_{i,t-3};$
$X_{i,t-4}; X_{i,t-5})$ denotes the observation vector of 3~5-period-lagged financial indicators for firm i;
n represents the number of observations; t_0 and d denote the beginning and length of the observation
period, respectively.

By introducing the hinge loss function, the optimization problem (14) has the equivalent form
as follows [63]:

$$\underset{\alpha_*}{min} \sum_{t=t_0+5}^{t_0+d} \sum_{i=1}^{n} [1 - Y_{i,t}\left(\alpha_*{}^T X_{it}\right)]_+ + \lambda\|\alpha_*\|_2^2 \tag{15}$$

where $\alpha_* = (\alpha_0; \alpha)$, $[\cdot]_+$ indicates the positive part, i.e., $[x]_+ = \max\{x,0\}$, and the turning parameter $\lambda = 1/2C$.

Considering that it is regularized by l_2-norm, the SVM forces all nonzero coefficient estimates, which leads to the problem of its inability to select significant features. Thus, to prevent the influence of noise features, we replace l_2-norm in the optimization problem (15) with l_1-norm, which is able to simultaneously conduct feature selection and classification. Furthermore, for computational convenience, we replace the hinge loss function in (15) with the form of the sum of square, and present the optimization problem combining the SVM model and the lasso method (l_1 regularization) as follows:

$$\hat{\alpha}_* = \underset{\alpha_*}{argmin} \sum_{t=t_0+5}^{t_0+d} \sum_{i=1}^{n} \left([1 - Y_{i,t}\alpha_*^T X_{it}]_+\right)^2 + \lambda\|\alpha_*\|_1 \tag{16}$$

In (16), $\hat{\alpha}_*$ is the optimal estimated value for the coefficients of the SVM model, and the others are defined as above. Similarly with the process of the solution to the problem (5) as presented previously, first by introducing an auxiliary variable $\beta \in R^{3p+1}$, the lasso–SVM model (16) can be explicitly rewritten as follows:

$$\underset{\alpha_*,\beta}{min} \sum_{t=t_0+5}^{t_0+d} \sum_{i=1}^{n} \left([1 - Y_{i,t}\alpha_*^T X_{it}]_+\right)^2 + \lambda\|\beta_*\|_1 \ \ s.t. \ \alpha_* = \beta_* \tag{17}$$

Then, the augmented Lagrangian function of the optimization problem (17) can be accordingly specified as

$$L_\rho(\alpha_*, \beta_*, \theta_*) = \sum_{t=t_0+5}^{t_0+d} \sum_{i=1}^{n} \left([1 - Y_{i,t}\alpha_*^T X_{it}]_+\right)^2 + \lambda\|\beta_*\|_1 - \theta_*^T(\alpha_* - \beta_*) + \frac{\rho}{2}\|\alpha_* - \beta_*\|_2^2 \tag{18}$$

where $\theta \in R^{3p+1}$ and $\rho \in R$ are the Lagrange and the augmented Lagrange multipliers, respectively. Then, the iterative scheme of ADMM for the optimization problem (18) is similar with (8a)–(8c) and can be accordingly specified as

$$\alpha_*^{k+1} = \underset{\alpha_*}{argmin} \sum_{t=t_0+5}^{t_0+d} \sum_{i=1}^{n} \left([1 - Y_{i,t}(\alpha_*^T X_{it})]_+\right)^2 - (\theta_*^k)^T(\alpha_* - \beta_*^k) + \frac{\rho}{2}\|\alpha_* - \beta_*^k\|_2^2 \tag{19a}$$

$$\beta_*^{k+1} = \underset{\beta_*}{argmin}\lambda\|\beta_*\|_1 - \theta^k(\alpha_*^{k+1} - \beta_*) + \frac{\rho}{2}\|\alpha_*^{k+1} - \beta_*\|_2^2 \tag{19b}$$

$$\theta_*^{k+1} = \theta_*^k - \rho(\alpha_*^{k+1} - \beta_*^{k+1}) \tag{19c}$$

The finite Armijo–Newton algorithm [61] is applied for solving the α-sub-problem (19a), which is a convex piecewise quadratic optimization problem. Its objective function is first-order differentiable but not twice-differentiable with respect to α_*, which precludes the use of a regular Newton method. $F(\alpha_*)$ is the objective function of the sub-optimization problem (19a) and its gradient and generalized Hessian matrix are presented as follows Equations (20) and (21):

$$\nabla F(\alpha_*) = -2 \sum_{t=t_0+5}^{t_0+d} \sum_{i=1}^{n} Y_{i,t}X_{it}(1 - Y_{i,t}\alpha_*^T X_{it})_+ - \theta^k + \rho(\alpha_* - \beta_*^k) \tag{20}$$

$$\partial^2 F(\alpha_*) = 2 \sum_{t=t_0+5}^{t_0+d} \sum_{i=1}^{n} diag(1 - Y_{i,t}\alpha_*^T X_{it})_* X_{it} X_{it}^T + \rho I \tag{21}$$

where $I \in R^{3p+1}$ is identity matrix and $diag(1 - Y_{i,t} \alpha_*^T X_{it})_*$ is a diagonal matrix in that the j-th ($j = 1, 2, \ldots, 3p + 1$) diagonal entry is a sub-gradient of the step function $(\cdot)_+$ as

$$(diag(1 - Y_{i,t}\alpha_*{}^T X_{it})_*)_{jj} \begin{cases} = 1 & if\ 1 - Y_{i,t}\alpha_*{}^T X_{it} > 0, \\ \in [0,1] & if\ 1 - Y_{i,t}\alpha_*^T X_{it} = 0, \\ = 0 & if\ 1 - Y_{i,t}\alpha_*^T X_{it} < 0. \end{cases} \tag{22}$$

The whole optimization procedure applied to solve the α-sub-problem (19a) is described in Algorithm 2.

Algorithm 2. A finite Armijo–Newton algorithm for the sub-problem (19a). [1]: δ is the parameter associated with finite Armijo Newton algorithm and between 0 and 1.

Require:

1. Training data $\{X_{i,t-3}, X_{i,t-4}, X_{i,t-5}, Y_{i,t}\}$, where $X_{i,t-l} \in R^P$, $l = 3, 4, 5$ and $Y_{i,t} \in \{1,-1\}$, $I = 1,2,\ldots,n$, $t = t_0 + 5, t_0 + 6, \ldots, t_0 + d$

2. Turining parameter λ

3. Choose augmented Lagrange multiplier $\rho = 1$. Set initial $(\theta_*{}^0, \beta_*{}^0, \alpha_*{}^0) \in R \times R^{3P+1} \times R^{3P+1}$ and stopping criterion $\varepsilon = 10^{-6}$

Ensure:

4. **While** not converging (i.e., $\|\nabla F[(\alpha_*{}^i) - \partial^2 F(\alpha_*{}^i)^{-1}\nabla F(\alpha_*{}^i)]\|_2 \geq \varepsilon$) **do**

5. Calculate the Newton direction $d^i = -\partial^2 F(\alpha_*{}^i)^{-1}\nabla F(\alpha_*{}^i)$ following (20)–(22)

6. Choose $\delta^1 = 0.4$ and find stepsize $\tau_i = \max\{1, 1/2, 1/4, \ldots\}$ such that $F(\alpha_*{}^i) - F(\alpha_*{}^i + \tau_i d^i) \geq -\delta\tau_i\nabla F(\alpha_*{}^i)^T d^i$ is satisfied

7. Update $(\alpha_*)^{i+1} \leftarrow (\alpha_*)^i + \tau_i d^i$, $i \leftarrow I + 1$

8. **End while**

9. Output $\alpha_*{}^{k+1} = \alpha_*{}^i$

The finite Armijo–Newton algorithm can guarantee the unique global minimum solution in a finite number of iterations. The details of proof of the global convergence of the sequence to the unique solution can be found in [61]. For the sub-problem (19b), its solution can be also analytically given by (11) presented above, after replacing α, β and θ with α_*, β_* and θ_*.

So far, the lasso estimators for the SVM model (16), including 3~5-period-lagged financial ratios, have been obtained by following the above procedures. For the convenience of readers, we summarize the whole optimization procedures in training the lasso–SVM with lagged variables and describe them in Algorithm 3. It is worth to note that the estimators for the lasso–SVM model that contain 3~5-period-lagged financial ratios and macro-economic indicators can be also obtained by the following algorithm similarly.

Algorithm 3. An ADMM algorithm framework for lasso–support vector machine (SVM) with lagged variables (16)

Require:

1. Training data $\{X_{i,t-3}, X_{i,t-4}, X_{i,t-5}, Y_{i,t}\}$, where $X_{i,t-l} \in R^P$, $l = 3, 4, 5$ and $Y_{i,t} \in \{1,-1\}$, $i = 1, 2, \ldots, n$, $t = t_0 + 5, t_0 + 6, \ldots, t_0 + d$

2. Turining parameter λ

3. Choose augmented Lagrange multiplier $\rho = 1$. Set initial $(\theta_*{}^0, \beta_*{}^0, \alpha_*{}^0) \in R \times R^{3P+1} \times R^{3P+1}$ and stopping criterion $\varepsilon = 10^{-6}$

Ensure:

4. **While** not converging (i.e., either $\|\beta^{k+1} - \beta^k\|_2$ or $\|\alpha^{k+1} - \beta^{k+1}\|_2$ is greater than stopping criterion of 10^{-6}) **do**

5. **For** $k = 0, 1, \ldots, N$ **do**

6. Calculate $\alpha_*{}^{k+1}$ following finte Armijo–Newton algorithm displayed in Algorithm 2

7. Calculate $\beta_*{}^{k+1}$ following (11)

8. Update $\theta_*{}^{k+1} \leftarrow \theta_*{}^k - \rho(\alpha_*{}^{k+1} - \beta_*{}^{k+1})$

9. **End for**

10. **End while**

---

4. Data

4.1. Sample Description

The data used in the study are limited to manufacturing corporations. The manufacturing sector plays an important role in contributing to the economic growth of a country, especially a developing country [64]. According to the data released by the State Statistical Bureau of China, manufacturing accounts for 30% of the country's GDP. China's manufacturing sector has the largest number of listed companies as well as the largest number of ST companies each year. On the other hand, according to the data disclosed by the China Banking Regulatory Commission, in the Chinese manufacturing sector, the non-performing loan ratio has been increasing. For example, there was a jump in the non-performing loan ratio from 3.81% in December of 2017 to 6.5% in June of 2018. Therefore, it is quite important to establish an effective early warning system aiming to assess financial stress and prevent potential financial fraud of a listed manufacturing company for market participants, including investors, creditors and regulators.

In this paper, we selected 234 listed manufacturing companies from the Wind database. Among these, 117 companies are financially healthy and 117 are financially distressed, i.e., the companies being labeled as "special treatment". The samples were selected from 2007 to 2017, since the Ministry of Finance of the People's Republic of China issued the new "Accounting Standards for Business Enterprises" (new guidelines), which required that all listed companies be fully implemented from January 1, 2007. Similar to [7], [16] and [45], all 117 financially distressed companies receive ST due to negative net profit for two consecutive years. There were respectively 10, 9, 17, 24, 26 and 31 companies labeled as ST or *ST in each year from 2012 to 2017. The same number of financially healthy companies were selected in each year. Considering the regulatory requirement and qualified data of listed companies, our data sample enforces the use of 2007 (t_0) as the earliest estimation window available in forecasting a listed company's financial distress. Meanwhile, the maximum order lag used in our models is as long as 5 (years); that is, the maximum horizon is 5 years, so the number of special-treated (ST) companies was counted since 2012 ($t_0 + 5$). Furthermore, we divided the whole sample group into two groups: the training sample and the testing sample. The training sample is from 2012 to 2016, includes the data of 172 companies and is used to construct the models and estimate the coefficients. Correspondingly, the testing sample is from 2017, includes the data of 62 companies and is used to evaluate the predicting performance of the models.

4.2. Covariate

In this paper, we use the factors measured in consecutive time windows $t - 3$, $t - 4$ and $t - 5$ to predict a listed company's financial status at time t ($t = 2012, 2013, \ldots, 2017$). Therefore, we define response y as whether a Chinese manufacturing listed company was labeled as "special treatment" by China Securities Regulatory Commission at time t ($t = 2012, 2013, \ldots, 2017$) and input explanatory variables as their corresponding financial indicators based on financial statements reported at $t - 3$, $t - 4$ and $t - 5$. For example, we define response y as whether a Chinese manufacturing listed company was labeled as "special treatment" during the period of from January 1, 2017 to December 31, 2017 (denoted as year t) and (1) input explanatory variables as their corresponding financial indicators based on financial statements reported on December 31, 2014 (denoted as year $t - 3$), in December, 2013 (denoted as year $t - 4$) and in December, 2012 (denoted as year $t - 5$); through this way, the time lags of the considered financial indicators and the responses are between 3 to 5 years; (2) input explanatory variables as macroeconomic indicators based on the statements reported on December 31, 2014, 2013 and 2012 by the Chinese National Bureau of Statistics; through this way, the time lags of the considered macroeconomic indicators and the response are also between 3 to 5 years. The effect of time lags of 3 to 5 years of financial indicators on the likelihood of occurrence of financial distress is separately suggested by some previous research of early warnings of listed companies' financial distress, but the varying effects of these time lags that occur in one prediction model are not yet considered in the existing studies.

4.2.1. Firm-Idiosyncratic Financial Indicator

An original list of 43 potentially helpful ratios is compiled for prediction and provided in Table 1 because of the large number of financial ratios found to be significant indicators of corporate problems in past studies. These indicators are classified into five categories, including solvency, operational capability, profitability, structural soundness and business development and capital expansion capacity. All variables used for calculation of financial ratios are obtained from the balance sheet, income statements or cash flow statements of the listing companies. These financial data for financially distressed companies are collected in year 3, 4 and 5 before the companies receive the ST label. For example, the considered year when the selected financially distressed companies receive ST is 2017; the financial data are obtained in 2014, 2013 and 2012. Similarly, the data for financially healthy companies are also collected in 2014, 2013 and 2012. Model 1 (the accounting-only model) will be constructed using all the data in the following context. The model is used to predict whether a company is labeled in year t, incorporating the financial data of three consecutive time windows, $t - 3$, $t - 4$ and $t - 5$ ($t = 2012, 2014, \ldots, 2017$).

Table 1. List of financial indicators.

Solvency	Operational Capabilities
1 Total liabilities/total assets (TL/TA)	9 Sales revenue/average net account receivable (SR/ANAR)
2 Current assets/current liabilities (CA/CL)	10 Sales revenue/average current assets (SR/ACA)
3 (Current assets–inventory)/current liabilities (CA-I)/CL	11 Sales revenue/average total assets (AR/ATA)
4 Net cash flow from operating activities/current liabilities (CF/CL)	12 Sales cost/average payable accounts (SC/APA)
5 Current liabilities/total assets (CL/TA)	13 Sales cost/sales revenue (SC/SR)
6 Current liabilities/shareholders' equity (CL/SE)	14 Impairment losses/sales profit (IL/SP)
7 Net cash flow from operating and investing activities/total liabilities (NCL/TL)	15 Sales cost/average net inventory (SC/ANI)
8 Total liabilities/total shareholders' equity (TSE/TL)	16 Sales revenue/average fixed assets (SR/AFA)
Profitability	Structural Soundness
17 Net profit/average total assets (NP/ATA)	27 Net asset/total asset (NA/TA)
18 Shareholder equity/net profit (SE/NP)	28 Fixed assets/total assets (FA/TA)
19 (Sales revenue–sales cost)/sales revenue (SR-SC)/SR	29 Shareholders' equity/fixed assets (SE/FA)
20 Earnings before interest and tax/average total assets (EIA/ATA)	30 Current liabilities/total liabilities (CL/TL)
21 Net profit/sales revenue (NP/SR)	31 Current assets/total assets (CA/TA)
22 Net profit/average fixed assets (NP/AFA)	32 Long-term liabilities/total liabilities (LL/TL)
23 Net profit attributable to shareholders of parent company/sales revenue (NPTPC/SR)	33 Main business profit/net income from main business (MBP/NIMB)
24 Net cash flow from operating activities/sales revenue (NCFO/SR)	34 Total profit/sales revenue (TP/SR)
25 Net profit/total profit (NP/TP)	35 Net profit attributable to shareholders of the parent company/net profit (NPTPC/NP)
26 Net cash flow from operating activities/total assets at the end of the period (NCFO/TAEP)	36 Operating capital/total assets (OC/TA)
	37 Retained earnings/total assets (RE/TA)
Business Development and Capital Expansion Capacity	
38 Main sales revenue of this year/main sales revenue of last year (MSR(t)/MSR(t-1))	41 Net assets/number of ordinary shares at the end of year (NA/NOS)
39 Total assets of this year/total assets of last year (TA(t)/TA(t-1))	42 Net cash flow from operating activities/number of ordinary shares at the end of year (NCFO/NOS)
40 Net profit of this year/net profit of last year (NP(t)/NP(t-1))	43 Net increase in cash and cash equivalents at the end of year/number of ordinary shares at the end of year (NICCE/NOS)

4.2.2. Macroeconomic Indicator

Besides considering three consecutive period-lagged financial ratios for the prediction of financial distress of Chinese listed manufacturing companies, we also investigated the associations between macro-economic conditions and the possibility of falling into financial distress of these companies. The macro-economic factors include GDP growth, inflation, unemployment rate in urban areas and consumption level growth, as described in Table 2. GDP growth is widely understood to be an important variable to measure economic strength and prosperity; the increase in GDP growth may decrease the likelihood of distress. High inflation and high unemployment that reflect a weaker economy may increase the likelihood of financial distress. Consumption level growth reflects the change in consumption level and its increase may reduce the likelihood of financial distress.

Table 2. List of macroeconomic factors.

Figure [1]	Description
1 Real GDP growth (%)	Growth in the Chinese real gross domestic product (GDP) compared to the corresponding period of previous year (GDP growth is documented yearly and by province).
2 Inflation rate (%)	Percentage changes in urban consumer price compared to the corresponding period of the previous year (inflation rate is documented regionally).
3 Unemployment rate (%)	The data derived from the Labor Force Survey (population between 16 years old and retirement age, unemployment rate is documented yearly and regionally).
4 Consumption level growth (%)	Growth in the Chinese consumption level index compared to the corresponding period of the previous year (consumption level growth is documented yearly and regionally).

[1]: All data of the macro-economic covariates are collected from the National Bureau of Statistics of China.

In the following empirical part, Model 2 represents the "accounting plus macroeconomic indicators" model and includes, in addition to the accounting variables, 3-period-lagged macroeconomic indicators. We collected the corresponding macroeconomic data in each year from 2007 to 2012 for all 234 company samples and the raw macroeconomic data are from the database of the Chinese National Bureau of Statistics.

4.3. Data Processing

The results in the existing studies suggest that the predicting models of standardized data yield better results in general [65]. Therefore, before the construction of the models, a standardization processing is implemented based on the following linear transformations:

$$x_{ij}(t) = \frac{u_{ij}(t) - \min_{1 \leq i \leq 234}\left\{u_{ij}(t)\right\}}{\max_{1 \leq i \leq 234}\left\{u_{ij}(t)\right\} - \min_{1 \leq i \leq 234}\left\{u_{ij}(t)\right\}} \tag{23}$$

where $x_{ij}(t)$ denotes the standardized value of the j-th financial indicator for the i-th firm in year t, and $j = 1, 2, \ldots, 43, i = 1, 2, \ldots, 234$, and $t = 2007, 2008, \ldots, 2012$; $u_{ij}(t)$ denotes the original value of the j-th indicator of the i-th company in year t. Linear transformation scales each variable into the interval $[0, 1]$. Similarly, the following formula is used for data standardization of the macro-economic factor:

$$z_{ij}(t) = \frac{v_{ij}(t) - \min_{1 \leq i \leq 234}\left\{v_{ij}(t)\right\}}{\max_{1 \leq i \leq 234}\left\{v_{ij}(t)\right\} - \min_{1 \leq i \leq 234}\left\{v_{ij}(t)\right\}} \tag{24}$$

In formula (24), $z_{ij}(t)$ denotes the standardized value of the j-th macro-economic factor in year t; $v_{ij}(t)$ denotes the original value of the j-th indicator of the i-th company in year t, where $j = 1, 2, 3, 4$, $i = 1, 2, \ldots, 234$, and $t = 2007, 2008, \ldots, 2012$. It is worth noting that the assignment to $v_{ij}(t)$ for each company is based on the data of the macroeconomic condition of the province where the company operates (registration location).

5. Empirical Results and Discussion

In this chapter, we establish a financial earning prediction system for Chinese listed manufacturing companies by using two groups of lasso-generalized distributed lag models, i.e., a logistic model and an SVM model including 3~5-period-lagged explanatory variables, and implement financial distress prediction and feature selection simultaneously. For the selected sample set, the sample data from 2007 to 2016 were used as the training sample and the sample from 2017 as the test sample. The tuning parameter was identified from cross-validation in the training set, and the performance of the chosen method was evaluated on the testing set by the area under the receiver operating characteristics curve (AUC), G-mean and Kolmogorov–Smirnov (KS) statistics.

5.1. Preparatory Work

It is necessary to choose a suitable value for the tuning parameter λ that controls the trade-off of the bias and variance. As mentioned before, 10-fold cross-validation is used on the training dataset in order to obtain the optimal tuning parameter, λ. First, we compare prediction performance of the lasso–logistic-distributed lag model (5) including only 43 firm-level financial indicators (the accounting-only model) when the turning parameter λ changes. The results show that the mean AUCs of validation data are 0.9075, 0.9095, 0.9091, 0.9112, 0.8979, 0.8902 and 0.8779, respectively, corresponding to $\lambda = 0.01, 0.1, 0.5, 1, 2, 3, 4$. Second, we compare the prediction performance of the logistic-distributed lag model (4) incorporating lasso penalty with 43 firm-level financial indicators and 4 macro-economic factors (the model of accounting plus macroeconomic variables). The results show that the mean AUCs of validation data are 0.9074, 0.8018, 0.9466, 0.9502, 0.9466, 0.9466 and 0.8498, respectively, corresponding to $\lambda = 0.01, 0.1, 0.5, 1, 2, 3, 4$. Panel (a) and (b) in Figure 1 also show the average predictive accuracy of cross-validation that results from using seven different values of the tuning parameter λ in the accounting model and the model of accounting plus macroeconomic variables.

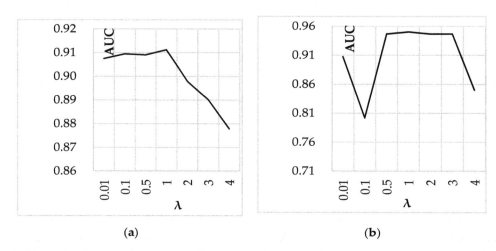

(a)   (b)

Figure 1. (a,b) are the Cross-validation performances that result from applying lasso–logistic-distributed lag regression to the listed manufacturing companies' data with various values of λ.

Generally speaking, the two kinds of models yield the best performance when $\lambda = 1$. Therefore, in the following, we fit and evaluate the lasso–logistic-distributed lag models by using the tuning parameter of 1.

5.2. Analyses of Results

This study develops a group of ex-ante models for estimating financial distress likelihood in the time window of t to test the contribution of financial ratios and macroeconomic indicators in the consecutive time windows of $t - 3$, $t - 4$ and $t - 5$. In the followings, Table 3 presents the results from lasso–logistic-distributed lag (LLDL) regressions of the financial distress indicator on the predictor variables and Table 4 presents the results from the lasso–SVM-distributed lag model. Furthermore, we compare predictive performance of the existing widely used ex-ante models, including neural networks (NN), decision trees (DT), SVM, and logistic models estimated in a time period from $t - 3$ to $t - 5$ with our models. The comparative results are shown in Table 5, Table 6 as well as Figure 2.

Table 3. The indicator selection and the estimates for lasso–logistic-distributed lag models.

Selected Indicator	Model 1 (Financial Ratios Only)			Model 2 (Financial Plus Macroeconomic Factor)		
	$t-3$[2]	$t-4$	$t-5$[1]	$t-3$	$t-4$	$t-5$
1 Total liabilities/total assets	×[2]	×	3.1671 (0.07) ***,[3]	×	×	3.5519 (0.07) ***
2 Current liabilities/total assets	×	−3.356 (0.27) ***	×	×	−1.2292 (0.26) ***	×
3 Sales revenue/average current assets	×	−0.5988 (0.19).	×	×	−3.887 (0.19) ***	×
4 Sales revenue/average total assets	−0.4367 (0.14) ***	−5.7393 (0.24) ***	−1.8312 (0.14) **	−0.5428 (0.14) **	−0.3907 (0.23) **	−3.5193 (0.14) ***
5 Sales cost/sales revenue	5.1892 (0.08) **	×	×	3.9211 (17.57)	×	×
6 Impairment losses/sales profit	−0.4496 (0.08) ***	×	×	−0.5777 (0.08) ***	×	×
7 Sales cost/average net inventory	−1.3265 (0.12) ***	×	×	−1.1143 (0.12) *	×	×
8 Net profit/average total assets	×	−1.1919 (0.14)	×	×	−3.3509 (0.14) **	×
9 Shareholders' equity/net profit	5.4466 (0.17) ***	×	×	4.0804 (0.18) ***	×	×
10 (Sales revenue-sales cost)/sales revenue (net income/revenue)	×	×	×	−1.2209 (17.7)	×	×
11 Net profit/average fixed assets	1.3912 (0.31) **	×	×	×	×	×
12 Net profit/total profit	×	0.2856 (0.14) ***	0.0422 (0.09) *	×	0.0371 (0.14) ***	×
13 Net cash flow from operating activities/total assets	−4.8561 (0.11) ***	−2.6798 (0.11) **	−1.0999 (0.12)	−3.005 (0.1) *	−2.7581 (0.1) **	−0.0304 (0.12)
14 Fixed assets/total assets	1.6395 (0.1)	0.9142 (0.11) **	×	1.5972 (0.09)	×	0.5416 (0.09)

Table 3. *Cont.*

Selected Indicator	Model 1 (Financial Ratios Only)			Model 2 (Financial Plus Macroeconomic Factor)		
	$t-3$	$t-4$	$t-5$[1]	$t-3$	$t-4$	$t-5$
15 Shareholders' equity/fixed assets	×	1.0914 (0.09)***	×	×	0.0472 (0.09)**	×
16 Current liabilities/total liabilities	2.2516 (0.06)*	×	2.2987 (0.07)***	3.1472 (0.06)***	×	2.1535 (0.07)***
17 Current assets/total assets	−1.5197 (0.11)	×	×	−3.081 (0.11)*	×	×
18 Long−term liabilities/total liabilities	×	1.6 (0.07)*	×	×	1.8855 (0.06)**	×
19 Main business profit/net income from main business	−3.3814 (0.1)***	−1.0212 (0.1)***	5.2777 (0.1)***	−4.0263 (0.1)***	−0.9392 (0.1)***	5.876 (0.1)***
20 Net profit attributable to shareholders of the parent company/net profit	−3.5409 (0.13)***	×	×	−2.159 (0.13)***	×	×
21 Operating capital/total assets	−2.1682 (0.16)***	×	×	−0.328 (0.16)*	×	×
22 Main sales revenue of this year/main sales revenue of last year	×	×	2.9534 (0.1)**	×	×	2.5545 (0.11)**
23 Net assets/number of ordinary shares at the end of year	×	−6.255 (0.07)***	×	×	−5.8881 (0.07)***	×
24 Real Consumer Price Index (CPI) growth (%)	×	×	×	×	−0.2536 (0.06)	0.7531 (0.05)
25 Real GDP growth (%)	×	×	×	−2.4867 (0.09)***	−1.6404 (0.11)	−0.9319 (0.1)
26 Consumption level growth (%)	×	×	×	−0.9931 (0.08)**	−1.8625 (0.06)	×
27 Unemployment rate (%)	×	×	×	2.7262 (0.07)***	×	×

[1]: "$t-3$, $t-4$ and $t-5$" represent the estimates for the coefficient vectors of financial and macroeconomic indicators with lag length of 3–5 in the lasso–logistic–distributed lag model, respectively, when $\lambda = 1$. [2]: "×" in the table means that the corresponding factor cannot be selected. [3]: The values in brackets are standard error for the estimated coefficients. "*", "**", and "***" indicate that the corresponding variable being significant is accepted at significance levels of 0.1, 0.05 and 0.01, respectively.

Table 4. The indicator selection and the estimates for the lasso–SVM-distributed lag models.

Selected Indicator	Model 1			Model 2		
	$t-3$	$t-4$	$t-5$	$t-3$	$t-4$	$t-5$
1 Total liabilities/total assets	32.1469	7.7613	×	10.7109	7.8039	×
2 Current assets/current liabilities	×	13.7838	−23.2184	×	27.1895	−14.1113
3 Current liabilities/total assets	×	−28.6108	−25.7518	×	−11.9697	×
4 Net cash flow from operating and investing activities/total liabilities	−11.7710	−9.2197	−4.7334	−10.8928	−4.2075	−4.0695
5 Sales revenue/average current assets	−13.2180	−5.5190	−2.3310	×	−3.5302	−2.3478
6 Impairment losses/sales profit	−3.8743	−0.8378	−0.1417	−5.0528	×	−2.1980
7 Sales cost/average net inventory	−4.2927	×	×	−8.5432	×	×
8 Sales revenue/average fixed assets	7.5395	4.0548	4.3177	×	×	×
9 (Sales revenue–sales cost)/sales revenue	×	−4.1270	5.6701	−1.3797	−4.4148	×
10 Net profit attributable to shareholders of the parent company/sales revenue	3.8270	×	×	6.1038	×	×
11 Net cash flow from operating activities/sales revenue	×	−15.5682	×	×	−6.9168	×
12 Net profit/total profit	−1.6296	5.6995	1.6336	−2.4791	2.4036	−0.4364
13 Net cash flow from operating activities/total assets at the end of the period	−12.3631	−19.5928	−4.4420	−2.1426	×	−0.1701
14 Fixed assets/total assets	0.2474	3.0676	8.7795	5.4054	×	1.7320
15 Current liabilities/total liabilities	×	×	9.6303	5.1482	4.3620	10.0672
16 Current assets/total assets	−12.3003	−6.7341	−0.4332	−9.4098	×	−0.5753
17 Long-term liabilities/total liabilities	−5.7781	0.8473	2.0308	×	6.4801	4.2084
18 Main business profit/net income from main business	−7.3785	−7.8631	−9.5525	−2.7997	−4.3300	−4.3107
19 Net profit attributable to shareholders of the parent company/net profit	−10.7914	−6.3596	9.1739	−5.9123	1.7203	1.9460
20 Operating capital/total assets	×	19.8833	×	×	×	8.6408
21 Retained earnings/total assets	×	×	30.8895	×	×	0.9384
22 Main sales revenue of this year/main sales revenue of last year	×	×	25.2376	0.7510	0.0517	13.5974

Table 4. *Cont.*

Selected Indicator	Model 1			Model 2		
	t – 3	*t* – 4	*t* – 5	*t* – 3	*t* – 4	*t* – 5
23 Net profit of this year/net profit of last year	−16.5430	17.9966	−7.8113	×	5.9123	−6.9035
24 Net increase in cash and cash equivalents at the end of year/number of ordinary shares	14.4968	0.2728	11.3146	7.6436	×	0.2771
25 Real CPI growth (%)	×	×	×	−2.4001	−0.7880	2.6728
26 Real GDP growth (%)	×	×	×	−1.0391	−4.5598	×
27 Consumption level growth (%)	×	×	×	−1.0196	−1.1848	−2.8019
28 Unemployment rate (%)	×	×	×	16.3215	×	14.3059

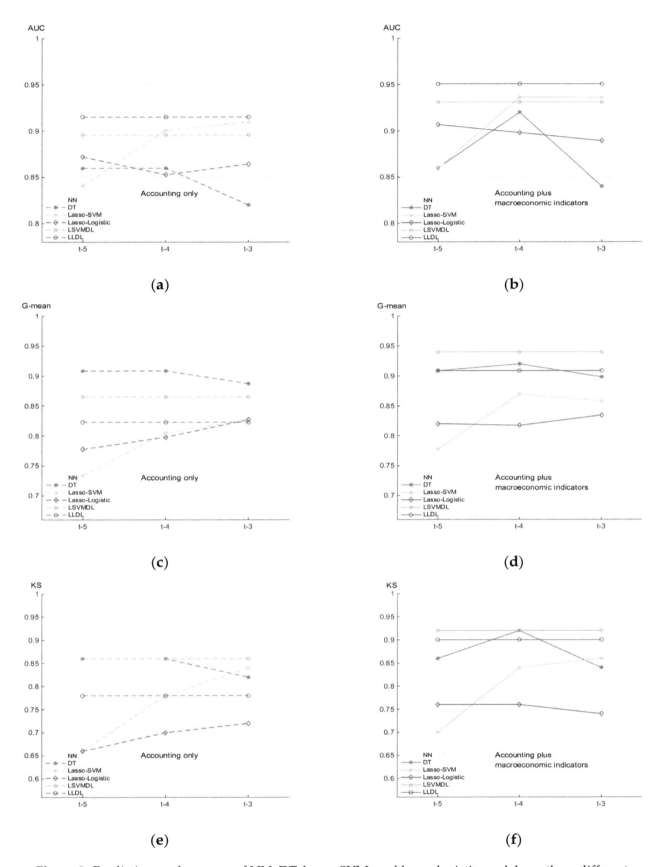

Figure 2. Predictive performance of NN, DT, lasso–SVM, and lasso–logistic models on three different time window datasets, respectively, and our models on three consecutive time window datasets, evaluated by AUC for (**a**) and (**b**), G-Mean for (**c**) and (**d**), and KS for (**e**) and (**f**).

Table 5. Prediction results of the neural network (NN), decision tree (DT), lasso–SVM and lasso–logistic in the single year time window versus the lasso–SVM-distributed lag (LSVMDL) and lasso–logistic-distributed lag (LLDL) models (financial ratios only).

	NN	DT	Lasso–SVM	Lasso–Logistic	LSVMDL	LLDL
Panel A: prediction performance of the existing models in time period $t - 3$						
AUC	0.9356	0.8200	0.9100	0.8644	0.8956	0.9152
G-mean	0.8673	0.8874	0.8272	0.8272	0.8655	0.8230
KS	0.8800	0.8200	0.8400	0.7200	0.8600	0.7800
Panel B: prediction performance of the existing models in time period $t - 4$						
AUC	0.9224	0.8600	0.9008	0.8528	0.8956	0.9152
G-mean	0.8580	0.9087	0.8052	0.7979	0.8655	0.8230
KS	0.8200	0.8600	0.7800	0.7000	0.8600	0.7800
Panel C: prediction performance of the existing models in time period $t - 5$						
AUC	0.8700	0.8600	0.8408	0.8720	0.8956	0.9152
G-mean	0.8780	0.9087	0.7336	0.7778	0.8655	0.8230
KS	0.8000	0.8600	0.6600	0.6600	0.8600	0.7800

Table 6. Prediction results of NN, DT, lasso–SVM and lasso–logistic models in the single year time window versus the lasso–SVM-distributed lag (LSVMDL) model and the lasso–logistic-distributed lag (LLDL) model (financial ratios plus macroeconomic indicators).

	NN	DT	Lasso–SVM	Lasso–Logistic	LSVMDL	LLDL
Panel A: prediction performance of the existing models in time period $t - 3$						
AUC	0.9400	0.8400	0.9360	0.8892	0.9312	0.9508
G-mean	0.9087	0.8981	0.8580	0.8343	0.9398	0.9087
KS	0.8900	0.8400	0.8600	0.7400	0.9200	0.9000
Panel B: prediction performance of the existing models in time period $t - 4$						
AUC	0.9340	0.9200	0.9364	0.8980	0.9312	0.9508
G-mean	0.8874	0.9198	0.8695	0.8171	0.9398	0.9087
KS	0.8600	0.9200	0.8400	0.7600	0.9200	0.9000
Panel C: prediction performance of the existing models in time period $t - 5$						
AUC	0.9160	0.8600	0.8592	0.9068	0.9312	0.9508
G-mean	0.8765	0.9085	0.7778	0.8200	0.9398	0.9087
KS	0.8200	0.8600	0.7000	0.7600	0.9200	0.9000

5.2.1. The Results of the Accounting-Only Model and Analyses

In Table 3, Model 1 represents the "accounting-only" lasso–logistic-distributed lag (LLDL) regression model including the 43 financial statement ratios in 3 adjacent years; the results of financial indicator selection and the estimations for the coefficients are listed in the first three columns. By using Algorithm 1, 23 indicators are in total chosen from the original indicator set. More specifically, two indicators, i.e., indicator number 1 and 2, are selected from the solvency category, five indicators (number 3 to 7) are selected from the operational capability category; six indicators (8-13) from operational capability, eight indicators (13–21) from profitability and two indicators (21-23) from structural soundness and business development and capital expansion capacity. It also can be found that nine financial indicators, namely, sales revenue/average total assets(1), impairment losses/sales profit(2), sales cost/average net inventory(3), shareholders' equity/net profit(4), net profit/total profit(5), net cash flow from operating activities/total assets(6), main business profit/net income from main business(7), net profit attributable to shareholders of the parent company/net profit(8) and operating capital/total assets(9), not used in the paper of [7] have quite significant influence on the future financial distress risk.

The potentially helpful ratios, such as the leverage ratio (total liabilities/total assets), shareholders' equity/net profit (ROE), net profit/average total assets (ROA), current liabilities/total liabilities etc., have significant effects on the occurrence of financial distress of Chinese listed manufacturing companies. For example, as shown in Table 3, the indicator of the leverage ratio in year $t - 3$—a very early time period—is selected as a significant predictor, and the estimated value for the coefficient is 3.1671. This implies that the increase in value of the Leverage ratio in the fifth previous ST year increases the financial risk of the listed manufacturing companies. The indicator of ROA for year $t - 4$ is selected, and the estimated value of the coefficient of the indicator is −1.1919, which implies the probability of falling into financial distress for a company will decrease with the company's ROA value, i.e., net profit/average total assets increasing.

Besides, the results in Table 3 also show that all changes in the indicator of sales revenue/average total assets for three consecutive time periods have significant effects on the future financial distress risk. It can be found that different weights are assigned to the variables of sales revenue/average total assets with different time lags, and the coefficient estimates for the indicator in the time windows of $t - 3$, $t - 4$ and $t - 5$ are −0.4367, −5.7393 and −1.8312, respectively. This implies that increases in sale revenue in different time windows have positive and significant (but different) effects on the future financial status of a listed company. The result for the indicator of "net cash flow from operating activities/total assets" presented in row 13 and the first 3 columns of Table 3 illustrate that changes in this indicator in different time windows have different effects on the future occurrence of financial distress at a significance level and magnitude of influence. The estimated coefficients for the variable measured in the previous time windows, $t - 3$, $t - 4$ and $t - 5$, are −4.8561, −2.6798 and −1.0999, at the significance level of 0.01, 0.05 and (>) 0.1, respectively. This indicates that (1) the higher the ratio of net cash flow from operating activities to total assets for a listed manufacturing company, the lower the likelihood of the firm's financial distress; (2) the changes in net cash flow from operating activities/total assets in the time windows $t - 3$ and $t - 4$ have significant influence on the risk of financial distress, and the magnitude of influence increases as the length of lag time decreases; (3) the influence of this indicator declines over time and change in this indicator in the 5 years before the observation of the financial distress event has no significant effect on financial risk when compared with relatively recent changes.

5.2.2. The Results and Analyses of the Model of Accounting Plus Macroeconomic Variables

In Table 3, Model 2 represents the "accounting plus macroeconomic factor" model, including the original 43 financial ratios and 4 macroeconomic indicators in 3 adjacent years, and the results of indicator selection and the coefficient estimates are listed in the last three columns. It can be found that for Model 2, the same group of financial variables is selected and included in the final model. Time lags of the selected financial variables and the signs (but not magnitudes) of the estimated coefficients for the variables are almost consistent for Model 1 and 2.

In addition to the accounting ratios, three macroeconomic factors are selected as significant predictors and included in the final model: GDP growth, consumption level growth and unemployment rate in time window of $t - 3$. The estimate for the coefficients of the selected GDP growth and unemployment rate are −2.4867 and 2.7262, respectively, which means that high GDP growth should decrease the financial distress risk, but high unemployment will deteriorate the financial condition of a listed manufacturing company. These results are consistent, which was expected. The estimate for the coefficient of consumption level growth is −0.9931, which implies that the high consumption level growth should decrease the possibility of financial deterioration of a listed company. Finally, it cannot be found that Consumer Price Index (CPI) growth has a significant influence on the financial distress risk.

The 4 year-lagged and 5 year-lagged GDP growth and 4 year-lagged consumption level growth are also selected and included in the final model but not as very significant predictors, which implies the following: (1) the changes in macroeconomic conditions have a continuous influence on the financial distress risk; (2) however, the effect of the macroeconomic condition' changes on the financial distress risk declines with the length of the lag window increasing.

5.2.3. The Results of Lasso–SVM-Distributed Lag (LSVMDL) Models and Analyses

We introduce 3-period lags of financial indicators presented in Table 1, i.e., TL/TA_{t-3}, TL/TA_{t-4} and TL/TA_{t-5}, CA/CL_{t-3}, CA/CL_{t-4} and CA/CL_{t-5} ... , $NICCE/NOS_{t-3}$, $NICCE/NOS_{t-4}$ and $NICCE/NOS_{t-5}$ into the model (16) and implement the indicator selection and the coefficient estimates by using Algorithm 3. The corresponding results are presented in first three columns of Table 4. Then, we introduce 3-period lags of financial and macroeconomic indicators presented in Tables 1 and 2 into the model (16) and the coefficient estimate of selected indicators are presented in the last three columns of Table 4.

Twenty-four financial indicators are selected and included in the final SVM-distributed lag model, denoted as Model 1 in Table 4; 17 indicators among them are also included in the final logistic-distributed lag model. For convenience of comparison, the 17 indicators, such as total liabilities/total assets, current liabilities/total assets and sales revenue/average current assets etc., are italicized and shown in the "selected indicator" column of Table 4.

According to the relation between response variables and predictors in the SVM model, as mentioned before, the increase (decrease) in the factors should increase (decrease) the financial distress risk when the coefficient estimates are positive. Therefore, let us take the estimated results in the first three rows and columns as an example: (1) the increase in the total liabilities to total assets ratio should increase the financial distress risk of a listed manufacturing company; (2) the increase in current liabilities to total assets ratio should decrease the financial distress risk; (3) the changes in the indicators in the period closer to the time of obtaining ST have a more significant effect on the likelihood of financial distress in terms of magnitudes of estimates of the coefficients.

Four macroeconomic factors, in addition to 24 financial indicators, are selected and included in the final SVM-distributed lag model, denoted as Model 2 in Table 4. The results show that (1) the effects of the selected financial ratios on the response, i.e., the financial status of a company, is consistent with the results in the SVM-distributed lag model including only financial ratios, i.e., Model 1, in terms of time lags of the selected financial variables and the signs of the estimated coefficients for the explanatory variables; (2) high GDP growth and high consumption level growth should decrease the financial distress risk, but high unemployment will deteriorate the financial condition of a listed manufacturing company.

From Table 4, it can be found that different indicators have different influence on the financial status of a company. The effects of some indicators on financial distress risk increase with the decrease in the time lag, e.g., total liabilities to total assets ratio, current liabilities/total assets and net cash flow from operating and investing activities/total liabilities etc., while the effects of some other indicators should decrease with the decrease in the time lag, e.g., fixed assets/total assets, GDP growth and consumption level growth etc. However, for some indicators, the effects of different time windows on financial status change. For example, the coefficients for current assets/current liabilities (current ratio) in Model 1 are 13.7838 for time window $t - 4$ and -23.2184 for time window $t - 5$, which implies that a high current ratio in time window $t - 5$ should decrease the financial distress risk; this, however, would be not the case in time $t - 4$. Similar case can be found for CPI growth in Model 2. Thus, SVM-distributed lag models may not interpret well; therefore, it would be inferior to the logistic-distributed lag models in terms of in terms of interpretability.

5.2.4. Comparison with Other Models

For the purpose of comparison, the prediction performances of the ex-ante models for the estimation of financial distress likelihood developed by the existing studies are shown in Tables 5 and 6. The existing widely used ex-ante models include the neural network (NN), decision tree (DT), SVM, and logistic models estimated in different time periods of $t - 3$, $t - 4$, and $t - 5$, called $t - 3$ models,

$t-4$ models and $t-5$ models. The construction of these three groups of models is similar to [7]. Let us take the construction of $t-5$ model as example. For 10 financially distressed companies that received ST in 2012 and the selected 10 healthy companies until 2012 as a control group, their financial and macroeconomic data in 2007 (5 years before 2012) were collected. For 9 financially distressed companies that received ST in 2013 and the selected 9 healthy companies, their financial and macroeconomic data in 2008 (5 years before 2013) were collected. Similarly, for 17, 24, 26 financial distressed companies that receive the ST label respectively in 2014, 2015 and 2016 and the non-financial companies randomly selected at a 1:1 ratio in each year for matching with the ST companies, their data in 2009 (5 years before 2014), 2010 (5 years before 2015) and in 2011 (5 years before 2016) were collected. By using the labels of 172 companies and the data that were obtained 5 years prior to the year when the companies received the ST label, we construct $t-5$ financial distress forecast models combined with a neural network (NN), decision tree (DT), SVM, and logistic regression. Similarly, $t-3$ models and $t-4$ models can be built. The data of financially distressed companies that received ST in 2017 and non-financial distressed companies were used to evaluate these models' predicting performance.

As mentioned in the beginning of this section, three measures of prediction performances are reported in these two tables, namely, AUC, G-mean, and Kolmogorov–Smirnov statistics. In the above scenarios based on different time periods as well as division of the whole dataset, we compare respectively the predicting performance of those one-time window models ($t-3$ models, $t-4$ models and $t-5$ models) including financial ratios only and financial ratios plus macroeconomic factors with our lasso–SVM-distributed lag (LSVMDL) model and lasso–logistic-distributed lag (LLDL). The prediction results are presented in Table 5 for the case of "financial ratios only" and Table 6 for the case of "financial ratio plus macroeconomic factors".

In Table 5, panel A presents the predictive performances of NN, DT, lasso–SVM and lasso–logistic models including the original 43 financial ratios shown in Table 1 in the period $t-3$ as predictors of financial distress status in period t, while the results in the last two columns are the performances of the two groups of distributed lag financial distress predicting models including the same original 43 financial ratios but in periods $t-3$, $t-4$ and $t-5$, i.e., our models. Panel B and C of Table 5 present the prediction performance of the models used for comparison purposes estimated in $t-4$ and $t-5$, respectively. The results for our models retain the same values because these models include simultaneously the 3-year-, 4-year- and 5-year-lagged financial ratios.

The only difference between Tables 5 and 6 is that all models, in addition to the 43 original accounting rations, incorporate 4 macroeconomic indicators in different time windows. For example, for time window $t-3$, the NN, DT, lasso–SVM and lasso–logistic models include 3-year-lagged macroeconomic indicators shown in Table 2 in addition to the financial statement ratios shown in Table 1. The cases of time windows $t-4$ and $t-5$ are similar for these models. As for the LSVMDL and LLDL models, i.e., our models, they include 3-periods-lagged macroeconomic indicators in the time windows $t-3$, $t-4$ and $t-5$ in addition to the accounting ratios.

From Table 5, the prediction accuracy of NN or DT is highest in the time windows $t-3$ and $t-4$; our models outperform the others in time window $t-5$ for predicting accuracy. Generally speaking, the accuracy for time period $t-3$ is relatively higher than the other two time periods for the NN, lasso–SVM and lasso–logistic models. Furthermore, the prediction results based on time period $t-3$ are the most precise for NN when compared with other models in a single time period and even our models, which implies that the selected financial ratios in the period closer to the time of obtaining ST may contain more useful information for the prediction of financial distress, and may be applicable to NN. The AUC of 91.52% of the lasso–logistic-distributed lag model (LLDL) ranked second, close to the accuracy of 93.56% obtained by using NN. Therefore, the LLDL model should be competitive in terms of interpretability and accuracy in the case of "accounting ratio only".

From Table 6, the prediction accuracy of all used models is higher than the results in Table 5. For example, the AUC, G-mean and KS of the NN model in time window $t-3$ increases from 93.56%, 86.73% and 88.00% in Table 5 to 94.00%, 90.87% and 89.00% in Table 6, respectively. The changing tendency of the prediction accuracy is retained for the other models, including macroeconomic indicators in addition to the accounting ratios. All results in Table 6 indicate that the introduction of the macroeconomic variables can improve predictive performance of all used models for the purpose of comparison; the changes in macroeconomic conditions do affect the likelihood of financial distress risk. On the other hand, the LLDL model performs best with the AUC of over 95% when compared with the best NN (in time period $t - 3$, 94%), the best DT (in time period $t - 4$, 92.24%), the best lasso–SVM (in time period $t - 4$, 93.64%), the best lasso–logistic (in time period $t - 5$, 90.68%) and LSVMDL (93.12%). The LSVMDL model is the best performing model in terms of G-mean and KS statistics.

Figure 2 also shows the comparative results of the accuracy of the six models. The predictive performances of all the models including accounting ratios only, indicated by the dotted lines (a), (c) and (e) in Figure 2, are worse than the models including macroeconomic indicators as well as accounting ratios, which are illustrated by the solid lines (b), (d) and (f) in Figure 2. Figures (a) and (b), G-Mean for (c) and (d), and KS for (e) and (f) present AUC, G-mean and KS for all of the examined models, respectively. The models used for comparison, namely, NN, DT, lasso–SVM and lasso–logistic models, were those that yielded the highest accuracy based on the different time window dataset. For example, based on the results of panel (b), AUC of NN (the yellow solid line), DT (the pink solid line), and lasso–logistic (the red one) models are highest in time window $t - 3$, $t - 4$ and $t - 5$, respectively. We cannot conclude that the prediction results based on financial and macroeconomic data of one specific time window, e.g., $t - 3$ (see [7]), are the most accurate. However, from the results in (b), (d) and (f), our models, the LLDL or LSVMDL model incorporating financial and macroeconomic data in three consecutive time-windows, yielded relatively robust and higher prediction performances.

Put simply, the two groups of generalized distributed lag financial distress predicting models proposed by this paper outperform the other models in each time period, especially when the accounting ratios and macroeconomic factors were introduced into the models. We demonstrated that our models provide an effective way to deal with multiple time period information obtained from changes in accounting and macroeconomic conditions.

5.2.5. Discussion

Logistic regression and multivariate discriminant methods should be the most popular statistical techniques used in financial distress risk prediction modelling for different countries' enterprise, e.g., American enterprises [1] and European enterprises [4,30,31], because of their simplicity, good predictive performance and interpretability. The main statistical approach involved in this study is logistic regression, but rather multivariate discriminant analysis, given that strict assumptions regarding normal distribution of explanatory variables are used in multivariate discriminant analysis. The results in this study conform that logistic regression models still perform well for predicting Chinese listed enterprises' financial distress risks.

The major contribution to financial distress prediction literature made by this paper is that an optimally distributed lag structure of macroeconomic data in the multi-periods, in addition to financial ratio data, are imposed on the logistic regression model through minimizing loss function, and the heterogenous lagged effects of the factors in the different period are presented. The results unveil that financial indicators, such as total liabilities/total assets, sales revenue/total assets, and net cash flow from operating activities/total assets, tend to have a significant impact over relatively longer periods, e.g., 5 years before the financial crisis of a Chinese listed manufacturing company. This finding is in accordance with the recent research of [30,31] in that the authors claim the process of going bankrupt is not a sudden phenomenon; it may take as long as 5–6 years. In the very recent study of Korol et al. [30], the authors built 10 group models comprising 10 periods: from 1 year to 10 years prior to bankruptcy. The results in [30] indicate that a bankruptcy prediction model such as the fuzzy set model maintained an effectiveness level above 70% until the eighth year prior to bankruptcy. Therefore, our model can be extended through introducing more lagged explanatory variables, e.g., 6- to 8-year-lagged financial variables, which may bring a better distributive lag structure of explanatory variables and predicting ability of the models.

The findings of this study allow managers and corporate analysts to prevent financial crisis of a company by monitoring early changes in a few sensitive financial indicators and taking actions, such as optimizing the corporate's asset structure, increasing cash flow and sales revenue, etc. They are also helpful for investors to make investment decision by tracking continuous changes in accounting conditions of a company of interest and predicting its risk of financial distress.

Another major contribution of this study is the confirmation of the importance of macroeconomic variables in predicting the financial distress of a Chinese manufacturing company, although scholars still argue about the significance of macro variables. For example, Kacer et al. [66] did not recommend the use of macro variables in the financial distress prediction for Slovak Enterprises, while Hernandez Tinoco et al. [4] confirmed the utilization of macro variables in the financial distress prediction for listed enterprises of the United Kingdom. The results in Section 5.2.4 of this study show that the prediction performance of all models (including both the models used for comparison and our own models) was increased when the macro variables were included in each model. The findings of this study allow regulators to tighten the supervision of Chinese listed companies when macroeconomic conditions change, especially in an economic downturn.

One of the main limitations of this study is that we limited the research only to the listed manufacturing companies. Both Korol et al. [28] and Kovacova [30] emphasized that the type of industry affects the risk of deterioration in the financial situation of companies. More specifically, distinguished by factors such as intensity of competition, life cycle of products, demand, changes in consumer preferences, technological change, reducing entry barriers into the industry and susceptibility of the industry to business cycles, different industries are at different levels of risk [28]. The manufacturing sector, which includes the metal, mining, automotive, aerospace and housing industries, is highly susceptible to demands, technological changes and macroeconomic conditions, thus making it at a high level of risk, while agriculture may be at a relatively low risk level. The risk parameter assigned to the service sector, including restaurants, tourism, transport and entertainment etc., has seen significant changes following the outbreak of the Coronavirus. Therefore, applicability and critique to our models for predicting financial distress risk of the companies operating in other industry and even other countries need to be further detected.

6. Conclusions

In this paper, we propose a new framework of a financial early warning system through introducing a distributed lag structure to be widely used in financial distress prediction models such as the logistic regression and SVM models. Our models are competitive when compared with the conventional financial distress forecast models, which incorporates data from only one-period of $t-3$ or $t-4$ or $t-5$, in terms of predictive performance. Furthermore, our models are superior to the conventional one-time window financial distress forecast models, in which macroeconomic indicators of GDP growth, consumption level growth and unemployment rate, in addition to accounting factors, are incorporated. The empirical findings of this study indicate that the changes in macroeconomic conditions do have significant and continuous influence on the financial distress risk of a listed manufacturing company. This paper may provide an approach of examining the impacts of macroeconomic information from multiple periods and improving the predictive performance of financial distress models.

We implement feature selection to remove redundant factors from the original list of 43 potentially helpful ratios and their lags by introducing lasso penalty into the financial distress forecast logistic models with lags and SVM models with lags. Furthermore, we provide an ADMM algorithm framework that yields the global optimum for convex and the non-smooth optimization problem to obtain the optimal estimation for the coefficients of these financial distress forecast models with financial and macroeconomic factors and their lags. Results from the empirical study show that not only widely used financial indicators (calculated from accounting data), such as leverage ratio, ROE, ROA, and current liabilities/total liabilities, have significant influence on the financial distress risk of a listed manufacturing company, but also the indicators that are rarely seen in the existing literature, such as net profit attributable to shareholders of the parent company and net cash flow from operating activities/total assets, may play very important roles in financial distress prediction. The closer to the time of financial crisis, the more net profit attributable to shareholders of the parent company and net cash flow from operating activities may considerably decrease the financial distress risk. These research findings may provide more evidence for company managers and investors in terms of corporate governance or risk control.

The main limitation of this research is that we limited the research only to listed manufacturing companies. Sensitivity of financial distress models and suitability of both financial and macroeconomic variables to the enterprises that operate in other industries, e.g., service companies, need to be further discussed. On the other hand, given that the utilization of financial and macroeconomic variables in predicting the risk of financial distress of Chinese listed manufacturing companies is confirmed, we intend to continue the research toward the use of interaction terms of financial and macroeconomic variables in the context of the multiple period. Furthermore, the heterogeneous effect of changes in macroeconomic conditions on the financial distress risk of a company under different financial conditions can be discovered.

Author Contributions: We attest that all authors contributed significantly to the creation of this manuscript. The conceptualization and the methodology were formulated by D.Y., data curation was completed by G.C., and the formal analysis was finished by K.K.L. All authors have read and agreed to the published version of the manuscript.

References

1. Altman, E.I. Financial ratios, discriminant analysis and the prediction of corporate bankruptcy. *J. Financ.* **1968**, *23*, 589–609. [CrossRef]
2. Lau, A.H.L. A five-state financial distress prediction model. *J. Account. Res.* **1987**, *25*, 127–138. [CrossRef]
3. Jones, S.; Hensher, D.A. Predicting firm financial distress: A mixed logit model. *Account. Rev.* **2004**, *79*, 1011–1038. [CrossRef]
4. Hernandez Tinoco, M.; Holmes, P.; Wilson, N. Polytomous response financial distress models: The role of accounting, market and macroeconomic variables. *Int. Rev. Financ. Anal.* **2018**, *59*, 276–289. [CrossRef]
5. Zmijewski, M.E. Methodological issues related to the estimation of financial distress prediction models. *J. Account. Res.* **1984**, *22*, 59–82. [CrossRef]
6. Ross, S.; Westerfield, R.; Jaffe, J. *Corporate Finance*; McGraw-Hill Irwin: New York, NY, USA, 2000.
7. Geng, R.; Bose, I.; Chen, X. Prediction of financial distress: An empirical study of listed Chinese companies using data mining. *Eur. J. Oper. Res.* **2015**, *241*, 236–247. [CrossRef]
8. Westgaard, S.; Van Der Wijst, N. Default probabilities in a corporate bank portfolio: A logistic model approach. *Eur. J. Oper. Res.* **2001**, *135*, 338–349. [CrossRef]
9. Balcaen, S.; Ooghe, H. 35 years of studies on business failure: An overview of the classic statistical methodologies and their related problems. *Br. Account. Rev.* **2006**, *38*, 63–93. [CrossRef]
10. Martin, D. Early warnings of bank failure: A logit regression approach. *J. Bank. Financ.* **1977**, *1*, 249–276. [CrossRef]
11. Liang, D.; Tsai, C.F.; Wu, H.T. The effect of feature selection on financial distress prediction. *Knowl. Based Syst.* **2015**, *73*, 289–297. [CrossRef]
12. Frydman, H.; Altman, E.I.; Kao, D.L. Introducing recursive partitioning for financial classification: The case of financial distress. *J. Financ.* **1985**, *40*, 269–291. [CrossRef]
13. Leshno, M.; Spector, Y. Neural network prediction analysis: The bankruptcy case. *Neurocomputing* **1996**, *10*, 125–147. [CrossRef]
14. Shin, K.S.; Lee, T.S.; Kim, H.J. An application of support vector machines in bankruptcy prediction model. *Expert Syst. Appl.* **2005**, *28*, 127–135. [CrossRef]
15. Sun, J.; Li, H. Data mining method for listed companies' financial distress prediction. *Knowl. Based Syst.* **2008**, *21*, 1–5. [CrossRef]

16. Jiang, Y.; Jones, S. Corporate distress prediction in China: A machine learning approach. *Account. Financ.* **2018**, *58*, 1063–1109. [CrossRef]
17. Purnanandam, A. Financial distress and corporate risk management: Theory and evidence. *J. Financ. Econ.* **2008**, *87*, 706–739. [CrossRef]
18. Almamy, J.; Aston, J.; Ngwa, L.N. An evaluation of Altman's Z-score using cash flow ratio to predict corporate failure amid the recent financial crisis: Evidence from the UK. *J. Corp. Financ.* **2016**, *36*, 278–285. [CrossRef]
19. Liang, D.; Lu, C.C.; Tsai, C.F.; Shih, G.A. Financial ratios and corporate governance indicators in bankruptcy prediction: A comprehensive study. *Eur. J. Oper. Res.* **2016**, *252*, 561–572. [CrossRef]
20. Scalzer, R.S.; Rodrigues, A.; Macedo, M.Á.S.; Wanke, P. Financial distress in electricity distributors from the perspective of Brazilian regulation. *Energy Policy* **2019**, *125*, 250–259. [CrossRef]
21. Altman, I.E.; Haldeman, G.R.; Narayanan, P. ZETA^{TM} analysis A new model to identify bankruptcy risk of corporations. *J. Bank. Financ.* **1977**, *1*, 29–54. [CrossRef]
22. Inekwe, J.N.; Jin, Y.; Valenzuela, M.R. The effects of financial distress: Evidence from US GDP growth. *Econ. Model.* **2018**, *72*, 8–21. [CrossRef]
23. Ohlson, J. Financial ratios and the probabilistic prediction of bankruptcy. *J. Account. Res.* **1980**, *18*, 109–131. [CrossRef]
24. Hillegeist, S.; Keating, E.; Cram, D.; Lundstedt, K. Assessing the probability of bankruptcy. *Rev. Account. Stud.* **2004**, *9*, 5–34. [CrossRef]
25. Teresa, A.J. Accounting measures of corporate liquidity, leverage, and costs of financial distress. *Financ. Manag.* **1993**, *22*, 91–100.
26. Shumway, T. Forecasting bankruptcy more accurately: A simple hazard model. *J. Bus.* **2001**, *74*, 101–124. [CrossRef]
27. Hosaka, T. Bankruptcy prediction using imaged financial ratios and convolutional neural networks. *Expert Syst. Appl.* **2019**, *117*, 287–299. [CrossRef]
28. Korol, T. Dynamic Bankruptcy Prediction Models for European Enterprises. *J. Risk Financ. Manag.* **2019**, *12*, 185. [CrossRef]
29. Gregova, E.; Valaskova, K.; Adamko, P.; Tumpach, M.; Jaros, J. Predicting Financial Distress of Slovak Enterprises: Comparison of Selected Traditional and Learning Algorithms Methods. *Sustainability* **2020**, *12*, 3954. [CrossRef]
30. Kovacova, M.; Kliestik, T.; Valaskova, K.; Durana, P.; Juhaszova, Z. Systematic review of variables applied in bankruptcy prediction models of Visegrad group countries. *Oeconomia Copernic.* **2019**, *10*, 743–772. [CrossRef]
31. Kliestik, T.; Misankova, M.; Valaskova, K.; Svabova, L. Bankruptcy Prevention: New Effort to Reflect on Legal and Social Changes. *Sci. Eng. Ethics* **2018**, *24*, 791–803. [CrossRef]
32. López, J.; Maldonado, S. Profit-based credit scoring based on robust optimization and feature selection. *Inf. Sci.* **2019**, *500*, 190–202. [CrossRef]
33. Maldonado, S.; Pérez, J.; Bravo, C. Cost-based feature selection for Support Vector Machines: An application in credit scoring. *Eur. J. Oper. Res.* **2017**, *261*, 656–665. [CrossRef]
34. Li, J.; Qin, Y.; Yi, D. Feature selection for Support Vector Machine in the study of financial early warning system. *Qual. Reliab. Eng. Int.* **2014**, *30*, 867–877. [CrossRef]
35. Duffie, D.; Saita, L.; Wang, K. Multi-Period Corporate Default Prediction with Stochastic Covariates. *J. Financ. Econ.* **2004**, *83*, 635–665. [CrossRef]
36. Greene, W.H.; Hensher, D.A.; Jones, S. An Error Component Logit Analysis of Corporate Bankruptcy and Insolvency Risk in Australia. *Econ. Rec.* **2007**, *83*, 86–103.
37. Figlewski, S.; Frydman, H.; Liang, W.J. Modeling the effect of macroeconomic factors on corporate default and credit rating transitions. *Int. Rev. Econ. Financ.* **2012**, *21*, 87–105. [CrossRef]
38. Tang, D.Y.; Yan, H. Market conditions, default risk and credit spreads. *J. Bank. Financ.* **2010**, *34*, 743–753. [CrossRef]
39. Chen, C.; Kieschnick, R. Bank credit and corporate working capital management. *J. Corp. Financ.* **2016**, *48*, 579–596. [CrossRef]
40. Jermann, U.; Quadrini, V. Macroeconomic effects of financial shocks. *Am. Econ. Rev.* **2012**, *102*, 238–271. [CrossRef]

41. Carpenter, J.N.; Whitelaw, R.F. The development of China's stock market and stakes for the global economy. *Annu. Rev. Financ. Econ.* **2017**, *9*, 233–257. [CrossRef]

42. Hua, Z.; Wang, Y.; Xu, X.; Xu, X.; Zhang, B.; Liang, L. Predicting corporate financial distress based on integration of support vector machine and logistic regression. *Expert Syst. Appl.* **2007**, *33*, 434–440. [CrossRef]

43. Li, H.; Sun, J. Hybridizing principles of the Electre method with case-based reasoning for data mining: Electre-CBR-I and Electre-CBR-II. *Eur. J. Oper. Res.* **2009**, *197*, 214–224. [CrossRef]

44. Cao, Y. MCELCCh-FDP: Financial distress prediction with classifier ensembles based on firm life cycle and Choquet integral. *Expert. Syst. Appl.* **2012**, *39*, 7041–7049. [CrossRef]

45. Shen, F.; Liu, Y.; Wang, R. A dynamic financial distress forecast model with multiple forecast results under unbalanced data environment. *Knowl. Based Syst.* **2020**, *192*, 1–16. [CrossRef]

46. Gasparrini, A.; Armstrong, B.; Kenward, M.G. Distributed lag non-linear models. *Stat. Med.* **2010**, *29*, 2224–2234. [CrossRef]

47. Gasparrini, A.; Scheipl, B.; Armstrong, B.; Kenward, G.M. Penalized Framework for Distributed Lag Non-Linear Models. *Biometrics* **2017**, *73*, 938–948. [CrossRef] [PubMed]

48. Wilson, A.; Hsu, H.H.L.; Chiu, Y.H.M. Kernel machine and distributed lag models for assessing windows of susceptibility to mixtures of time-varying environmental exposures in children's health studies. *arXiv* **2019**, arXiv:1904.12417.

49. Nelson, C.R.; Schwert, G.W. Estimating the Parameters of a Distributed Lag Model from Cross-Section Data: The Case of Hospital Admissions and Discharges. *J. Am. Stat. Assoc.* **1974**, *69*, 627–633. [CrossRef]

50. Hammoudeh, S.; Sari, R. Financial CDS, stock market and interest rates: Which drives which? *N. Am. J. Econ. Financ.* **2011**, *22*, 257–276. [CrossRef]

51. Lahiani, A.; Hammoudeh, S.; Gupta, R. Linkages between financial sector CDS spreads and macroeconomic influence in a nonlinear setting. *Int. Rev. Econ. Financ.* **2016**, *43*, 443–456. [CrossRef]

52. Almon, S. The distributed lag between capital appropriations and expenditures. *Econometrica* **1965**, *33*, 178–196. [CrossRef]

53. Dominici, F.; Daniels, M.S.L.; Samet, Z.J. Air pollution sand mortality: Estimating regional and national dose—Response relationships. *J. Am. Stat. Assoc.* **2002**, *97*, 100–111. [CrossRef]

54. Wooldridge, J.M. *Econometric Analysis of Cross Section and Panel Data*; MIT Press: Cambridge, MA, USA, 2010.

55. Park, H.; Sakaori, F. Lag weighted lasso for time series model. *Comput. Stat.* **2013**, *28*, 493–504. [CrossRef]

56. Glowinski, R.; Marroco, A. Sur l'approximation, par éléments finis d'ordre un, et la résolution, par pénalisation-dualité d'une classe de problèmes de Dirichlet non linéaires. *ESAIM Math. Model. Numer.* **1975**, *9*, 41–76. [CrossRef]

57. Dantzig, G.; Wolfe, J. Decomposition principle for linear programs. *Oper. Res.* **1960**, *8*, 101–111. [CrossRef]

58. Hestenes, M.R. Multiplier and gradient methods. *J. Optim. Theory. Appl.* **1969**, *4*, 302–320. [CrossRef]

59. Chambolle, A.; Pock, T. A first-order primal-dual algorithm for convex problems with applications to imaging. *J. Math. Imaging Vis.* **2011**, *40*, 120–145. [CrossRef]

60. Boyd, S.; Parikh, N.; Chu, E.; Peleato, B.; Eckstein, J. Distributed Optimization and Statistical Learning via the Alternating Direction Method of Multipliers. *Found. Trends. Mach. Learn.* **2011**, *3*, 1–122. [CrossRef]

61. Mangasarian, O.L. A finite Newton method for classification. *Optim. Methods Softw.* **2002**, *17*, 913–929. [CrossRef]

62. Shon, T.; Moon, J. A hybrid machine learning approach to network anomaly detection. *Inf. Sci.* **2007**, *177*, 3799–3821. [CrossRef]

63. Liu, D.; Qian, H.; Dai, G.; Zhang, Z. An iterative SVM approach to feature selection and classification in high-dimensional datasets. *Pattern Recognit.* **2013**, *46*, 2531–2537. [CrossRef]

64. Tiwari, R. Intrinsic value estimates and its accuracy: Evidence from Indian manufacturing industry. *Future Bus. J.* **2016**, *2*, 138–151. [CrossRef]

65. Shanker, M.; Hu, M.Y.; Hung, M.S. Effect of data standardization on neural network training. *Omega Int. J. Manag. Sci.* **1996**, *24*, 385–397. [CrossRef]

66. Kacer, M.; Ochotnicky, P.; Alexy, M. The Altman's revised Z'-Score model, non-financial information and macroeconomic variables: Case of Slovak SMEs. *Ekon. Cas.* **2019**, *67*, 335–366.

5

A Proposal to Fix the Number of Factors on Modeling the Dynamics of Futures Contracts on Commodity Prices

Andrés García-Mirantes [1], Beatriz Larraz [2,*] and Javier Población [3]

[1]   IES Juan del Enzina, 24001 Leon, Spain; andres.web.publicar@gmail.com
[2]   Statistics Department/Faculty of Law and Social Sciences, Universidad de Castilla-La Mancha, 45071 Toledo, Spain
[3]   Banco de España, 28014 Madrid, Spain; Javier.poblacion@bde.es
*   Correspondence: beatriz.larraz@uclm.es
†   This paper should not be reported as representing the views of the Banco de España (BdE) or European Central Bank (ECB). The views expressed herein are those of the authors and should not be attributed to the BdE or ECB.

Abstract: In the literature on modeling commodity futures prices, we find that the stochastic behavior of the spot price is a response to between one and four factors, including both short- and long-term components. The more factors considered in modeling a spot price process, the better the fit to observed futures prices—but the more complex the procedure can be. With a view to contributing to the knowledge of how many factors should be considered, this study presents a new way of computing the best number of factors to be accounted for when modeling risk-management of energy derivatives. The new method identifies the number of factors one should consider in the model and the type of stochastic process to be followed. This study aims to add value to previous studies which consider principal components by assuming that the spot price can be modeled as a sum of several factors. When applied to four different commodities (weekly observations corresponding to futures prices traded at the NYMEX for WTI light sweet crude oil, heating oil, unleaded gasoline and Henry Hub natural gas) we find that, while crude oil and heating oil are satisfactorily well-modeled with two factors, unleaded gasoline and natural gas need a third factor to capture seasonality.

Keywords: commodity prices; futures prices; number of factors; eigenvalues

---

1. Introduction

Forecasting is not a highly regarded activity for economists and financiers. For some, it evokes images of speculators, chart analysts and questionable investor newsletters. For others, there are memories of the grandiose econometric forecasting failures of the 1970's. Nevertheless, there is a need for forecasting in risk management. A prudent corporate treasurer or fund manager must have some way of measuring the risk of earnings, cash flows or returns. Any measure of risk must incorporate some estimate of the probability distribution of the futures asset prices on which financial performance depends. Consequently, forecasting is an indispensable element of prudent financial management.

When a company is planning to develop a crude oil or natural gas field, the investment is significant, and production usually lasts many years. However, there must be an initial investment for there to be any return (see, for example, [1,2], among others). Assuming that futures values are not known after a certain date because there is no trade, it makes it difficult to measure the risk of these projects. Since commodities (crude oil, gas, gasoline, etc.) are physical assets, their price dynamic is much more complex than financial assets because their prices are affected by storage and transportation cost (cost of carry). Due to such complexity, in order to model this price dynamic we need factor models such as in [3–9]. In addition, in the transport sector [10] and [11] use different factor models for modeling bulk shipping prices and freight prices.

In order to measure exposure to price risk due to a single underlying asset, it is necessary to know the dynamics of the term structure of asset prices. Specifically, the value-at-risk (VaR, [12]) of the underlying asset price, the most widely known measure of market risk [13], is characterized by knowing the stochastic dynamic of the price, the volatility of the price and the correlation of different prices at different times. For these reasons, to date, the behavior of commodity prices has been modeled under the assumption that the spot price and/or the convenience yield of the commodity follow a stochastic process.

In the literature we find that the spot price is considered as the sum of both short-term and long-term components (see, for example, [14,15]). Short-term factors account for the mean reverting components in commodity prices, while long-term factors account for the long-term dynamics of commodity prices, assuming they follow a random walk. Sometimes a deterministic seasonal component needs to be added [16].

Following this approach, some multifactor models have been proposed in the literature. Focusing on the number of factors initially considered, [17] developed a two-factor model to value oil-linked assets. Later, [14] planned a one-factor model, two-factor model and a three-factor model, adding stochastic interest rates to the previous factors. This was superseded by a new formulation which appeared in [15], enhancing the latter article and developing a short-term/long-term model. [18] added the long-term spot price return as a third risk factor. Finally, [19] offered researchers a general N-factor model.

At this point, it should be stressed that the decision regarding the number of factors to be used in the model needs to be made a priori. According to the above literature consulted, the models are usually planned with two, three or four factors. However, in this study, the need to assume a fixed number of factors in the model is discounted. We propose a new method that identifies the number of factors one should consider in the model and the type of stochastic process to be followed. This method avoids the necessity of inaccurately suggesting a concrete number of factors in the model. This is very useful for researchers and practitioners because the optimal number of factors could change, depending on the accuracy needed in each problem. Clearly, if we do not use the optimal number of factors in modeling the commodity price dynamics, the results will not be optimal.

To the best of our knowledge, there are three previous studies applying principal component analysis [20] to the modeling of commodity futures price dynamics [21–23]. However, they only model the futures prices dynamic and ignore the dynamic followed by the spot price and, consequently carrying the risk of being incoherent, since futures price are the spot price expected value under the Q measure.

This study aims to add value to previous contributions by assuming that is the spot price can be modeled as a sum of several factors (long term and short term, seasonality, etc.). Therefore, since it is widely accepted (see, for example, [24]) that the futures price is the spot price expected value under the Q measure ($F_{t,T} = E^*[S_{t+T}|I_t]$), where S_{t+T} is the spot price at time $t + T$, I_t is the information available at time t and $E^*[\ ]$ is the expected value under the Q measure.), from the variance–covariance matrix of the futures prices we can deduce the best structure for modelling the spot prices dynamic.

The remainder of this study is organized as follows. Section 2 presents a general theoretical model and explains the methodology proposed to set an optimal set of factors. In Section 3, we describe the datasets used to show the methodology and these results are described. Finally, Section 4 sets out the conclusions.

2. Theoretical Model

2.1. Theoretical Model

In the main literature to date (for example, [19]), it is assumed that the commodity log spot price is the sum of several stochastic factors: $S_t = \exp(\mathbf{C}\mathbf{X}_t)$, $t = 0,\ldots,n$ where the vector of state variables $\mathbf{X}_t = (x_{1t},\ldots,x_{Nt})$ follows the process: $d\mathbf{X}_t = \mathbf{M}dt + \mathbf{A}\mathbf{X}_t dt + \mathbf{R}d\mathbf{W}_t$, being $\mathbf{C}, \mathbf{M}, \mathbf{A}$ and $\mathbf{R}$ vectors' and matrices' parameters.

It is widely accepted that, for the model to be identifiable, some restrictions must be imposed. This means that if we assume that $\mathbf{A}$ is diagonalizable and all its eigenvalues are real (a different formula is available if some are complex), we can take $\mathbf{C} = (1,\ldots,1)$, $\mathbf{M}' = (\mu,0,\ldots,0)$ and $\mathbf{A} =$

$$\begin{pmatrix} 0 & 0 & \cdots & 0 \\ 0 & k_2 & \cdots & 0 \\ \vdots & \vdots & \ddots & \vdots \\ 0 & 0 & \cdots & k_N \end{pmatrix}$$, with $k_i, i = 1,\ldots,N$ the eigenvalues and $k_1 = 0$, by simply changing the state space

basis. Therefore, we already have $\mathbf{M}, \mathbf{A}$ and $\mathbf{C}$.

It is also easy to prove that as $d\mathbf{W}_t$ is a $N \times 1$ vector of correlated Brownian motion increments,

$\mathbf{R}$ can be assumed as $\mathbf{R} = \begin{pmatrix} \sigma_1 & 0 & \cdots & 0 \\ 0 & \sigma_2 & \cdots & 0 \\ \vdots & \vdots & \ddots & \vdots \\ 0 & 0 & \cdots & \sigma_N \end{pmatrix}$. Note that $\mathbf{R}$ is not important, but the product $\mathbf{R}\mathbf{R}'$

is what appears in all formulae. In fact, it can be proved that any factorization of $\mathbf{R}\mathbf{R}'$ corresponds to a different definition of the noise, so we can safely take $\mathbf{R}$ as any Choleski factorization of $(\mathbf{R}\mathbf{R}')$. In the Black–Scholes world (risk-neutral world), knowing the real dynamics, the risk neutral one is $d\mathbf{X}_t = \mathbf{M}^* dt + \mathbf{A}\mathbf{X}_t dt + \mathbf{R}d\mathbf{W}_t^*$ where $\mathbf{M}^* = \mathbf{M} - \boldsymbol{\lambda}$ being $\boldsymbol{\lambda}' = (\lambda_1, \lambda_2, \ldots, \lambda_N)$ the vector formed from each state variable's risk premium).

Following [25], the futures price is given by $F_{t,T} = \exp\big(g(T) + \mathbf{C}e^{\mathbf{A}T}\mathbf{X}_t\big)$, where we know explicitly

$g(T) = \mathbf{C}\int_0^T e^{\mathbf{A}(T-s)}\mathbf{M}^* ds + \mathbf{C}\Big(\int_0^T e^{\mathbf{A}(T-s)}\mathbf{R}\mathbf{R}'\big(e^{\mathbf{A}(T-s)}\big)' ds\Big)\mathbf{C}'$ and where both $g(T)$ and $C(T) = e^{\mathbf{A}T}$ are known deterministic functions independent of t and $\mathbf{X}_t$ is a stochastic process with known dynamics.

Defining in a more compact form, we have:
$$\begin{cases} d\mathbf{X}_t = (\mathbf{M} + \mathbf{A}\mathbf{X}_t)dt + \mathbf{R}d\mathbf{W}_t \\ F_{t,T} = \exp[\delta(T) + \phi(T)\mathbf{X}_t + \varphi(T)\mathbf{M}^* + \varepsilon_{t,T}] \end{cases}$$

2.2. A General Procedure to Determine the Stochastic Factors

In the previous subsection, we have presented the general model for characterizing the commodity price dynamics based on the assumption that the log commodity spot price is the sum of several factors. However, to the best of the authors' knowledge, the optimal number of stochastic factors has not yet been studied, for these models.

This subsection presents a theoretical procedure to establish the optimal number of factors. It also presents a way to determine how those factors should be aligned (long-term, short-term, seasonal, etc.).

To address this problem, let us suppose that there are M futures maturities and n observations of the forward curve, that is, the matrix $\mathbf{U} = \log\big(F_{t,T_i}\big)$, $t = 0,\ldots,n$; $i = 1,\ldots,M$ has dimension $M \times (n+1)$. We further assume, as usual, that $n \gg M$. To determine the optimal number of stochastic factors needed to characterize the commodity price dynamic in the best way, first we must realize that the number of factors is equal to $rank(\mathbf{R})$ and, from the previous expression, $rank(\mathbf{R})$ has to be equal to the rank of the variance–covariance matrix of $\mathbf{U}$. If, as usual, the process $\mathbf{X}_t$ has a unit root, so it is non-stationary and the variance and covariances are infinity, we need another matrix to determine the rank of the variance–covariance matrix of $\mathbf{U}$.

If we define volatility (instantaneous variance) as $\sigma_{T_i}^2 = \lim\limits_{h \to 0} \dfrac{Var\left(\log F_{t+h,T_i} - \log F_{t,T_i}\right)}{h}$, $i = 1, \ldots, M$

and cross-volatility (instantaneous covariance) as $\sigma_{T_i,T_j} = \lim\limits_{h \to 0} \dfrac{Cov\left(\log F_{t+h,T_i} - \log F_{t,T_i}, \log F_{t+h,T_j} - \log F_{t,T_j}\right)}{h}$,

$i, j = 1, \ldots, M$ (as expected, $\sigma_{T_i}^2 = \sigma_{T_i,T_j}$), we have the necessary matrix. Although we cannot compute the limit from the data, we can set h as the shortest time period available and estimate it directly as

$\hat{\sigma}_{T_i,T_j} = \left[\dfrac{\hat{Cov}\left(\log F_{t+h,T_i} - \log F_{t,T_i}, \log F_{t+h,T_j} - \log F_{t,T_j}\right)}{h} \right]$, where $\hat{Cov}$ is the sample covariance.

We thus define the matrix $\boldsymbol{\Theta} = \left(\Theta_{ij}\right)$ (dim $M \times M$) as $\Theta_{ij} = \sigma_{T_i,T_j}$, $i, j = 1, \ldots, M$. We can estimate it directly from our database and we can also estimate its rank. Once we have this rank, as stated above $rank(\boldsymbol{\Theta}) = rank(\mathbf{R}) = N$, we know the number of stochastic factors (N) that define the commodity price dynamics.

From a practical point of view, however, if we follow this procedure as explained above, unless one futures maturity is a linear combination of the rest (which is not likely), we obtain $rank(\boldsymbol{\Theta}) = rank(\mathbf{R}) = N$. Nevertheless, the weights of these factors are going to be different and most of them will have an insignificant weight.

Fortunately, from this procedure, we can also estimate the eigenvalues $k_1, \ldots, k_N$ and, from there, determine the factor weight through the eigenvalues' relative weight. We can estimate the eigenvalues of $\mathbf{A}$ via a nonlinear search procedure by using the fact that $\sigma_{T_i,T_j} = \mathbf{C}e^{\mathbf{A}T_i}\mathbf{R}\mathbf{R}'\left(e^{\mathbf{A}T_j}\right)'\mathbf{C}'$ (see García et

al. 2008) and therefore, $\boldsymbol{\Theta}$ can be expressed as $\boldsymbol{\Theta} = \mathbf{C}\begin{pmatrix} e^{\mathbf{A}T_1} & \cdots & e^{\mathbf{A}T_M} \end{pmatrix}\mathbf{R}\mathbf{R}'\begin{pmatrix} e^{\mathbf{A}T_1} \\ \vdots \\ e^{\mathbf{A}T_M} \end{pmatrix}'\mathbf{C}'$. σ_{T_i,T_j} is a

linear combination of products of $e^{k_1 T}, \ldots, e^{k_N T}$. In other words, if $k_1, \ldots, k_N$ are the eigenvalues of $\mathbf{A}$, $e^{k_1 T}, \ldots, e^{k_N T}$ must be the eigenvalues of $\boldsymbol{\Theta}$.

Moreover, from the eigenvalues of matrix $\mathbf{A}$, it is also easy to determine the factors. Taking into account that factors' Stochastic Differential Equation (SDE) is $d\mathbf{X}_t = \mathbf{M}dt + \mathbf{A}\mathbf{X}_t dt + \mathbf{R}d\mathbf{W}_t$, if, for example, the eigenvalue is $k = 0$, the factor is a long-term one because the SDE associated with this factor is a random walk (General Brownian Motion (GBM)): $dx_{it} = \mu_i dt + \sigma_i dW_{it}$. On the other hand, if the eigenvalue is $k \in (-1, 0)$, the factor is a short-term one because the SDE associated with this factor is an Ornstein–Uhlenbeck: $dx_{it} = \lambda x_{it}dt + \sigma_i dW_{it}$. If the eigenvalue is complex, the factor is a seasonal one.

From a practical point of view, when we carry out this procedure we get N eigenvalues and we need to decide how many of them to optimally choose. The way to decide this is through the relative weight of the eigenvalues. By normalizing the largest one to 1, the smallest eigenvalues represent negligible factors. This allows us to decide how many factors must be optimally chosen.

In order to clarify concepts, the following example could be useful, if we have $M = 9$ futures with maturities at times $T_1, \ldots, T_9$. The method is as follows.

1. Compute $\hat{\Theta}_{ij} = \left[\dfrac{\hat{Cov}\left(\log F_{t+h,T_i} - \log F_{t,T_i}, \log F_{t+h,T_j} - \log F_{t,T_j}\right)}{h} \right]$.

2. Compute the rank of $\hat{\Theta}$. Let us assume that this is 3.

3. As a result, we have three eigenvalues k_1, k_2 and k_3. It is usual to assume that $k_1 = 0$ as the futures process is not stationary, but k_1 can nevertheless be estimated. If we do assume it, however, we obtain that σ_{T_i,T_j} is a linear combination of the products of $e^{0T} = 1$, $e^{k_2 T}$ and $e^{k_3 T}$. Therefore, we obtain the general equation $\Theta_{ij} = \alpha_{11} + \alpha_{12}e^{k_2 T_j} + \alpha_{13}e^{k_3 T_j} + \alpha_{21}e^{k_2 T_i} + \alpha_{31}e^{k_3 T_i} + \alpha_{22}e^{k_2 (T_i+T_j)} + \alpha_{23}e^{k_2 T_i + k_3 T_j} + \alpha_{23}e^{k_2 T_j + k_3 T_i} + \alpha_{33}e^{k_3 (T_i+T_j)}$ which can be estimated numerically as:

   a. Select an initial estimate of (k_2, k_3).
   b. Regress $\hat{\Theta}_{ij}$ and compute the error.

c.   Iteratively select another estimate of (k_2, k_3) and get back to b.

To the best of the authors' knowledge, no method has combined the knowledge of this concrete specification $G = \Phi(T)$ with a nonlinear search procedure to identify factors, which is one of the contributions made by this article.

Once we have determined the optimal number and form of the stochastic factors to characterize the commodity price dynamics, we can estimate model parameters using standard techniques. The Kalman filter (see, for example, [26]) uses a complex calibration technique. Other techniques include approximations such as [18] or [27]. Finally, the recently published option by [28] presents an optimal way of estimating model parameters by avoiding the use of the Kalman filter. Model parameters are estimated in the papers and so, for the sake of brevity we do not estimate the parameters in this study.

3. Data and Main Results

3.1. Data

In this subsection, we briefly describe the datasets used in this study. The datasets include weekly observations corresponding to futures prices for four commodities: WTI light sweet crude oil, heating oil, unleaded gasoline (RBOB) and Henry Hub natural gas. These futures were taken into consideration because they are the most representative and classic among the products. They are futures with many historical series and futures at many maturities. Therefore, they are considered as ideal for studying the optimal number of factors that should be chosen.

In this study, two data sets were considered for each commodity. Data set 1 contains less futures maturities, but more years of observations considered while data set 2 contains more futures maturities, but less years of observations. For dataset 1 (Table 1A), related to WTI crude oil, it comprised contracts from 4 September 1989 to 3 June 2013 (1240 weekly observations) for futures maturities from F1 to F17, F1 being the contract for the month closest to maturity, F2 the contract for the second-closest month to maturity, etc. In the case of heating oil, it contained contracts from 21 January 1991 to 3 June 2013 (1168 weekly observations) for futures maturities from F1 to F15. Meanwhile, RBOB gasoline first data set comprised contracts from 3 October 2005 to 3 June 2013 (401 weekly observations) for futures maturities from F1 to F12 and in the case of Henry Hub natural gas, it contained contracts from 27 January 1992 to 3 June 2013 (1115 weekly observations) for futures maturities from F1 to F16.

Looking at the dataset 2 (Table 1B), in the case of WTI crude oil, it comprised contracts from 18 September 1995 to 3 June 2013 (925 weekly observations) for futures maturities from F1 to F28 and in the case of heating oil it comprised contracts from 9 September 1996 to 3 June 2013 (874 weekly observations) for futures maturities from F1 to F18. In the meantime, RBOB gasoline comprised contracts from 2 February 2007 to 3 June 2013 (330 weekly observations) for futures maturities from F1 to F36 and, to end with, in the case of Henry Hub natural gas, dataset 2 (Table 1B) contained contracts from 24 March 1997 to 3 June 2013 (856 weekly observations) for futures maturities from F1 to F36.

Table 1 shows the main descriptive statistics of the futures, particularly the mean and volatility, for each dataset. It is interesting to note that the lack of low-cost transportation and the limited storability of natural gas made its supply unresponsive to seasonal variation in demand. Thus, natural gas prices were strongly seasonal [3]. The unleaded gasoline was also seasonal.

Table 1. Descriptive statistics.

	(A) Dataset 1							
	WTI Crude Oil		**Gasoline**		**Natural Gas**		**Heating Oil**	
	Mean ($/bbl)	**Volatility (%)**	**Mean ($/bbl)**	**Volatility (%)**	**Mean ($/MMBtu)**	**Volatility (%)**	**Mean ($/bbl)**	**Volatility (%)**
F1	43.1	30%	96.7	32%	4.2	45%	63.6	28%
F2	43.3	27%	96.5	30%	4.3	40%	63.8	26%
F3	43.3	25%	96.4	29%	4.3	36%	64.0	24%
F4	43.4	24%	96.3	27%	4.4	32%	64.1	23%
F5	43.3	23%	96.1	27%	4.4	29%	64.1	22%
F6	43.3	22%	95.9	26%	4.4	27%	64.2	21%
F7	43.3	21%	95.7	25%	4.5	26%	64.2	20%
F8	43.2	20%	95.6	26%	4.5	24%	64.1	19%
F9	43.2	20%	95.6	25%	4.5	24%	64.1	19%
F10	43.1	19%	95.4	26%	4.5	22%	64.1	18%
F11	43.1	19%	95.5	25%	4.5	22%	64.1	18%
F12	43.0	18%	95.5	25%	4.5	21%	64.0	17%
F13	43.0	18%			4.5	20%	63.7	17%
F14	42.9	18%			4.5	20%	63.4	17%
F15	42.9	17%			4.5	20%	63.0	17%
F16	42.8	17%			4.5	20%		
F17	42.8	17%						

	(B) Dataset 2							
	WTI Crude Oil		**Gasoline**		**Natural Gas**		**Heating oil**	
	Mean ($/bbl)	**Volatility (%)**	**Mean ($/bbl)**	**Volatility (%)**	**Mean ($/MMBtu)**	**Volatility (%)**	**Mean ($/bbl)**	**Volatility (%)**
F1	50.9	30%	101.1	32%	4.9	45%	53.3	30%
F2	51.2	28%	100.6	30%	5.0	40%	53.5	28%
F3	51.3	26%	100.3	30%	5.1	38%	53.6	26%
F4	51.3	25%	100.1	28%	5.1	33%	53.7	25%
F5	51.3	24%	99.8	28%	5.2	31%	53.7	24%
F6	51.3	23%	99.6	27%	5.2	28%	53.7	23%
F7	51.3	22%	99.3	26%	5.3	27%	53.7	22%
F8	51.3	21%	99.2	26%	5.3	26%	53.7	21%
F9	51.2	21%	99.1	25%	5.3	25%	53.7	21%
F10	51.2	20%	99.1	27%	5.3	24%	53.6	20%
F11	51.1	20%	99.1	26%	5.3	22%	53.6	19%
F12	51.1	19%	99.1	26%	5.3	21%	53.5	19%
F13	51.0	19%	99.1	26%	5.3	21%	53.3	19%
F14	50.9	19%	99.0	25%	5.3	21%	53.0	19%
F15	50.8	18%	98.9	25%	5.3	21%	53.0	18%
F16	50.8	18%	98.8	23%	5.3	20%	53.5	18%
F17	50.7	18%	98.5	24%	5.3	20%	55.4	18%
F18	50.7	18%	98.3	23%	5.3	19%	58.4	18%
F19	50.6	17%	98.1	23%	5.3	20%		
F20	50.5	17%	98.0	23%	5.3	19%		
F21	50.5	17%	98.0	23%	5.3	19%		
F22	50.4	17%	97.9	24%	5.3	20%		
F23	50.4	17%	97.9	23%	5.2	18%		
F24	50.3	17%	97.9	24%	5.2	18%		
F25	50.3	16%	97.9	24%	5.2	18%		
F26	50.2	16%	97.8	23%	5.2	18%		
F27	50.2	16%	97.8	24%	5.2	18%		
F28	50.1	16%	97.7	23%	5.2	18%		
F29			97.6	23%	5.2	18%		
F30			97.5	22%	5.2	18%		
F31			97.4	22%	5.2	18%		
F32			97.4	23%	5.2	19%		
F33			97.3	22%	5.2	18%		
F34			97.1	23%	5.2	19%		
F35			97.0	23%	5.2	18%		
F36			97.0	23%	5.2	17%		

3.2. Main Results

We now present the results after applying the method proposed to the 4 commodities (2 datasets per commodity) described above in order to select the number of factors to model the behavior of commodity prices. The results correspond to the eigenvalues in decreasing order, the percentage of the overall variability that they explain and the cumulative proportion of explained variance. These are reported in Tables 2–5.

Table 2. Eigenvalues for both datasets of the WTI light sweet crude oil.

Dataset 1			Dataset 2		
Eigenvalues	Percentage of Total Variance	Cumulative Variance (%)	Eigenvalues	Percentage of Total Variance	Cumulative Variance (%)
100	99.6713	99.6713	100	99.5448	99.5448
0.3202	0.3191	99.9904	0.4428	0.4408	99.9855
0.0084	0.0084	99.9988	0.0126	0.0125	99.9980
0.0010	0.0010	99.9998	0.0017	0.0017	99.9997
0.0001	0.0001	99.9999	0.0002	0.0002	99.9998
2.9905×10^{-5}	2.9806×10^{-5}	100	0.0001	0.0001	99.9999
1.2209×10^{-5}	1.2169×10^{-5}	100	3.7318×10^{-5}	3.7148×10^{-5}	100
5.4907×10^{-6}	5.4727×10^{-6}	100	1.6898×10^{-5}	1.6821×10^{-5}	100
2.7838×10^{-6}	2.7746×10^{-6}	100	8.7477×10^{-6}	8.7079×10^{-6}	100
1.5250×10^{-6}	1.5200×10^{-6}	100	4.4713×10^{-6}	4.4509×10^{-6}	100
7.5290×10^{-7}	7.5043×10^{-7}	100	3.0355×10^{-6}	3.0217×10^{-6}	100
4.3460×10^{-7}	4.3317×10^{-7}	100	2.3004×10^{-6}	2.2899×10^{-6}	100
3.3010×10^{-7}	3.2901×10^{-7}	100	1.3628×10^{-6}	1.3566×10^{-6}	100
1.8100×10^{-7}	1.8041×10^{-7}	100	8.7940×10^{-7}	8.7540×10^{-7}	100
1.1490×10^{-7}	1.1452×10^{-7}	100	4.7100×10^{-7}	4.6886×10^{-7}	100
1.0350×10^{-7}	1.0316×10^{-7}	100	3.6450×10^{-7}	3.6284×10^{-7}	100
3.9300×10^{-8}	3.9171×10^{-8}	100	2.3880×10^{-7}	2.3771×10^{-7}	100
			1.8840×10^{-7}	1.8754×10^{-7}	100
			1.4180×10^{-7}	1.4115×10^{-7}	100
			1.1480×10^{-7}	1.1428×10^{-7}	100
			1.0070×10^{-7}	1.0024×10^{-7}	100
			7.7800×10^{-8}	7.7446×10^{-8}	100
			5.4200×10^{-8}	5.3953×10^{-8}	100
			4.7800×10^{-8}	4.7582×10^{-8}	100
			3.8600×10^{-8}	3.8424×10^{-8}	100
			2.3000×10^{-8}	2.2895×10^{-8}	100
			2.1600×10^{-8}	2.1502×10^{-8}	100
			8.9000×10^{-9}	8.8595×10^{-9}	100

As a general rule, we can consider that the first factor, which corresponds to the first eigenvalue, was clearly dominant in the sense that it can explain a percentage of the total variance ranging between 95.2% and 99.7%, depending on the commodity. It captures qualitative long-run effects. However, it is always necessary to consider a second factor capable of taking up short-term effects. Both the first and second factors explain a cumulative proportion of overall variance between 97.5% and 99.9%, depending on the case under study. In WTI light sweet crude oil, these two factors explain more than a 99.99% of the total variance is explained, while in heating oil case studies, these percentages were approximately 99.88% and in unleaded gasoline and Henry Hub natural gas, they were approximately 97–98%.

Consequently, in the first commodity (crude oil) it is recommended that just the first two factors are considered. The reason is that a third factor will impose a larger estimating effort and a minimum reduction in terms of error measures. The first factor will capture long-term effects, such as world economic events, which significantly impact on commodity prices. The second factor will capture the nature of short-term components such as temporary issues and unforeseen situations. The third and following stochastic factors can be considered as seasonal factors [28] and, as we know, crude oil is a non-seasonal commodity. This matter reinforces the idea that it is suitable to consider a model with only the first two factors.

The next commodity, heating oil, presents some seasonal behavior, which could be captured by a third factor. The fact that the gain in the percentage of cumulative proportion of overall variance goes from 99.88 to 99.94 and from 99.90 to 99.94 in its respective datasets suggest the inclusion of a third factor was not necessary.

Table 3. Eigenvalues for both datasets of the heating oil.

Dataset 1			Dataset 2		
Eigenvalues	Percentage of Total Variance	Cumulative Variance (%)	Eigenvalues	Percentage of Total Variance	Cumulative Variance (%)
100	99.6133	99.6133	100	99.5365	99.5365
0.2698	0.2687	99.8820	0.3666	0.3649	99.9014
0.0658	0.0655	99.9475	0.0475	0.0472	99.9486
0.0474	0.0472	99.9947	0.0448	0.0446	99.9932
0.0028	0.0028	99.9975	0.0037	0.0037	99.9969
0.0013	0.0013	99.9988	0.0012	0.0012	99.9981
0.0009	0.0008	99.9997	0.0011	0.0011	99.9992
0.0001	0.0001	99.9998	0.0005	0.0005	99.9997
0.0001	0.0001	99.9999	0.0001	0.0001	99.9998
4.7937×10^{-5}	4.7752×10^{-5}	99.9999	0.0001	0.0001	99.9999
1.9734×10^{-5}	1.9658×10^{-5}	100	4.1450×10^{-5}	4.1257×10^{-5}	99.9999
1.1626×10^{-5}	1.1581×10^{-5}	100	2.8767×10^{-5}	2.8633×10^{-5}	99.9999
1.0482×10^{-5}	1.0441×10^{-5}	100	1.5784×10^{-5}	1.5711×10^{-5}	100
9.6273×10^{-6}	9.5901×10^{-6}	100	1.3478×10^{-5}	1.3416×10^{-5}	100
6.3346×10^{-6}	6.3101×10^{-6}	100	9.3425×10^{-6}	9.2992×10^{-6}	100
			7.9877×10^{-6}	7.9507×10^{-6}	100
			6.1859×10^{-6}	6.1572×10^{-6}	100
			5.7507×10^{-6}	5.7240×10^{-6}	100

Conversely, for the unleaded gasoline and Henry hub natural gas, at least a third factor seemed to be necessary. Both were seasonal commodities (see, for example, [3]). They were characterized by very limited storability and their prices were highly dependent on the commodity demand. Third and fourth factors will acknowledge this behavior. It seems necessary to capture more than long-term and short-term dynamics. Depending on the cumulative variance, if we would like to explain (98–99%), we need to consider at least a third factor or two more. In the unleaded gasoline case, the inclusion of a third factor would increase the cumulative proportion of overall variance from 98.48% to 99.73% and from 97.49% to 98.73%. However, with a fourth factor, we would reach 99.86% and 99.76%, respectively. When we apply the methodology proposed to Henry Hub natural gas datasets, we also verify the need to consider a third and even a fourth factor to explain 99.80% and 99.65% of the total variance, respectively.

Table 4. Eigenvalues for both datasets of the unleaded gasoline (RBOB).

Dataset 1			Dataset 2		
Eigenvalues	Percentage of Total Variance	Cumulative Variance (%)	Eigenvalues	Percentage of Total Variance	Cumulative Variance (%)
100	96.8591	96.8591	100	95.2473	95.2473
1.6748	1.6222	98.4813	2.3570	2.2450	97.4924
1.2901	1.2496	99.7308	1.3050	1.2429	98.7353
0.1334	0.1292	99.8600	1.0762	1.0250	99.7603
0.0558	0.0540	99.9140	0.0639	0.0608	99.8212
0.0386	0.0374	99.9515	0.0599	0.0570	99.8782
0.0217	0.0210	99.9724	0.0437	0.0416	99.9198
0.0156	0.0151	99.9876	0.0217	0.0206	99.9405
0.0093	0.0090	99.9966	0.0208	0.0198	99.9602
0.0022	0.0022	99.9988	0.0171	0.0163	99.9765
0.0009	0.0009	99.9997	0.0074	0.0070	99.9835
0.0003	0.0003	100	0.0049	0.0047	99.9882
			0.0030	0.0029	99.9910
			0.0025	0.0024	99.9935
			0.0019	0.0018	99.9953
			0.0012	0.0011	99.9964
			0.0008	0.0008	99.9972
			0.0006	0.0006	99.9978
			0.0004	0.0004	99.9982
			0.0004	0.0003	99.9986
			0.0003	0.0003	99.9989
			0.0003	0.0003	99.9991
			0.0002	0.0002	99.9993
			0.0001	0.0001	99.9995
			0.0001	0.0001	99.9996
			0.0001	0.0001	99.9997
			0.0001	0.0001	99.9997
			0.0001	0.0001	99.9998
			0.0001	0.0000	99.9999
			3.8439×10^{-5}	3.6612×10^{-5}	99.9999
			2.8300×10^{-5}	2.6955×10^{-5}	99.9999
			2.4205×10^{-5}	2.3055×10^{-5}	99.9999
			1.9530×10^{-5}	1.8602×10^{-5}	100
			1.5016×10^{-5}	1.4303×10^{-5}	100
			1.2694×10^{-5}	1.2091×10^{-5}	100
			9.9475×10^{-6}	9.4747×10^{-6}	100

These results are coherent with the patterns shown in the futures contracts of each commodity. By considering seasonality as a stochastic factor instead of a deterministic one, we can choose from two- to four-factor models to better model the behavior of commodity prices. It should be noted that the long-term and short-term effects, captured by the first two factors, are clearly dominant in terms of their eigenvalues' relative weight. However, the seasonality should be considered if necessary.

It is important to bear in mind that the distinction between long term and short term is not always direct. It is related to the eigenvalue of the factor, which, as we have stated, is always in the form e^k with $k \leq 0$ (a positive k would mean an explosive process, which is clearly not observed in the data).

If $k = 0$, we have a long-term effect (a unit root). The more negative k is, the shorter the effect. Therefore, $k = -1$ means a much shorter effect than $k = -0.01$, for example.

Explanation capacities of each factor are measured according to their (relative) contribution to the global variance. For example, if there is a unique factor related to eigenvalue $k = 0$ that gives 90% of variance, we would conclude that long term dynamics explain 90% of the variance.

Table 5. Eigenvalues for both datasets of the henry hub natural gas.

Dataset 1			Dataset 2		
Eigenvalues	Percentage of Total Variance	Cumulative Variance (%)	Eigenvalues	Percentage of Total Variance	Cumulative Variance (%)
100	97.8179	97.8179	100	95.8957	95.8957
1.1564	1.1311	98.9491	2.7972	2.6824	98.5782
0.4785	0.4681	99.4172	0.5993	0.5747	99.1529
0.3960	0.3874	99.8046	0.5221	0.5007	99.6535
0.0839	0.0821	99.8867	0.1178	0.1130	99.7665
0.0730	0.0714	99.9580	0.0993	0.0952	99.8617
0.0223	0.0218	99.9798	0.0782	0.0750	99.9367
0.0052	0.0050	99.9849	0.0166	0.0159	99.9527
0.0039	0.0038	99.9887	0.0074	0.0071	99.9598
0.0031	0.0030	99.9917	0.0070	0.0067	99.9665
0.0027	0.0027	99.9944	0.0060	0.0057	99.9722
0.0023	0.0023	99.9967	0.0051	0.0049	99.9772
0.0012	0.0012	99.9979	0.0048	0.0046	99.9818
0.0010	0.0010	99.9988	0.0038	0.0037	99.9854
0.0007	0.0007	99.9995	0.0032	0.0031	99.9886
0.0005	0.0005	100	0.0024	0.0023	99.9908
			0.0020	0.0019	99.9927
			0.0018	0.0017	99.9944
			0.0017	0.0016	99.9961
			0.0013	0.0012	99.9973
			0.0010	0.0009	99.9983
			0.0006	0.0006	99.9988
			0.0003	0.0003	99.9991
			0.0002	0.0002	99.9993
			0.0002	0.0002	99.9995
			0.0001	0.0001	99.9996
			0.0001	0.0001	99.9997
			0.0001	0.0001	99.9998
			0.0001	0.0001	99.9998
			0.0001	0.0001	99.9999
			3.2345×10^{-5}	3.1018×10^{-5}	99.9999
			2.8128×10^{-5}	2.6974×10^{-5}	100
			1.5565×10^{-5}	1.4926×10^{-5}	100
			1.2489×10^{-5}	1.1977×10^{-5}	100
			9.3473×10^{-6}	8.9637×10^{-6}	100
			7.6972×10^{-6}	7.3813×10^{-6}	100

It should be noted that this article focuses on the econometric theory and identifies the optimal number of factors to characterize the dynamics of commodity prices. Apart from this econometric approach, where each factor represents a component—long term, short term, seasonal, etc.—these factors may also capture economic forces [29–31]. In other words, there are economic forces that are being captured by these factors, such as technology effects (long term) or the functioning of the market (short term). Following [15], we argue that the long-term factor reflects expectations of the exhaustion of the existing supply, improvements in technology for the production and discovery of the commodity, inflation, as well as political and regulatory effects. The short-term factor reflects short-term changes in demand or intermittent supply disruptions. An interpretation of seasonal factors can be found in [3].

This method provides a new selection criterion for obtaining the optimal number of factors. It is always important to keep in mind the purpose of modeling such commodity prices. If we need more accuracy because, for example, we are designing investment strategies, the consideration of more factors is understandable. We could also use fewer factors in a different case.

This is important because, on one hand, if we use too many factors the model will be too complex and parameter estimation may not be accurate. On the other hand, if we use too few factors the model will not be acceptable because it will not capture all the characteristic of the price dynamics that we need to consider in order to solve our problem.

We believe our findings to be very useful for researchers and practitioners. Based on our findings, a researcher who needs to model a commodity price dynamic can use our method to identify the number and the characteristics of the factors to be included in the model. Moreover, a practitioner who is investing or measuring risk can also use our methodology in order to identify the optimal number of factors needed and their characteristics.

Finally, as stated above, we have chosen to order the factors according to their relative (joint) contribution to variance because it is a direct and simple way to interpret the results. We are aware that collinearity and, in general, correlation structures can modify the results. However, since the first eigenvalue explains around 95% of variance, it seems unlikely that results are going to change substantially by a more refined analysis.

4. Summary and Conclusions

In this article, we propose a novel methodology for choosing the optimal number of stochastic factors to be included in a model of the term structure of futures commodity prices. With this method, we add to the research related to the way we characterize commodity price dynamics.

The procedure is based on the eigenvalues of the variance–covariance matrix. Moreover, in deciding how many of them to choose, we propose using the relative weight of the eigenvalues and the percentage of the total variance explained by them and balancing this with the effort of estimating more parameters.

In this article, we applied our method to eight datasets, corresponding with four different commodities: crude oil, heating oil, unleaded gasoline and natural gas. Results indicate that to model the first two commodity prices two factors are suitable, which corresponds with the two biggest eigenvalues, since they are sufficient to account for both long-term and short-term structures. Nevertheless, in the case of unleaded gasoline and natural gas, a third or even fourth factor is needed. We think that, in accordance with the literature, this is related to their seasonal behavior.

Our results support the notion that including too many or too few factors or factors with characteristics which are not optimal in a model for commodity prices could lead to results which may not be as accurate as they should be.

Author Contributions: Conceptualization, B.L. and J.P.; methodology, A.G.-M.; software, A.G.-M.; validation, Población and A.G.-M.; formal analysis, A.G.-M.; investigation, J.P. and A.G.-M.; resources, A.G.-M., B.L. and J.P.; data curation, A.G.-M., B.L. and J.P.; writing—original draft preparation, B.L.; writing—review and editing, B.L. y Población; visualization, B.L.; supervision, Población; project administration, B.L.; funding acquisition, B.L. All authors have read and agreed to the published version of the manuscript.

Acknowledgments: This study should not be reported as representing the views of the Banco de España (BdE) or European Central Bank (ECB). The views in this study are those of the author and do not necessarily reflect those of the Banco de España (BdE) or European Central Bank (ECB). We thank the anonymous referees. Any errors are caused by the authors.

References

1. Jahn, F.; Cook, M.; Graham, M. *Hydrocarbon Exploration and Production*; Elsevier: Aberdeen, UK, 2008.
2. Smit, H.T.J. Investment analysis of offshore concessions in the Netherlands. *Financ. Manag.* **1997**, *26*, 5–17. [CrossRef]
3. García, A.; Población, J.; Serna, G. The Stochastic Seasonal Behaviour of Natural Gas Prices. *Eur. Financ. Manag.* **2012**, *18*, 410–443.
4. García, A.; Población, J.; Serna, G. The stochastic seasonal behavior of energy commodity convenience yields. *Energy Econ.* **2013**, *40*, 155–166.
5. García, A.; Población, J.; Serna, G. Analyzing the dynamics of the refining margin: Implications for valuation and hedging. *Quant. Financ.* **2013**, *12*, 1839–1855.
6. Alquist, R.; Bhattarai, S.; Coibion, O. Commodity-price comovement and global economic activity. *J. Monet. Econ.* **2019**. [CrossRef]

7.   Jacks, D.S. From boom to bust: A typology of real commodity prices in the long run. *Cliometrica* **2019**, *13*, 201–220. [CrossRef]
8.   Nazlioglu, S. Oil and Agricultural Commodity Prices. In *Routledge Handbook of Energy Economics*; Soytas, U., San, R., Eds.; Routledge: London, UK, 2020; pp. 385–405.
9.   Ayres, J.; Hevia, C.; Nicolini, J.P. Real exchange rates and primary commodity prices. *J. Intern. Econ.* **2020**, *122*. [CrossRef]
10. Población, J.; Serna, G. A common long-term trend for bulk shipping prices. *Marit. Econ. Logist.* **2018**, *20*, 421–432. [CrossRef]
11. García, A.; Población, J.; Serna, G. Hedging voyage charter rates on illiquid routes. *Intern. J. Shipp. Transp. Logist.* **2020**, *12*, 197–211.
12. Morgan, J.P. *Risk Metrics–Technical Document*; Reuters: New York, NY, USA, 1996.
13. Echaust, K.; Just, M. Value at Risk Estimation Using the GARCH-EVT Approach with Optimal Tail Selection. *Mathematics* **2020**, *8*, 114. [CrossRef]
14. Schwartz, E.S. The stochastic behavior of commodity prices: Implication for valuation and hedging. *J. Financ.* **1997**, *52*, 923–973. [CrossRef]
15. Schwartz, E.S.; Smith, J.E. Short-term variations and long-term dynamics in commodity prices. *Manag. Sci.* **2000**, *46*, 893–911. [CrossRef]
16. Sorensen, C. Modeling seasonality in agricultural commodity futures. *J. Futures Mark.* **2002**, *22*, 393–426. [CrossRef]
17. Gibson, R.; Schwartz, E.S. Stochastic convenience yield and the pricing of oil contingent claims. *J. Financ.* **1990**, *45*, 959–976. [CrossRef]
18. Cortazar, G.; Schwartz, E.S. Implementing a stochastic model for oil futures prices. *Energy Econ.* **2003**, *25*, 215–218. [CrossRef]
19. Cortazar, G.; Naranjo, L. An N-Factor gaussian model of oil futures prices. *J. Futures Mark.* **2006**, *26*, 209–313. [CrossRef]
20. Camiz, S.; Pillar, V.D. Identifying the Informational/Signal Dimension in Principal Component Analysis. *Mathematics* **2018**, *6*, 269. [CrossRef]
21. Cortazar, G.; Schwartz, E.S. The valuation of commodity-contingent claims. *J. Deriv.* **1994**, *1*, 27–39. [CrossRef]
22. Clewlow, L.; Strickland, C. *Energy Derivatives, Pricing and Risk Management*; Lamina Publication: London, UK, 2000.
23. Tolmasky, C.; Hindanov, D. Principal components analysis for correlated curves and seasonal commodities: The case of the petroleum market. *J. Futures Mark.* **2002**, *22*, 1019–1035. [CrossRef]
24. Hull, J. *Options, Futures and Other Derivatives*, 5th ed.; Prentice Hall: Upper Saddle River, NJ, USA, 2003.
25. García, A.; Población, J.; Serna, G. A Note on Commodity Contingent Valuation. *J. Deriv. Hedge Fund.* **2008**, *13*, 311–320. [CrossRef]
26. Harvey, A.C. *Forecasting Structural Time Series Models and the Kalman Filter*; Cambridge University Press: Cambridge, UK, 1989.
27. Kolos, S.P.; Rohn, E.I. Estimating the commodity market price of risk for energy prices. *Energy Econ.* **2008**, *30*, 621–641. [CrossRef]
28. García, A.; Larraz, B.; Población, J. An alternative method to estimate parameters in modeling the behavior of commodity prices. *Quant. Financ.* **2016**, *16*, 1111–1127. [CrossRef]
29. Coles, J.L.; Li, Z.F. An Empirical Assessment of Empirical Corporate Finance. *SSRN* **2019**. [CrossRef]
30. Coles, J.L.; Li, Z.F. Managerial Attributes, Incentives, and Performance. *Rev. Corp. Financ. Stud.* **2019**. [CrossRef]
31. Dang, C.; Foerster, S.R.; Li, Z.F.; Tang, Z. Analyst Talent, Information, and Insider Trading. *SSRN* **2020**. [CrossRef]

6

Discounted and Expected Utility from the Probability and Time Trade-Off Model

Salvador Cruz Rambaud *,† and **Ana María Sánchez Pérez** †

Departamento de Economía y Empresa, Universidad de Almería, La Cañada de San Urbano, s/n, 04120 Almería, Spain; amsanchez@ual.es
* Correspondence: scruz@ual.es
† La Cañada de San Urbano, s/n, 04120 Almería, Spain.

Abstract: This paper shows the interaction between probabilistic and delayed rewards. In decision-making processes, the Expected Utility (EU) model has been employed to assess risky choices whereas the Discounted Utility (DU) model has been applied to intertemporal choices. Despite both models being different, they are based on the same theoretical principle: the rewards are assessed by taking into account the sum of their utilities and some similar anomalies have been revealed in both models. The aim of this paper is to characterize and consider particular cases of the Time Trade-Off (PPT) model and show that they correspond to the EU and DU models. Additionally, we will try to build a PTT model starting from a discounted and an expected utility model able to overcome the limitations pointed out by Baucells and Heukamp.

Keywords: risk; delay; decision-making process; probability; discount

---

1. Introduction

The main objective of this paper is to present the Probability and Time Trade-Off Model [1] as an accurate framework where risk and intertemporal decisions can be separately considered.

The methodology used in this paper consists of considering some particular cases of the PTT model and show that they correspond to EU and DU models. Moreover, the possibility of reversing the process is provided, i.e., obtaining a PTT model starting from an EU and a DU model.

The decision-making process is relatively simple when the alternatives differ only in one dimension (e.g., the amount, the probability of occurrence or the delay) while the rest of the variables remain constant [2]. However, decision-making problems frequently involve alternatives which differ in more than one dimension [3]. Along these lines, there are two traditional models to assess choices which differ in risk or time, in addition to the amount of their reward. Despite risk and delay initially appearing quite different, the individual behavior when facing risky and delayed outcomes is analogous [4]. Currently, due to the fact that most real-world decisions are made on alternatives which are both uncertain and delayed [4], there is a growing interest in understanding and modelling how risk and delay interact in the individual behavior. In this way, there are some scholars as Luckman [5] who show the attempts to explain the complex individual behaviors when facing alternatives which differ in more than two dimensions.

The decision-making process has been analyzed in psychophysics, neuroscience and social and behavioral sciences, such as economics or psychology. From an academic point of view, one of the most studied processes in decision-making is intertemporal choice which concerns those alternatives which differ in maturities (the choice between a smaller, sooner outcome, and a larger, later one) [3]. On the other hand, the decision-making under uncertainty involves alternatives whose rewards differ in relation to the probability of being received (the choice between "a smaller reward, to be received with greater probability, and a larger one, but less likely") [3].

Both kinds of decisions have been traditionally analyzed by using two main systems of calculation: the Discounted Utility model and the Expected Utility theory which describe the present value of delayed rewards and the actuarial value of risky rewards, respectively. Both models are simple, widely accepted, and with a similar structure, since they use the same theoretical principle: the rewards are assessed by the sum of their utilities [6,7]. In the decision-making process, individuals choose the alternative which maximizes their current utility value (denoted by U_0).

As seen in Table 1, DU and EU are the basic models employed in the decision-making process which represent the rational choice over time and under risk, respectively.

Table 1. Classical models to obtain the utility value. Source: Own elaboration.

	Discounted Utility (DU)	Expected Utility (EU)
Pioneer work	Samuelson [8]	Von Neumann and Morgenstern [9]
Result	The present value of delayed rewards	The expected value of risky rewards
Formula	$U_0 = \sum_{t=0}^{T} \delta^t u_t$	$U_0 = \sum_{k=0}^{n} p_k u_k$
Parameters	u_t: utility from the reward at t t: reward maturity ($t = 0, 1, \ldots, T$) δ: discount factor ($0 < \delta < 1$)	u_k: utility from the k-th reward p_k: probability of the k-th reward ($\sum_{k=0}^{n} p_k = 1$)

On the other hand, the Discounted Expected Utility (DEU) model (see Table 2) is employed in decision environments involving both intertemporal and risky decisions (Schoemaker [10] points out nine variants of the Expected Utility model). DEU model has been deeply analyzed in several recent works by Coble and Lusk [11] and Andreoni and Sprenger [12].

Table 2. DEU model. Source: Own elaboration.

Pioneer work	Jamison [13]
Result	The value of risky and delayed rewards
Formula	$V(c_0, \ldots, c_r) = \sum_{t=0}^{T} D(t)u(c_t)$
Parameters	V: valuation of consumption in different periods t: reward maturity ($t = 0, 1, \ldots, T$) $D(t)$: discount function $u(c_t)$: utility of consumption at t (c_t)

The accuracy of DU and EU models has been questioned to explain actual behaviors given that they are a simplification of reality [14]. In the same way, [15,16] show that DEU model fails as a predictor of intertemporal-risky choices. From an experimental point of view, Coble and Lusk [11] prove that the data does not support the DEU model assumption of a unique parameter that explain risk and time preferences. Usually, individuals' preferences cannot be so easily determined and then several anomalies of these models must be taken into account when a real decision is analyzed. Some of these effects or anomalies are the consequence of psychophysical properties of time, probability and pay-out dimensions [17].

Indeed, several studies, such as [6,18], compare the analogies and the anomalies present in DU (intertemporal choices) and EU (risky choices) models, by observing that some risky choice inconsistencies are parallel to delay choice inconsistencies. In this line, it should be stressed the contribution by Prelec and Loewenstein [19] where a one-to-one correspondence is shown between the behavioral anomalies of Expected and Discounted Utility models. Nevertheless, Green, Myerson and Ostaszewski [20] findings suggest that processes involving delayed and probabilistic rewards, despite being similar, are not identical.

The main contribution of this paper is the demonstration of that both the Expected Utility (EU) and the Discounted Utility (DU) models can be embedded in the Probability and Time Trade-Off (PTT) model. Moreover, preliminary thoughts are provided on the possibility of reversing the process, i.e., obtaining a PTT starting from an EU or a DU model.

The relevance of this contribution is that the existence of the proved equivalence can be used to explain and relate behavioral inconsistencies in real choices. In effect, most existing literature presents the anomalies in intertemporal and probabilistic choices as separate inconsistencies [21] and, indeed, this paper can be used to clarify the equivalence between certain anomalies analyzed in the context of the DU and the EU models. A precedent can be found in the paper by Cruz Rambaud and Sánchez Pérez about the so-called peanuts effects [7]. This methodology could be applied to other anomalies present in both aforementioned models.

This paper has been organized as follows. After this Introduction, Section 2 presents an extensive revision of the existing literature on this topic, divided into three subsections to facilitate its reading. Section 3 has been structured into four subsections. Section 3.1 provides some basic definitions, properties and examples related to reward choices where both time and probability are involved. Sections 3.2 and 3.3 are devoted to obtaining the EU and DU from the PTT model, respectively. Section 3.4 is an essay to generate PTT starting from DU and EU models, and represents the framework in which further research is needed. In Section 4, the main obtained results are discussed regarding other works which aim to relate the properties of decisions under risk and under time. Finally, Section 5 summarizes and concludes.

2. Literature Review

Most of the previous research analyzing delay and risk parameters do so separately. Only a few papers study the individual preferences in decisions involving time-delayed and risky rewards. Initially, Prelec and Loewenstein [19] study uncertainty and delay from a common approach. In this sense, Weber and Chapman [4] and Gollier [22] analyze the relationship between choice under risk and time from a global perspective.

There have been several attempts to introduce a new model which explains individual preferences in decisions involving time-delayed and risky rewards [5,21]. Specifically, in some of these models, delayed rewards are studied from the perspective of the subjective probability [23,24].

These descriptive psychophysics models need to be empirically implemented. However, from a practical point of view, few publications, such as [25,26], have analyzed the risk and discount attitudes simultaneously. Specifically, some of them [11,27] explain the relationship between the risk and time in the decision-making process from an experimental point of view. From this perspective, it is necessary to highlight that uncertainty underlying time delays may be undermined when data is obtained through laboratory experiments [28].

Despite risk and delay being perceived as concepts psychologically distinct, in some contexts, decision-makers may identify both concepts as psychologically interchangeable since they influence preferences [17]. This is because behavioral patterns facing risk and delay are based on a common underlying dimension [17,23]. Even though time delay and uncertainty are interrelated, their interaction is controversial. Below, we can find some examples of studies that have analyzed the relation between time and risk preferences to assess delayed and probabilistic choices. In Section 2.1, uncertainty is treated as the fundamental concept and delays are transformed into risky terms. Next, in Section 2.2, by assuming that uncertainty is linked to delayed rewards, the reward probability is expressed as additional waiting time. Finally, in Section 2.3, the new models to assess risky intertemporal choices are pointed out.

2.1. Uncertainty as Central Concept. Transformation of Delays into Probability Terms

Keren and Roelofsma [28] defend that uncertainty is the psychologically central concept, given that decisions are affected by delay only if this delay entails uncertainty. They propose that the delay effect is actually the effect of the uncertainty inherent to delay. Indeed, they defend that the immediacy effect and the certainty effect are the same effects given that decision-makers are based on the implicit uncertainty, not the delay itself. In intertemporal choice, the immediate outcome entails no uncertainty while the delayed outcome is perceived as uncertain. In this way, "if delay implies risk, then risk should have the same effects as delay—the two are interchangeable" [4].

In this sense, Rachlin [23] translates reward delay into the probability of receiving it. Delays act like less-than-unit probabilities; longer delays correspond to lower probabilities, given that uncertainty increases as delay increases. In this way, intertemporal discount models may be translated into probabilistic discount functions (called "odds against" Θ, i.e., the average number of trials until a win). They are calculated as follows:

$$\Theta = \frac{1}{p} - 1,$$

where p is the probability of receiving an uncertain outcome.

2.2. Uncertainty is Inherent to Intertemporal Choice. Interpretation of Reward Probability as Waiting Time

When applying the DU model, sometimes future outcomes are modelled as though non-stochastic by ignoring its uncertainty. However, as stated by Fisher [29], "future income is always subject to some uncertainty, and this uncertainty must naturally have an influence on the rate of time preference, or degree of impatience, of its possessor". In this vein, some recent studies consider the relation between behavior under risk and over time with the premise that uncertainty is inherent to intertemporal choices, given that any event may interfere in the process of acquiring the reward between the current and the promised date [30].

This implies that the "decision-maker's valuation of delayed outcomes not only depends on her pure time preference, i.e., her preference for immediate utility over delayed utility, but also on her perception of the uncertainty and, consequently, on her risk preferences" [31]. Under the assumption that only present consumption is certain while any future consumption may be considered to be uncertain, risk preferences could influence intertemporal choice patterns. In this way, Takahashi [32] studies the aversion to subjective uncertainty associated with delay.

Soares dos Santos et al. [3] propose a generalized function for the probabilistic discount process by using time preferences. Specifically, probabilistic rewards are transformed into delayed rewards as follows: instead of using the probability of occurrence, they use the mean waiting time before a successful draw of the corresponding reward.

Probabilities are converted into comparable delays according to the constant of proportionality by [23] and through the examination of the indifference points of hypothetical rewards which are both delayed and risky. Once the probabilities are transformed into delays, this delay is added to the explicit delay, being this delay/probability combination the total delay used to assess delayed and risky rewards. The similar structure of time and risk shows that if the risk is interpreted as waiting time, both magnitudes may be combined into a single metric which is consistent with the hyperbolic discount function (better than exponential function given that as delay increases, there is a hyperbolic decay of probabilities of obtaining it). Furthermore, this metric may explain some of the observed behavior in choice under risk, such as the certainty effect [33].

2.3. Models to Assess Risky Intertemporal Choices

Traditionally, risky intertemporal rewards have been evaluated by applying the EU and DU models separately. First, risky rewards are assessed by the EU model, and then their expected value at maturity is discounted by using a constant discount rate. More flexibility in the assessment of risky delayed rewards is requested from a descriptive point of view by [34]. This flexibility is necessary given that the consequences of delayed rewards do not only affect the present utility but also the future utility. In the same way, the probability implementation red has an influence on the discount rates [35].

Luckman [5] has shown that there are three specific unifying models to deal with delayed and probabilistic choices: the Probability and Time Trade-off model [36], the Multiplicative Hyperboloid Discounting model [37], and the Hyperbolic Discounting model [38]. These three models have a common feature as they consider two special risky intertemporal choices: pure risky choices and pure intertemporal choices. These special risky intertemporal choices are consistent with the results from traditional models.

In the assessment of delayed but certain rewards, the DU model is employed. However, for those alternatives whose maturity is unknown or uncertain at the beginning, i.e., when the decision-maker does not know the exact realization time of the future outcome, the DEU model may be implemented [30]. Specifically, when there are different possible delays for a reward and their probabilities are known, its "timing risk" [16] is identified. Meanwhile, the term "timing uncertainty" is employed to denote those outcomes which possible delays are vaguely known or unknown [30]. Time lotteries which pay a specific prize at uncertain future dates are a clear example of this kind of rewards [39]. Onay and Öncüler [16] and Coble and Lusk [11] demonstrate that DEU model is not accurate enough to forecast intertemporal choice behavior under timing risk.

In 2012, Han and Takahashi [40] proposed that psychophysical time commonly explains anomalies in decision both over time and under risk. Moreover, they introduce the non-linear psychophysical time into the time discount function according to the Weber-Fechner law. Green and Myerson [2] show that a single process to assess risky and intertemporal operations is inconsistent. Apart from the fact that risk and time are not equivalent parameters, "the interaction between them is complex and not easily understood" [17]. Nevertheless, recent studies show that it is necessary to introduce a common framework to understand people's perception of risk and delay when making decisions [41]. In this way, there is still room to improve the methodology and results.

Summarizing the introduction and the literature review, Figure 1 shows the existing methodologies to assess the delayed and uncertain rewards which differ in one, two or more dimensions.

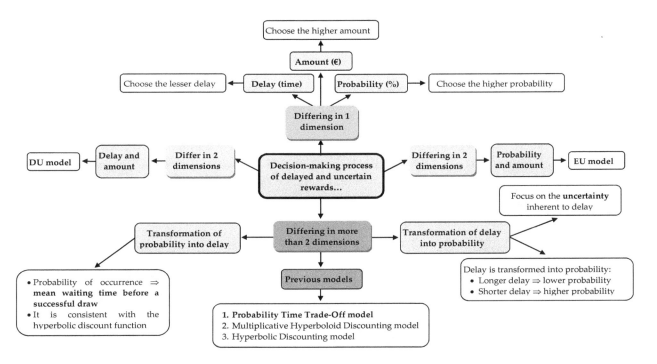

Figure 1. Decision-making process of delayed and uncertain rewards. Source: Own elaboration.

3. Deriving DU and EU from the Probability and Time Trade-Off Model

3.1. Introduction

It will prove useful to begin with the following definition in the ambit of the Probability and Time Trade-off (PTT) model [1].

Definition 1. *Let $\mathcal{M}$ be the set $X \times P \times T$, where $X = [0, +\infty)$, $P = [0,1]$, and $T = [0, +\infty]$. A discount function in the context of the PTT model is a continuous real-valued map $V(x, p, t)$, defined on $\mathcal{M}$, which is strictly increasing with respect to the first and second components, and strictly decreasing according to the third. Moreover, it satisfies that $V(x, 1, 0) = x$, for every $x \in X$.*

Example 1. $V(x, p, t) = (xp + 1)^{\exp\{-kt\}} - 1$, $k > 0$, *is a discount function in the context of the PTT model.*

Definition 1 guarantees that $V(x, p, t) \leq x$. In effect, $x = V(x, 1, 0) \geq V(x, p, 0) \geq V(x, p, t)$. The triple (x, p, t) denotes the prospect of receiving a reward x at time t with probability p. Obviously,

1. If $p = 1$, then the concept of a discount function *in the context of the DU model* arises: $F(x, t) := V(x, 1, t)$ is a continuous real-valued map defined on $X \times T$, which is strictly increasing in the first component, strictly decreasing in the second component, and satisfies $F(x, 0) = x$, for every $x \in X$.
2. If $t = t_0$, then the concept of a discount function *in the context of the EU model* arises: $V(x, p) := V(x, p, t_0)$ is a continuous real-valued map defined on $X \times P$, which is strictly increasing in the two components, and satisfies $V(x, 1) = x$, for every $x \in X$.

Definition 2. *Given a discount function $V(x, p, t)$ in the context of the PTT model, the domain of V is the maximum subset, $\mathcal{D}$, of $\mathcal{M}$ where V satisfies all conditions of Definition 1.*

Example 2. *The domain of the discount function $V(x, p, t) = (xp + 1)^{\exp\{-kt\}} - 1$, $k > 0$, is $\mathcal{D} = \mathcal{D}$. On the other hand, the domain of the discount function*

$$V(x, p, t) = \frac{xp + it}{1 + jt},$$

where $i > 0$ and $j > 0$, is:

$$\mathcal{D} = \left\{ (x, p) \in X \times P : xp > \frac{i}{j} \right\} \times T.$$

Baucells and Heukamp [1] require that V converges to zero when xpe^{-t} converges to zero. However, in the present paper this restriction will be removed, and we will allow that V tends to zero only when $x \to 0$, or $p \to 0$:

$$\lim_{t \to +\infty} V(x, p, t) := L(x, p) > 0,$$

provided that $T \subseteq \text{proy}_3(\mathcal{D})$.

Definition 3. *A discount function in the context of the PTT model, V, is said to be regular if $L(x, p) = 0$, while V is said to be singular if $L(x, p) > 0$.*

Example 3. *The discount function $V(x, p, t) = (xp + 1)^{\exp\{-kt\}} - 1$ is regular since*

$$L(x, p) = (xp + 1)^0 - 1 = 0.$$

On the other hand, the discount functions $V(x,p,t) = \frac{xp+it}{1+jt}$ and $V(x,p,t) = \frac{xp+x^2p^2it}{1+jt}$, where $i > 0$ and $j > 0$, are singular as

$$L(x,p) = \frac{i}{j} > 0$$

and

$$L(x,p) = \frac{x^2p^2i}{j} > 0,$$

respectively.

Thus, the paper by Baucells and Heukamp [1] implicitly assumes the regularity of V. However, in this work, this requirement will not necessarily hold.

Now, we are going to provide an interpretation of probability in the context of a prospect (x,p,t). In effect, let $V(x,p,t)$ be a discount function in the context of the PTT model and consider a given value, x, of the amount. Therefore, $V_x(p,t) := V(x,p,t)$ is now a two-variable function. Consider the indifference line given by $V_x(p,t) = k$ ($0 < k \leq x$) (observe that $k = V_x(p_0, 0)$, for some p_0), which eventually can give rise to an explicit function, denoted by $p_{k,x}(t)$ (see Figure 2). Obviously, $p_x(t)$ is an increasing function which has 1 as upper bound and 0 as lower bound. Moreover, $p_{k,x}(0) = p_0 = k$. Let

$$t_{k,x}^{\min} = \min\{t : V_x(p,t) = k, \text{ for some } p\}$$

and

$$t_{k,x}^{\max} = \max\{t : V_x(p,t) = k, \text{ for some } p\}.$$

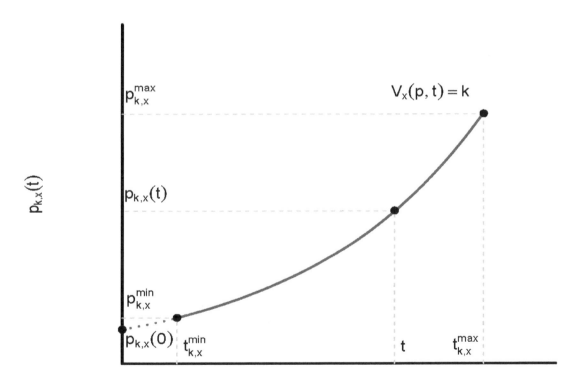

Figure 2. Indifference line $V_x(p,t) = k$ ($0 < k \leq x$). Source: Own elaboration.

Lemma 1. *The following statements hold:*

(i) $t_{k,x}^{\min}$ is the solution of $V_x(0,t) = k$ if, and only if, $0 \in proy_2(\mathcal{D})$.
(ii) $t_{k,x}^{\max}$ is the solution of $V_x(1,t) = k$ if, and only if, $1 \in proy_2(\mathcal{D})$.

Proof. Take into account that $V_x(0,t)$ and $V_x(1,t)$ are lower and upper bounded functions in time. This guarantees the existence of both a minimum and a maximum time. □

Proposition 1. *If V is regular or V is singular and $0 < L(x,p) < k$, then $1 \in proy_2(\mathcal{D})$.*

Proof. In effect, by the definition of a discount function in the context of the PTT model, one has $V_x(1,0) = x$. Moreover, if V is regular or V is singular and $0 < L(x,p) < k$, the following chain of inequalities holds:

$$0 \leq L(x,1) < k < x.$$

Therefore, as V is continuous and decreasing with respect to time, by the Intermediate Value Theorem, there exists t_1, such that $V_x(1,t_1) = k$. Consequently, $1 \in \text{proy}_2(\mathcal{D})$. □

Example 4. *Let us consider the following discount function in the context of the PTT model:*

$$V(x,p,t) = \frac{xp}{1 + ixpt},$$

where $i > 0$. If $V(x,p,t) = k$ ($0 < k \leq x$), then

$$p_{k,x}(t) = \frac{k}{x - ikxt} = \frac{p_{k,x}(0)}{1 - ip_{k,x}(0)xt},$$

which is obviously increasing with respect to t. The minimum value of t is $t_{k,x}^{\min} = 0$, and the maximum value of t is

$$t_{k,x}^{\max} = \frac{x - k}{ikx} = \frac{1 - p_{k,x}(0)}{ip_{k,x}(0)x}.$$

The corresponding minimum and maximum values of p are $p_{k,x}^{\min} = p_{k,x}(0) = k$ and $p_{k,x}^{\max} = 1$, respectively.

Finally, the map of indifference curves $V_x(p,t) = k, 0 < k \leq x$, gives rise to a family of distribution functions, denoted by $p_{k,x}(t)$, corresponding to a stochastic process, satisfying:

$$V(x, p_{k,x}(t), t) = k.$$

More, specifically, Figure 2 represents all couples (t, p) such that $(x, p, t) \in X \times P \times T$, for given values of x and $0 < k \leq x$. Moreover, it shows that there exists a functional relationship between p and t, given by $p_{k,x}(t)$, with $0 < k \leq x$. Indeed, $p_{k,x}(t)$ is a distribution function. In effect, let us consider the random variable $T_{k,x}$: "Time period in which the reward x can be delivered, at a discounting level k". In other words, each random variable $T_{k,x}$ is a stopping time depending on k and x. Specifically, $p_{k,x}(t)$ is the distribution function of $T_{k,x}$:

$$p_{k,x}(t) = \Pr(T_{k,x} \leq t).$$

Consequently, starting from X, a continuous stochastic process has been obtained for every $x \in X$, giving rise to the following family of stochastic processes:

$$\left\{ \{T_{k,x}\}_{0 < k \leq x} \right\}_{x \in X}.$$

Assume that $x_1 < x_2$. Then $T_{k,x_1} < T_{k,x_2}$, $0 < k \leq x_1 < x_2$, i.e., the stochastic process $\{T_{k,x}\}_{x \in X}$ is increasing with respect to x. Moreover, if $0 < k_1 < k_2 \leq x$, then $T_{k_1,x} < T_{k_2,x}$ and so $\{T_{k,x}\}_{0 < k \leq x}$ is increasing with respect to k. In this case, we can define a discount function where time is stochastic in the following way.

Definition 4. *A discount function with stochastic time is a real function*

$$F : \{\{(x, T_{k,x})\}_{0 < k \leq x}\}_{x \in X} \longrightarrow \mathbb{R}$$

such that

$$(x, T_{k,x}) \mapsto F(x, T_{k,x}),$$

defined by:

$$F(x, T_{k,x}) = V(x, p_0, t_0),$$

such that $p_{k,x}(t_0) = p_0$.

Obviously, function F is well defined. Therefore, we can state the following theorem.

Theorem 1. *A discount function $V(x, p, t)$ is equivalent to the discount function with stochastic time $F(x, T_{k,x})$, where $T_{k,x}$ is the random variable: "Time period in which the reward x can be delivered, at a discounting level k".*

Remark 1. *Observe that for every $x \in X$, the random variables $T_{k,x}$ could be indexed, instead of by k, by another parameter in one-to-one correspondence with k. For example, for a given value p of probability, there is a biunivocal correspondence between k-values and calendar times. Thus, by denoting the calendar time as τ, the random variable $T_{k,x}$ becomes $T_{\tau,x}$, in whose case we will say that the discount function of Definition 4 is time-dependent (in the particular case in which time is age, the discount function is said to be age-dependent [42]).*

In the same way, for a given value pt of time, there is a bijective correspondence between k-values and probabilities. Thus, by denoting the probability as q, the random variable $T_{k,x}$ becomes $T_{q,x}$, in whose case we will say that the discount function of Definition 4 is risk-dependent.

On this question, we will return later in Section 3.3. Observe that now there is an extra force of discount given by the probability p. This statement can be shown in the following proposition.

Proposition 2. *Assume that V is differentiable. Then, the instantaneous discount rate of V, denoted by δ_V, is greater than the instantaneous discount, δ_F, of the discount function in the context of the DU model, $F(x, t) := V(x, p, t)$, where p is constant.*

Proof. In effect, the derivative of the implicit function $V(x, p_{k,x}(t), t) = k$ $(0 < k \leq x)$, results in:

$$dV = \frac{\partial V}{\partial x} dx + \frac{\partial V}{\partial p} \frac{\partial p_{k,x}(t)}{\partial x} dx + \frac{\partial V}{\partial p} \frac{\partial p_{k,x}(t)}{\partial t} dt + \frac{\partial V}{\partial t} dt = 0,$$

from where the instantaneous discount rate of V at (x, p, t) is (see [43]):

$$\delta_V(x, p, t) := \frac{dx}{x dt} = -\frac{1}{x} \frac{\frac{\partial V}{\partial t} + \frac{\partial V}{\partial p} \frac{\partial p_{k,x}(t)}{\partial t}}{\frac{\partial V}{\partial x} + \frac{\partial V}{\partial p} \frac{\partial p_{k,x}(t)}{\partial x}}.$$

As

$$\frac{\partial V}{\partial p} \frac{\partial p_{k,x}(t)}{\partial t} > 0$$

and

$$\frac{\partial V}{\partial p}\frac{\partial p_{k,x}(t)}{\partial x} < 0,$$

then, for every $(x, p, t) \in \mathcal{M}$,

$$\delta_V(x, p, t) > -\frac{1}{x}\frac{\frac{\partial V}{\partial t}}{\frac{\partial V}{\partial x}},$$

which is the instantaneous discount rate when p is constant. Therefore,

$$\delta_V(x, p, t) > \delta_F(x, t),$$

as expected. □

3.2. Deriving EU from PTT Model

The following result has been inspired in [7].

Lemma 2. *Given $x \in X$, let us consider the real function $V_x : P \times T \to \mathbb{R}$, defined as $V_x(p, t) := V(x, p, t)$. Then, for every $(p, t) \in P \times T$ and every $s < t$, there exists $k = k(x, p, s, t)$ $(0 < k < 1)$ such that $V_x(kp, s) = V_x(p, t)$.*

Proof. In effect, given $x \in X$ and $(p, t) \in P \times T$, for every s $(s < t)$, let us consider the following real-valued function:

$$V_{x,s} : P \to \mathbb{R}$$

defined as:

$$V_{x,s}(q) := V_x(q, s).$$

By the definition of V, the inequality

$$V_x(p, t) < V_{x,s}(p) \tag{1}$$

holds. Moreover, when $q \to 0$, $V_{x,s}(q) \to 0$. Therefore, there exists q_0, small enough, such that

$$V_{x,s}(q_0) \le V_x(p, t). \tag{2}$$

Putting together inequalities (1) and (2), one has:

$$V_{x,s}(q_0) \le V_x(p, t) < V_{x,s}(p).$$

As V is continuous and increasing in probability, by the Intermediate Value Theorem, there exists a value $k = k(x, p, t, s)$ $(0 < k < 1)$, such that $V_{x,s}(kp) = V_x(p, t)$, i.e., $V_x(kp, s) = V_x(p, t)$.

Time s is well defined. In effect, starting now from another couple (p', t'), such that $V_x(p, t) = V_x(p', t')$, for every s under t and t', one has:

$$V_x(kp, s) = V_x(p, t)$$

and

$$V_x(k'p', s) = V_x(p', t'),$$

from where $kp = k'p'$. □

Analogously, it could be shown that under the same conditions as Lemma 2, for every $(p, t) \in P \times T$ and every $u > t$, there exists k $(k > 1)$ such that $V_x(kp, u) = V_x(p, t)$. However, it is possible that this result is restricted for some values of p and t whereby, for every $x \in X$, we are going to consider the values $p_x^{\max}$ and $t_x^{\max}$ such that

$$V(x, p, t) = V(x, p_x^{\max}, t_x^{\max}).$$

Example 5. *With the discount function of Example 1:*

$$V(x, p, t) = \frac{xp}{1 + ixpt},$$

where $i > 0$, for every (p, t) and s, the equation in q:

$$V(x, p, t) = V(x, q, s)$$

gives the following solution:

$$q = \frac{p}{1 + ixp(t - s)}.$$

Observe that q makes sense for every $s \leq t$, and even for every s such that

$$1 + ixp(t - s) \geq p,$$

from where:

$$t < s \leq t + \frac{1 - p}{ixp}.$$

However, we will assume that always $t_x^{\min} = 0$, for every $x \in X$. To derive EU model, let

$$(x_1, p_1, t_1), (x_2, p_2, t_2), \ldots, (x_n, p_n, t_n)$$

be a sequence of n outcomes in the context of the PTT model. According to Lemma 1, there exist $p_0^1, p_0^2, \ldots, p_0^n$ ($p_0^k \leq p_k$, $k = 1, 2, \ldots, n$), such that:

$$V(x_k, p_k, t_k) = V(x_k, p_0^k, 0),$$

for every $k = 1, 2, \ldots, n$. Consequently, the present value of these outcomes is:

$$V_0 := \sum_{k=1}^{n} V(x_k, p_k, t_k) = \sum_{k=1}^{n} V(x_k, p_0^k, 0).$$

Independently of the shape of function V, the PTT model has been transformed into an EU model because time has been removed from the prospect (x, p, t). Observe that probabilities are not linear with respect to the discounted amounts.

Remark 2 (On non-linear probabilities). *Chew and Epstein [44] proposed some alternative theories with non-linear probabilities which may explain many behavioral paradoxes while holding normatively properties; for instance, consistency with stochastic dominance and risk aversion. In this vein, Halevy [45] provided a function for the discounted utility based on the non-linear probability weighting to evaluate the diminishing impatience related with the uncertainty of delayed rewards. These theories are useful, analytical tools in the decision-making process which allow separating the risk aversion from the elasticity of substitution.*

To explain the non-linear psychological distance, Baucells and Heukamp [1] stated that it is necessary a non-linear probability weighing bonded with non-exponential discounting.

With the aim of illustrating the non-linear probability weighing, the mathematical description by Brandstätter, Kühberger and Schneider [46] is shown to reflect the elation and disappointment in probabilities.

In effect, being $1 - p$ the utility after a success and $-p$ the disutility after a failure, the expected success is calculated as follows:

$$\text{utility after a success} \times \text{probability of a success} = p(1 - p),$$

meanwhile the expected failure is:

$$\text{disutility after a failure} \times \text{probability of a failure} = -p(1 - p),$$

To take into account the non-linearity of the utility after a success (that is, elation) and the disutility after a failure (that is, disappointment), new utilities may be implemented to obtain the expected success and failure. In this way, the utility after a success and the disutility after a failure are $c_e s(1 - p)$ and $c_d s p$, respectively, where c_e and c_d are constants and s is a non-linear surprise function. Since disappointment is an aversive emotional state, c_d is expected to be negative. A steeper slope for disappointment than for elation is assumed (this means that $c_d > c_e$).

3.3. Deriving DU from PTT Model

Analogously to Lemma 2, we can show the following statement.

Lemma 3. *Given an $x \in X$, let us consider the real function $V_x : P \times T \to \mathbb{R}$, defined as $V_x(p, t) := V(x, p, t)$. If V is regular, then, for every $(p, t) \in P \times T$ and every $q < p$, there exists $k = k(x, p, q, t)$ ($0 < k < 1$) such that $V_x(q, kt) = V_x(p, t)$.*

Analogously, it could be shown that under the same conditions as Lemma 3, for every $(p, t) \in P \times T$ and every $q > p$, there exists $k = k(x, p, q, t)$ ($k > 1$) such that $V_x(q, kt) = V_x(p, t)$. However, as in Section 3.2, it is possible that this result is restricted for some values of p and t. In this section, we will always assume that $p_x^{\max} = 1$, for every $x \in X$.

To derive DU model, let

$$(x_1, p_1, t_1), (x_2, p_2, t_2), \ldots, (x_n, p_n, t_n)$$

be a sequence of n outcomes in the context of the PTT model. If V is regular, according to Lemma 3, there exist $t_1^1, t_1^2, \ldots, t_1^n$ ($t_1^k \geq t_k$, $k = 1, 2, \ldots, n$), such that:

$$V(x_k, p_k, t_k) = V(x_k, 1, t_1^k),$$

for every $k = 1, 2, \ldots, n$. Consequently, the present value of these outcomes is:

$$V_0 := \sum_{k=1}^{n} V(x_k, p_k, t_k) = \sum_{k=1}^{n} V(x_k, 1, t_1^k).$$

Independently of the shape of function V, the PTT model has been transformed into a DU model because probability is constant and equal to 1 whereby all outcomes are sure.

Corollary 1. *A specific PTT model of the form $V(x, p, t) := V(xp, t)$ gives rise to both a DU and an EU model.*

Proof. In effect, the equation:

$$V(xp, t) = V(xq, s)$$

implies:

1. For $q = 1$, $V(xp, t) = V(x1, t_x^{\max}) = V(x, t_x^{\max})$, which is the DU model.
2. For $t = 0$, $V(xp, t) = V(xp_x^{\min}, 0) = xp_x^{\min}$, which is the EU model.

$\square$

3.4. Deriving PTT from DU or EU Model

In this context, it could be interesting to think about the converse construction, i.e., to generate a function $V(x, p, t)$ starting from $V(x, t)$ and $V(x, p)$ coming from a DU and an EU model, respectively. In effect,

(A) Given a DU model, $V(x, t)$, it can be assumed that all prospects (x, t) have probability $p = 1$. In this case, we can construct a PTT model which coincides with the DU model when $p = 1$:

$$V(x, p, t) := V(x, t)p$$

or

$$V(x, p, t) := V(xp, t).$$

(B) Analogously, given an EU model, $V(x, p)$, it can be understood that all prospects (x, p) expire at the same instant $t = t_0$. In this case, we can construct a PTT model which coincides with the EU model when $t = t_0$:

$$V(x, p, t) := x \left[\frac{V(x, p)}{x} \right]^{\frac{t}{t_0}}.$$

Observe that for the sake of generality, neither of the two PTT proposed models are of the form $V(x, p, t) = w(p)f(t)v(x)$ nor $V(x, p, t) = g(p, t)v(x)$ pointed out by [1].

(C) Given a DU model, $V(x, t)$, and an EU model, $V(x, p)$, if $V(x, 0) = x$ and $V(x, 1) = x$, respectively, we can construct a PTT model which coincides with both models, at $t = 0$ and $p = 1$, respectively:

$$V(0, p, t) = 0$$

and

$$V(x, p, t) = \frac{1}{x} V(x, t) V(x, p),$$

otherwise.

4. Discussion

In this paper, it has been mathematically demonstrated that the PTT model is general enough to explain intertemporal and risky decisions separately. The shown association between PTT model and DU and EU models allows explaining and relating the behavioral properties and inconsistencies in real choices.

It must be mentioned that most previous literature studies anomalies in intertemporal and probabilistic choices separately. In this way, the analysis of the equivalence between certain anomalies in the context of the DU and EU models may be analyzed under the wide setting provided by the PTT model.

A way to study the similarity between time delay and uncertainty in the decision-making process is through the analysis of the immediacy and certainty effects. These effects reflect the tendency of individuals to overestimate the significance of immediacy or certainty, relative to delayed or probable outcomes, respectively. The relation between both effects allows glimpsing the analogies and the influence of time and delay on the decision-making process. Some of the main findings are listed below:

* In the seminal paper by Allais [47], the disproportionate preference for present outcomes of the immediacy effect is shown, consequently not only of the intrinsic temptation but the certainty on the payment.
* Keren and Roelofsma [28] analyze the effect of risk on the immediacy effect and the effect of time delay on the certainty effect. They suggest that time distance makes outcomes seem more uncertain by eliminating the certainty advantage of the immediate outcome. Thereof, they reveal that the introduction of uncertainty reduces the importance of time delay (if two certain rewards

are transformed to be equally probable (i.e., $p = 0.50$), the delayed one is generally preferred). In the same way, time distance decreases the influence of the probability on preferences.

- Chapman and Weber [17] prove that when the delay is introduced to sure outcomes, the certainty effect is almost eliminated just as when uncertainty is added. On the other hand, in a similar way, when explicit risk is introduced to immediate rewards, the immediacy effect is almost eliminated just as if time delay is added. It is necessary to clarify that presently there is no consensus on this topic, while Pennesi [48] confirms that when the immediate payoff becomes uncertain, the immediacy effect disappears, Abdellaoui et al. [35] claim that the immediacy effect persists under risk.
- Epper et al. [31] stress that previous papers, in most cases, determine that there are interaction effects between time and risk, such as risk tolerance increases with delay.
- Andreoni and Sprenger [49] conclude that risk preference is not time preference: "subjects exhibit a preference for certainty when it is available, but behave largely as discounted expected utility maximizers away from certainty".

Another way to conclude that delay and risk choices have non-parallel decision mechanisms has been proved by Cruz Rambaud and Sánchez Pérez [7] and Chapman and Weber [17]. The effect of the reward size on the treatment of delayed and probabilistic outcomes moves in the opposite direction. On one hand, in intertemporal choices, as the reward amount increases, decision-makers prefer the delayed but greater reward (this is called the "magnitude effect"). On the other hand, in risky choices, the reward size increase implies a decreasing sensitivity; decision-makers prefer the more probable but lower reward (this is called the "peanut effect").

Despite some previous papers claiming that DU and EU models anomalies move in the opposite direction, the findings of our research are in line with most part of the previous literature linking the anomalies exhibited by both models. Given that the PTT model considers a unique framework to deal with uncertainty and delayed rewards, it may imply that risk and time anomalies can be captured by a unique model. Thus, the results of this research contribute to clearly understanding the aforementioned relationship by considering risk and time anomalies inside the same framework.

Specifically, Leland and Schneider [14] pointed that "the PTT model accounts for three systematic interaction effects between risk and time preferences when choices involve both risk and time delays as well as some other fundamental behaviors such as the common ratio and common difference effects".

In effect, Schneider [21] introduces the two following dual concepts:

- *Time interacts with risk preference* if, for every $x \in (0, z)$, $\alpha \in (0, 1)$, and $s > t$,

$$(x, p, t) \sim (z, \alpha p, t) \text{ implies } (x, p, s) \prec (z, \alpha p, s).$$

- *Risk interacts with time preference* if, for every $x \in (0, z)$, $t, \Delta > 0$, and $q < p$,

$$(x, p, t) \sim (z, p, t + \Delta) \text{ implies } (x, q, t) \prec (z, q, t + \Delta).$$

By applying Lemmas 2 and 3, it can be shown that the former definitions are equivalent in the presence of the so-called *reverse sub-endurance* (see [7]):
For every $x \in (0, z)$, $t, \Delta > 0$, and $\alpha \in (0, 1)$,

$$(z, p, t + \Delta) \sim (z, \alpha p, t) \text{ implies } (x, p, t + \Delta) \succ (x, \alpha p, t).$$

In this way, our objective will be to investigate the possible equivalence between other dual concepts in the ambit of risk and time preferences. However, this issue will be left for further research in the context of the PTT model.

5. Conclusions

In this paper, an extensive review of the previous methodologies which assess risk and delayed rewards in a unique framework has been made. It reveals that there is still room to improve the existing methodologies to reach this goal. Specifically, this paper has dealt with the classical problem of the possible relationship between the DU and the EU models but treated from the joint perspective of the PTT model.

In this paper, the equivalence of the PTT model with the DU is demonstrated and the EU models separately considered. In this sense, this paper's main findings are three-fold:

- On the one hand, the DU model has been derived from the PTT model, by taking a specific value of probability. Specifically, we have found that the PTT model is equivalent to the discount function with stochastic time $F(x, T_{k,x})$, where $T_{k,x}$ is the random variable: "Time period in which the reward x can be delivered, at a discounting level k".

- Analogously, given a concrete value of time, the EU model can be derived from the PTT model.

- Finally, this paper provides some insights into the construction of a PTT model starting from a DU and an EU model. However, more future research is needed on this topic.

Thus, this paper shows the validity of the PTT model to assess risky and delayed rewards separately. As pointed out, a limitation of the paper is the difficulty of building a complete PTT model starting from DU and EU models in a same framework. However, a solution to do this is provided: the construction of the PTT model starting from DU and EU models by using specific models able to satisfy the appropriate patterns of time and probability pointed out by Baucells and Heukamp [1].

As a future line of research, we stress that it is necessary to continue analyzing the equivalence between the PTT and DU and EU models from the perspective of the different effects or anomalies when considering delay and time individually (in DU and EU models, respectively) and jointly (PTT model). A second future research line is to check the validity of the PTT model and its relationship with DU and EU models from an experimental point of view.

Author Contributions: The individual contribution of each author has been as follows: formal analysis, funding acquisition, investigation and writing–original draft, S.C.R.; conceptualization, methodology, writing–review & editing and supervision, A.M.S.P. All authors have read and agreed to the published version of the manuscript.

Acknowledgments: We are very grateful for the valuable comments and suggestions offered by the Academic Editor and three anonymous referees.

Abbreviations

The following abbreviations are used in this manuscript:

DU   Discounted Utility
EU   Expected Utility
DEU   Discounted Expected Utility
PTT   Probability and Time Trade-Off

References

1. Baucells, M.; Heukamp, F.H. Probability and time trade-off. *Manag. Sci.* **2012**, *58*, 831–842. [CrossRef]
2. Green, L.; Myerson, J. A discounting framework for choice with delayed and probabilistic rewards. *Psychol. Bull.* **2004**, *130*, 769–792. [CrossRef] [PubMed]
3. Soares dos Santos, L.; Destefano, N.; Souto Martinez, A. Decision making generalized by a cumulative probability weighting function. *Phys. Stat. Mech. Its Appl.* **2018**, *490*, 250–259. [CrossRef]

4. Weber, B.J.; Chapman, G.B. The combined effects of risk and time on choice: Does uncertainty eliminate the immediacy effect? *Organ. Behav. Hum. Decis.* **2005**, *96*, 104–118. [CrossRef]

5. Luckman, A.; Donkin, C.; Newell, B.R. Can a single model account for both risky choices and inter-temporal choices? Testing the assumptions underlying models of risky inter-temporal choice. *Psychon. Bull. Rev.* **2018**, *25*, 785–792. [CrossRef]

6. Baucells, M.; Heukamp, F.H.; Villasis, A. Risk and time preferences integrated. In Proceedings of the Foundations of Utility and Risk Conference, Rome, Italy, 30 April 2006.

7. Cruz Rambaud, S.; Sánchez Pérez, A.M. The magnitude and peanuts effects: Searching implications. *Front. Appl. Math. Stat.* **2018**, *4*, 36. [CrossRef]

8. Samuelson, P.A. A note on measurement of utility. *Rev. Econ. Stud.* **1937**, *4*, 155–161. [CrossRef]

9. Von Neumann, J.; Morgenstern, O. *Theory of Games and Economic Behavior*, 2nd ed.; Princeton University Press: Princeton, NJ, USA, 1947.

10. Schoemaker, P.J.H. The Expected Utility model: Its variants, purposes, evidence and limitations. *J. Econ. Lit.* **1982**, *20*, 529–563.

11. Coble, K.H.; Lusk, J.L. At the nexus of risk and time preferences: An experimental investigation. *J. Risk Uncertain.* **2010**, *41*, 67–79. [CrossRef]

12. Andreoni, J.; Sprenger, C. *Risk Preferences Are Not Time Preferences: Discounted Expected Utility with a Disproportionate Preference for Certainty*; Working Paper 16348; National Bureau of Economic Research: Cambridge, MA, USA, 2010.

13. Jamison, D.T. *Studies in Individual Choice Behavior*; RAND Memorandum No. P-4255; RAND Corporation: Santa Monica, CA, USA, 1970.

14. Leland J.; Schneider M. *Risk Preference, Time Preference, and Salience Perception*; ESI Working Papers 17-16; ESI: Orange, CA, USA, 2017.

15. Lanier, J.; Miao, B.; Quah, J.K.H.; Zhong, S. Intertemporal Consumption with Risk: A Revealed Preference Analysis. Available online: http://dx.doi.org/10.2139/ssrn.3168361 (accessed on 28 February 2020).

16. Onay, S.; Öncüler, A. Intertemporal choice under timing risk: An experimental approach. *J. Risk Uncertain.* **2007**, *34*, 99–121. [CrossRef]

17. Chapman, G.B.; Weber, B.J. Decision biases in intertemporal choice and choice under uncertainty: Testing a common account. *Mem. Cogn.* **2006**, *34*, 589–602. [CrossRef]

18. Quiggin, J.; Horowitz, J. Time and risk. *J. Risk Uncertain.* **1995**, *10*, 37–55. [CrossRef]

19. Prelec, D.; Loewenstein, G. Decision making over time and under uncertainty: A common approach. *Manag. Sci.* **1991**, *37*, 770–786. [CrossRef]

20. Green, L., Myerson, J.; Ostaszewski, P. Amount of reward has opposite effects on the discounting of delayed and probabilistic outcomes. *J. Exp. Psychol. Mem. Cogn.* **1999**, *2*, 418–427. [CrossRef]

21. Schneider, M. *Dual-Process Utility Theory: A Model of Decisions Under Risk and Over Time*; ESI Working Paper; ESI: Orange, CA, USA, 2016.

22. Gollier, C. *The Economics of Risk and Time*; MIT Press: Cambridge, MA, USA, 2004.

23. Rachlin, H.; Raineri, A.; Cross, D. Subjective probability and delay. *J. Exp. Anal. Behav.* **1991**, *55*, 233–244. [CrossRef] [PubMed]

24. Takahashi, T.; Ikeda, K.; Hasegawa, T. A hyperbolic decay of subjective probability of obtaining delayed rewards. *Behav. Brain Funct.* **2007**, *3*, 1–11. [CrossRef] [PubMed]

25. Issler, J.V.; Piqueira, N.S. Estimating relative risk aversion, the discount rate, and the intertemporal elasticity of substitution in consumption for Brazil using three types of utility function. *Braz. Rev. Econom.* **2000**, *20*, 201–239. [CrossRef]

26. Van Praag, B.M.S.; Booij, A.S. *Risk Aversion and the Subjective Time Preference: A Joint Approach*; CESifo Working Paper Series 923; CESifo Group: Munich, Germany, 2003.

27. Anderhub, V.; Güth, W.; Gneezy, U.; Sonsino, D. On the interaction of risk and time preferences: An experimental study. *Ger. Econ. Rev.* **2001**, *2*, 239–253. [CrossRef]

28. Keren, G.; Roelofsma, P. Immediacy and certainty in intertemporal choice. *Organ. Behav. Hum. Decis. Process.* **1995**, *63*, 287–297. [CrossRef]

29. Fisher, I. *The Theory of Interest*; Macmillan: New York, NY, USA, 1930.

30. Dai, J.; Pachur, T.; Pleskac, T.J.; Hertwig, R. What the future holds and when: A description-experience gap in intertemporal choice. *Psychol. Sci.* **2019**, *30*, 1218–1233. [CrossRef]

31. Epper, T.; Fehr-Duda, H.; Bruhin, A. Viewing the future through a warped lens: Why uncertainty generates hyperbolic discounting. *J. Risk Uncertain.* **2011**, *43*, 169–203. [CrossRef]

32. Takahashi, T. A comparison of intertemporal choices for oneself versus someone else based on Tsallis' statistics. *Phys. Stat. Mech. Its Applications* **2007**, *385*, 637–644. [CrossRef]

33. Ericson, K.M.; Laibson, D. Intertemporal choice (No. w25358). In *Handbook of Behavioral Economics*; Elsevier: Amsterdam, The Netherlands, 2018.

34. Loewenstein, G.; Prelec, D. Anomalies in intertemporal choice: Evidence and an interpretation. *Q. J. Econ.* **1992**, *107*, 573–597. [CrossRef]

35. Abdellaoui, M.; Kemel, E.; Panin, A.; Vieider, F.M. Measuring time and risk preferences in an integrated framework. *Games Econ. Behav.* **2019**, *115*, 459–469. [CrossRef]

36. Baucells, M.; Heukamp, F.H. Common ratio using delay. *Theory Decis.* **2010**, *68*, 149–158. [CrossRef]

37. Vanderveldt, A.; Green, L.; Myerson, J. Discounting of monetary rewards that are both delayed and probabilistic: Delay and probability combine multiplicatively, not additively. *J. Exp. Psychol. Learn. Cogn.* **2015**, *41*, 148–162. [CrossRef]

38. Yi, R.; de la Piedad, X.; Bickel, W.K. The combined effects of delay and probability in discounting. *Behav. Process.* **2006**, *73*, 149–155. [CrossRef]

39. DeJarnette, P.; Dillenberger, D.; Gottlieb, D.; Ortoleva, P. Time lotteries, second version (No. 15-026v2). *Penn Institute for Economic Research*; Department of Economics, University of Pennsylvania: Philadelphia, PA, USA, 2018.

40. Han, R.; Takahashi, T. Psychophysics of time perception and valuation in temporal discounting of gain and loss. *Phys. Stat. Mech. Its Appl.* **2012**, *391*, 6568–6576. [CrossRef]

41. Konstantinidis, E.; Van Ravenzwaaij, D.; Güney, Ş; Newell, B.R. Now for sure or later with a risk? Modeling risky intertemporal choice as accumulated preference. *Decision* **2020**, *7*, 91–120. [CrossRef]

42. Caliendo, F.N.; Findley, T.S. Discount functions and self-control problems. *Econ. Lett.* **2014**, *122*, 416–419. [CrossRef]

43. Cruz Rambaud, S.; Parra Oller, I.M.; Valls Martínez, M.C. The amount-based deformation of the *q*-exponential discount function: A joint analysis of delay and magnitude effects. *Phys. Stat. Mech. Its Applications* **2019**, *508*, 788–796. [CrossRef]

44. Chew, S.H.; Epstein, L.G. Nonexpected utility preferences in a temporal framework with an application to consumption-savings behaviour. *J. Econ. Theory* **1990**, *50*, 54–81. [CrossRef]

45. Halevy, Y. Strotz meets Allais: Diminishing impatience and the certainty effect. *Am. Econ.* **2008**, *98*, 1145–1162. [CrossRef]

46. Brandstätter, E.; Kühberger, A.; Schneider, F. A cognitive-emotional account of the shape of the probability weighting function. *J. Behav. Decis. Mak.* **2002**, *15*, 79–100. [CrossRef]

47. Allais, M. Le comportement de l'homme rationnel devant le risque: Critique des postulats et axiomes de l'école américaine. *Econometrica* **1953**, *21*, 503–546. [CrossRef]

48. Pennesi, D. Uncertain discount and hyperbolic preferences. *Theory Decis.* **2017**, *83*, 315–336. [CrossRef]

49. Andreoni, J.; Sprenger, C. Risk preferences are not time preferences. *Am. Econ. Rev.* **2012**, *102*, 3357–3376. [CrossRef]

7

US Policy Uncertainty and Stock Market Nexus Revisited through Dynamic ARDL Simulation and Threshold Modelling

Muhammad Asif Khan [1,*], Masood Ahmed [1,2,*], József Popp [3,4] and Judit Oláh [4,5]

[1]   Faculty of Management Sciences, University of Kotli, Azad Jammu and Kashmir, Kotli 11100, Pakistan
[2]   Lee Kuan Yew School of Public Policy, National University of Singapore, Kent Ridge, 469C Bukit Timah Road, Singapore 259772, Singapore
[3]   Faculty of Economics and Social Sciences, Szent István University, 2100 Gödöllő, Hungary; Popp.Jozsef@szie.hu
[4]   TRADE Research Entity, Faculty of Economic and Management Sciences, North-West University, Vanderbijlpark 1900, South Africa; olah.judit@econ.unideb.hu
[5]   Faculty of Economics and Business, University of Debrecen, 4032 Debrecen, Hungary
*   Correspondence: khanasif82@uokajk.edu.pk (M.A.K.); masoodahmed@u.nus.edu (M.A.)

Abstract: Since the introduction of the measure of economic policy uncertainty, businesses, policymakers, and academic scholars closely monitor its momentum due to expected economic implications. The US is the world's top-ranked equity market by size, and prior literature on policy uncertainty and stock prices for the US is conflicting. In this study, we reexamine the policy uncertainty and stock price nexus from the US perspective, using a novel dynamically simulated autoregressive distributed lag setting introduced in 2018, which appears superior to traditional models. The empirical findings document a negative response of stock prices to 10% positive/negative shock in policy uncertainty in the short-run, while in the long-run, an increase in policy uncertainty by 10% reduces the stock prices, which increases in response to a decrease with the same magnitude. Moreover, we empirically identified two significant thresholds: (1) policy score of 4.89 (original score 132.39), which negatively explain stock prices with high magnitude, and (2) policy score 4.48 (original score 87.98), which explains stock prices negatively with a relatively low magnitude, and interestingly, policy changes below the second threshold become irrelevant to explain stock prices in the United States. It is worth noting that all indices are not equally exposed to unfavorable policy changes. The overall findings are robust to the alternative measures of policy uncertainty and stock prices and offer useful policy input. The limitations of the study and future line of research are also highlighted. All in all, the policy uncertainty is an indicator that shall remain ever-important due to its nature and implication on the various sectors of the economy (the equity market in particular).

Keywords: policy uncertainty; stock prices; dynamically simulated autoregressive distributed lag (DYS-ARDL); threshold regression; United States

1. Introduction

The field of mathematical finance is one of the most rapidly emerging domains in the subject of finance. Dynamically Simulated Autoregressive Distributed Lag (DYS-ARDL) [1] is an influential tool that may help an investor analyze and benefit by understanding the positive and negative shocks in policy indicators. This strategy enables investors to observe the reaction of equity prices to positive and negative shocks of various magnitude (1%, 5%, 10%, and others). More importantly, it may assist the diversification of potential portfolios across various equities based on predicted reaction. Coupled with DYS-ARDL, the few other effective strategies include statistical arbitrage strategies (SAS) and pairs trading strategy (PTS) that are empirically executed in mathematical finance literature; see for example [1–6]. Stübinger and Endres [2] developed and applied PTS to minute-by-minute data of oil companies constituting the S&P 500 market index for the US and revealed that the statistical arbitrage strategy enables intraday and overnight trading. Similarly, Stübinger, Mangold, and Krauss [6] developed SAS (based on vine copulas), which is a highly flexible instrument with multivariate dependence modeling under the linear and nonlinear setting. The authors find it promising in the context of the S&P 500 index of the United States (US) equities. Using SAS, Avellaneda and Lee [3] related the performance of mean-reversion SAS with the stock market cycle and found it effective in studying stock performance during the liquidity crisis. Empirical evidence from the US equity market on PTS links trading cost documents that PTS is profitable among well-matched portfolios [5]. Liu, Chang, and Geman [4] argue that PTS can facilitate stakeholders to capture inefficiencies in the local equity market using daily data. Interestingly, we find that SAS and PTS strategies are successfully employed in the context of the US, while to the best of our knowledge, we do not find the use of DYS-ARDL, which is surprising. Each of the described strategies has unique features in a given scenario in which they are used, yet it worthwhile to add little value to mathematical finance literature by empirically examining the DYS-ARDL specification in the US context.

Given the economic implications of financial markets and eventual behavior [7–10], this piece of research empirically examines the short- and long-run impacts of policy uncertainty (hereafter PU) on stock prices of the US using a novel DYS-ARDL setting proposed by Jordan and Philips [1] and of threshold relation using the Tong [11] model. The study is motivated by conflicting literature on policy risk stock price and shortcomings associated with the traditional cointegration model (e.g., Autoregressive Distributed Lag (ARDL)).

Since the introduction of the measure of PU by Baker et al. [12], the effects of the PU on macro variables have gained substantial attention. PU is closely monitored and analyzed by businesses, policymakers, and academic scholars, as the global economy is now more closely interconnected than ever [13]. Intuitively, an increase in PU is expected to negatively influence the stock market, while on the contrary, stock market indicators may react positively to a decline in PU [14]. This intuition is consistent with the findings of Baker, Bloom, and Davis [12], who have shown its adverse effects on economic activities, which is confirmed by the recent literature [14–27].

According to Baker, Bloom, and Davis [12], economic PU refers to *"a non-zero probability of changes in the existing economic policies that determine the rules of the game for economic agents"*. The impact of changes in PU may potentially rout the following channels:

- First, it can change or delay important decisions made by companies and other economic actors, such as investment [28], employment, consumption, and savings decisions [14,29].
- Second, it increases financing and production costs by affecting supply and demand channels, exacerbating investment decline, and economic contraction [14,17,30,31].
- Third, it can increase the risks in financial markets, especially by reducing the value of government protection provided to the market [17].
- Lastly, PU also affects inflation, interest rates, and expected risk premiums [32,33].

Importantly, in the context of the US, the phenomena are also captured by a few studies [14,21–23,27] with conflicting findings. For example, some of them [14,15,21,23,34] found a negative relationship, while others reported no effect [22,27]. The conflicting referred literature on the US [14,15] relies on the classical approach [35] to capture the cointegration relationship. From the symmetry assumption perspective drawn on this approach [35], it follows that an increase in PU will negatively affect the other macroeconomic variables and that a decrease in PU will increase this variable. However, this may not be the case, as investors' responses may differ from increasing PU versus decreasing PU. It is possible that, due to an increase in uncertainty, investors move their equity assets to safer assets and that a decrease in uncertainty may cause them to shift their portfolio towards the stock market (assume the change in PU is less than increase) if they expect that a decrease in uncertainty is short-lived and then that asymmetry originates.

The shortcomings associated with Pesaran, Shin, and Smith [35] are, to some extent, addressed by nonlinear extension by Shin et al. [36], which generates two separate series (positive and negative) from the core explanatory variable. Thus, the asymmetric impact may be estimated; however, this approach overlooks the simulation features while estimating the short- and long-run asymmetries. The package is given by Jordan and Philips [1], known as the DYS-ARDL approach, which takes into account the simulation mechanism and liberty to use positive and negative shocks in an explanatory variable and captures the impact in a variable of interest. According to recent literature [37,38], this novel approach is capable of predicting the actual positive and negative changes in the explanatory variable and its subsequent impact on the dependent variable. Moreover, it can stimulate, estimate, and automatically predict, and graph said changes. The authors also believe that classical ARDL can only estimate the long-term and short-term relationships of the variables. Contemplating the limitations associated with traditional estimators, this study uses Jordan and Philips [1] inspirational DYS-ARDL estimator to examine the relationship between PU and US stock prices.

In addition, this study extends the analysis beyond the DYS-ARDL estimator [1] by using Tong [11] threshold regression Although DYS-ARDL [1] is a powerful tool to capture the dynamic cointegration between an independent variable and dependent variable, and its unique feature automatically generates the simulation-based graph of changes to SP as a result of a certain positive/negative shock in PU, it is beyond its capacity to figure out a certain level (point) where the relationship (magnitude of coefficient) changes. For example, literature shows that the general stock market is linearity correlated with the changes in PU [14–27]. An increase in PU brings a negative influence on SP, in which a decrease translates into a positive change.

Threshold models have recently paid attention to modeling nonlinear behavior in applied economics. Part of the interest in these models is in observable models, followed by many economic variables, such as asymmetrical adjustments to the equilibrium [39]. By reviewing a variety of literature, Hansen [40] recorded the impact of the Tong [11] threshold model on the field of econometrics and economics and praised Howell Tong's visionary innovation that greatly influenced the development of the field of econometrics and economics.

Concisely, this small piece of research extends the financial economics and mathematical finance literature on PU and SP in the context of the United States, which is the world's top-ranked equity market [41] in three distinct ways. First, the novelty stems from the use of DYS-ARDL [1], which produces efficient estimation using simulations mechanism (which traditional ARDL departs), and auto-predicts the relationship graphically alongside empirical mechanics. To the best of our knowledge, this is the first study to verify traditional estimation with this novel and robust method. The empirical findings of DYS-ARDL document a negative response of stock prices in the short-run for a 10% positive and negative change (shock) in PU, while a linear relationship is observed in case of the long-run in response to said change.

Second, coupled with novel DYS-ARDL, this study adds value to relevant literature by providing evidence from threshold regression [11], which provides two significant thresholds in the nexus of PU-SP that may offer useful insight into policy matters based upon identified threshold(s). It is worth noting that SP negatively reacts to PU until a certain level (threshold-1), where the magnitude of such reaction changes (declines) to another point (threshold-2) with relatively low magnitude (still negative). Interestingly, below threshold-2, the PU became irrelevant to the US-SP nexus.

Third, this is a compressive effort to provide a broader picture of the US stock market reaction to policy changes. In this regard, prior literature is confined to the New York Stock Exchange Composite Index and S&P 500, while this study empirically tested seven major stock indices: S&P 500, Dow Jones Industrial Average, Dow Jones Composite Average, NASDAQ composite, NASDAQ100, and Dow Jones Transpiration Average. Expending analysis of these indices potentially provides useful insights to investors and policymakers because all are not equally exposed to adverse changes in PU. Some of them are nonresponsive to such changes, which may help a group of investors diversifying their investments to avoid unfavorable returns and to construct the desired portfolio with low risk. On the other hand, risk-seeking investors may capitalize on risk premiums, where understanding the identified thresholds may help to diversify their investments reasonably.

The rest of the work is organized as follows. Section 2 outlines the related literature; Section 3 illustrates the material and methods; results and discussion are covered by Section 4; the study is concluded in Section 5.

2. Literature Review

Bahmani-Oskooee and Saha [15] assessed the impact of PU on stock prices in 13 countries, including the United States, and find that, in almost all 13 countries, increased uncertainty has negative short-term effects on stock prices but not in the long term. Sum [18] utilized the ordinary least squares method to analyze the impact of PU on stock markets (from January 1993 to April 2010) of Ukraine, Switzerland, Turkey, Norway, Russia, Croatia, and the European Union. The study finds that PU negatively impacts EU stock market returns, except for in Slovenia, Slovakia, Latvia, Malta, Lithuania, Estonia, and Bulgaria. The analysis does not identify any negative impact of stock market returns of non-EU countries included in the study. Sum [24] used a vector autoregressive model with Granger-causality testing and impulse response function and founds that PU negatively impacts stock market returns for most months from 1985 to 2011.

Another study [34] analyzed monthly data of PU and stock market indices of eleven economies, including China, Russia, the UK, Spain, France, India, Germany, the US, Canada, Japan, and Italy. The study found that PU negatively impacts stock prices mostly except periods of low-to-high frequency cycles. The study used data from 1998 to 2014. Using data from 1900 to 2014, Arouri, Estay, Rault, and Roubaud [14] measured PU's impact on the US stock market and found a weak but persistent negative impact of PU on stock market returns. Inflation, default spread, and variation in industrial production were the control variables used. The study also found that PU has a greater negative impact on stock market returns during high volatility.

Pastor and Veronesi [17] estimated how the government's economic policy announcement impacts stock market prices and reported that stock prices go up when the government makes policy announcements and that more unexpected announcement brings in greater volatility. Li, Balcilar, Gupta, and Chang [19] found a weak relationship between PU and stock market returns in China and India. For China, the study used monthly data from 1995 to 2013, and for India, it used monthly data from 2003 to 2013. The study employed two methods (i) bootstrap Granger full-sample causality testing and (ii) subsample rolling window estimation. The first method did not find any relationship between stock market returns and PU, while the second method showed a weak bidirectional relationship for many sub-periods. Employing the time-varying parameter factor-augmented vector autoregressive (VAR) model on data from January 1996 to December 2015, Gao, Zhu, O'Sullivan, and Sherman [20] estimated the impact of PU on the UK stock market returns. The study considered both domestic and international economic PU factors. The paper maintains that PU explains the cross-section of UK stock market returns.

Wu, Liu, and Hsueh [22] analyzed the relationship between PU and performance of the stock markets of Canada, Spain, the UK, France, Italy, China, India, the US, and Germany. Analyzing monthly data from January 2013 to December 2014, the study found that not all stock markets under investigation react similarly to PU. According to the study, the UK stock market falls most with negative PU, but the markets of Canada, the US, France, China, and Germany remain unaffected. Asgharian, Christiansen, and Hou [21] measured the relationship between PU and the US (S&P 500) and the UK (FTSE 100) stock markets. The study used daily data for stock market indices and monthly data for PU. The paper found that stock market volatility in the US depends on PU in the US and that stock market volatility in the UK depends on PU in both the US and UK.

Christou, Cunado, Gupta, and Hassapis [23] estimated the impact of PU on the stock markets of the US, China, Korea, Canada, Australia, and Japan. Using monthly data from 1998 to 2014 and employing a panel VAR model with impulse response function, the study found that own country PU impacts stock markets negatively in all aforementioned countries. The study also found that PU in the US also negatively impacts all other countries' stock markets in the analysis, except Australia. Debata and Mahakud [25] found a significant relationship between PU and stock market liquidity in India. The study used monthly data from January 2013 to Granger 2016 and employed VAR Granger causality testing, variance decomposition analysis, and impulse response function. The impulse response function showed that PU and stock market liquidity are negatively related.

Liu and Zhang [42] investigated PU's impact on stock market volatility of the S&P 500 index from January 1996 to June 2013. The study found that PU and stock market volatility are interconnected and that PU has significant predictive power on stock market volatility. Pirgaip [27] focused on the relationship between stock market volatility for fourteen OECD countries, subject to monthly data from March 2003 to April 2016 for Japan, France, Germany, Chile, Canada, Italy, Australia, the US, UK, Sweden, Spain, Netherlands, Australia, and South Korea. Employing the bootstrap panel Granger causality method, the study found that PU impacts stock prices in all countries except the US, Germany, and Japan.

Škrinjarić and Orlović [26] estimated the spillover effects of PU shocks on stock market returns and risk for nine Eastern and Central European countries, including Bulgaria, Estonia, Lithuania, Croatia, Slovenia, Hungary, Czech Republic, Poland, and Slovakia. The paper employed a rolling estimation of the VAR model and the spillover indices. The study's findings suggest that Poland, the Czech Republic, Slovenia, and Lithuania are more sensitive to PU shocks compared to other markets in the study. In contrast, the Bulgarian stock market is least impacted by PU shocks. Other countries' stock markets have an individual reaction to PU shocks.

Ehrmann and Fratzscher [43] examined how the US monetary policy shocks are transmitted stock market returns over February 1994 to December 2004, with a weak association in India, China, and Malaysia's stock markets while strong on Korea, Hong Kong, Turkey, Indonesia, Canada, Finland, Sweden, and Australia. Brogaard and Detzel [44] examined the relationship between PU and asset prices using a monthly Center for Research in Security Prices (CRSP) value-weighted index as the US stock market's performance measure and PU. The findings suggest that a one standard deviation increase in PU decreases stock returns by 1.31% and increases 3-month log excess returns by 1.53%. The study also found that dividend growth is not affected by PU. Antonakakis et al. [45] estimated co-movements between PU and the US stock market returns and stock market volatility using S&P 500 stock returns data and S&P 500 volatility index data. The study found a negative dynamic correlation between PU and stock returns except during the financial crisis of 2008, for which the correlation became positive.

Stock market volatility also negatively impacts the stock market returns, according to the study. Dakhlaoui and Aloui [46] scrutinized the relationship between the US PU and Brazil, Russia, India, and China stock markets, estimating daily data from July 1997 to July 2011. The study found a negative relationship between the US PU and the returns, but the volatility spillovers were found to oscillate between negative and positive making, it highly risky for investors to invest in US and BRIC stock markets simultaneously. Yang and Jiang [47] used data from the Shanghai stock index from January 1995 to December 2014 to investigate the relationship between PU and china stock market returns and suggest that stock market returns and PU are negatively correlated and that the negative impact of PU lasts for about eight months after the policy announcement.

Das and Kumar [16] estimated the impacts of domestic PU and the US PU on the economies of 17 countries. The analysis included monthly data from January 1998 to February 2017 and found that emerging markets are less prone and vulnerable to domestic and US PU than developed economies while Chile and Korea are relatively more sensitive to both Domestic PU and US PU, whereas China is least affected. Estimation reveals that except Canada and Australia, stock prices and all other developed economies in the analysis are quite sensitive to US PU. Australia and Canada stock prices are more reliant on domestic PU. Stock prices of all the emerging economies are more reliant on domestic PU except for the marginal exception of Russia and Brazil.

We conclude that the reviewed literature on policy-stock prices is conflicting. See, for example, Bahmani-Oskooee and Saha [15]; Asgharian, Christiansen, and Hou [21]; Christou, Cunado, Gupta, and Hassapis [23]; Ko and Lee [34]; and Arouri, Estay, Rault, and Roubaud [14], who found that the US stock market is negatively correlated to changes in PU, and Wu, Liu, and Hsueh [22], and Pirgaip [27], who documented no effect of US. Sum [13] revealed a cointegration relationship that exists between the economic uncertainty of the US and Europe, showing a spillover effect across financial markets across the national borders. The literature referred to the US with few exceptions including Arouri, Estay, Rault, and Roubaud [14], and Bahmani-Oskooee and Saha [15], who assumed a linear relationship between PU and stock prices and relied on Pesaran, Shin, and Smith [35] for the traditional cointegration approach to finding the long-run dynamics of the PU and stock prices. Amongst these, Arouri, Estay, Rault, and Roubaud [14] found a long-run weak negative impact in general and persistent negative impact during high volatility regimes. However, Bahmani-Oskooee and Saha [15] found short-run negative impacts and no effect in the long-run.

The strand of literature relied on traditional cointegration [35] for modeling policy-stock price connection follows the symmetry assumption perspective holding that an increase in PU will negatively affect the other macroeconomic variable and a decrease in PU will increase this variable. However, this may not be the case, as investors' responses may differ from increasing PU versus decreasing PU. It is possible that, due to an increase in uncertainty, investors move their equity assets to safer assets and that a decrease in uncertainty may cause them to shift their portfolio towards the stock market (assume the change in PU is less than increase) if they expect that a decrease in uncertainty is short-lived and then that asymmetry originates. Figure 1 plots the theoretical framework based on reviewed papers [14,15].

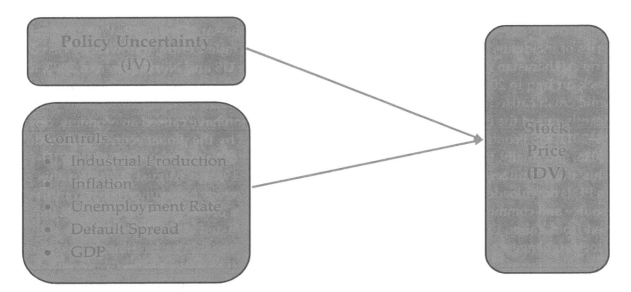

Figure 1. Theoretical framework, IV: independent variable (measured by news-based policy uncertainty—PU_NB) and DV: dependent variable. Source: Drawn from the literature (Arouri et al., [14], and Bahmani-Oskooee and Saha, [15]).

We conclude that empirical literature on PU and stock prices is conflicting, with no consensus on its empirical impact, as the literature shows mixed results (positive, negative, and no effect). This may be attributable to the differences in methodological strategies used, time coverage, and other controls used in the estimation process. Among empirical methods used, ARDL is commonly used to arrive at short- and long-run cointegration relationships. Moreover, it is surprising that threshold identification in PU and stock price connection is an unaddressed phenomenon. Thus, it is imperative to go ahead and comprehensively examine the short- and the long-run association between PU and stock prices using an updated dataset coupled with DYS-ARDL and the threshold strategy in the context of the United States, the world top-ranked financial market (in terms of market size) [41].

3. Materials and Methods

3.1. Description of Variables and Data Source

The independent variable is economic PU, which is an index built by Baker, Bloom, and Davis [12] from three types of underlying components. The first component quantifies the news coverage of policy-related economic uncertainties. A second component reflects the number of federal tax legislation provisions that will expire in the coming years. The third component uses the disagreement among economic meteorologists as an indicator of uncertainty. The first component is an index of the search results of 10 major newspapers, which includes *US Today, Miami Herald, Chicago Tribune, Washington Post, Los Angeles Times, Boston Globe, San Francisco Chronicle, Dallas Morning News, New York Times*, and *Wall Street Diary*. From these documents, Baker, Bloom, and Davis [12] create a normalized index of the volume of news articles discussing PU. The second component of this index is based on reports from the congressional budget office, which compiles lists of temporary provisions of federal tax legislation. We compile an annual number of weighted US dollar tax laws that expire over the next 10 years and provide a measure of uncertainty on which path federal tax laws will follow in the future.

The third component of the PU index is based on the Federal Reserve Bank of Philadelphia's survey of professional meteorologists. Here, it uses the dispersion between individual meteorologists' forecasts of future consumer price index levels, federal spending, and state and local spending to create indices of uncertainty for policy-related macroeconomic variables. This study uses news-based PU (PU_NB) for the main analysis, while robustness is performed using three component-based PU index (PU_3C). Figure 2 provides a glimpse of historical US monthly PU indices (both PU_NB and PU_3C). A rise in PU indices is shown by the second half of the sample period. We may attribute it to a series of incidents, such as the 9/11 attack on the World Trade Centre, followed by US coalition attack on Afghanistan in 2001, mounted tension between the US and North Korea in 2003, and the US attack on Iraq in 2003. Later, the major event was the 2007–2009 recession in the form of a US economic crash caused by the subprime crisis in 2008, and aftershocks in subsequent years have significantly raised the PU. The efforts to reduce carbon emission have caused an economic downturn in 2010–2011, US economic slowdown was heavily weighted by the global economic slowdown in 2015–2016, and finally, the sizable swaths of US economic shutdown were a result of COVID-19.

This study utilizes monthly data ranging from January 1985 to August 2020. For this period, data on PU is downloaded from the economic PU website (http://www.policyuncertainty.com/), which is open-source and commonly used in related literature, while data on seven US stock market indices are accessed from Yahoo Finance [48]. This includes monthly adjusted closing stock prices of the New York Stock exchange composite index (NYSEC) as a dependent variable for baseline analysis; however, the same measure of S&P500, Dow Jones Industrial Average (DJI), Dow Jones Composite Average (DJA), NASDAQ composite, NASDAQ100, and Dow Jones Transpiration Average (DJT) are utilized as robustness. Following Arouri, Estay, Rault, and Roubaud [14], and Bahmani-Oskooee and Saha [15], we consider Industrial production (IP), default spread (DS), inflation (INF), and unemployment rate (UE) as potential controls, and monthly data are sourced from Federal Reserve Economic Data (FRED https://fred.stlouisfed.org/) [49]. FRED is an open-source database that maintains various frequency datasets on more than 0.07 million in the United States and international time-series data from above 100 date sources.

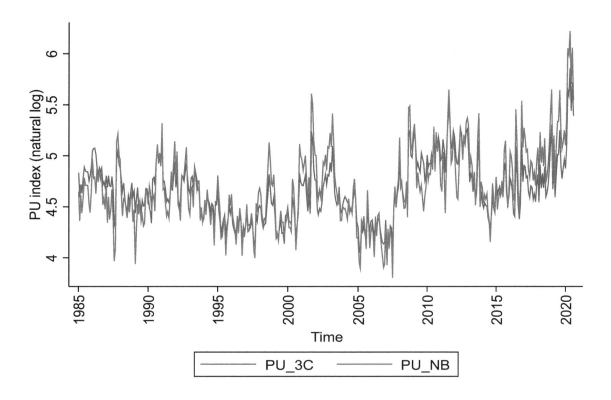

Figure 2. US monthly policy uncertainty index. Source: Baker, Bloom, and Davis [12].

The choice of the US's stock market as a potential unit for analysis is led by its top rank in terms of size among world exchanges [41]. Figure 3 shows a list of the world's largest stock exchanges as per the market capitalization of listed companies. The New York stock exchange and NASDAQ are ranked first and second with 25.53 and 11.23 trillion US dollars, respectively, among world exchanges [41]. Table 1 shows the descriptive properties of the underlying variables.

Figure 3. World largest stock exchanges by market. Source: Szmigiera [41].

Table 1. Descriptive Statistics.

Abbreviation	Description	Measurement	Mean	Std.Dev.	Min	Max	Data Source
SP	Stock price	Natural log of adjusted closing prices of NYSE composite index	8.538	0.702	7.000	9.541	Yahoo Finance https://finance.yahoo.com/
PU_NB	News-based policy uncertainty	Natural log of news-based policy uncertainty index	4.692	0.378	3.802	6.223	http://www.policyuncertainty.com/
INF	Inflation	Natural log	5.181	0.260	4.659	5.560	
IP	Industrial production	Natural log	4.439	0.248	1.716	4.705	FRED https://fred.stlouisfed.org/
UE	Unemployment rate	%	5.947	1.647	3.500	14.700	
DS	Default spread	Moody's Seasoned Baa Corporate Bond Minus Federal Funds Rate	3.847	1.596	0.500	8.820	

Jordan and Philips's [1] DYS-ARDL can be expressed in the following standard pathway:

$$\Delta(y)_t = \alpha_0 + \theta_0(y)_{t-1} + \theta_1(x_1)_{t-1} + \ldots + \theta_k(x_k)_{t-1} + \sum_{i=1}^{p} \alpha_{0i}\Delta(y)_{t-1} + \sum_{j=0}^{q1} \beta_{1j}\Delta(x_1)_{t-j} + \ldots$$
$$+ \sum_{j=0}^{qk} \beta_{kj}\Delta(x_k)_{t-j} + \varepsilon_t \tag{1}$$

where the change in the dependent variable (y) is a function of the intercept (α_0), and all the independent variables at time $t-1$ are the levels of the maximum of p and qk lags in respective first difference (Δ) along with error term (ε) at time t. The study uses Pesaran, Shin, and Smith's [35] ARDL bounds testing approach for a level relationship using Kwiatkowski–Phillips–Schmidt–Shin (2018) critical values as a benchmark. The null hypothesis for no level relationship obtained by joint F-statistics from the estimation is rejected against the critical bounds, in particular, when estimated F-statistics is greater than the upper bound I(1). Drawn on the empirical specification illustrated in Equation (1), the error correction transformation of the ARDL bounds estimators are estimated under the following:

The change in the dependent variable (y) is a function of intercept (α_0), and all the independent variables at time $t-1$ are levels to the maximum of p and qk lags in respective first difference (Δ) along with error term (ε) at time t. The study uses Pesaran, Shin, and Smith's [35] ARDL bounds testing approach for a level relationship using Kwiatkowski–Phillips–Schmidt–Shin (2018) critical values as a benchmark. The null hypothesis for no level relationship obtained by joint F-statistics from the estimation is rejected against the critical bounds, in particular, when estimated F-statistics is greater than the upper bound I(1). Drawn on the empirical specification illustrated in Equation (1), the error correction transformation of the ARDL bounds estimators are estimated as under the following:

$$\Delta ln(SP)_t = \alpha_0 \quad + \theta_0 \, ln\,(SP)_{t-1} + \beta_1\Delta \, ln\,(PU\_NB)_t + \theta_1 \, ln\,(PU\_NB)_{t-1} + \beta_2\Delta \, ln\,(INF)_t$$
$$+\theta_2 \, ln\,(INF)_{t-1} + \beta_3\Delta \, ln\,(IP)_t + \theta_3 \, ln\,(IP)_{t-1} + \beta_4\Delta\,(UE)_t + \theta_4(UE)_{t-1} \tag{2}$$
$$+\beta_5\Delta\,(DS)_t + \theta_5(DS)_{t-1} + \varepsilon_t$$

In Equation (2), θ_0 denotes error correction term (ECT), $\beta_1 - \beta_5$ capture the short-tun coefficient, and $\theta_1 - \theta_5$ indicate a long-run coefficient for each of the regressors respectively.

3.2. Threshold Regression

The DYS-ARDL [1] is a powerful tool for capturing the dynamic cointegration between the independent variable and the dependent variable. Its unique function is to simulate the automatic generation of graphs based on changes in the dependent variable as a result of a certain positive/negative shock in the explanatory variable. However, any particular degree (point) of change in the relationship cannot be imagined. For example, the literature shows that linearity on the general stock market is related to changes in PU. The increase in PU harms the stock market, while the decrease in PU leads to positive changes.

The threshold model extends linear regression to allow the coefficients to vary among regions/regimes. These regions are identified by threshold variables that are greater or less than the threshold value. The model can have multiple thresholds; you can specify a known number of thresholds, or you can allow it to use Bayesian Information Criteria (BIC), Akaike Information Criteria (AIC), or Hannan–Quinn Information Criteria (HQIC to determine the number for you). It includes region-varying coefficients for specified covariates for each identified threshold, and it is efficient in automatically estimating the possible thresholds using *the n thresholds(#)* function. Moreover, it creates a variable with a sum of squared residuals for each tentative threshold. Thus, single threshold regression [11] is modeled by Equation (3).

The threshold model provides a systematic method of tracking the turning point in the relationship that can help decision-makers make better decisions [50–53]. Therefore, the threshold regression model for a single threshold [11] is modeled by Equation (3) for regions defined by threshold γ.

$$
\begin{aligned}
y_t &= X_t\beta + Z_t\delta_1 + \varepsilon_t \ if \ w_t \ \le \ \gamma \\
y_t &= X_t\beta + Z_t\delta_2 + \varepsilon_t \ if \ \gamma \ < \ w_t
\end{aligned}
\tag{3}
$$

where y_t is a dependent variable (SP in our case), X_t represents the vector consisting of region-invariant parameters (INF, IP, UE, and DS), Z_t is a vector of exogenous variables with region-specific coefficient vectors ($\delta_1 \ and \ \delta_2$), and w_t is the threshold variable, PU_NB (that may be one of the variables in X_t or Z_t.

4. Results

4.1. Unit-Root Analysis

The preliminary step to test the level relationship between the dependent variable (SP) and respective regressors is to satisfy the stationarity condition of the individual series; in particular, the dependent variables must be integrated at the first difference, I(1). Furthermore, all the independent variables must not be stationary at the second difference, I(2). To determine the integration order aligned with recent literature [37], this study uses the Augmented Dickey–Fuller (ADF) and Kwiatkowski–Phillips–Schmidt–Shin (KPSS) test [54]. The null hypothesis for ADF assumes unit-root, while Baum [55] STATA module for KPSS, on the other hand, is tested under the null hypothesis of stationarity. The results are reported in Table 2, which reveals that the null hypothesis for most of the underlying variables cannot be rejected at level, which is rejected at first difference. Both tests (ADF and KPSS) witness that the dependent variable is stationary at the first difference and that none of the regressors is integrated at second order. The situation calls for the potential use of ARDL bounds testing for cointegration. After determining the stationarity conditions, the selection of optimal lag is another essential and challenging task, for which there is no hard and fast rule. However, following Bahmani-Oskooee and Saha [15], and Bahmani-Oskooee and Saha [56], we allow 8–12 lags for monthly data in this study. The lag-order is determined using AIC, SC, and HQ.

Table 2. Unit-root analysis.

Variable	Augmented Dickey–Fuller Test		Kwiatkowski–Phillips–Schmidt–Shin Test	
	Level	1st Difference	Level	1st Difference
SP	−2.450	−10.413 ***	0.425	0.037 ***
PU_NB	−2.676	−4.950 ***	0.336	0.011 ***
INF	−1.270	−10.619 ***	0.879	0.030 ***
IP	−3.513 **	−4.637 ***	0.141 **	0.097 ***
UE	−2.798	−12.726 ***	0.499	0.041 ***
DS	−3.477 ***	−8.201 ***	0.134 **	0.063 ***

***, and ** indicate that the null hypothesis of unit-root rejected at 1%, 5%, and 10% levels of significance, respectively.

4.2. Baseline Analysis—ARDL Bounds Test

The study estimates the baseline relationship between PU_NB and SP using ordinary least squared regression (OLS) in a series of estimation. Referring to Table A1 (Appendix A), initially in the model (1), PU_NB shows a positive impact on SP; however, when controls are introduced, the relationship becomes negative and consistent across all estimators (2–5). This shows the relevance of controls, and the inclusion of each control has increased the R-squared.

Pesaran, Shin, and Smith;s [35] bounds test reveals the existence of a cointegration relationship between PU_NB and SP along with controls. Table 3 shows the ARDL bounds test and diagnostic testing for baseline estimation. Computed absolute F-statistics and t-statistics in Table 3 (upper part) are greater than upper bounds at all significance levels (10%, 5%, and 1%) of Kripfganz and Schneider (2018) critical values.

Table 3. ARDL bounds test and diagnostic testing.

Test Statistics	Value					
F-statistics	6.574					
t-statistics	−4.654					
Confidence interval	10%			5%		1%
Bounds	I(0)	I(1)	I(0)	I(1)	I(0)	I(1)
F-stat *	2.130	3.240	2.459	3.640	3.155	4.470
t-stat *	−2.557	−4.065	−2.857	−4.399	−3.439	−5.023
Diagnostic testing						
Diagnostic test	Jarque-Bera		ARCH	Breusch-Pagan/Cook-Weisberg	Breusch-Godfrey LM	Ramsey RESET
p-value	0.188		0.101	0.102	0.418	0.452
Inference	Estimated residuals are normal		No heteroskedasticity problem		No serial correlation problem	Model correctly specified
Variance inflation factor						
Variable	INF	IP	UE	DS	PU_NB	Mean VIF
VIF	2.94	2.8	2.18	1.85	1.43	2.15

* indicates Kripfganz and Schneider (2018) critical values.

After establishing the ARDL bounds test, we proceed to check for diagnostic testing. Table 3 (middle part) shows the p-values for each of the estimated tests, which affirms that baseline, and ARDL estimation satisfies the diagnostic properties, such as normality of estimated residuals, heteroskedasticity, serial correlation, and correct specification of the model. The bottom part of Table 3 incorporates the multicollinearity results of the variance inflation factor (VIF). The benchmark to draw inference is the individual VIF value for each regressor not being greater than 5. In our case, none of the regressors violate these criteria, which signifies that the multicollinearity problem does not exist in our estimation and that the obtained results are correctly estimated.

4.3. Dynamic ARDL Simulations and Robustness

Table 4 documents the results of DYS-ARDL [1], using PU_NB as a baseline measure (Table 4, model-1) and PU_3C as its near alternative for robustness (Table 4, model-2); 5000 simulations are estimated for both models. Khan, Teng, and Khan [37], and Khan et al. [57] affirm that the novel DYS-ARDL model can stimulate, estimate, and graph to automatically predict the graphs of negative and positive changes occurring in variables and their short- and long-term relationships, which are beyond the capacity of classical ARDL. The significant and negative coefficient of error correction term (ECT) in each of the estimated model stratifies the existence of a cointegration relationship between variables under consideration. The system corrects the previous period disequilibrium at a monthly rate of 6.7%. The negative and significant PU_NB coefficient illustrates that equity markets in the US do not like a mounting risk in the form of PU.

Table 4. Dynamically simulated autoregressive distributed lag (DYS-ARDL) results.

	(1)	(2)
Variables	**SP**	**SP**
	PU_NB	**Robustness: PU_3C**
ECT(−1)	−0.067 ***	−0.072 ***
	(0.021)	(0.021)
ΔPU	−0.044 ***	−0.068 ***
	(0.008)	(0.012)
PU	−0.014 **	−0.024 **
	(0.007)	(0.010)
ΔINF	−0.096	−0.224
	(0.651)	(0.649)
INF	0.088 **	0.092 **
	(0.035)	(0.043)
ΔIP	−0.008	−0.010
	(0.015)	(0.015)
IP	0.128 **	0.129 **
	(0.056)	(0.055)
ΔUE	0.008 **	0.008 **
	(0.004)	(0.004)
UE	0.005 **	0.006 ***
	(0.002)	(0.002)
ΔDS	−0.030 ***	−0.029 ***
	(0.007)	(0.007)
DS	−0.007 ***	−0.007 ***
	(0.002)	(0.002)
Constant	−0.368 ***	−0.360 ***
	(0.134)	(0.134)
Obs.	427	427
F-statistics	10.95 ***	10.21 ***
Simulations	5000	5000

Standard errors are in parenthesis. *** $p < 0.01$, and ** $p < 0.05$. All the abbreviations are defined in Table 1. SP refers to the NYSE composite index.

This study performed several robustness checks using an alternative measure of PU_NB and SP. A three component-based measure of PU is used as an alternative measure (it is explained in detail in the variable description section of the Material and Methods section). Table 4 (model-2) incorporates the results of DYS-ARDL, where the dependent variable is SP from the NYSEC index and the independent variable is PU_3C. The results are consistent with the main analysis. The disequilibrium is corrected at a monthly speed of adjustment of 7%, while both in the short- and long-run, increasing PU negatively drives the SP. Similar to the main analysis, the behavior of defaults spread is aligned to the implication of PU both in the short- and long-run. We find inflation, industrial production, and unemployment as stock-friendly indicators in the long-run with positive stimulus.

The impulse response function of the PU_NB impact on SP in the United States for the sampling period is shown in Figure 4. The results of the impulse response graph show that a 10% increase in PU_NB negatively affects the SP in the US both in the short- and long term while a 10% drop in the PU_NB shows negative effects in the US in the short term and positive effects in the long term. A short-term decline in SP because of PU_NB may be attributable to standard investment behavior, which is depicted by declining risk premium, which constitutes a substantial part of security prices. However, in the long run, the disequilibrium is corrected as shown by ECT in Table 4, and investment patterns are adjusted according to the risk.

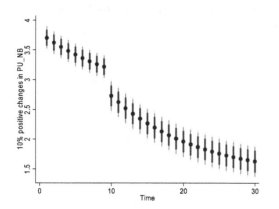
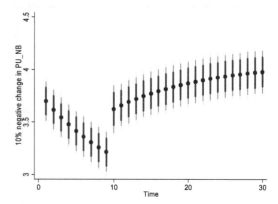

Figure 4. Graphical illustration of the response of stock prices (NYSE composite index) to a 10% increase (in the left portion of the Figure) and 10% decrease (in the right portion of the Figure) in PU_NB.

4.4. Robustness: Alternative Measures of Stock Prices

Apart from the main analysis, the study explores the matter in depth by using six alternative stock indices (S&P 500, Dow Jones Industrial Average, Dow Jones Composite Average, NASDAQ Composite, NASDAQ 100, and Dow Jones Transpiration Average) from the United States for robustness. Table A2 (Appendix B) uncovers interesting scenarios across the alternative measure so stock prices. Out of six alternatives, DJI, DJA, and DJT show a cointegration relationship to changes in PU, while other measures show negative but insignificant coefficients. One important phenomenon is the persistent negative reaction of all these measures to policy change in the short-run, while in the long-run, the response is negligible, and in particular, S&P 500, NASDAQ composite, and NASDAQ 100 are even not exposed to such a risk. These findings are encouraging for potential investors to diversify the investment across potential portfolios considering these reactions.

4.5. Threshold Regression

Table 5 summarizes the threshold regression results for both measures of PU (PU_NB, and PU_3C). Columns (1–2) carry the results of PU_NB regressed as an independent variable on NYSEC, and S&P 500, while columns (3–4) incorporate the robustness with an alternative measure, PU_3C. First, we estimate a single threshold model for PU_NB as a threshold variable and found 4.89 to be a significant threshold, which enables us to go ahead and estimate, double, and tribble thresholds. Second, a threshold of 4.48 was also significant, while the third one is found insignificant. Single threshold shows that a policy score of 4.89 (PU ≥ Th-1) negatively explains the stock prices in the US with coefficients −0.291 and −0.270 for models (1–2), respectively. For a double threshold level of 4.48 (PU ≥ Th-2& ≤ TH-1), the PU still negatively translates the stock prices, but the magnitude has relatively declined with coefficients of −0.074, and −0.005 for models (1–2), respectively. Interestingly, below 4.48 (PU ≤ TH-2), the relationship between PU and stock price becomes irrelevant, which has no statistical and economic implications. Likewise, the results are consistent (in terms of the direction of relationship and significance) and robust across alternative measure, PU_3C.

Identified thresholds through threshold regression are also shown in Figure 5, where the black horizontal line (a) indicates the single threshold of ≥4.89 (132.39 PU score), for which PU negatively explains stock prices with relatively high magnitude, whereas the second horizontal black line (b) denotes the double threshold value of 4.48 (87.98 PU score), the point where the coefficient of PU translates to a negative reaction in stock prices (less than the single threshold magnitude which remains unchanged between 4.89–4.48—the area covered by two lines). On the Y-axis, both thresholds corresponding to a) and b) are indicated by solid black circles. Interestingly, the area below 4.48 is the region in which PU becomes irrelevant to stock prices in our sample period.

Table 5. Threshold regression results.

Variables	PU_NB		Robustness: PU_3C	
	(1)	(2)	(3)	(4)
	SP	SP_S&P 500	SP	SP_S&P 500
TH-1		4.89 **		4.89 **
TH-2		4.48 **		4.48 **
INF	0.873 ***	1.017 ***	0.877 ***	0.987 ***
	(0.123)	(0.184)	(0.125)	(0.187)
IP	2.291 ***	2.080 ***	2.278 ***	2.098 ***
	(0.150)	(0.223)	(0.152)	(0.228)
GDP	−4.167 ***	−7.293 ***	−3.921 ***	−6.560 ***
	(0.983)	(1.467)	(0.914)	(1.366)
DS	−0.016 ***	0.008	−0.015 **	−0.043 ***
	(0.006)	(0.009)	(0.006)	(0.010)
UE	−0.023 *	−0.104 ***	−0.020 *	−0.048 ***
	(0.012)	(0.017)	(0.011)	(0.009)
PU ≥ Th-1	−0.291 ***	−0.270 ***	−0.174 **	−0.092 ***
	(0.077)	(0.093)	(0.093)	(0.016)
PU ≥ Th-2& ≤ TH-1	−0.074 **	−0.005 ***	−0.071 ***	−0.038 ***
	(0.034)	(0.002)	(0.011)	(0.014)
PU < TH-2	0.031	0.104	0.026	0.067
	(0.046)	(0.069)	(0.077)	(0.055)
Constant	13.086 ***	25.987 ***	12.111 ***	22.783 ***
	(4.459)	(6.657)	(4.219)	(6.304)
Obs.	428	428	428	428

Standard errors are in parenthesis. *** $p < 0.01$, ** $p < 0.05$, and * $p < 0.1$. The economic meanings of thresholds 4.89 and 4.48 are equivalent to the original PU_NB scores of 132.39, and 87.98, respectively. SP refers to the NYSE composite index.

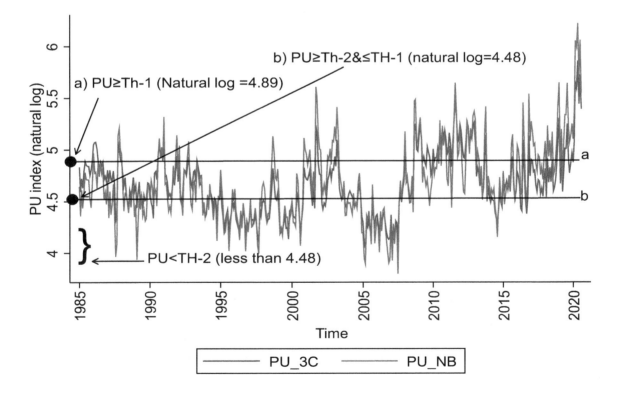

Figure 5. Illustration of identified thresholds (PU). Source: Baker, Bloom, and Davis [12].

5. Discussion

The empirical findings document a declining trend in stock prices in the short-run for both an increase and a decrease in PU. We have found that increased PU hurts stock prices while decreasing uncertainty increases them in the long-run. Following relevant literature, the study uses the New York Stock exchange composite index for baseline analysis and provides a comprehensive insight by extending the analysis to alternative stock indices (S&P 500, Dow Jones Industrial Average, Dow Jones Composite Average, NASDAQ Composite, NASDAQ 100, and Dow Jones Transpiration Average) for the United States. Moreover, besides the news-based measure of PU, we use three component-based uncertainties to affirm the baseline results. Interestingly, the findings produced by the alternative measures of stock prices (Dow Jones Industrial Average, Dow Jones Composite Average, and Dow Jones Transpiration Average) and PU are found consistent and robust.

For convenient discussion, the overall findings are categorized into three groups, namely, (1) DYS-ARDL output, (2) threshold points, and (3) channels following which PUs influence the stock prices.

(1)   It is observed that a 10% shock in PU_NB (both positive/negative) negatively drives the stock prices in the short- and long-run (as depicted by Figure 4). This may be attributable to standard investment behavior differentials, depicted by declining risk premiums, which constitutes a substantial part of security prices. More specifically, a decline in PU also reduces the risk premium, which was part of security prices before the decline in PU. In this scenario, risk-seeking investors may shift investments to relatively high-risk securities while risk-averse investors may continue trading in existing securities. This behavior causes disequilibrium to the traditional demand and supply metaphor; however, in the long run, this disequilibrium is automatically rectified with monthly rates of around 6.7, and 7%, respectively (see Table 4), and investment patterns are corrected accordingly.

(2)   The threshold(s) levels identified through threshold regression are interesting for policy matters. The PU score above the threshold point of 4.89 (natural log—equals 132.39 of original score) compels the pessimistic investors to be involved in selling their securities, which results in high supply and low demand, which causes a decline in stock prices and vice-versa for a decline in such risk. It is important to understand that a high level of PU appears to include most of the investors in shifting investments to relatively safe heavens, which, in contrast, behave differently for the second threshold. This difference denotes a relatively low magnitude in the explanation power of PU, which is still negative. In this stream between two threshold points (4.89–4.48 (132.39–87.98, original score)—the area covered between points a and b in Figure 2), the policy risk is not extremely high, which eventually influence the stock prices with relatively low magnitudes (Table 5, model (1), where coefficient changes from −0.291 to −0.07). This channel holds for models (2–4). While the stock price reaction to changes in PU below the second threshold appears to be irrelevant to decision making, it still carries a positive coefficient (which is statistically insignificant).

(3)   It may take any one or a combination of more than one to influence the stock prices. The impact of changes in PU may theoretically take any combination or one of the following avenues to trigger stock prices. It can cause a delay in important decisions (e.g., employment, investment, consumption, and savings) by stakeholders (policymakers, regulators, and businesses, and economic agents) [29]. It increases financing and production costs by affecting the supply and demand channels, exacerbating the decline in investments and economic contraction [17,30,31]. Finally, the financial risk may be amplified due to such changes, as it is argued that the jump risk premium associated with policy decisions should be positive on average [17], which also influences inflation, interest rates, and expected risk premiums [32,33]. Therefore, the firms facing increased uncertainty in economic policy will reduce their investments in the short- and long-term [28]. This argument is supported by [58], who recorded a negative reaction in

accounting-based performance measures of firm performance in response to an increase in PU in the context of listed non-financial corporations in the United States.

The readers may carefully interpret the results of the threshold by understanding the original PU scores of 132.39 and 87.98 for single and double thresholds, respectively.

Summing up this section, we find that the literature supports our findings, for example, Asgharian, Christiansen, and Hou [21]; Bahmani-Oskooee and Saha [15]; Christou, Cunado, Gupta, and Hassapis [23]; Ko and Lee (2015); and Arouri, Estay, Rault, and Roubaud [14]. However, the findings of Wu, Liu, and Hsueh [22]; Pirgaip [27]; and Bahmani-Oskooee and Saha [15] are not in the same line, documenting no effect of the US stock market to changes in PU. Therefore, the PU-stock market dilemma shall remain debatable in the future.

6. Conclusions

This study revisits the PU-stock prices nexus and extends the equity market modeling beyond traditional cointegration specification by providing short- and long-run implications of PU on stock prices of the United Stated using the novel DYS-ARDL setting proposed by Jordan and Philips [1]. The next vital contribution of this study is the identification of two significant thresholds of PU (see Figure 2 and Table 5), which is a useful addition to the equity market literature. Finally, we provide a comprehensive picture of the PU and stock price relationship in the US perspective by expanding the analysis across seven stock market indices. Because related literature mostly opts for S&P 500 and NYSEC indices as representative of the US equity market, it is worth mentioning that all indices of the United States stock market are not equally exposed to rising PU, which may help effective diversification of portfolio and associated riskiness.

One important conclusion is the significant negative impact of PU on stock prices across all measures in the short-run, which needs to be considered by stakeholders while making an investment decision or policy formulation. Nevertheless, under dynamic ARDL simulations perspectives, the study extends the equity market literature by producing evidence from the world's largest equity by size and tosses the debate to be examined across other major financial markets of the world.

This research empirically examines the PU and stock price connection in the context of the United States, which is ranked first in terms of market size [41], using Jordan and Philips's [1] novel estimator and threshold setting. Particularly, there may be some other economic factors that influence stock prices; this study followed recent literature [14,15] to include industrial production, default spread, inflation, and the unemployment rate as potential controls. To be specific in capturing the PU impact on US stock indices, this study departs from examining the response of stock prices to positive/negative shocks in each of the control variables. Besides controls, the study excludes other medium and small equity indices in the present analysis, which may be of sound interest for policy matters for small investors. In future research, such considerations may produce interesting findings. Another grey area may be the extension of the present methodology to a cross-country level, based on the development and/or income level. Such an extension, with a comparative image, may be beneficial to those who want to diversify the security market investment across national borders.

Author Contributions: Conceptualization, M.A.K., and M.A.; methodology, software and data curation, M.A.K.; writing—original draft preparation, M.A.K., and M.A.; writing—review and editing, J.P. and J.O. All authors have read and agreed to the published version of the manuscript.

Acknowledgments: We are grateful to Kamran Khan, a doctoral candidate at Northeast Normal University, School of Economics and Management for guidance in estimating the DYS-ARDL model and its technicalities. We are also appreciative of Juan, guest editor, for consistent guidance throughout the review process and finally of the constructive and encouraging suggestions by anonymous reviewers at the core of this manuscript, which we endorse vigorously.

Appendix A

Table A1. OLS baseline results.

	(1)	(2)	(3)	(4)	(5)
	SP	**SP**	**SP**	**SP**	**SP**
PU_NB	0.443 ***	−0.220 ***	−0.186 ***	−0.124 ***	−0.105 ***
	(0.072)	(0.021)	(0.029)	(0.022)	(0.022)
INF		0.717 ***	0.481 ***	0.531 ***	0.556 ***
		(0.023)	(0.228)	(0.186)	(0.150)
IP			0.301	0.269	0.176
			(0.280)	(0.226)	(0.189)
DS				−0.053 ***	−0.029 ***
				(0.005)	(0.007)
UE					−0.040 ***
					(0.009)
Constant	0.460 ***	−0.505 ***	−0.776 ***	−0.986 ***	−0.646 ***
	(0.343)	(0.130)	(0.205)	(0.165)	(0.208)
Obs.	428	428	428	428	428
R-squared	0.057	0.944	0.948	0.961	0.965

Standard errors are in parenthesis. *** $p < 0.01$. All the abbreviations are defined in Table 1.

Appendix B

Table A2. Robustness: alternative measures of SP.

	(1)	(2)	(3)	(4)	(5)	(6)
	SP_DJI	**SP_DJA**	**SP_SP**	**SP_NASDAQC**	**SP_NASDAQ100**	**SP_DJT**
ECT(−1)	−0.027 *	−0.048 ***	−0.016	−0.012	−0.011	−0.075 ***
	(0.016)	(0.018)	(0.014)	(0.012)	(0.011)	(0.023)
ΔPU_NB	−0.045 ***	−0.041 ***	−0.042 ***	−0.066 ***	−0.068 ***	−0.054 ***
	(0.008)	(0.008)	(0.008)	(0.012)	(0.014)	(0.012)
PU_NB	−0.006 ***	−0.007 **	0.004	0.006	0.006	−0.008 ***
	(0.002)	(0.003)	(0.007)	(0.010)	(0.012)	(0.003)
Constant	−0.162	−0.338 **	−0.127	−0.167	−0.195	−0.510 ***
	(0.127)	(0.137)	(0.125)	(0.154)	(0.212)	(0.187)
Obs.	427	427	427	427	418	343
F-statistics	5.92 ***	6.11 ***	5.95 ***	5.48 ***	4.51***	4.52 ***
Simulations	5000	5000	5000	5000	5000	5000

Standard errors are in parenthesis. *** $p < 0.01$, ** $p < 0.05$, and * $p < 0.1$. DJI: Dow Jones Industrial Average, DJA: Dow Jones Composite Average, S&P: S&P 500, NASDAQ Composite, NASDAQ100, and DJT: Dow Jones Transpiration Average. Controls are not shown in this table as they are the same as estimated in the baseline model.

References

1. Jordan, S.; Philips, A.Q. Cointegration testing, and dynamic simulations of autoregressive distributed lag models. *Stata J.* **2018**, *18*, 902–923. [CrossRef]
2. Stübinger, J.; Endres, S. Pairs trading with a mean-reverting jump—Diffusion model on high-frequency data. *Quant. Financ.* **2018**, *18*, 1735–1751. [CrossRef]
3. Avellaneda, M.; Lee, J.-H. Statistical arbitrage in the US equities market. *Quant. Financ.* **2010**, *10*, 761–782. [CrossRef]
4. Liu, B.; Chang, L.-B.; Geman, H. Intraday pairs trading strategies on high frequency data: The case of oil companies. *Quant. Financ.* **2017**, *17*, 87–100. [CrossRef]
5. Do, B.; Faff, R. Are Pairs Trading Profits Robust to Trading Costs? *J. Financ. Res.* **2012**, *35*, 261–287. [CrossRef]
6. Stübinger, J.; Mangold, B.; Krauss, C. Statistical arbitrage with vine copulas. *Quant. Financ.* **2018**, *18*, 1831–1849. [CrossRef]

7.   Khan, M.A.; Domicián, M.; Abdulahi, M.E.; Sadaf, R.; Khan, M.A.; Popp, J.; Oláh, J. Do Institutional Quality, Innovation and Technologies Promote Financial Market Development? *Eur. J. Int. Manag.* **2020**, *14*. [CrossRef]

8.   Khan, M.A.; Ilyas, R.M.A.; Hashmi, S.H. Cointegration between Institutional Quality and Stock Market Development. *NUML Int. J. Bus. Manag.* **2018**, *13*, 90–103.

9.   Khan, M.A.; Khan, M.A.; Abdulahi, M.E.; Liaqat, I.; Shah, S.S.H. Institutional quality and financial development: The United States perspective. *J. Multinatl. Financ. Manag.* **2019**, *49*, 67–80. [CrossRef]

10. Shah, S.S.H.; Khan, M.A.; Meyer, N.; Meyer, D.F.; Oláh, J. Does Herding Bias Drive the Firm Value? Evidence from the Chinese Equity Market. *Sustainability* **2019**, *11*, 5583. [CrossRef]

11. Tong, H. Threshold models in time series analysis—30 years on. *Stat. Interface* **2011**, *4*, 107–118. [CrossRef]

12. Baker, S.R.; Bloom, N.; Davis, S.J. Measuring economic policy uncertainty. *Q. J. Econ.* **2016**, *131*, 1593–1636. [CrossRef]

13. Sum, V. Economic policy uncertainty in the United States and Europe: A cointegration test. *Int. J. Econ. Financ.* **2013**, *5*, 98–101. [CrossRef]

14. Arouri, M.; Estay, C.; Rault, C.; Roubaud, D. Economic policy uncertainty and stock markets: Long-run evidence from the US. *Financ. Res. Lett.* **2016**, *18*, 136–141. [CrossRef]

15. Bahmani-Oskooee, M.; Saha, S. On the effects of policy uncertainty on stock prices. *J. Econ. Financ.* **2019**, *43*, 764–778. [CrossRef]

16. Das, D.; Kumar, S.B. International economic policy uncertainty and stock prices revisited: Multiple and Partial wavelet approach. *Econ. Lett.* **2018**, *164*, 100–108. [CrossRef]

17. Pastor, L.; Veronesi, P. Uncertainty about government policy and stock prices. *J. Financ.* **2012**, *67*, 1219–1264. [CrossRef]

18. Sum, V. Economic policy uncertainty and stock market performance: Evidence from the European Union, Croatia, Norway, Russia, Switzerland, Turkey and Ukraine. *J. Money Invest. Bank.* **2012**, *25*, 99–104. [CrossRef]

19. Li, X.-l.; Balcilar, M.; Gupta, R.; Chang, T. The causal relationship between economic policy uncertainty and stock returns in China and India: Evidence from a bootstrap rolling window approach. *Emerg. Mark. Financ. Trade* **2016**, *52*, 674–689. [CrossRef]

20. Gao, J.; Zhu, S.; O'Sullivan, N.; Sherman, M. The role of economic uncertainty in UK stock returns. *J. Risk Financ. Manag.* **2019**, *12*, 5. [CrossRef]

21. Asgharian, H.; Christiansen, C.; Hou, A.J. Economic Policy Uncertainty and Long-Run Stock Market Volatility and Correlation. Available online: https://papers.ssrn.com/sol3/papers.cfm?abstract_id=3146924 (accessed on 29 October 2020).

22. Wu, T.-P.; Liu, S.-B.; Hsueh, S.-J. The causal relationship between economic policy uncertainty and stock market: A panel data analysis. *Int. Econ. J.* **2016**, *30*, 109–122. [CrossRef]

23. Christou, C.; Cunado, J.; Gupta, R.; Hassapis, C. Economic policy uncertainty and stock market returns in PacificRim countries: Evidence based on a Bayesian panel VAR model. *J. Multinatl. Financ. Manag.* **2017**, *40*, 92–102. [CrossRef]

24. Sum, V. Economic Policy Uncertainty and Stock Market Returns. *SSRN Electron. J.* **2012**. [CrossRef]

25. Debata, B.; Mahakud, J. Economic policy uncertainty and stock market liquidity: Does financial crisis make any difference? *J. Financ. Econ. Policy* **2018**, *10*, 112–135. [CrossRef]

26. Škrinjarić, T.; Orlović, Z. Economic policy uncertainty and stock market spillovers: Case of selected CEE markets. *Mathematics* **2020**, *8*, 1077. [CrossRef]

27. Pirgaip, B. The causal relationship between stock markets and policy uncertainty in OECD countries. In Proceedings of the RSEP International Conferences on Social Issues and Economic Studies, Barcelona, Spain, 7–10 November 2017.

28. Chen, P.-F.; Lee, C.-C.; Zeng, J.-H. Economic policy uncertainty and firm investment: Evidence from the U.S. market. *Appl. Econ.* **2019**, *51*, 3423–3435. [CrossRef]

29. Gulen, H.; Ion, M. Policy uncertainty and corporate investment. *Rev. Financ. Stud.* **2016**, *29*, 523–564. [CrossRef]

30. Julio, B.; Yook, Y. Corporate financial policy under political uncertainty: International evidence from national elections. *J. Financ.* **2012**, *67*, 45–84. [CrossRef]

31. Leduc, S.; Liu, Z. Uncertainty shocks are aggregate demand shocks. *J. Monet. Econ.* **2016**, *82*, 20–35. [CrossRef]

32. Pástor, L'.; Veronesi, P. Political uncertainty and risk premia. *J. Financ. Econ.* **2013**, *110*, 520–545. [CrossRef]

33. Bernal, O.; Gnabo, J.-Y.; Guilmin, G. Economic policy uncertainty and risk spillovers in the Eurozone. *J. Int. Money Financ.* **2016**, *65*, 24–45. [CrossRef]

34. Ko, J.-H.; Lee, C.-M. International economic policy uncertainty and stock prices: Wavelet approach. *Econ. Lett.* **2015**, *134*, 118–122. [CrossRef]

35. Pesaran, M.H.; Shin, Y.; Smith, R.J. Bounds testing approaches to the analysis of level relationships. *J. Appl. Econom.* **2001**, *16*, 289–326. [CrossRef]

36. Shin, Y.; Yu, B.; Greenwood-Nimmo, M. Modelling asymmetric cointegration and dynamic multipliers in a nonlinear ARDL framework. In *Festschrift in Honor of Peter Schmidt*; Springer: Berlin/Heidelberg, Germany, 2014; pp. 281–314.

37. Khan, M.I.; Teng, J.Z.; Khan, M.K. The impact of macroeconomic and financial development on carbon dioxide emissions in Pakistan: Evidence with a novel dynamic simulated ARDL approach. *Environ. Sci. Pollut. Res.* **2020**, *27*, 39560–39571. [CrossRef] [PubMed]

38. Khan, M.K.; Teng, J.-Z.; Khan, M.I.; Khan, M.O. Impact of globalization, economic factors and energy consumption on CO_2 emissions in Pakistan. *Sci. Total Environ.* **2019**, *688*, 424–436. [CrossRef] [PubMed]

39. Zapata, H.O.; Gauthier, W.M. Threshold models in theory and practice. In Proceedings of the 2003 Annual Meeting of the Southern Agricultural Economics Association, Mobile, AL, USA, 1–5 February 2003.

40. Hansen, B.E. Threshold autoregression in economics. *Stat. Interface* **2011**, *4*, 123–127. [CrossRef]

41. Szmigiera, M. Largest Stock Exchange Operators, Listed by Market Cap of Listed Companies 2020. 2020. Available online: https://www.statista.com/statistics/270126/largest-stock-exchange-operators-by-market-capitalization-of-listed-companies/ (accessed on 20 May 2020).

42. Liu, L.; Zhang, T. Economic policy uncertainty and stock market volatility. *Financ. Res. Lett.* **2015**, *15*, 99–105. [CrossRef]

43. Ehrmann, M.; Fratzscher, M. Global financial transmission of monetary policy shocks. *Oxf. Bull. Econ. Stat.* **2009**, *71*, 739–759. [CrossRef]

44. Brogaard, J.; Detzel, A. The asset-pricing implications of government economic policy uncertainty. *Manag. Sci.* **2015**, *61*, 3–18. [CrossRef]

45. Antonakakis, N.; Chatziantoniou, I.; Filis, G. Dynamic co-movements of stock market returns, implied volatility and policy uncertainty. *Econ. Lett.* **2013**, *120*, 87–92. [CrossRef]

46. Dakhlaoui, I.; Aloui, C. The interactive relationship between the US economic policy uncertainty and BRIC stock markets. *Int. Econ.* **2016**, *146*, 141–157. [CrossRef]

47. Yang, M.; Jiang, Z.-Q. The dynamic correlation between policy uncertainty and stock market returns in China. *Phys. A Stat. Mech. Appl.* **2016**, *461*, 92–100. [CrossRef]

48. Yahoo-Finance. 2020. Available online: https://finance.yahoo.com/ (accessed on 1 September 2020).

49. FRED, Federal Reserve Economic Data. 2020. Available online: https://fred.stlouisfed.org/ (accessed on 28 September 2020).

50. Abdulahi, M.E.; Shu, Y.; Khan, M.A. Resource rents, economic growth, and the role of institutional quality: A panel threshold analysis. *Resour. Policy* **2019**, *61*, 293–303. [CrossRef]

51. Khan, M.A.; Gu, L.; Khan, M.A.; Oláh, J. Natural Resources and Financial Development: The Role of Institutional Quality. *J. Multinatl. Financ. Manag.* **2020**, *56*, 100641. [CrossRef]

52. Khan, M.A.; Islam, M.A.; Akbar, U. Do economic freedom matters for finance in developing economies: A panel threshold analysis. *Appl. Econ. Lett.* **2020**, 1–4. [CrossRef]

53. Liu, H.; Islam, M.A.; Khan, M.A.; Hossain, M.I.; Pervaiz, K. Does financial deepening attract foreign direct investment? Fresh evidence from panel threshold analysis. *Res. Int. Bus. Financ.* **2020**, *53*, 101198. [CrossRef]

54. Kwiatkowski, D.; Phillips, P.C.B.; Schmidt, P.; Shin, Y. Testing the null hypothesis of stationarity against the alternative of a unit root. *J. Econom.* **1992**, *54*, 159–178. [CrossRef]

55. Baum, C. *KPSS: Stata Module to Compute Kwiatkowski-Phillips-Schmidt-Shin Test for Stationarity*; Boston College Department of Economics: Boston, MA, USA, 2000.

56. Bahmani-Oskooee, M.; Saha, S. On the effects of policy uncertainty on stock prices: An asymmetric analysis. *Quant. Financ. Econ.* **2019**, *3*, 412–424. [CrossRef]

57. Khan, M.K.; Teng, J.-Z.; Khan, M.I. Effect of energy consumption and economic growth on carbon dioxide emissions in Pakistan with dynamic ARDL simulations approach. *Environ. Sci. Pollut. Res.* **2019**, *26*, 23480–23490. [CrossRef]

58. Iqbal, U.; Gan, C.; Nadeem, M. Economic policy uncertainty and firm performance. *Appl. Econ. Lett.* **2020**, *27*, 765–770. [CrossRef]

8

A Novel Methodology to Calculate the Probability of Volatility Clusters in Financial Series: An Application to Cryptocurrency Markets

Venelina Nikolova [1,†], Juan E. Trinidad Segovia [1,*,†], Manuel Fernández-Martínez [2,†] and Miguel Angel Sánchez-Granero [3,†]

[1]   Department of Accounting and Finance, Faculty of Economics and Business, Universidad de Almería, 04120 Almería, Spain; vdn088@inlumine.ual.es

[2]   University Centre of Defence at the Spanish Air Force Academy, MDE-UPCT, 30720 Santiago de la Ribera, Región de Murcia, Spain; manuel.fernandez-martinez@cud.upct.es

[3]   Department of Mathematics, Faculty of Science, Universidad de Almería, 04120 Almería, Spain; misanche@ual.es

*   Correspondence: jetrini@ual.es

†   These authors contributed equally to this work.

Abstract: One of the main characteristics of cryptocurrencies is the high volatility of their exchange rates. In a previous work, the authors found that a process with volatility clusters displays a volatility series with a high Hurst exponent. In this paper, we provide a novel methodology to calculate the probability of volatility clusters with a special emphasis on cryptocurrencies. With this aim, we calculate the Hurst exponent of a volatility series by means of the FD4 approach. An explicit criterion to computationally determine whether there exist volatility clusters of a fixed size is described. We found that the probabilities of volatility clusters of an index (S&P500) and a stock (Apple) showed a similar profile, whereas the probability of volatility clusters of a forex pair (Euro/USD) became quite lower. On the other hand, a similar profile appeared for Bitcoin/USD, Ethereum/USD, and Ripple/USD cryptocurrencies, with the probabilities of volatility clusters of all such cryptocurrencies being much greater than the ones of the three traditional assets. Our results suggest that the volatility in cryptocurrencies changes faster than in traditional assets, and much faster than in forex pairs.

Keywords: volatility cluster; Hurst exponent; FD4 approach; volatility series; probability of volatility cluster; S&P500; Bitcoin; Ethereum; Ripple

1. Introduction

It is easy to observe that large fluctuations in stock market prices are followed by large ones, whereas small fluctuations in prices are more likely to be followed by small ones. This property is known as volatility clustering. Recent works, such as [1,2], have shown that while large fluctuations tend to be more clustered than small ones, large losses tend to lump together more severely than large gains. The financial literature is interested in modeling volatility clustering since the latter is considered as a key indicator of market risk. In fact, the trading volume of some assets, such as derivatives, increases over time, making volatility their most important pricing factor.

It is worth mentioning that both, high and low volatilities, seem to be a relevant factor for stock market crises according to Danielsson et al. [3]. They also found that the relation between unexpected volatility and the incidence of crises became stronger in the last few decades. In the same line, Valentine et al. [4] showed that market instability is not only the result of large volatility, but also of small volatility.

The classical approach for volatility clusters lies in nonlinear models, based on heteroskedastic conditionally variance. They include ARCH [5], GARCH [6–8], IGARCH [9], and FIGARCH [10,11] models.

On the other hand, agent-based models allow reproducing and explaining some stylized facts of financial markets [12]. Interestingly, several works have recently been appeared in the literature analyzing a complete order book by real-time simulation [13–15]. Regarding the volatility clustering, it is worth mentioning that Lux et al. [16] highlighted that volatility is explained by market instability. Later, Raberto et al. [17] introduced an agent-based artificial market whose heterogeneous agents exchange only one asset, which exhibits some key stylized facts of financial markets. They found that the volatility clustering effect is sensitive to the model size, i.e., when the number of operators increases, the volatility clustering effect tends to disappear. That result is in accordance with the concept of market efficiency.

Krawiecki et al. [18] introduced a microscopic model consisting of many agents with random interactions. Then the volatility clustering phenomenon appears as a result of attractor bubbling. Szabolcs and Farmer [19] empirically developed a behavioral model for order placement to study endogenous dynamics of liquidity and price formation in the order book. They were able to describe volatility through the order flow parameters.

Alfarano et al. [20] contributed a simple model of an agent-based artificial market with volatility clustering generated due to interaction between traders. Similar conclusions were obtained by Cont [21], Chen [22], He et al. [23], and Schmitt and Westerhoff [24].

Other findings on the possible causes of volatility clusters are summarized below. Cont [21] showed that volatility is explained by agent behavior; Chen [22] stated that return volatility correlations arise from asymmetric trading and investors' herding behavior; He et al. [23] concluded that trade between fundamental noise and noise traders causes the volatility clustering; and Schmitt and Westerhoff [24] highlighted that volatility clustering arises due to the herding behavior of speculators.

Chen et al. [25] proposed an agent-based model with multi-level herding to reproduce the volatilities of New York and Hong Kong stocks. Shi et al. [26] explained volatility clustering through a model of security price dynamics with two kind of participants, namely speculators and fundamental investors. They considered that information arrives randomly to the market, which leads to changes in the viewpoint of the market participants according to a certain ratio. Verma et al. [27] used a factor model to analyze how market volatility could be explained by assets' volatility.

An interesting contribution was made by Barde in [28], where the author compared the performance of this kind of model with respect to the ARCH/GARCH models. In fact, the author remarked that the performance of three kinds of agent-based models for financial markets is better in key events. Population switching was found also as a crucial factor to explain volatility clustering and fat tails.

On the other hand, the concept of a volatility series was introduced in [2] to study the volatility clusters in the S&P500 series. Moreover, it was shown that the higher the self-similarity exponent of the volatility series of the S&P500, the more frequent the volatility changes and, therefore, the more likely that the volatility clusters appear. In the current article, we provide a novel methodology to calculate the probability of volatility clusters of a given size in a series with special emphasis on cryptocurrencies.

Since the introduction of Bitcoin in 2008, the cryptocurrency market has experienced a constant growth, just like the use of crypto assets as an investment or medium of exchange day to day. As of June 2020, there are 5624 cryptocurrencies, and their market capitalization exceeds 255 billion USD according to the website CoinMarketCap [29]. However, one of the main characteristics of cryptocurrencies is the high volatility of their exchange rates, and consequently, the high risk associated with their use.

Lately, Bitcoin has received more and more attention by researchers. Compared to the traditional financial markets, the cryptocurrency market is very young, and because of this, there are relatively few research works on their characteristics, and all of them quite recent. Some of the authors analyzed the Bitcoin market efficiency by applying different approaches, including the Hurst exponent (cf. [30] for a detailed review), whereas others investigated its volatility using other methods. For instance, Letra [31] used a GARCH model for Bitcoin daily data; Bouoiyour and Selmi [32] carried out many extensions of GARCH models to estimate Bitcoin price dynamics; Bouri, Azzi, and Dyhberg [33] analyzed the relation between volatility changes and price returns of Bitcoin based on an asymmetric GARCH model; Balcilar et al. [34] analyzed the relation between the trading volume of Bitcoin and its returns and volatility by employing, in contrast, a non-parametric causality in quantiles test; and Baur et al. [35] studied the statistical properties of Bitcoin and its relations with traditional asset classes.

Meanwhile, in 2017, Bariviera et al. [36] used the Hurst exponent to compare Bitcoin dynamics with standard currencies' dynamics and detected evidence of persistent volatility and long memory, facts that justify the GARCH-type models' application to Bitcoin prices. Shortly after that, Phillip et al. [37] provided evidence of slight leverage effects, volatility clustering, and varied kurtosis. Furthermore, Zhang et al. [38] analyzed the first eight cryptocurrencies that represent almost 70% of cryptocurrency market capitalization and pointed out that the returns of cryptocurrencies exhibit leverage effects and strong volatility clustering.

Later, in 2019, Kancs et al. [39], based on the GARCH model, estimated factors that affect Bitcoin price. For it, they used hourly data for the period between 2013 and 2018. After plotting the data graphically, they suggested that periods of high volatility follow periods of high volatility, and periods of low volatility follow periods of low volatility, so in the series, large returns follow large returns and small returns small returns. All these facts indicate evidence of volatility clustering and, therefore, that the residue is conditionally heteroscedastic.

The structure of this article is as follows. Firstly, Section 2 contains some mathematical basic concepts on measure theory and probability (Section 2.1), the FD4 approach Section 2.2), and the volatility series (Section 2.3). The core of the current paper is provided in Section 3, where we explain in detail how to calculate the probability of volatility clusters of a given size. A study of volatility clusters in several cryptocurrencies, as well as in traditional exchanges is carried out in Section 4. Finally, Section 5 summarizes the main conclusions of this work.

2. Methods

This section contains some mathematical tools of both measure and probability theories (cf. Section 2.1) that allow us to mathematically describe the FD4 algorithm applied in this article (cf. Section 2.2) to calculate the self-similarity index of time series. On the other hand, the concept of a volatility series is addressed in Section 2.3.

2.1. Random Functions, Their Increments, and Self-Affinity Properties

Let $t \geq 0$ denote time and $(X, \mathcal{A}, P)$ be a probability space. We shall understand that $\mathbf{X} = \{X_t \equiv X(t, \omega) : t \geq 0\}$ is a random process (also a random function) from $[0, \infty) \times \Omega$ to $\mathbb{R}$, if X_t is a random variable for all $t \geq 0$ and $\omega \in \Omega$, where Ω denotes a sample space. As such, we may think of $\mathbf{X}$ as defining a sample function $t \mapsto X_t$ for all $\omega \in \Omega$. Hence, the points in Ω do parameterize the functions $\mathbf{X} : [0, \infty) \to \mathbb{R}$ with P being a measure of probability in the class of such functions.

Let X_t and Y_t be two random functions. The notation $X_t \sim Y_t$ means that the finite joint distribution functions of such random functions are the same. A random process $\mathbf{X} = \{X_t : t \geq 0\}$ is said to be self-similar if there exists a parameter $H > 0$ such that the following power law holds:

$$X_{at} \sim a^H X_t \tag{1}$$

for each $a > 0$ and $t \geq 0$. If Equation (1) is fulfilled, then H is named the self-similarity exponent (also index) of the process $\mathbf{X}$. On the other hand, the increments of a random function X_t are said to be stationary as long as $X_{a+t} - X_a \sim X_t - X_0$ for all $t \geq 0$ and $a > 0$. We shall understand that the increments of a random function are self-affine of the parameter $H \geq 0$ if the next power law stands for all $h > 0$ and $t_0 \geq 0$:

$$X_{t_0+\tau} - X_{t_0} \sim h^{-H} \left(X_{t_0+h\tau} - X_{t_0} \right).$$

Let X_t be a random function with self-affine increments of the parameter H. Then, the following T^H-law holds:

$$\mathcal{M}_T \sim T^H \, \mathcal{M}_1,$$

where its (T-period) cumulative range is defined as:

$$\mathcal{M}_{t,T} := \sup \left\{ X(s, \omega) - X(t, \omega) : s \in [t, t+T] \right\} - \inf \left\{ X(s, \omega) - X(t, \omega) : s \in [t, t+T] \right\},$$

and $\mathcal{M}_T := \mathcal{M}_{0,T}$ (cf. Corollary 3.6 in [40]).

2.2. The FD4 Approach

The FD4 approach was first contributed in [41] to deal with calculations concerning the self-similarity exponent of random processes. It was proven that the FD4 generalizes the GM2 procedure (cf. [42,43]), as well as the fractal dimension algorithms (cf. [44]) to calculate the Hurst exponent of any process with stationary and self-affine increments (cf. Theorem 3.1 in [41]). Moreover, the accuracy of such an algorithm was analyzed for samples of (fractional) Brownian motions and Lévy stable processes with lengths ranging from 2^5 to 2^{10} points (cf. Section 5 in [41]).

Next, we mathematically show how that parameter could be calculated by the FD4 procedure. First of all, let $\mathbf{X} = \{ X_t : t \geq 0 \}$ be a random process with stationary increments. Let $q > 0$, and assume that for each $X_t \in \mathbf{X}$, there exists $m_q(X_t) := \mathrm{E}\left[|X_t|^q \right]$, its (absolute) q-order moment. Suppose, in addition, that there exists a parameter $H > 0$ for which the next relation, which involves (τ-period) cumulative ranges of $\mathbf{X}$, holds:

$$\mathcal{M}_\tau \sim \tau^H \, \mathcal{M}_1. \tag{2}$$

Recall that this power law stands for the class of (H-)self-similar processes with self-affine increments (of parameter H; see Section 2.1), which, roughly speaking, is equivalent to the class of processes with stationary increments (cf. Lemma 1.7.2 in [45]). Let us discretize the period by $\tau_n = 2^{-n} : n \in \mathbb{N}$ and take q-powers on both sides of Equation (2). Thus, we have:

$$\mathcal{M}_{\tau_n}^q \sim \tau_n^{qH} \, \mathcal{M}_1^q \text{ for all } n \in \mathbb{N}. \tag{3}$$

Clearly, the expression in Equation (3) could be rewritten in the following terms:

$$X_n^q \sim \tau_n^{qH} X_0^q = 2^{-nqH} X_0 \tag{4}$$

where, for short, the notation $X_n := \mathcal{M}_{\tau_n} = \mathcal{M}_{2^{-n}}$ is used for all $n \in \mathbb{N}$. Since the two random variables in Equation (4) are equally distributed, their means must be the same, i.e.,

$$m_q(X_n) = \mathrm{E}\left[X_n^q \right] = 2^{-nqH} \, \mathrm{E}\left[X_0^q \right] = 2^{-nqH} m_q(X_0). \tag{5}$$

Taking (2-base) logarithms on both sides of Equation (5), the parameter H could be obtained by carrying out a linear regression of:

$$H = \frac{1}{nq} \log_2 \frac{m_q(X_0)}{m_q(X_n)}. \tag{6}$$

vs. q. Alternatively, observe that the expression in Equation (4) also provides a relation between cumulative ranges of consecutive periods of $\mathbf{X}$, i.e.,

$$X_n^q \sim 2^{qH} X_{n+1}^q. \tag{7}$$

Since the random variables on each side of Equation (7) have the same (joint) distribution function, their means must be equal, namely,

$$m_q(X_n) = \mathrm{E}\,[X_n^q] = 2^{q\,H}\,\mathrm{E}\,[X_{n+1}^q] = 2^{q\,H}\,m_q(X_{n+1}) \text{ for all } n \in \mathbb{N}, \tag{8}$$

which provides a strong connection between consecutive moments of order q of $\mathbf{X}$. If (two-base) logarithms are taken on both sides of Equation (8), a linear regression of the expression appearing in Equation (9) vs. q allows calculating the self-similarity exponent of $\mathbf{X}$ (whenever self-similar patterns do exist for such a process):

$$H = \frac{1}{q}\,\log_2 \frac{m_q(X_n)}{m_q(X_{n+1})}. \tag{9}$$

Hence, the FD algorithm is defined as the approach whose running is based on the expressions appearing in either Equation (5) or Equation (8). The main restriction underlying the FD algorithm consists of the assumption regarding the existence of the q-order moments of the random process $\mathbf{X}$. At first glance, any non-zero value could be assigned to q to calculate the self-similarity exponent (provided that the existence of that sample moment could be guaranteed). In the case of Lévy stable motions, for example, given q_0, it may occur that $m_q(X_n)$ does not exist for any $q > q_0$. As such, we shall select $q = 0.01$ to calculate the self-similarity index of a time series by the FD algorithm, thus leading to the so-called FD4 algorithm. Equivalently, the FD4 approach denotes the FD algorithm for $q = 0.01$. In this paper, the self-similarity exponent of a series by the FD4 approach is calculated according to the expression in Equation (6). Indeed, since it is equivalent to:

$$\log_2 m_q(X_n) = \log_2 m_q(X_0) - nqH,$$

the Hurst exponent of the series is obtained as the slope of a linear regression, which compares $\log_2 m_q(X_n)$ with respect to n. In addition, notice that a regression coefficient close to one means that the expression in Equation (5) is fulfilled. As such, the calculation of $m_q(X_n)$ becomes necessary to deal with the procedure described above, and for each n, it depends on a given sample of the random variable $X_n \in \mathbf{X}$. For computational purposes, the length of any sample of X_n is chosen to be equal to 2^n. Accordingly, the greater n, the more accurate the value of $m_q(X_n)$ is. Next, we explain how to calculate $m_q(X_n)$. Let a log-price series be given, and divide it into 2^n non-overlapping blocks, $\mathcal{B}_i : i = 1, \ldots, 2^n$. The length of each block is $k := 2^{-n} \cdot \text{length(series)}$, so for each $i = 1, \ldots, 2^n$, we can write $\mathcal{B}_i = \{B_1, \ldots, B_k\}$. Then:

1. Determine the range of each block $\mathcal{B}_i$, i.e., calculate $R_i = \max\{B_j : j = 1, \ldots, k\} - \min\{B_j : j = 1, \ldots, k\}$ for each $i = 1, \ldots, 2^n$.
2. The (q-order) sample moment is given by $m_q(X_n) = 2^{-n} \sum_{i=1}^{2^n} R_i^q$.

According to the step (1), both the minimum and the maximum values of each period are required to calculate each range R_i. In this way, notice that such values are usually known for each trading period in the context of financial series. It is also worth noting that when n takes the value $\log_2(\text{length(series)})$, then each block only consists of a single element. In this case, though, each range R_i can be still computed.

2.3. The Volatility Series

The concept of a volatility series was first contributed in Section 2.2 of [2] as an alternative to classical (G)ARCH models with the aim to detect volatility clusters in series of asset returns from the S&P500 index. It was found, interestingly, that whether clusters of high (resp., low) volatility appear in the series, then the self-similarity exponent of the associated volatility series increases (resp., decreases).

Let r_n denote the log-return series of a (index/stock) series. In financial series, the autocorrelation function of the r_n's is almost null, though the $|r_n|$ series is not. The associated volatility series is defined as $s_n = |r_n| + s_{n-1} - m$, where $|\cdot|$ refers to the absolute value function, m is a constant, and $s_0 = 0$. For practical purposes, we set $m = \text{mean } |r_n|$.

Next, we explain how the Hurst exponent of the volatility series, s_n, could provide a useful tool to detect volatility clusters in a series of asset returns. Firstly, assume that the volatility of the series is constant. Then, the values of the associated volatility series would be similar to those from a sample of a Brownian motion. Hence, the self-similarity exponent of that volatility series would become close to 0.5. On the contrary, suppose that there exist some clusters of high (resp., low) volatility in the series. Thus, the graph of its associated volatility series becomes smoother, as illustrated in Figure 1, which also depicts the concept of a volatility series. Hence, almost all the values of the volatility series are greater (resp., lower) than the mean of the series. Accordingly, the volatility series turns out to be increasing (resp., decreasing), so its self-similarity exponent also increases (resp., decreases).

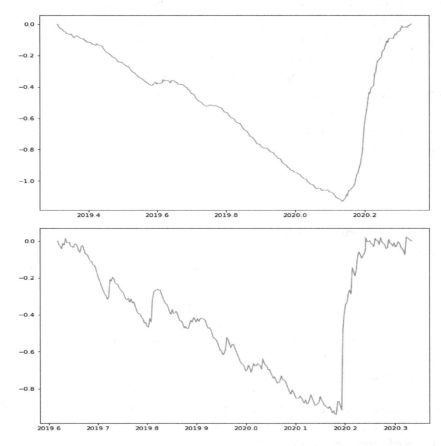

Figure 1. The picture at the top depicts the volatility series of the S&P500 index in the period ranging from March 2019 to March 2020. A self-similarity exponent equal to 0.94 is obtained by the FD4 approach. The graph below illustrates the volatility series of the Bitcoin/USD index in a similar period (both series contain 250 data (one year of trading), but recall that the Bitcoin/USD currency remains active also on weekends). In that case, a self-similarity exponent equal to 0.65 is obtained.

Following the above, the Hurst exponent of the volatility series of an index or asset provides a novel approach to explore the presence of volatility clusters in series of asset returns.

3. Calculating the Probability of Volatility Clusters of a Given Size

In this section, we explore how to estimate the probability of the existence of volatility clusters for blocks of a given size. Equivalently, we shall address the next question: What is the probability that a volatility cluster appears in a period of a given size? Next, we show that the Hurst exponent of a volatility series (see Sections 2.2 and 2.3) for blocks of that size plays a key role.

We know that the Hurst exponent of the volatility series is high when there are volatility clusters in the series [2]. However, how high should it be?

To deal with this, we shall assume that the series of (log-)returns follows a Gaussian distribution. However, it cannot be an i.i.d. process since the standard deviation of the Gaussian distribution is allowed to change. This hypothesis is more general than an ARCH or GARCH model, for example. Since we are interested in the real possibility that the volatility changes and, in fact, there exist volatility clusters, a static fixed distribution cannot be assumed. In this way, it is worth noting that the return distribution of these kinds of processes (generated from Gaussian distributions with different standard deviations) is not Gaussian, and it is flexible enough to allow very different kinds of distributions.

As such, let us assume that the series of the log-returns, r_n, follows a normal distribution, $N(0, \sigma(n))$, where its standard deviation varies over time via the function $\sigma(n)$. In fact, some classical models such as ARCH, GARCH, etc., stand as particular cases of that model. As such, we shall analyze the existence of volatility clusters in the following terms. We consider that there exist volatility clusters as long as there are, at least, both, a period of high volatility and a period of low volatility. Figure 2 illustrates that condition. Indeed, two broad periods could be observed concerning the volatility series of the S&P500 index. The first one has a low volatility (and hence, a decreasing volatility series) and the second one a high volatility (and hence, an increasing volatility series). In this case, the effect of the higher volatility (due to the COVID-19 crisis) is evident, thus being confirmed by a very high Hurst exponent of the corresponding volatility series (equal to 0.94).

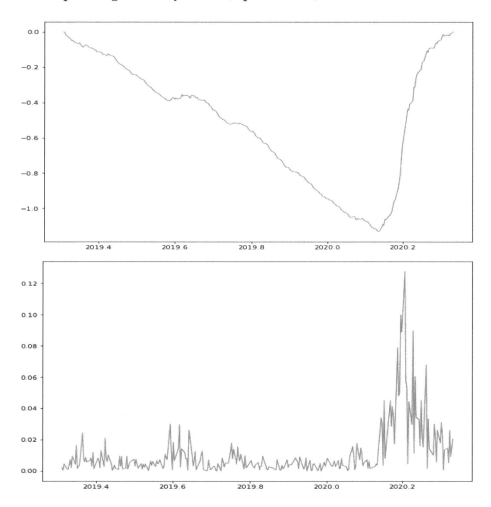

Figure 2. The graph at the top depicts the volatility series of the S&P500 index in the period ranging from March 2019 to March 2020. On the other hand, the chart at the bottom shows the series of absolute values of the log-returns of the S&P500 in the same period. That period, the self-similarity index of the volatility series of the S&P500, was found to be equal to 0.94 by the FD4 algorithm.

On the other hand, Figure 3 depicts the volatility series of the S&P500 index in the period ranging from January 2017 to January 2018. A self-similarity index equal to 0.55 was found by the FD4 algorithm. In this case, though, it is not so clear that there are volatility clusters, which is in accordance with the low Hurst exponent of that volatility series.

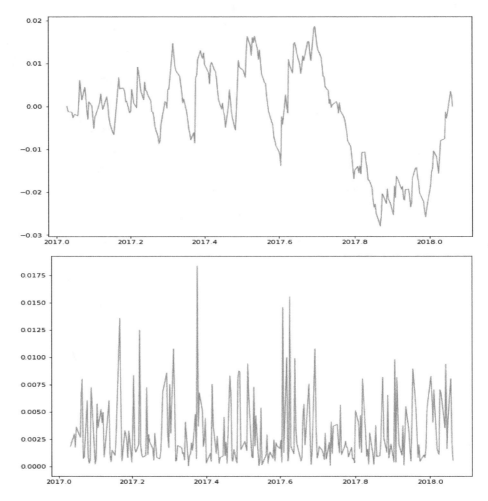

Figure 3. The plot at the top illustrates the volatility series of the S&P500 index in the period ranging from January 2017 to January 2018, whereas the graph at the bottom depicts the series of absolute values of the log-returns of the S&P500 index in the same period. In this case, the self-similarity exponent of the volatility series was found to be equal to 0.55 by the FD4 approach.

As such, the Hurst exponent of the volatility series of a Brownian motion will be considered as a benchmark in order to decide whether there are volatility clusters in the series. More precisely, first, by Monte Carlo simulation, a collection of Brownian motions was generated. For each Brownian motion, the Hurst exponents (by FD4 approach) of their corresponding volatility series were calculated. Hence, we denote by $H_{\lim}(n)$ the value that becomes greater than 90% of those Hurst exponents. Observe that $H_{\lim}(n)$ depends on n, the length of the Brownian motion sample. In fact, for a short series, the accuracy of the FD4 algorithm to calculate the Hurst exponent is lower. Accordingly, the value of $H_{\lim}(n)$ will be higher for a lower value of n. Figure 4 illustrates (for the 90th percentile) how the benchmark given by $H_{\lim}(n)$ becomes lower as the length of the Brownian motion series increases.

Therefore, we will use the following criteria. We say that there are volatility clusters in the series provided that the Hurst exponent of the corresponding volatility series is greater than $H_{\lim}$. Then, we will measure the probability of volatility clusters for subseries of a given length as the ratio between the number of subseries with volatility clusters to the total amount of subseries of the given length.

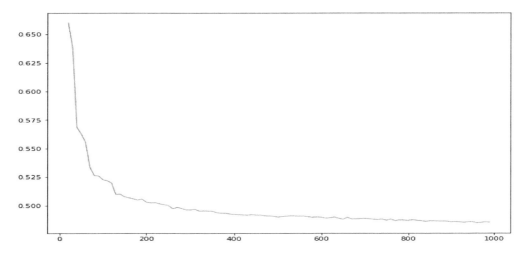

Figure 4. The 90th percentile, $H_{\lim}(n)$, of the Hurst exponents of the volatility series of Brownian motions for several values of the length of the series, n.

In order to check that measure of the probability of volatility clusters, we will test it by artificial processes with volatility clusters of a fixed length (equal to 200 data). A sample from that process is generated as follows. For the first 200 data, generate a sample from a normal distribution $N(0, 0.01)$; for the next 200 data, generate a sample from a normal distribution $N(0, 0.03)$; for the next 200 data, generate a sample from a normal distribution $N(0, 0.01)$, and so on. It is worth pointing out that a mixture of (samples from) normal distributions with distinct standard deviations can lead to (a sample from) a heavy-tailed distribution. Following that example, Figure 5 depicts the distribution of that artificial process with volatility clusters compared to the one from a Gaussian distribution and also to the S&P500 return distribution (rescaled). It is clear that the process is far from Gaussian even in that easy example.

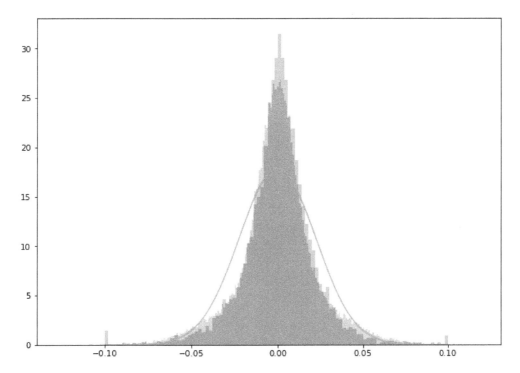

Figure 5. Histogram or density function of: (orange) return distribution of the S&P500 (rescaled and clipped to the interval $[-0.1, 0.1]$); (blue) process with volatility clusters of a fixed length (200 data); (green) normal distribution.

For that process, consider one random block of length 50. It may happen that such a block fully lies in a 200 block of fixed volatility. In this case, there will be no volatility clusters. However, if the first 20 data lie in a block of volatility equal to 0.01, with the remaining 30 data lying in a block of volatility equal to 0.03, then such a block will have volatility clusters. On the other hand, it is clear that if we have one block of length 50 with the first 49 data lying in a block of volatility equal to 0.01, whereas the remaining one datum lies in a block of 0.03 volatility, we cannot say that there are volatility clusters in such a block. Therefore, we shall consider that there are volatility clusters if there are at least 10 data in blocks with distinct volatilities. In other words, we shall assume that we cannot detect clusters with less that 10 data.

On the other hand, note that we are using a confidence level of 90%, and hence, if we get a probability of volatility clusters of, say, $x\%$, that means that there are no volatility clusters regarding the $(100 - x)\%$ of the blocks of the given size. However, for that confidence level of 90%, we are missing 10% of that $(100 - x)\%$, and hence, we will have the following theoretical estimates.

- Theoretical probability of volatility clusters considering clusters of at least 10 data: $(x - 20)/200$.
- Theoretical probability of volatility clusters considering clusters of at least 10 data detected at a confidence level of 90%: $(x - 20)/200 + (1 - (x - 20)/200) \cdot 0.1$.

Figure 6 graphically shows that the proposed model for estimating the probability of volatility clusters could provide a fair approximation to the actual probability of volatility clusters for such an artificial process.

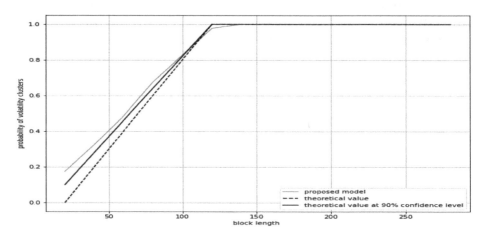

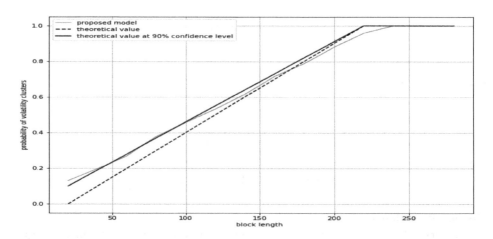

Figure 6. *Cont.*

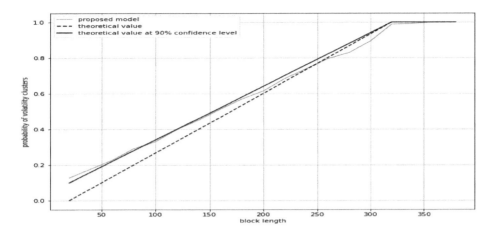

Figure 6. Probability of the existence of volatility clusters for an artificial process with volatility clusters of a fixed length (equal to 100, 200, and 300, from top to bottom).

4. Volatility Clusters in Cryptocurrencies

One of the main characteristics of cryptocurrencies is the high volatility of their exchange rates, and consequently, the high risk associated with their use.

In this section, the methodology provided in Section 3 to calculate the probability of volatility clusters is applied to different financial assets, with a special interest in cryptocurrency markets.

First, Figure 7 shows a similar profile in regard to the probabilities of volatility clusters of an index (S&P500) and a stock (Apple). On the other hand, the probability of volatility clusters of the Euro/USD exchange results in being quite lower.

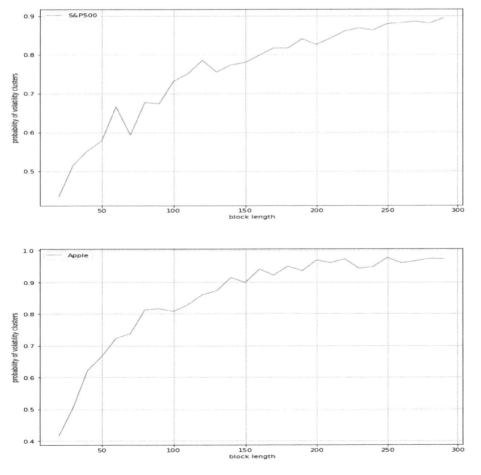

Figure 7. *Cont.*

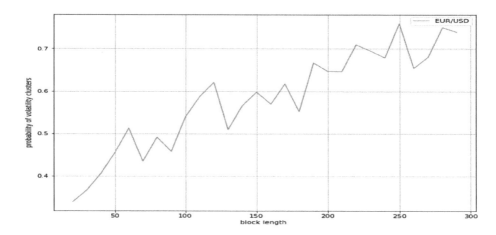

Figure 7. Probabilities of volatility clusters of the next assets. From top to bottom, an index (S&P500), a stock (Apple), and a forex pair (Euro/USD).

On the other hand, Figure 8 depicts the probability of volatility clusters of the three main cryptocurrencies, namely Bitcoin/USD, Ethereum/USD, and Ripple/USD. A similar profile appears for all such cryptocurrencies with the probabilities of their volatility clusters much greater than the ones for the three asset classes displayed in Figure 7.

These results suggest that the volatility in cryptocurrencies changes faster than in traditional assets, and much faster than in forex pairs.

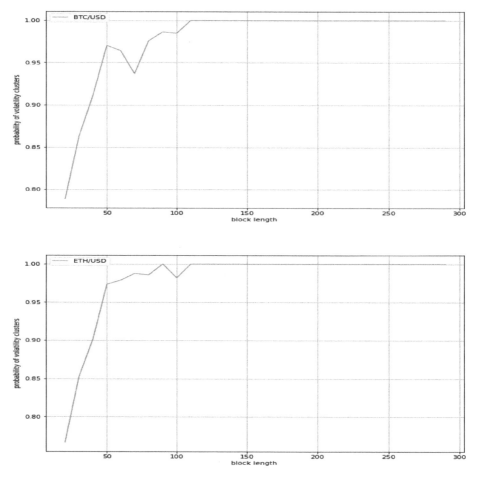

Figure 8. *Cont.*

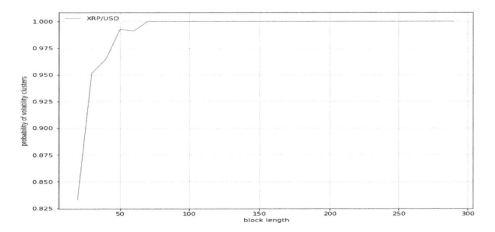

Figure 8. Probabilities of volatility clusters of the following cryptocurrencies. From top to bottom, Bitcoin/USD, Ethereum/USD, and Ripple/USD.

5. Conclusions

One of the main characteristics of cryptocurrencies is the high volatility of their exchange rates. In a previous work, the authors found that a process with volatility clusters displays a volatility series with a high Hurst exponent [2].

In this paper, we provide a novel methodology to calculate the probability of the volatility clusters of a series using the Hurst exponent of its associated volatility series. Our approach, which generalizes the (G)ARCH models, was tested for a class of processes artificially generated with volatility clusters of a given size. In addition, we provided an explicit criterion to computationally determine whether there exist volatility clusters of a fixed size. Interestingly, this criterion is in line with the behavior of the Hurst exponent (calculated by the FD4 approach) of the corresponding volatility series.

We found that the probabilities of volatility clusters of an index (S&P500) and a stock (Apple) show a similar profile, whereas the probability of volatility clusters of a forex pair (Euro/USD) results in being quite lower. On the other hand, a similar profile appears for Bitcoin/USD, Ethereum/USD, and Ripple/USD cryptocurrencies, with the probabilities of volatility clusters of all such cryptocurrencies being much greater than the ones of the three traditional assets. Accordingly, our results suggest that the volatility in cryptocurrencies changes faster than in traditional assets, and much faster than in forex pairs.

Author Contributions: Conceptualization, V.N., J.E.T.S., M.F.-M., and M.A.S.-G.; methodology, V.N., J.E.T.S., M.F.-M., and M.A.S.-G.; validation, V.N., J.E.T.S., M.F.-M., and M.A.S.-G.; formal analysis, V.N., J.E.T.S., M.F.-M., and M.A.S.-G.; writing—original draft preparation, V.N., J.E.T.S., M.F.-M., and M.A.S.-G.; writing—review and editing, V.N., J.E.T.S., M.F.-M., and M.A.S.-G.; These authors contributed equally to this work. All authors have read and agreed to the published version of the manuscript.

Acknowledgments: The authors would also like to express their gratitude to the anonymous reviewers whose suggestions, comments, and remarks allowed them to enhance the quality of this paper.

References

1. Tseng, J.-J.; Li, S.-P. Asset returns and volatility clustering in financial time series. *Phys. A Stat. Mech. Appl.* **2011**, *390*, 1300–1314. [CrossRef]

2. Trinidad Segovia, J.E.; Fernández-Martínez, M.; Sánchez-Granero, M.A. A novel approach to detect volatility clusters in financial time series. *Phys. A Stat. Mech. Appl.* **2019**, *535*, 122452. [CrossRef]

3. Danielsson, J.; Valenzuela, M.; Zer, I. Learning from History: Volatility and Financial Crises. *Rev. Financ.* **2018**, *21*, 2774–2805. [CrossRef]

4. Valenti, D.; Fazio, G.; Spagnolo, B. The stabilizing effect of volatility in financial markets. *Phys. Rev. E* **2018**, *97*, 062307. [CrossRef]

5.   Engle, R.F. Autoregressive Conditional Heteroscedasticity with Estimates of the Variance of United Kingdom Inflation. *Econometrica* **1982**, *50*, 987–1007. [CrossRef]
6.   Bollerslev, T. Generalized autoregressive conditional heteroskedasticity. *J. Econom.* **1986**, *31*, 307–327. [CrossRef]
7.   Taylor, S.J. *Modelling Financial Time Series*; John Wiley & Sons, Ltd.: Chichester, UK, 1986.
8.   Kim, Y.S.; Rachev, S.T.; Bianchi, M.L.; Fabozzi, F.J. Financial market models with Lévy processes and time-varying volatility. *J. Bank. Financ.* **2008**, *32*, 1363–1378. [CrossRef]
9.   Engle, R.F.; Bollerslev, T. Modelling the persistence of conditional variances. *Econom. Rev.* **1986**, *5*, 1–50. [CrossRef]
10.   Baillie, R.T.; Bollerslev, T.; Mikkelsen, H.O. Fractionally integrated generalized autoregressive conditional heteroskedasticity. *J. Econom.* **1996**, *74*, 3–30. [CrossRef]
11.   Bentes, S.R. Long memory volatility of gold price returns: How strong is the evidence from distinct economic cycles? *Phys. A Stat. Mech. Appl.* **2016**, *443*, 149–160.

      [CrossRef]
12.   Patterson, G.; Sornette, D.; Parisi, D. Properties of balanced flows with bottlenecks: Common stylized facts in finance and vibration-driven vehicles. *Phys. Rev. E* **2020**, *101*, 042302. [CrossRef]
13.   Biondo, A.E. Order book microstructure and policies for financial stability. *Stud. Econ. Financ.* **2018**, *35*, 196–218.

      [CrossRef]
14.   Biondo, A.E. Order book modeling and financial stability. *J. Econ. Interact. Coord.* **2019**, *14*, 469–489.

      [CrossRef]
15.   Sueshige, T.; Sornette, D.; Takayasu, H.; Takayasu, M. Classification of position management strategies at the order-book level and their influences on future market-price formation. *PLoS ONE* **2019**, *14*, e0220645. [CrossRef] [PubMed]
16.   Lux, T.; Marchesi, M. Volatility clustering in financial markets: A microsimulation of interacting agents. *Int. J. Theor. Appl. Financ.* **2000**, *3*, 675–702. [CrossRef]
17.   Raberto, M.; Cincotti, S.; Focardi, S.M.; Marches, M. Agent-based simulation of a financial market. *Phys. A Stat. Mech. Appl.* **2001**, *299*, 319–327. [CrossRef]
18.   Krawiecki, A.; Hołyst, J.A.; Helbing, D. Volatility Clustering and Scaling for Financial Time Series due to Attractor Bubbling. *Phys. Rev. Lett.* **2002**, *89*, 158701. [CrossRef]
19.   Szabolcs, M.; Farmer, J.D. An empirical behavioral model of liquidity and volatility. *J. Econ. Dyn. Control* **2008**, *32*, 200–234
20.   Alfarano, S.; Lux, T.; Wagner, F. Estimation of Agent-Based Models: The Case of an Asymmetric Herding Model. *Comput. Econ.* **2005**, *26*, 19–49 [CrossRef]
21.   Cont, R. Volatility Clustering in Financial Markets: Empirical Facts and Agent-Based Models. In *Long Memory in Economics*; Teyssière, G., Kirman, A.P., Eds.; Springer: Berlin/Heidelberg, Germany, 2007.
22.   Chen, J.J.; Zheng, B.; Tan, L. Agent-Based Model with Asymmetric Trading and Herding for Complex Financial Systems. *PLoS ONE* **2013**, *8*, e79531. [CrossRef]
23.   He, X.Z.; Li, K.; Wang, C. Volatility clustering: A nonlinear theoretical approach. *J. Econ. Behav. Organ.* **2016**, *130*, 274–297. [CrossRef]
24.   Schmitt, N.; Westerhoff, F. Herding behavior and volatility clustering in financial markets. *Quant. Financ.* **2017**, *17*, 1187–1203. [CrossRef]
25.   Chen, J.-J.; Tan, L.; Zheng, B. Agent-based model with multi-level herding for complex financial systems. *Sci. Rep.* **2015**, *5*, 8399. [CrossRef] [PubMed]
26.   Shi, Y.; Luo, Q.; Li, H. An Agent-Based Model of a Pricing Process with Power Law, Volatility Clustering, and Jumps. *Complexity* **2019**, *2019*, 3429412. [CrossRef]
27.   Verma, A.; Buonocore, R.J.; di Matteo, T. A cluster driven log-volatility factor model: A deepening on the source of the volatility clustering. *Quant. Financ.* **2018**, 1–16. [CrossRef]
28.   Barde, S. Direct comparison of agent-based models of herding in financial markets. *J. Econ. Dyn. Control* **2016**, *73*, 329–353 [CrossRef]
29.   CoinMarketCap, 2020. Available online: https://coinmarketcap.com/all/views/all/ (accessed on 24 March 2020).
30.   Dimitrova, V.; Fernández-Martínez, M.; Sánchez-Granero, M.A.; Trinidad Segovia, J.E. Some comments on Bitcoin market (in)efficiency. *PLoS ONE* **2019**, *14*, e0219243. [CrossRef]

31. Letra, I. What Drives Cryptocurrency Value? A Volatility and Predictability Analysis. 2016. Available online: https://www.repository.utl.pt/handle/10400.5/12556 (accessed on 24 March 2020).
32. Bouoiyour, J.; Selmi, R. Bitcoin: A beginning of a new phase? *Econ. Bull.* **2016**, *36*, 1430–1440.
33. Bouri, E.; Azzi, G.; Dyhrberg, A.H. On the return-volatility relationship in the Bitcoin market around the price crash of 2013. *Economics* **2017**, *11*, 1–16.
34. Balcilar, M.; Bouri, E.; Gupta, R.; Roubaud, D. Can volume predict Bitcoin returns and volatility? A quantiles-based approach. *Econ. Model.* **2017**, *64*, 74–81. [CrossRef]
35. Baur, D.G.; Hong, K.; Lee, A.D. Bitcoin: Medium of exchange or speculative assets? *J. Int. Financ. Mark. Inst. Money* **2018**. Available online: https://papers.ssrn.com/sol3/papers.cfm?abstract_id=2561183 (accessed on 1 May 2020)
36. Bariviera, A.F.; Basgall, M.J.; Hasperué, W.; Naiouf, M. Some stylized facts of the Bitcoin market. *Physics A* **2017**, *484*, 82–90. [CrossRef]
37. Phillip, A.; Chan, J.S.K.; Peiris, S. A new look at cryptocurrencies. *Econ. Lett.* **2018**, *163*, 6–9. [CrossRef]
38. Zhang, W.; Wang, P.; Li, X.; Shen, D. Some stylized facts of the cryptocurrency market. *Appl. Econ.* **2018**, *50*, 5950–5965. [CrossRef]
39. Kancs, D.; Rajcaniova, M.; Ciaian, P. *The Price of Bitcoin: GARCH Evidence from High Frequency Data*; 29598 EN; Publications Office of the European Union: Luxembourg, 2019; ISBN 978-92-7998570-6, JRC115098. [CrossRef]
40. Mandelbrot, B.B. (Ed.) *Gaussian Self-Affinity and Fractals*; Springer-Verlag: New York, NY, USA, 2002.
41. Fernández-Martínez, M.; Sánchez-Granero, M.A.; Trinidad Segovia, J.E.; Román-Sánchez, I.M. An accurate algorithm to calculate the Hurst exponent of self-similar processes. *Phys. Lett. A* **2014**, *378*, 2355–2362. [CrossRef]
42. Sánchez-Granero, M.A.; Trinidad Segovia, J.E.; García Pérez, J. Some comments on Hurst exponent and the long memory processes on capital markets. *Phys. A Stat. Mech. Appl.* **2008**, *387*, 5543–5551. [CrossRef]
43. Trinidad Segovia, M.; Fernández-Martínez, J.E.; Sánchez-Granero, M.A. A note on geometric method-based procedures to calculate the Hurst exponent, *Phys. A Stat. Mech. Appl.* **2012**, *391*, 2209–2214. [CrossRef]
44. Sánchez-Granero, M.A.; Fernández-Martínez, M.; Trinidad Segovia, J.E. Introducing fractal dimension algorithms to calculate the Hurst exponent of financial time series. *Eur. Phys. J. B* **2012**, 85–86. [CrossRef]
45. Fernaández-Martíínez, M.; Guirao, J.L.G.; Sánchez-Granero, M.A.; Trinidad Segovia, J.E. *Fractal Dimension for Fractal Structures: With Applications to Finance*, 1st ed.; Springer Nature: Cham, Switzerland, 2019; pp. 1–204.

9

Exploring the Link between Academic Dishonesty and Economic Delinquency: A Partial Least Squares Path Modeling Approach

Elena Druică [1,*], Călin Vâlsan [2], Rodica Ianole-Călin [1], Răzvan Mihail-Papuc [1] and Irena Munteanu [3]

[1]   Faculty of Business and Administration, University of Bucharest, 030018 Bucharest, Romania; rodica.ianole@faa.unibuc.ro (R.I.-C.) razvanmihail.papuc@faa.unibuc.ro (R.M.-P.)

[2]   Williams School of Business, Bishop's University, Sherbrooke, QC J1M1Z7, Canada; cvalsan@ubishops.ca

[3]   Faculty of Economic Sciences, Ovidius University, 900470 Constanta, Romania; irena.munteanu@365.univ-ovidius.ro

*   Correspondence: elena.druica@faa.unibuc.ro

Abstract: This paper advances the study of the relationship between the attitude towards academic dishonesty and other types of dishonest and even fraudulent behavior, such as tax evasion and piracy. It proposes a model in which the attitudes towards two types of cheating and fraud are systematically analyzed in connection with a complex set of latent construct determinants and control variables. It attempts to predict the tolerance towards tax evasion and social insurance fraud and piracy, using academic cheating as the main predictor. The proposed model surveys 504 student respondents, uses a partial least squares—path modeling analysis, and employs two subsets of latent constructs to account for context and disposition. The relationship between the outcome variable and the subset of predictors that account for context is mediated by yet another latent construct—Preoccupation about Money—that has been shown to strongly influence people's attitude towards a whole range of social and economic behaviors. The results show academic dishonesty is a statistically significant predictor of an entire range of unethical and fraudulent behavior acceptance, and confirm the role played by both contextual and dispositional variables; moreover, they show that dispositional and contextual variables tend to be segregated according to how they impact the outcome. They also show that money priming does not act as a mediator, in spite of its stand-alone impact on the outcome variables. The most important result, however, is that the effect size of the main predictor is large. The contribution of this paper is two-fold: it advances a line of research previously sidestepped, and it proposes a comprehensive and robust model with a view to establish a hierarchy of significance and effect size in predicting deviance and fraud. Most of all, this research highlights the central role played by academic dishonesty in predicting the acceptance of any type of dishonest behavior, be it in the workplace, at home, or when discharging one's responsibilities as a citizen. The results presented here give important clues as to where to start intervening in order to discourage the acceptance of deviance and fraud. Educators, university professors, and academic administrators should be at the forefront of targeted campaigns and policies aimed at fighting and reducing academic dishonesty.

Keywords: academic cheating; tax evasion; informality

1. Introduction

Academic cheating and workplace cheating are like two peas in a pod. Those who engage in dishonest behavior during university are more likely to lie, cheat, and steal later on during their professional career [1,2]. These findings echo the widely-held belief that early cheating in school and university is a good predictor of dishonesty in the workplace later on. The relationship among academic dishonesty, workplace unethical behavior, and integrity standards is well documented [3].

If people cheat in school, and they cheat later on, at work, why would dishonesty, fraud, and cheating stop there? It makes sense to assume that once people become accustomed to disrespecting academic integrity, they might show lack of integrity in every aspect of their lives, be it at work, at home, or in public. However, there is very little academic research in this direction. This issue has received little attention and the evidence is still sketchy. This paper takes the relationship between the attitude towards academic dishonesty and other types of dishonest and even fraudulent behavior one step further. It proposes a study in which the attitudes towards two types of cheating and fraud are systematically analyzed in connection with a complex set of latent construct determinants and control variables. It attempts to predict the tolerance towards tax evasion and social insurance fraud, and piracy using academic cheating as the main predictor. The proposed model uses a subset of latent constructs that account for context, and another subset to account for disposition. The relationship between the outcome variable and the subset of predictors that account for context is mediated by yet another latent construct—Preoccupation about Money—that has been shown to strongly influence people's attitude towards a whole range of social and economic behaviors.

The contribution of this paper is two-fold: it advances a line of research previously sidestepped, and it proposes a comprehensive and robust model with a view to establishing a hierarchy of significance and effect size in predicting deviance and fraud. As it will be shown here, it turns out that the significance and the effect size of the main predictor, i.e., academic dishonesty, is huge compared with the rest of the other predictors.

Our results have theoretical as well as practical implications. The results confirm the role played by both contextual and dispositional variables; moreover, they show that dispositional and contextual variables tend to be segregated according to how they impact the outcome [3]. They also show that money priming does not act as a mediator in spite of its stand-alone impact on the outcome variables. Most of all, they buttress the important role played by academic dishonesty in predicting the acceptance of any type of dishonest behavior, be it in the workplace, at home, or when discharging one's responsibilities as a citizen.

The results presented here give important clues as to where to start intervening in order to discourage the acceptance of deviance and fraud. By far, the first choice should be tackling the issue of academic dishonesty. There is a respectable body of evidence showing that ethical education and moral sensitivity training tend to work in lowering the acceptance and incidence of academic cheating [2,4,5]. Educators, university professors, and academic administrators should be at the forefront of targeted campaigns and policies aimed at fighting and reducing academic dishonesty.

A word of caution is in order: the results show where to direct the intervention in order to reduce the acceptance of unethical behavior and fraud. The unambiguous course of action is to tackle academic dishonesty, but the findings do not illuminate the manner in which this should be done, which is a different matter altogether and not the subject of the current paper.

The paper is organized as follows. The next section discusses the literature, while Section three presents the sample of respondents and the methodology used to construct the latent variables. Section four presents the results of the partial least squares – path model (PLS-PM henceforth). Section five provides a brief discussion and interpretation of the findings. Section 6 concludes the paper.

2. Literature Review

It is truly worrisome that academic cheating is more prevalent than most people think. It seems that almost all university students have engaged in or witnessed academic dishonesty at some point during their studies [6,7]. There are many studies using a diverse methodology, including but not limited to surveys, factor analysis, structural equation modelling, and cross-lagged regressions, which show how truly widespread academic cheating is. They also show how academic cheating is linked to workplace cheating. Nursing students cheat in large proportion [8–10]; engineering students cheat [11]; psychology students cheat [12]; IT students cheat [13]; and business students seem to outdo everyone else; they have the worst reputation for academic integrity standards among all other students [14–16]

More recently, other researchers [17] found that personality traits defined according to the reinforcement sensitivity theory (RST) are predictors for the extent to which individuals engage in academic dishonesty. Among these predictors, impulsivity and Fight–Flight–Freeze behaviors appear to play an important role.

Other authors [18] administered the Academic Honesty Scale, the Brief Self-Control Scale, the Social Success Index, the Normalcy Feeling Scale, the Social Comparison Scale, and the Satisfaction With Life Scale to a sample of 631 Polish respondents, and found self-regulation to be inversely related to academic cheating. The study also found a gender gap when engaging in academic cheating. Moreover, social comparison appears to be directly related to plagiarism.

Yet, in other cases [19] the investigation was based on a cross-lagged model to describe a complex dynamic between academic cheating on the one hand, and regulatory self-efficacy and moral disengagement on the other hand. The authors found a negative relationship between academic cheating and regulatory self-efficacy, and a positive relationship between academic cheating and moral disengagement. The results are not surprising; moral disengagement encourages academic dishonesty, which in turn legitimizes a shift in attitudes towards cheating. This repositioning leads to an increasing acceptance of cheating as a normal state of affairs.

Using a survey of 185 faculty and 295 students, other authors found a significant difference in perception and attitudes between students and faculty when it comes to assessing the consequences and implication of academic dishonesty [20].

There is a rich literature on the link between academic cheating and workplace deviance. However, there are almost no studies linking academic cheating to economic delinquency beyond the workplace. In [21], the authors argue that individuals who are more tolerant of academic dishonesty also tend to be less reliable, engage in risky behaviors, and accept more readily illegal behaviors. They are also among the very few who link academic dishonesty to dishonesty in politics, athletics, and even tax evasion [22]. This current paper differs from previous research because it takes over where [22] left, and concentrates on tax evasion and piracy, using a well-rounded system of predictors, among which academic cheating represents the most important element.

3. Materials and Methods

The data consists of 504 respondents aged 18–25 (mean 19.82, SD = 1.55), all of whom are students from various national university centers. The distribution is 74.2% females and 25.8% males, with 71.3% originating from urban areas and 28.7% from rural areas. The data was collected via an online questionnaire applied between March and April 2019. Participation in the study was voluntarily.

There are two versions of the same variance-based, structural equation model. There are eight latent variables, and four observed variables. The difference between the two models is in the outcome variable. The first version uses tax evasion and social insurance fraud acceptance as the outcome, while the second version uses piracy acceptance as the outcome. Both versions of the model have ten predictors and one mediator variable.

The items used in the measurement of tax evasion, social insurance fraud, and piracy are taken from a survey on attitudes and behavior towards tax evasion and compliance implemented in Ireland in 2008/2009 by the Office of the Revenue Commissioners (the government body responsible for tax administration and customs regime) [23]. The original survey question contained 14 items, but following an exploratory factor analysis, only six items were retained, as shown in Table 1.

Table 1. Six questionnaire items and two latent (outcome) variables: tax evasion & social insurance fraud acceptance, and piracy acceptance.

	Items [23]	Dimension
ATT1	To claim credits or tax/payment reliefs that you are not entitled to	Tax Evasion and Social Insurance Fraud
ATT2	To deliberately not pay the taxes you are supposed to pay	Acceptance
ATT3	To deliberately claim state social benefits that you are not entitled to	(TESIFA)
ATT4	To knowingly buy counterfeit goods (e.g., clothing, handbags)	
ATT5	To knowingly buy pirated goods (e.g., books, CDs, DVDs)	Piracy Acceptance
ATT6	To use a computer software without having a valid license for it	(PA)

The attitude toward money scale developed by Lim and Teo [24] is used to extract the first of the four observed predictors: "I believe that a person's pay is related to their ability and effort", is deemed as "fairness" (FAIR). The second observed predictor is taken from the money scale developed by Yamauchi and Templer [25]. The item is part of a broader measure of power, but here, "money makes people respect you" is assigned to a variable deemed "money as social status" (MASS). It can be argued that a stronger belief in fairness would result in a weaker acceptance of any deviant or fraudulent behavior [26]. On the other hand, one expects that a greater need to express social status through a display of wealth is associated with more cynicism, a stronger sense of entitlement, and eventually more acceptance of cheating and fraudulent behavior [27]. It could even be the case that cheating becomes a compulsive behavior when driven by social status [28].

The third and fourth predictors are two latent variables called hard work as the path to achievement (HAWPACH) and valuing leisure time (VLT), adapted from Mudrack and McHoskey [29,30]. Both predictors contain items belonging to the work attitudes construct, and are taken directly from the Protestant ethics scale [31]. In the original work, the scale used to measure valuing leisure time is reversed, in an attempt to capture negative judgment against idleness [32]. Here, a 1–7 Likert scale is used, where 1 corresponds to "total disagreement", and 7 means "total agreement," to ensure higher scores are associated with higher valuation of leisure time (Table 2). It is expected that a strong predilection for hard work would lower the acceptance of any type of cheating or fraudulent behavior [33]. There is no prior expectation about the relationship between VLT and the two outcome variables.

Table 2. The structure of two latent variable predictors: hard work as the path to achievement (HAWPACH) and valuing leisure time (VLT).

Items from the Protestant Ethic Scale [31]		
Item	Latent Variable	Manifest Variable
WORK1	Hard Work as the Path to Achievement (HAWPACH) [30]	Any person who is able and willing to work hard has a good chance of succeeding
WORK2		If one works hard enough they are likely to make a good life for themselves
WORK3	Valuing leisure time (VLT) [30]	People should have more leisure time to spend in relaxation
WORK4		Life would be more meaningful if we had more leisure time

Academic dishonesty (ACADISH), the main predictor, is a latent variable using only two items [34]: "cheating during an exam in order to obtain a better grade" (DIS1), and "cheating during an exam in order to obtain a passing grade" (DIS2). There is a difference between these two instances stemming from the nature of the consequences. Cheating in order to obtain a passing grade seems to be perceived as more acceptable because it thwarts failure [13]. On the other hand, cheating to merely get a good grade tends to be perceived as less acceptable [35].

The model adapts the Rosenberg self-esteem scale to the context of the current survey [36–38]. The scale is one-dimensional and has 10 items. The original measurement is on a 1–4 Likert scale, where items 2, 5, 6, 8, 9 have their scores reversed, and the total score is obtained by summing up the results of each item. Here, a 1–7 Likert scale is used (1—"total disagreement", 7—"total agreement"). Higher scores are an indication of higher levels of self-esteem. Factor analysis reveals the presence of two latent variables labeled, "positive feelings" (POF), and "negative feelings" (NEF), presented in Table 3. The two latent variables show a negative Pearson's correlation coefficient of 50%. While some findings suggest that the importance of self-esteem as a determinant for a wide array of behavior types has been overstated [36], POF and NEF are included in the model as two distinct dispositional control variables [39].

Table 3. Two latent predictors derived from the self-esteem scale.

Self-Esteem Scale [36]		Latent Variables—Feelings	
EST1	On the whole, I am satisfied with myself.	Positive	
EST2	At times I think I am no good at all.		Negative
EST3	I feel that I have a number of good qualities.	Positive	
EST4	I am able to do things as well as most other people.	Positive	
EST5	I feel I do not have much to be proud of.		Negative
EST6	I certainly feel useless at times.		Negative
EST7	I feel that I'm a person of worth, at least on an equal plane with others.	Positive	
EST8	I wish I could have more respect for myself.		Negative
EST9	All in all, I am inclined to feel that I am a failure.		Negative
EST10	I take a positive attitude toward myself.	Positive	

Self-efficacy (SELFEFF) is measured using the 10-item general self-efficacy scale [40]. Here, a 1–7 Likert scale is also used (1—"Not at all true", 7—"Exactly true"). There are 10 items (SELFEFF1–SELFEFF10) resulting in a single latent variable, following an exploratory parallel analysis based on maximum likelihood extraction. Cronbach's Alpha shows very good internal consistency at 0.92 and cannot be increased any further. The variance explained by this factor is 55.2%. Since self-efficacy is most often associated with an internal locus of control, one would expect to find a direct relationship between this latent construct and the acceptance of unethical and fraudulent behavior [41–43].

Preoccupation with money (PFM) is a latent variable predictor, based on the items presented in Table 4, and introduced as a mediator. It was extracted from the attitude toward money scale, and corresponds to one of the four dimensions found in the original study [44]. Money represents a powerful extrinsic motivator, and other studies have already found that it plays an important mediating role [45].

Money priming increases the acceptance of interactions based predominantly on market transactions at the expense of other types of social interaction. As such, money makes respondents endorse steeper hierarchical economic systems more readily. Because wealth and status are perceived as a reward for focusing on money and market transactions, money priming reduces the level of empathy and compassion towards more disadvantaged categories [27]. When reminded about money, individuals shift their frame of mind to a modus operandi in which efficiency and results take precedence over all other considerations [46].

It is expected that preoccupation with money is likely to increase the acceptance of cheating and fraudulent behavior for at least two reasons. When framed in terms of eliciting results and achieving performance measured in monetary terms, the focus of individuals is funneled towards obtaining the required results, while other contextual concerns fade into the background [47]. On the other hand, exposure to money and wealth makes people feel more entitled, and this is bound to increase the likelihood of engaging in, or more easily accepting unethical behavior [48,49].

Table 4. The latent variable "preoccupation with money".

Item	Latent Variable	Manifest Variable
PFM1		Compared to people I know, I believe I think about money more than they do.
PFM2	Preoccupation with money	I often fantasize about money and what I can do with it.
PFM3	[44]	Most of my friends have more money than I do.
PFM4		Money is the most important thing in my life.

Age represents a commonly used control variable. The segment of young adults used in the current study is relevant when exploring the relationships between money attitudes and materialism [50], and relationships among money attitudes, credit card usage, and compulsive buying [28,51,52]. Given the relatively narrow range of this observed variable, we do not expect to find a statistically significant effect. We include it, nevertheless, for the sake of following a consecrated methodology.

Gender represents another commonly used control variable. Previous research finds that money is less important for women than for men [53]; however, this finding has to be qualified by cross-cultural research, taking into account the role played by women in the financial management of the household [54]. This qualifier notwithstanding, it is expected that men are more likely to accept dishonest and fraudulent behavior than women.

Table 5 summarizes the latent variable predictors, constructed as a weighted average of their corresponding manifest variables [55]. Figure 1 presents the research model.

Table 5. A summary of latent predictors, with abbreviations and descriptors.

Latent Structure	Observed Variables
NEF	Negative feelings. Part of the self-esteem scale, the items capture negative feelings toward oneself: EST2, EST5, EST6, EST8, EST9
POF	Positive feelings. Part of the self-esteem scale, the items capture positive feelings toward oneself: EST1, EST3, EST4, EST7, EST10
HAWPACH	Hard work as the path to achievement. Hard work provides ground for success in life: WORK1, WORK2
VLT	Valuing leisure time. Appreciation for leisure time: WORK3, WORK4
ACADISH	Academic dishonesty. Motivators for academic cheating: DIS1, DIS2
SELFEFF	Self-efficacy. The level of self-efficacy: SELFEFF1–SELFEFF10
PFM	Preoccupation with money. Importance of money and fantasies around them: MON1, MON2, MON3, MON4
TESIFA	Tax evasion and social insurance fraud acceptance. The level of acceptance of active rule bending: ATT1, ATT2, ATT3
PA	Piracy acceptance. The level of piracy acceptance: ATT4, ATT5, ATT6

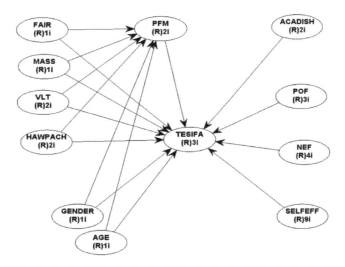

Figure 1. The research model.

Several items were subsequently dropped, either to increase internal consistency or to maintain factor loadings above 0.7. Eventually, MON3 and MON4 (preoccupation with money), EST3 and EST8 (self-esteem), and EFF2 and EFF3 (self-efficacy) were dropped from the final version of the model.

4. Results

The PLS-PM analysis is aimed at maximizing the explained variance of the dependent, endogenous latent variable [56]. The two outcome variables used here are tax evasion and social insurance fraud acceptance (TESIFA), and piracy acceptance (PA). Preoccupation with money (PFM) serves as a mediator in the relationship between contextual and dispositional constructs and the outcome variables. Academic dishonesty (ACADISH) represents the main predictor.

At its core, the estimation method is an iterative algorithm based on ordinary least squares (OLS). Any PLS-PM model consists of two parts: an outer, or measurement model, and an inner, or structural model. The outer model estimates the relationship between the latent constructs and their respective indicator manifest variables, assessed in terms of composite indices. The inner model estimates the relationships among the latent variables themselves.

One begins by estimating the model using R software version 3.4.3, with the "plspm" and the "plsdepot" packages. Subsequently, the results are cross-checked using WarpPLS software version 6.0. The statistical inference part is based on bootstrapping with 999 repetitions.

Table 6 provides the reliability results for the measurement model and shows the robustness of the measures. The composite reliability results range from 0.828 to 0.936 (self-efficacy). These values are above the threshold of 0.7 recommended in the literature [57]. Some alpha values are in the moderate range ("valuing leisure time" and "preoccupation with money"), but one might take the view that even an alpha of 0.5 or 0.6 could be acceptable, in particular when the number of scale items is small [55,58]. Also, the results are considered to be relevant when the average variance extracted (AVE) for each individual latent construct exceeds 0.50, a requirement that in this case is met across the board.

Table 6. Assessment of the measurement model.

Variable	Abbreviation	Composite Reliability (Dillon Goldstein rho)	Cronbach's Alpha	Average Variance Extracted (AVE)
Negative feelings	NEF	0.889	0.833	0.668
Positive feelings	POF	0.897	0.827	0.743
Valuing leisure time	VLT	0.867	0.692	0.765
Hard Work as the Path to Achievement	HAWPACH	0.873	0.710	0.775
Self-efficacy	SELFEFF	0.936	0.923	0,621
Preoccupation with money	PFM	0.828	0.583	0.706
Academic Dishonesty	ACADISH	0.955	0.906	0.914
Tax Evasion and Social Insurance Fraud	TESIFA	0.883	0.824	0.654
Piracy acceptance	PA	0.851	0.736	0.656

Table 7 shows the square roots of all the AVEs (the diagonal elements of the inter-correlation matrix) to be greater than the off-diagonal elements in their corresponding rows and columns. In addition, the off-diagonal correlations are all below the threshold value of 0.8 recommended by Kennedy [59].

Table 7. Discriminant validity (inter-correlations) of variable constructs.

Variable	NEF	POF	VLT	HAWPACH	SELFEFF	PFM	ACADISH	TESIFA	PA
NEF	0.817	0.593	−0.028	0.163	0.395	−0.114	−0.130	−0.272	−0.195
POF		0.862	0.081	0.288	0.583	0.030	−0.021	−0.096	−0.073
VLT			0.874	0.145	0.127	0.136	0.084	0.049	0.143
HAWPACH				0.881	0.347	0.031	−0.087	−0.197	−0.193
SELFEFF					0.788	0.112	−0.049	−0.224	−0.073
PFM						0.840	0.249	0.190	0.275
ACADISH							0.956	0.392	0.475
TESIFA								0.809	–
PA									0.810

Table 8 presents the loadings and cross-loadings of all manifest variables. All loadings are higher than 0.7, ranging from 0.708 to 0.874. It is easy to notice how clusters of indicators uniquely circumscribe each latent construct, with factor loadings of 0.7 or higher, and with high statistical significance ($p < 0.001$). At the same time, same-construct item loadings are higher than cross-construct loadings. This fact confirms the convergent validity of these indicators and suggests that they group into distinct latent constructs.

Table 8. Convergent validity (inter-correlations) of variable constructs.

Variable	NEF	POF	VLT	HAWPACH	SELFEFF	PFM	ACADISH	TESIFA	PA
EST2	0.854	−0.034	−0.059	−0.044	−0.005	−0.032	−0.010	0.066	0.008
EST5	0.722	0.016	0.049	0.041	−0.021	−0.055	0.039	−0.008	−0.037
EST6	0.851	−0.119	0.032	0.028	0.024	0.046	−0.016	0.063	0.075
EST9	0.835	0.142	−0.015	−0.019	−0.002	0.034	−0.006	−0.125	−0.053
EST1	−0.099	0.865	−0.009	−0.005	−0.008	−0.037	0.000	0.034	0.002
EST7	0.033	0.856	0.027	−0.003	−0.037	0.061	0.021	−0.052	0.045
EST10	0.066	0.866	−0.017	0.007	0.044	−0.023	−0.021	0.017	−0.047
WORK3	0.009	−0.035	0.874	0.049	0.009	−0.102	−0.009	0.016	0.003
WORK4	−0.009	0.035	0.874	−0.049	−0.009	0.102	0.009	−0.016	−0.003
WORK1	0.006	0.026	−0.011	0.881	0.016	0.055	0.013	−0.032	0.001
WORK2	−0.006	−0.026	0.011	0.881	−0.016	−0.055	−0.013	0.032	−0.001
SELFEFF1	−0.064	0.042	0.022	0.066	0.827	−0.012	0.018	−0.067	0.067
SELFEFF4	0.038	0.070	−0.004	−0.039	0.859	−0.053	0.050	0.020	−0.006
SELFEFF5	0.013	0.085	−0.019	−0.093	0.805	0.116	0.034	0.009	−0.003
SELFEFF6	−0.037	0.014	−0.000	0.162	0.788	0.029	−0.024	−0.034	−0.032
SELFEFF7	0.099	−0.077	0.005	−0.061	0.708	−0.123	−0.104	0.081	−0.095
SELFEFF8	−0.009	−0.015	0.032	−0.044	0.837	−0.066	−0.042	−0.059	−0.005
SELFEFF9	−0.059	−0.060	0.012	−0.025	0.724	0.028	−0.009	−0.085	0.037
SELFEFF10	−0.003	0.009	−0.038	−0.032	0.832	0.033	0.004	0.042	−0.016
MON1	−0.045	0.056	−0.071	−0.062	−0.010	0.840	0.013	0.006	0.039
MON2	0.045	−0.056	0.071	0.062	0.010	0.840	0.013	−0.006	−0.039
DIS1	−0.001	0.034	0.002	0.008	−0.014	0.008	0.956	0.018	−0.007
DIS2	0.001	−0.034	−0.002	−0.008	0.014	−0.008	0.956	−0.018	0.007
ATT1	0.060	−0.005	0.034	−0.059	0.032	0.054	0.107	0.823	–
ATT2	−0.025	−0.014	−0.031	0.074	0.010	−0.022	−0.054	0.834	–
ATT3	−0.008	0.011	0.015	0.049	0.002	0.037	0.008	0.780	–
ATT4	0.003	−0.001	0.006	−0.031	0.047	−0.046	0.098	–	0.839
ATT5	−0.001	−0.059	0.033	−0.038	−0.031	0.030	−0/065	–	0.739
ATT6	−0.002	0.053	−0.034	0.064	−0.019	0.019	−0.041	–	0.848

Table 9 presents the results for the first version of the structural model, using tax evasion and social insurance fraud as the endogenous variable. Table 10 presents the results for the second version of the structural model, using piracy as the endogenous variable.

Table 9. The results of the structural equations model—model 1.

	Direct Effects		Indirect Effects	Direct Effect Sizes (f2)		Total Effects (Direct Effect + Indirect Effect via Preoccupation for Money)
	Preoccupation for Money	TESIFA	TESIFA	Preoccupation for Money	TESIFA	PA
Preoccupation with money	–	0.100 * (0.011)			0.022	0.100 * (0.011)
FAIR	0.090 * (0.021)	0.048 (0.137)	0.009 (0.387)	0.015	0.005	0.057. (0.097)
MASS	0.353 *** (<0.001)	0.093 * (0.017)	0.035 (0.129)	0.141	0.018	0.129 ** (0.002)
HAWPACH	0.085 * (0.026)	−0.079 * (0.036)	0.009 (0.392)	0.007	0.006	−0.071. (0.054)
VLT	0.099 * (0.013)	0.058 (0.096)	0.010 (0.376)	0.014	0.016	0.068. (0.063)
Gender Male Female	Reference −0.128 ** (0.002)	Reference −0.083 * (0.030)	Reference −0.013 (0.341)	0.019	0.014	Reference −0.096 * (0.015)
Age	0.040 (0.181)	−0.105 ** (0.008)	0.004 (0.449)	0.003	0.015	−0.101 * (0.011)
ACADISH	–	0.296 *** (<0.001)	–	–	0.119	0.296 *** (<0.001)
NEF	–	−0.164 *** (<0.001)	–	–	0.047	−0.164 *** (<0.001)
POF	–	−0.062. (0.081)	–	–	0.008	−0.062. (0.081)
SELFEFF	–	−0.191 *** (<0.001)	–	–	0.048	−0.191 *** (<0.001)
R2/ Adjusted R2	20%/19%	31.8%/30.3%	–	–	–	–

Note: ***—p value < 0.001; **—p value < 0.01; *—p value < 0.05; .—p value < 0.10.

Table 10. The results of the structural equations model—model 2.

	Direct Effects		Indirect Effects	Direct Effect Sizes (f2)		Total Effects (Direct Effect + Indirect Effect via Preoccupation for Money)
	Preoccupation for Money	PA	PA	Preoccupation for Money	PA	PA
Preoccupation with money	–	0.139 *** (<0.001)	–		0.040	0.139 *** (<0.001)
FAIR	0.090 * (0.021)	0.017 (0.354)	0.012 (0.346)	0.015	0.001	0.029 (0.255)
MASS	0.353 *** (<0.001)	−0.015 (0.365)	0.049. (0.058)	0.141	0.003	0.034 (0.223)
HAWPACH	0.085 * (0.026)	−0.110 ** (0.003)	0.012 (0.353)	0.007	0.021	−0.099 * (0.013)
VLT	0.099 * (0.013)	0.122 ** (0.006)	0.014 (0.331)	0.014	0.022	0.136 *** (<0.001)
Gender Male Female	Reference −0.128 ** (0.002)	Reference −0.165 *** (<0.001)	Reference −0.018 (0.285)	0.019	0.046	Reference −0.183 *** (<0.001)
Age	0.040 (0.181)	0.131 ** (0.001)	0.006 (0.429)	0.003	0.023	0.137 *** (<0.001)
ACADISH	–	0.376 *** (<0.001)	–	–	0.180	0.376 *** (<0.001)
NEF	–	−0.088 * (0.023)	–	–	0.017	−0.088 * (0.023)
POF	–	0.026 (0.276)	–	–	0.003	0.026 (0.276)
SELFEFF	–	0.002 (0.486)	–	–	0.000	0.002 (0.486)
R2 /Adjusted R2	20%/19%	34.5%/33%	–	–	–	–

Note: ***—p value < 0.001; **—p value < 0.01; *—p value < 0.05; .—p value < 0.10.

These results show the estimated direct, indirect, and total effects, along with their statistical significance. The effect size for each of the direct paths is also reported. Tables 9 and 10 indicate good explanatory power with R-squared values of 19.6% (preoccupation with money), 21.1% (tax evasion and social insurance fraud), and 16.7% (piracy acceptance). The overall model fit, measured by the standardized root mean square residual (SRMR), is 0.06 for both versions of the model, well within the acceptable level. In general, it is considered that a SRMR < 0.08 indicates a very good fit [60].

Tables 11 and 12 summarize the results already presented in Tables 9 and 10 by indicating the direction and the significance of each relationship in simplified form, showing the two versions of the model side-by-side. FAIR has no significant impact—direct or indirect—on either outcome variable. It does, however, have a marginally significant total effect on TESIFA, and it is a significant predictor of the mediator variable. The belief in fairness does not appear to increase or reduce the level of tolerance towards deviant or fraudulent behavior. It does increase, however, the preoccupation with money, which makes sense if one perceives money as a means of keeping the score for effort and diligence.

Table 11. The results of the structural equations model, simplified and side-by-side (via the mediator).

Predictor	Preoccupation for Money	Direct Effects		Indirect Effects		Total Effects	
		TESIFA	PA	TESIFA	PA	TESIFA	PA
FAIR	+ (*)	None	None	None	None	+ (.)	None
MASS	+ (***)	+ (*)	None	None	+ (.)	+ (**)	None
HAWPACH	+ (*)	− (*)	− (**)	None	None	− (.)	− (*)
VLT	+ (*)	+ (.)	+ (***)	None	None	+ (.)	+ (***)
Gender Male Female	Reference − (***)	Reference − (*)	Reference − (***)	None	None	Reference − (*)	Reference − (***)
Age	None	− (**)	+ (**)	None	None	− (*)	+ (***)

Note: ***—p value < 0.001; **—p value < 0.01; *—p value < 0.05; .—p value < 0.10.

Table 12. The results of the structural equations model, simplified and side-by-side (predictors only).

Predictor	Tax Evasion and Security Insurance Fraud	Piracy Acceptance
PFM	+ (*)	+ (***)
ACADISH	+ (***)	+ (***)
NEF	− (***)	− (*)
POF	− (.)	None
SELFEFF	− (***)	None

Note: ***—p value < 0.001; **—p value < 0.01; *—p value < 0.05; .—p value < 0.10.

MASS is a positive and significant predictor of the mediator variable, and has a significant and positive total effect on TESIFA. There is a direct, significant, and positive effect on TESIFA, but there is no indirect effect. The total effect of MASS on the level of piracy acceptance is not statistically significant. However, when decomposed, the indirect effect (via the mediator, preoccupation about money) is marginally significant ($p = 0.058$), while the direct effect is not at all significant. Therefore, preoccupation with money marginally mediates the relationship between MASS and the level of piracy acceptance. Money as social status increases the level of tolerance towards tax evasion and social insurance fraud. As expected, this relationship appears to be mediated by the preoccupation with money.

Interestingly, money as social status does not increase the level of piracy acceptance, and one can only speculate as to why this is the case. Perhaps tax evasion pays better than piracy, and the opportunity cost expressed in terms of social status is higher. On the other hand, money as social status is associated with a stronger sense of entitlement that extends to defying the authority of the government, whereas piracy is merely petty behavior relegated to penny-pinching. People who need money to enhance their social status are more likely to wear an Armani suit and use an expensive MacBook Pro while dodging taxation; they are less likely to wear a knock-off pair of shoes and use a pirated version of Windows. Expensive notebooks and pirated software do not go together well.

HAWPACH has a negative total effect on both TESIFA and PA, yet the relationship is significant only in the case of PA, and is marginally significant in the case of TESIFA. Direct effects are significant in both cases, but indirect effects are not at all significant. Although HAWPACH is a predictor of Preoccupation with money, the latter does not mediate the relationship with the outcome variables.

This result is highly expected, because one would assume that valuing hard work is at loggerheads with any type of cheating. One can attribute the difference in significance between the two models to the fact that piracy is probably a tangible and real experience that students (who make up our entire sample) can relate to in daily life. On the other hand, most of the students probably have a good mental representation of tax evasion and social insurance fraud, but not yet the experience of engaging in such behavior. Piracy is at hand, while tax evasion is a potential.

VLT has a positive total effect on both outcome variables, yet the relationship is significant only in the case of PA. There are no indirect effects and the only significant direct effect is in the relationship with PA, while this is marginally significant in the case of TESIFA. Although VLT is a predictor of preoccupation with money, the latter does not mediate the relationship with the outcome variables. People valuing leisure time appear to be more tolerant towards cheating and fraudulent behavior. This might be explained by the perceived high opportunity cost of hard work.

Gender has a statistically significant total effect on both TESIFA and PA. There are no indirect effects, only direct effects. As is the case with the previous two variables, gender predicts preoccupation with money, yet the latter does not act as a mediator in the relationship with the outcome variables. As expected, women are less inclined to tolerate tax evasion, social insurance fraud, and piracy.

A relatively similar situation appears in the case of age—the total effects are significant and there are only direct effects on TESIFA and PA. However, the effects on the two outcome variables have opposite signs—TESIFA decreases, but PA increases with age. Moreover, age is not a predictor of preoccupation with money. Older students appear less tolerant towards tax evasion and social insurance fraud, yet more tolerant towards piracy. This is hard to explain without introducing additional assumptions and variables that cannot be pursued and tested here.

The relationship between ACADISH and the two outcome variables is positive and highly significant, as expected. NEF is negatively and significantly related to both TESIFA and PA, yet POF is only marginally related to TESIFA, and not at all to PA. Self-efficacy is negatively and significantly related to TESIFA, and not at all to PA.

5. Discussion

Contextual effect and dispositional effect predictors appear segregated according to the statistical significance of their relationship with the two outcome variables. If one sets aside the case of money as social status (for reasons discussed earlier), one notices that the entire set of contextual effects predictors show a stronger statistical significance in their relationship to piracy acceptance; and a weaker statistical significance in their relationship to tax evasion and social insurance fraud acceptance. One might interpret this in light of the fact that most of the students who answered our questionnaire are perhaps much more often exposed to, or engaged in piracy than in tax evasion and social insurance fraud at this stage in their life. Piracy represents a behavior one can easily relate to, while tax evasion is still a theoretical possibility.

On the other hand, dispositional effect predictors show a stronger statistical significance in their relationship with tax evasion and social insurance fraud acceptance than in the case of piracy acceptance. Perhaps the former variable is seen as more consequential and less socially acceptable than the latter; hence, a behavior such as tax evasion, by virtue of its perceived importance, is more likely to be at the center of thought processes associated with self-evaluation, self-cognition, and self-control.

Money priming has been shown to increase materialistic values and to make people more unscrupulous, yet contextual effects predict the outcomes without the mediation of PFM, although PFM, as expected, remains a predictor of both outcomes. Academic dishonesty is predicting cheating and fraudulent behavior well beyond the workplace, and size effects are the largest among all the predictors.

Both models have a good explanatory power. The predictors explain about 30% or more of the variation of the outcome constructs. Moreover, 20% of the variation of the mediator is explained by contextual and control variables (gender and age). From a practical perspective, the relative contribution of each individual predictor to the combined explanatory power of the model matters a lot. This contribution is usually measured in terms of effect sizes. In order for an intervention to be of any consequence, the effect size has to be above 0.02 [61]. By far, academic dishonesty displays the largest effect size of all predictors for both models. This is without any doubt one of the more important findings of this research.

In order to reduce the acceptance of tax evasion, social insurance fraud, piracy, and perhaps of other types of cheating and fraud, it helps to act on academic dishonesty first and foremost [62]. It has been shown that business students who are coached and sensitized about social responsibility and ethical management appear less inclined to engage in dishonest behavior and are less tolerant towards cheating [4]. Sometimes, simple, old-fashioned moral education and making people self-aware about cheating and deception in the context of social norms might be sufficient to effect a shift in attitudes. Short-circuiting self-deception through sensitivity training represents in itself a deterrent to cheating [5].

In the case of tax evasion and social insurance fraud, another lever appears to be self-efficacy. Boosting self-efficacy seemingly reduces the acceptance of tax evasion. However, this result is more or less trivial. In the case of piracy acceptance, gender and age also show small effect sizes, which are suitable for intervention. Both gender and age, however, represent control variables in this model, and they cannot be manipulated or acted upon in the same way as one might act upon other predictors.

In a similar vein, negative feelings also show relevant effect sizes (in the case of the first outcome variable) but cannot and should not be manipulated—without raising serious ethical concerns—merely for the sake of reducing the level of tolerance towards tax evasion.

Finally, preoccupation with money appears to have a small effect size on both outcome variables. Here, the path of intervention has to go through MASS, which also has a relevant effect size in its relationship with preoccupation with money.

6. Conclusions

An important body of literature shows that academic cheating is a good predictor of cheating and unethical behavior in the workplace. This paper takes this line of research one step further and investigates the relationship between academic dishonesty and other types of unethical and even fraudulent behaviors, well beyond the workplace; the focus is on tax evasion, social insurance fraud, and piracy. The source of data is a sample of 504 respondents, all students, aged 18–25. The PLS-PM analysis used in this research alternates the outcome variable between tax evasion and social insurance fraud acceptance, and piracy acceptance. The main predictor is academic dishonesty. The control variables are age, gender, and several latent constructs accounting for context and disposition. Preoccupation with money is used as a mediator between contextual predictors and our outcome variables.

It is contended that the results are consequential because they show that academic dishonesty is a statistically significant predictor of an entire range of unethical and fraudulent behavior acceptance. In addition, one finds that contextual constructs are segregated in the way they impact the two outcome variables. One explanation is that the sample is composed of students, and the respondents relate differently to tax evasion and social insurance fraud acceptance than to piracy acceptance for obvious reasons. The most important result, however, is that the effect size of the main predictor is large. This should shift the focus to a broader debate about how to fight academic dishonesty most efficiently. It is a question that should be taken very seriously, because there is a lot at stake—cheating has far-reaching implications, measured in billions of dollars. Yet again, the question of ethical behavior in general does not represent an esoteric, theoretical concept. It is consequential precisely because morality relates to real costs, some direct and tangible, other indirect and harder to ascertain, but which are nevertheless significant. The findings presented here have certain limitations. There is no doubt that vigorous intervention should be undertaken to influence the attitude towards academic dishonesty, but there is no obvious indication on how to achieve this. Effective intervention should start in school and university, but the most appropriate course of action should be the subject of other research. Last but not least, the focus of this study has been on attitudes rather than on behavior. It is unclear the extent to which the attitudes measured here would translate into actual behavior, be it academic cheating, tax evasion, or piracy.

Author Contributions: Conceptualization, E.D. and R.I.-C.; methodology, E.D. and C.V.; software, E.D. validation, I.M.; formal analysis, E.D.; investigation, R.I.-C., I.M., and R.M.-P.; resources, R.M.-P.; data curation, E.D.; writing—E.D., C.V., and R.I.-C.; writing—review and editing, E.D. and C.V.; funding acquisition, R.M.-P.

Acknowledgments: This research was supported by a Marie Curie Research and Innovation Staff Exchange scheme within the H2020 Programme (grant acronym: SHADOW, no: 778118).

References

1. LaDuke, R.D. Academic Dishonesty Today, Unethical Practices Tomorrow? *J. Prof. Nurs.* **2013**, *29*, 402–406. [CrossRef] [PubMed]
2. Nonis, S.; Swift, C.O. An Examination of the Relationship Between Academic Dishonesty and Workplace Dishonesty: A Multicampus Investigation. *J. Educ. Bus.* **2001**, *77*, 69–77. [CrossRef]
3. Lucas, G.M.; Friedrich, J. Individual Differences in Workplace Deviance and Integrity as Predictors of Academic Dishonesty. *Ethics Behav.* **2005**, *15*, 15–35. [CrossRef]
4. Chen, Y.-J.; Tang, T.L.-P. Attitude Toward and Propensity to Engage in Unethical Behavior: Measurement Invariance across Major among University Students. *J. Bus. Ethics* **2006**, *69*, 77–93. [CrossRef]
5. Mazar, N.; Ariely, D. Dishonesty in everyday life and its policy implications. *J. Public Policy Mark.* **2006**, *25*, 117–126. [CrossRef]
6. Harper, M.G. High tech cheating. *Nurse Educ. Pract.* **2006**, *6*, 364–371. [CrossRef]
7. Schmelkin, L.P.; Gilbert, K.; Spencer, K.J.; Pincus, H.S.; Silva, R. A Multidimensional Scaling of College Students' Perceptions of Academic Dishonesty. *J. High. Educ.* **2008**, *79*, 587–607. [CrossRef]
8. Brown, D.L. Cheating Must Be Okay—Everybody Does It! *Nurse Educ.* **2002**, *27*, 6. [CrossRef]
9. Faucher, D.; Caves, S. Academic dishonesty: Innovative cheating techniques and the detection and prevention of them. *Teach. Learn. Nurs.* **2009**, *4*, 37–41. [CrossRef]
10. Gaberson, K.B. Academic Dishonesty Among Nursing Students. *Nurs. Forum* **1997**, *32*, 14–20. [CrossRef]
11. Carpenter, D.D.; Harding, T.S.; Finelli, C.J.; Passow, H.J. Does academic dishonesty relate to unethical behavior in professional practice? An exploratory study. *Sci. Eng. Ethics* **2004**, *10*, 311–324. [CrossRef] [PubMed]
12. Li-Ping Tang, T.; Chen, Y.-J.; Sutarso, T. Bad apples in bad (business) barrels: The love of money, Machiavellianism, risk tolerance, and unethical behavior. *Manag. Decis.* **2008**, *46*, 243–263. [CrossRef]

13. Sheard, J.; Markham, S.; Dick, M. Investigating Differences in Cheating Behaviours of IT Undergraduate and Graduate Students: The maturity and motivation factors. *High. Educ. Res. Dev.* **2003**, *22*, 91–108. [CrossRef]
14. Gerlach, P. The games economists play: Why economics students behave more selfishly than other students. *PLoS ONE* **2017**, *12*, e0183814. [CrossRef] [PubMed]
15. Harris, J.R. A Comparison of the Ethical Values of Business Faculty and Students: How Different Are They? *Bus. Prof. Ethics J.* **1988**, *7*, 27–49. [CrossRef]
16. Wood, J.A.; Longenecker, J.G.; McKinney, J.A.; Moore, C.W. Ethical attitudes of students and business professionals: A study of moral reasoning. *J. Bus. Ethics* **1988**, *7*, 249–257. [CrossRef]
17. Bacon, A.M.; McDaid, C.; Williams, N.; Corr, P.J. What motivates academic dishonesty in students? A reinforcement sensitivity theory explanation. *Br. J. Educ. Psychol.* **2019**. [CrossRef]
18. Błachnio, A. Don't cheat, be happy. Self-control, self-beliefs, and satisfaction with life in academic honesty: A cross-sectional study in Poland. *Scand. J. Psychol.* **2019**, *60*, 261–266. [CrossRef]
19. Fida, R.; Tramontano, C.; Paciello, M.; Ghezzi, V.; Barbaranelli, C. Understanding the Interplay Among Regulatory Self-Efficacy, Moral Disengagement, and Academic Cheating Behaviour During Vocational Education: A Three-Wave Study. *J. Bus. Ethics* **2018**, *153*, 725–740. [CrossRef]
20. Keener, T.A.; Galvez Peralta, M.; Smith, M.; Swager, L.; Ingles, J.; Wen, S.; Barbier, M. Student and faculty perceptions: Appropriate consequences of lapses in academic integrity in health sciences education. *BMC Med. Educ.* **2019**, *19*, 209. [CrossRef]
21. Blankenship, K.L.; Whitley, B.E. Relation of General Deviance to Academic Dishonesty. *Ethics Behav.* **2000**, *10*, 1–12. [CrossRef]
22. Fass, R. Cheating and plagiarism. *Ethics High. Educ.* **1990**. Available online: https://eric.ed.gov/?id=ED324727 (accessed on 12 November 2019).
23. Walsh, K. Understanding Taxpayer Behaviour—New Opportunities for Tax Administration. *Econ. Soc. Rev.* **2012**, *43*, 451–475.
24. Lim, V.K.G.; Teo, T.S.H. Sex, money and financial hardship: An empirical study of attitudes towards money among undergraduates in Singapore. *J. Econ. Psychol.* **1997**, *18*, 369–386. [CrossRef]
25. Yamauchi, K.T.; Templer, D.J. The Development of a Money Attitude Scale. *J. Personal. Assess.* **1982**, *46*, 522–528. [CrossRef] [PubMed]
26. Fox, S.; Spector, P.E.; Miles, D. Counterproductive Work Behavior (CWB) in Response to Job Stressors and Organizational Justice: Some Mediator and Moderator Tests for Autonomy and Emotions. *J. Vocat. Behav.* **2001**, *59*, 291–309. [CrossRef]
27. Caruso, E.M.; Vohs, K.D.; Baxter, B.; Waytz, A. Mere exposure to money increases endorsement of free-market systems and social inequality. *J. Exp. Psychol. Gen.* **2013**, *142*, 301–306. [CrossRef]
28. Phau, I.; Woo, C. Understanding compulsive buying tendencies among young Australians: The roles of money attitude and credit card usage. *Mark. Intell. Plan.* **2008**, *26*, 441–458. [CrossRef]
29. McHoskey, J.W. Factor structure of the protestant work ethic scale. *Personal. Individ. Differ.* **1994**, *17*, 49–52. [CrossRef]
30. Mudrack, P.E. Protestant work-ethic dimensions and work orientations. *Personal. Individ. Differ.* **1997**, *23*, 217–225. [CrossRef]
31. Mirels, H.L.; Garrett, J.B. The Protestant Ethic as a personality variable. *J. Consult. Clin. Psychol.* **1971**, *36*, 40–44. [CrossRef]
32. Hassall, S.L.; Muller, J.J.; Hassall, E.J. Comparing the Protestant work ethic in the employed and unemployed in Australia. *J. Econ. Psychol.* **2005**, *26*, 327–341. [CrossRef]
33. Amos, C.; Zhang, L.; Read, D. Hardworking as a Heuristic for Moral Character: Why We Attribute Moral Values to Those Who Work Hard and Its Implications. *J. Bus. Ethics* **2019**, *158*, 1047–1062. [CrossRef]
34. Murdock, T.B.; Stephens, J.M. 10—Is Cheating Wrong? Students' Reasoning about Academic Dishonesty. In *Psychology Academic Cheating*; Anderman, E.M., Murdock, T.B., Eds.; Academic Press: Burlington, ON, Canada, 2007; pp. 229–251. ISBN 978-0-12-372541-7.
35. Jensen, L.A.; Arnett, J.J.; Feldman, S.S.; Cauffman, E. It's Wrong, But Everybody Does It: Academic Dishonesty among High School and College Students. *Contemp. Educ. Psychol.* **2002**, *27*, 209–228. [CrossRef]
36. Ciarrochi, J.; Heaven, P.C.; Davies, F. The impact of hope, self-esteem, and attributional style on adolescents' school grades and emotional well-being: A longitudinal study. *J. Res. Personal.* **2007**, *41*, 1161–1178. [CrossRef]

37. Mullen, S.P.; Gothe, N.P.; McAuley, E. Evaluation of the factor structure of the Rosenberg Self-Esteem Scale in older adults. *Personal. Individ. Differ.* **2013**, *54*, 153–157. [CrossRef]

38. Rosenberg, M. *Society and the Adolescent Self-Image*; Princeton University Press: Princeton, NJ, USA, 2015; ISBN 978-1-4008-7613-6.

39. Fox, S.; Spector, P.E. A model of work frustration–aggression. *J. Organ. Behav.* **1999**, *20*, 915–931. [CrossRef]

40. Schwarzer, R.; Jerusalem, M. The general self-efficacy scale (GSE). *Anxiety Stress Coping* **2010**, *12*, 329–345.

41. Luszczynska, A.; Scholz, U.; Schwarzer, R. The General Self-Efficacy Scale: Multicultural Validation Studies. *J. Psychol.* **2005**, *139*, 439–457. [CrossRef]

42. Reiss, M.C.; Mitra, K. The Effects of Individual Difference Factors on the Acceptability of Ethical and Unethical Workplace Behaviors. *J. Bus. Ethics* **1998**, *17*, 1581–1593. [CrossRef]

43. Scholz, U.; Doña, B.G.; Sud, S.; Schwarzer, R. Is general self-efficacy a universal construct? Psychometric findings from 25 countries. *Eur. J. Psychol. Assess.* **2002**, *18*, 242. [CrossRef]

44. Hoon, L.S.; Lim, V.K.G. Attitudes towards money and—for Asian management style following the economic crisis. *J. Manag. Psychol.* **2001**, *16*, 159–173. [CrossRef]

45. Chitchai, N.; Senasu, K.; Sakworawich, A. The moderating effect of love of money on relationship between socioeconomic status and happiness. *Kasetsart J. Soc. Sci.* **2018**. [CrossRef]

46. Vohs, K.D. Money priming can change people's thoughts, feelings, motivations, and behaviors: An update on 10 years of experiments. *J. Exp. Psychol. Gen.* **2015**, *144*, e86–e93. [CrossRef] [PubMed]

47. Mitchell, M.S.; Baer, M.D.; Ambrose, M.L.; Folger, R.; Palmer, N.F. Cheating under pressure: A self-protection model of workplace cheating behavior. *J. Appl. Psychol.* **2018**, *103*, 54–73. [CrossRef]

48. Kouchaki, M.; Smith-Crowe, K.; Brief, A.P.; Sousa, C. Seeing green: Mere exposure to money triggers a business decision frame and unethical outcomes. *Organ. Behav. Hum. Decis. Process.* **2013**, *121*, 53–61. [CrossRef]

49. Piff, P.K. Wealth and the Inflated Self: Class, Entitlement, and Narcissism. *Personal. Soc. Psychol. Bull.* **2014**, *40*, 34–43. [CrossRef]

50. Durvasula, S.; Lysonski, S. Money, money, money—How do attitudes toward money impact vanity and materialism?—The case of young Chinese consumers. *J. Consum. Mark.* **2010**, *27*, 169–179. [CrossRef]

51. Roberts, J.A.; Jones, E. Money Attitudes, Credit Card Use, and Compulsive Buying among American College Students. *J. Consum. Aff.* **2001**, *35*, 213–240. [CrossRef]

52. Roberts, J.A.; Sepulveda, M.C.J. Demographics and money attitudes: A test of Yamauchi and Templers (1982) money attitude scale in Mexico. *Personal. Individ. Differ.* **1999**, *27*, 19–35. [CrossRef]

53. Wernimont, P.F.; Fitzpatrick, S. The meaning of money. *J. Appl. Psychol.* **1972**, *56*, 218–226. [CrossRef]

54. Roberts, J.A.; Sepulveda, M.C.J. Money Attitudes and Compulsive Buying. *J. Int. Consum. Mark.* **1999**, *11*, 53–74. [CrossRef]

55. Fornell, C.; Bookstein, F.L. Two Structural Equation Models: LISREL and PLS Applied to Consumer Exit-Voice Theory. *J. Mark. Res.* **1982**, *19*, 440–452. [CrossRef]

56. Joreskog, K.G.; Wold, H. The ML and PLS techniques for modeling with latent variables: Historical and comparative aspects. In *Systems under Indirect Observation: Part I.*; Joreskog, K.G., Wold, H., Eds.; North–Holland: Amsterdam, The Netherland, 1982; pp. 263–270.

57. Nunnally, J.C.; Bernstein, I.H. *Psychometric Theory*, 3rd ed.; McGraw-Hill: New York, NY, USA, 1994; ISBN 978-0-07-047849-7.

58. Fornell, C.; Larcker, D.F. Evaluating structural equation models with unobservable variables and measurement error. *J. Mark. Res.* **1981**, *18*, 39–50. [CrossRef]

59. Kennedy, P. *A Guide to Econometrics*, 6st ed.; Wiley-Blackwell: Malden, MA, USA, 2008; ISBN 978-1-4051-8257-7.

60. Hu, L.; Bentler, P.M. Cutoff criteria for fit indexes in covariance structure analysis: Conventional criteria versus new alternatives. *Struct. Equ. Model. Multidiscip. J.* **1999**, *6*, 1–55. [CrossRef]

61. Cohen, J. *Statistical Power Analysis for the Behavioral Sciences*, 2nd ed.; Routledge: Hillsdale, MI, USA, 1988; ISBN 978-0-8058-0283-2.

62. Mirshekary, S.; Lawrence, A.D.K. Academic and Business Ethical Misconduct and Cultural Values: A Cross National Comparison. *J. Acad. Ethics* **2009**, *7*, 141–157. [CrossRef]

10

An Application of the SRA Copulas Approach to Price-Volume Research

Pedro Antonio Martín Cervantes [†], Salvador Cruz Rambaud [*,†] and María del Carmen Valls Martínez [†]

Department of Economics and Business, University of Almería, La Cañada de San Urbano, 04120 Almería, Spain; pmc552@ual.es (P.A.M.C.); mcvalls@ual.es (M.d.C.V.M.)
* Correspondence: scruz@ual.es
† These authors contributed equally to this work.

Abstract: The objective of this study was to apply the Sadegh, Ragno, and AghaKouchak (SRA) approach to the field of quantitative finance by analyzing, for the first time, the relationship between price and trading volume of the securities using four stock market indices: DJIA, FOOTSIE100, NIKKEI225, and IBEX35. This procedure is a completely new methodology in finance that consists of the application of a Bayesian framework and the development of a hybrid evolution algorithm of the Markov Chain Monte Carlo (MCMC) method to analyze a large number (26) of parametric copulas. With respect to the DJIA, the Joe's copula is the one that most efficiently models its succinct dependence structures. One of the copulas included in the SRA approach, the Tawn's copula, is jointly adjusted to the FOOTSIE100, NIKKEI225, and IBEX 35 indices to analyze the asymmetric relationship between price and trading volume. This adjustment can be considered almost perfect for the NIKKEI225, and a relatively different characterization for the IBEX35 seems to indicate the existence of endogenous patterns in the price and volume.

Keywords: copulas; Markov Chain Monte Carlo simulation; local optima vs. local minima; financial markets; SRA approach

1. Introduction

Current trends in quantitative finance reveal that econophysics has become an economic analysis discipline characterized not by its multidisciplinary but by its transdisciplinary nature [1], contributing to the formation of a common framework in the research of financial phenomena [2]. Traditionally, the link has been strong between the stochastic analysis of hydrological phenomena and the study of time series, especially in the field of quantitative finance. The best-known example is likely represented by the Hurst exponent, a procedure inspired by the floods of the Nile River [3], which is of unquestionable efficiency when estimating the long-term memory of time series. Hydrological phenomena are completely different to financial ones but, in general, they present certain common patterns of analysis. Thus, several works have transferred the applicability of the theory of copulas from the field of hydrology to finance [4–7]. Recently, Sadegh et al. [8] developed a specific methodology based on the joint use of 26 multivariate copulas applied in hydrology (hereinafter, SRA), which, in our opinion, offers huge potential for the analysis of the price–volume relationship. Therefore, our aim was to introduce this methodological approach within quantitative finance, summarizing its fundamental aspects as a step prior to its practical implementation.

The analysis of the joint dependence between economic and financial variables has found important support in the Sklar's theorem, through which it has been possible to specify, define, and contrast the latent or redundant dependence structures present in the bivariate and multivariate time series. Notably, Sklar's theorem, the starting point from which this theory departs, has been subject to continuous extensions that have improved the analysis of the structures of dependence between random variables or, in other words, of their succinct relationships when these are schematized in their minimal mathematical expression.

The emergent interest in copulas, detailed by [9], which increased in the field of finance after the paper by [10], does not correspond in reality to the use of several of the numerous types of pre-existing copulas, but to the systematic implementation of certain copulas types, either in economics and quantitative finance or in any other field. According to the compendium of copulas by [11], nonparametric and semiparametric models represent a minority that is largely surpassed by parametric models, amongst which almost 100 different types could be distinguished. Some of them have not been yet fully spread by the literature or, at least, they are not sufficiently well known, since most empirical studies opt for the application of a narrow number of copulas that could be classified as classic copulas.

Conversely, the analysis of the price–volume relationship (hereinafter, PVR) continues being a specific area of the financial literature that has not yet received a conclusive solution. In our opinion, the relationship between prices and trading volume can be derived by dissecting the dependence structure of both variables through the Sklar's theorem, that is, through the implementation of copulas. To accomplish this task, we followed the suggestion of [11] when implementing as many parametric copulas as possible to jointly analyze the same relationship, prices vs. trading or transaction volume, from different points of view (or dependence structures). Therefore, through this empirical work, we aimed to provide a new approach to the application of copulas in the context of PVR, implementing a large number of copulas that, to the best of our knowledge, have not been previously applied in the area of quantitative finance with the aim that these types of transdisciplinary approaches will transcend from the study of PVR to other areas of financial research in the future. This study was mainly based on [8], whose 26 parametric copulas, estimated according to a Bayesian uncertainty framework, were replicated in the price–volume variables of the DJIA, FTSE100, NIKKEI225, and IBEX35 indices.

The SRA was implemented in accordance with two different guidelines focused on two respective scenarios: first, this procedure was applied per se to price–volume data of the DJIA index over the period 1928–2009. Second, one of the 26 copulas included in this methodology, the Tawn's copula [12], was used to jointly compare the dependence structures derived from the PVR in the FTSE100, NIKKEI225, and IBEX35 indices using the period 2000–2018 as the time horizon (also in per se values). This copula was expressly used as it can be considered one of the new-generation copulas whose knowledge is not yet broadly applied in the literature and whose contribution to the analysis of the PVR may be crucial given its exhaustiveness in the estimation of parameters.

The rest of this article is organized as follows: first, Section 2 describes the current state of this research by outlining a literature review concerning the theory of copulas and the analysis of the PVR, detailing the works that expressly employed copulas in the determination of the relationship between prices and trading volume. In our opinion, with few exceptions such as [13,14], most of the works usually offer an excessively summarized and, in some cases, incomplete literature review of the PVR. For this reason, an extensive review of the literature was conducted by listing the four explanatory hypotheses that were mostly addressed in its study. Similarly, this section summarizes the plausible shortcomings derived from the utilization of copulas, pointing out a series of sociological weaknesses. In Section 3, the different databases used as well as a brief review of the theoretical bases presented in the SRA are described: its Bayesian perspective, later developed in Appendix A, and the Markov Chain Monte Carlo simulation used by this methodology. In Section 4, the results obtained are contextualized, finishing this investigation with Section 5, which is dedicated to the discussion of the results. The paper finishes with Section 6, which reflect our conclusions, supplemented with a proposal for future lines of investigation, congruent with the methodological scheme implemented in this manuscript, emphasizing the practical usefulness of the PVR analysis, both for investors and practitioners, from the perspective of the scheme proposed by Karpoff [13]. To ensure the maximum possible exhaustiveness, Appendix B provides an introductory summary of the main basis of the theory of copulas.

2. State of the Art

2.1. Related to the Theory of Copulas

From Sklar [15] until now, the theory of copulas has not stopped being an area under continuous development, to the point that copulas, as a concept, as well as their proven ability to determine parametric and nonparametric dependence measures, have been discovered and rediscovered during the last 50 years [16]. In this sense, Genest et al. [9] applied bibliometric methods to fix the end of the 1990s as the starting point of a growing interest, practically exponential, which, according to [17–19], was due to the seminal repercussion of several works of singular importance for its popularization. This would mean the rediscovery of Sklar's works. In the opinion of [20], this would include its involvement in quantitative finance areas and the opening of new lines of research in this field, which would serve as a trigger for its gradual generalization toward numerous multidisciplinary areas such as the insurance sector, actuarial science, meteorology, hydrology, and many other disciplines [5].

Daníelsson [21] highlighted three stylized findings commonly detected when implementing copulas: the volatility clustering, the phenomenon of fat tails [22], and the analysis of a nonlinear dependence between a given dataset of variables [23–26]. More generically, the application of copulas in economic-financial fields can be structured around a series of predominant research lines such as the valuation of collateralized debt obligations (CDOs) [10], the analysis of financial time series [27–29] (reinforced by the time-varying copulas approach [30,31]), the interpretation of the implicit asymmetries in the exchange rates [32], the successive contributions to the context of the portfolio management either from the construction of a simplified portfolio based on the theory of copulas [33] or from the application of the value-at-risk (VaR) methodology [30,34], or to the study of contingent claims, especially the valuation of financial options in turbulent environments, characterized by risk [35–37]. In addition to these research lines, the theory of copulas has been employed to address all kinds of specific aspects like the methodology proposed by [38] to obtain new copulas based on a given one or the creation of a new class of semiparametric copula-based multivariate dynamic models (SCOMDY), introduced by [39]. Analogously, García et al. [40] focused on building copulas in the contexts of marked uncertainty; the elaborated goodness-of-fit testing procedure for copulas suggested by [41] are also remarkable, as well as the development promoted by the vine-copulas to model dependence structures [42–44] in which the copulas are directly linked with the decision processes.

Limitations of the Copulæ Approach

Strictly, a complete literature review of the theory of copulas would not be objective enough if some of its perceptible limitations are not highlighted, often given by an erroneous conception and misuse of its theoretical basis and, to a lesser extent, by sociological factors. Embrechts et al. [45] listed three conceptual fallacies linked to the relative understanding and abuse when implementing copulas. However, although these have gradually been solved, the main limitation of copulas is the breach of the continuity condition [46], which a priori establishes a univocal relationship between any continuous multivariate distribution and a single resulting copula C [45]. So, in any case, Equation (A7) (see Appendix A) must be satisfied if all distribution functions $F_1(x_1), F_2(x_2), \ldots, F_n(x_n)$ are continuous. Schweizer and Sklar [47] showed that if there is at least one discrete F_i, the joint distribution function can continue being expressed as a function, as shown in Equation (A7); however, this would not be defining a copula per se, but a possible (or feasible) copula C. Several works have furthered the mitigation of this inconvenience; for example, Genest and Nešlehová [48] related copulas with discrete distribution functions, demonstrating how such links can invalidate some basic precepts of the theory of copulas (evidently, in the continuous case) or Mayor et al. [49], who performed a discrete extension of the Sklar's theorem in function of some operators similar to copulas, defined as a finite chain that they denominates "discrete copulas".

Similarly, others [50,51] emphasized that the justification of modeling the relationship of dependence between variables via copulas does not always have to be obvious or completely necessary as, in many cases, it may be more convenient to directly adjust the variables to a given multivariate distribution function (i.e., Gaussian or lognormal) to delimit the predictable stylized findings relative to their dependence structures. Another impediment, according to [52], is that copulas do not entirely correspond with the pre-existing stochastic framework because they are static models and, therefore, they are not completely adequate for modeling dependence structures over time.

The misuse of the Gaussian copula as a general indicator of credit risk should also be considered during the most recent period of economic boom, called "irrational exuberance" by Shiller [53], in whose case the procedure introduced by [10] practically became a standardized measure of the risk level of certain assets with high levels of volatility, being one of the indirect triggers in the expansion of the subprime mortgage crisis. Donnelly and Embrechts [54] metaphorically stated that "the devil is in the tails" when describing the main limitation of the models based on Gaussian copulas to fit extreme data values or outliers if compared with others like the Gumbel copula [55]. According to [45,56,57], there were many voices that, long enough in advance, warned about these models' inconsistencies that ignored the fact that the application of Gaussian copulas could be more or less viable in relatively stable financial environments but would be completely inefficient in detecting joint extreme events. This conclusion was personally confirmed by P. Embrechts to one of the coauthors of this work (November 2017):

> "[...] I insisted from the beginning, back in 1998, that credit risk models based on Gaussian copula are not capable of capturing joint credit defaults in a sufficiently realistic way. The mathematical result underlying this statement of mine dates back to the late fifties [...]"

Mikosch [52], Daníelsson [58], and Zimmer [59] also criticized the widespread application of this procedure and even Salmon [60] deduced that the interests, aims, and objectives of the banking industry overlapped with those of mathematics, pointing out a sociological limitation born from considering the mathematical methodology implicit in the theory of copulas as a *factotum* in the determination of the risk of financial assets. In this sense, Rogers [61] stated:

> "The problem is not that mathematics was used by the banking industry, the problem was that it was abused by the banking industry. Quants were instructed to build models which fitted the market prices. Now if the market prices were way out of line, the calibrated models would just faithfully reproduce those wacky values, and the bad prices get reinforced by an overlay of scientific respectability".

Daníelsson [21] considered that the a priori use of copulas can arbitrarily determine any structure of dependence so that an "optimal" adjustment of a copula does not mean an obligatory a sine qua non condition that leads to an optimal fit from the original distribution of the data. As no economic theory is explicitly linked to copulas, it is difficult to specify in advance what type of copulas are the most appropriate for each specific analysis given the total freedom in the choice of the underlying structures of dependence, which, in no case, are subrogated in a preliminary way to any economic theory.

2.2. Related to the Analysis of the Price-Volume Relationship

Osborne [62] was the first to address the concurrent relationship between prices and trading volume from a strictly quantitative perspective, estimating that the logarithm of the price of financial assets follows a diffusion process with a trend whose variance depends on the trading volume. Samuelson [63] was inspired by this research to infer that the prices of financial assets describe a specific random trajectory based on the Geometric Brownian motion. Thus, the primary roots of modern quantitative finance are based in the preliminary studies of the analysis of the PVR. Others [62,64,65] applied spectral analysis to determine that, in principle, there is no a significant relationship between prices and volumes (or it is too meager to take it into consideration).

These initial works provided the background to justify and empirically test the reconsidered theory of demand [66], a new conceptualization of the theory of supply and demand, openly contrary to classical postulates, which would anticipate the empirical basis of the Granger causality test [67]. Based on Godfrey et al. [65], Ying [68] presented a complete disagreement with the theory of conventional demand, performing a series of statistical tests whose results defined five empirical patterns that characterize the joint evolution of the price and volume variables. Clark [69] used a mixture of probabilistic distributions to describe what would be considered the first explanatory hypothesis of the PVR, the MDH (Mixture of Distribution Hypothesis), proposing that the number of operations that occur per unit of time is a random variable and the variation in prices per unit of time is the sum of the increments of the intraday price equilibrium. Thus, the mixed variable is hypothesized according to the information rate periodically reached by the markets, inferring that, in principle, price and volume must be positively correlated, varying in a contemporary basis, just before the arrival of new information. Others [70–74] used the basis of this approach, which were further expanded [75,76] by inputting the information rate into the GARCH (Generalized Autoregressive Conditional Heteroskedasticity models) primary specification of Bollerslev [77], hypothesizing that the daily trading volume behaves like a representative proxy variable when explaining the evolution of prices growth depending on the GARCH effects, or on the persistence of transitory volatility shocks. Practically as a counterpart to the MDH, the SAIH (Sequential Information Arrival Hypothesis) [78,79] arose as a probabilistic model based on a binomial distribution, according to which the information arrives the markets generating a noncontinuous or fragmented flow. Per Darrat et al. [80], this hypothesis should be only contrastable in those periods in which the information is public and whose empirical evidence is ascertained by all market participants. Copeland [78] argued that, as more than an effective explanatory hypothesis of the PVR, it should be reconsidered as "a new technique for the analysis of demand".

The DBH (Dispersion of Beliefs Hypothesis) and the NTH (Noise Trader Hypothesis) would complete, together with the MDH and the SIAH, the four major explanatory hypotheses of the PVR, being the common denominator of all information that reaches the markets, although analyzed from opposite points of view and finally convergent [81]. The NTH [82] states that prices and volumes are the result of positive and negative feedback strategies that degenerate into noise in the sense stated by Black [83], on which passive, rational, and speculative investors react positively to a feedback strategy. In other words, according to this hypothesis, all information of interest that arrives to the markets, or relevant in any investment process, would be equivalent to the paradigmatic [83] noise. In contrast, the DBH [84,85] defines an antagonistic theoretical scenario in which investors who interact exclusively for speculative reasons and their degree of risk aversion is neutral, collectively receive public information, which, in principle, is common and perceived in the form of market signals. Consequently, the consecutive changes in prices exhibit a negative serial correlation and trading volume is positively correlated [84].

Use of Copulas in the Price-Volume Research

Amongst the works that explicitly opted for the implementation of copulas in the study of the PVR are those by Gurgul, who focused on the Polish and central European stock markets (Austria and Germany). Gurgul and Syrek [86] implemented the family of Archimedean copulas to demonstrate that the volatility of (daily) returns of the companies listed on the DAX was positively related to the trading volume. Gurgul et al. [87] introduced a measure of dependences based on copulas to quantify the relationship between performance and volume, volatility and volume, and yield and performance of the benchmark Polish stock market (WIG) compared to three indices corresponding to other international financial markets (ATX, DAX, and DJIA). They concluded that each one of the proposed relationships is significant except for the volume traded in the Polish market vs. the volatility of DJIA returns. Gurgul et al. [88] used a Granger's nonlinear causality model based on the Bernstein's copula by applying the nonparametric test of conditional independence between two vector processes [89] in five selected ordinary shares of the ATX index, confirming the existence of several well-defined causal guidelines between the performance of shares, the volatility, and the trading volume (both expected and unexpected). This same copula, in conjunction with Hellinger's distance, was implemented [90] to study the high-frequency data of 10 central European companies (Austria and Poland), detecting a high degree of unidirectional causality, both linear and nonlinear, of the returns to the expected volume, which was not appreciable in the opposite direction. They also observed the existence of a linear causality from the volatility realized to the expected trading volume that, once again, was negligible in the opposite direction.

Gurgul and Syrek [91] studied the dependence structures of ordinary stock returns, volatility, and transaction volumes of several companies listed in the CAC40 and FTSE100 indices to verify the long-term memory of the MDH through the fractional cointegration of these series according to the procedure previously described [92]. In most cases, there is no structure of common dependence whereby the analyzed series would not be caused by a process of reaching a common information with long-term memory. Gurgul et al. [93] investigated the high-frequency data of 13 German companies included in the DAX index for a period of 33 days by selecting the copulas t and Gumbel to analyze their different underlying dependence structures according to the inference function for margins (IFM) method [94]. These scholars inferred that the contemporary relationship between the price duration and its associated trading volume depends on the distribution tails as unusual high volume accumulations tend to coincide with long durations and, conversely, dependence is minimal when any of the variables are delayed.

The Asian Financial Crisis of 1997 provided a empirical scenario from which Ning and Wirjanto [95] analyzed the structure of dependence between prices and volumes in a context of extreme volatility by examining the evolution of the most representative stock indices of the six countries in southern Asia, which were more seriously affected by the crisis. Gallant et al. [96] implemented several mixtures of copulas (Clayton, survival Clayton, and Frank) expressly focused on both tails. They obtained two conclusions: (1) In general terms, volume positively depends on the return exclusively in the upper tail of the distribution but not in the lower, which can be interpreted as volume is a key piece able to explain the periodical booms of the market, not its eventual collapses. (2) A marked asymmetric dependence exists between return and volume in the extremes of the distribution, evidenced by extremely high returns tending to be attached to extremely large volumes, but extremely low returns tending not to be associated with disproportionate trading volumes, whether high or low.

Naeem et al. [97] focused on the study of the PVR from the analysis of the asymmetric relationship between returns and trading volumes based on four stock indices also in Asia, developing an alternative measure of dependence by combining several copulas (Clayton, Survival Clayton, and Gumbel) with the univariate GARCH and FIGARCH (Fractionally Integrated GARCH models) in which the marginal distributions of the respective series of returns and volumes are adjusted, proving that the FIGARCH specification substantially improves the estimation of the parameters of each of the proposed copulas. As in [95], we remark that extraordinarily high trading volumes are often related to significant returns, which is due to sudden and sharp declines in the value of financial assets and, more specifically, within financial crisis environments.

3. Materials and Methods

Our objective was to present a multi-perspective design of Larkin's research [98] that enables the analysis of the PVR from different standpoints, depending on the use of different datasets, time horizons, and analytical tools (copulas). The SRA was applied to two different scenarios to provide a generic and a specific image of this methodology. Instead of using a representative hydrological or meteorological index as an empirical basis (i.e., the standardized precipitation index (SPI) [99]), per se values of four stock market indices commonly employed by the literature in the study of the PVR were selected: DJIA, FTSE100, NIKKEI225, and IBEX35.

In the first case, or generic scenario, all available copulas (26) were applied to a single index (DJIA). Later, in the specific scenario, a single copula was adjusted to three indices (FTSE100, NIKKEI225, and IBEX35). The copula chosen in the second case was the Tawn copula, a family of new-generation copulas derived from the Khoudraji's device copula [100]. In this way, we contribute to the analysis of the PVR with the inclusion of new copulas never or rarely implemented in this research, such as some of those included in the SRA approach. In relation to the construction of the generic scenario, we decided to use a wide database consisting of 20,219 stock trading sessions of the DJIA index, covering the period from 10 January 1928 to 4 August 2009, which were consecutively subdivided into quarterly periods until obtaining 490 observations representing the adjusted closing values of the DJIA at the end of each corresponding session and the final volume of the shares traded at each date.

This temporal accrual as well as the use of data per se allowed us to adapt the original datasets to the methodology proposed by [8]. The analysis of the specific scenario corresponding to the FTSE100, NIKKEI225, and IBEX35 indices involved monthly data of per se price and volume collected during the period from 31 October 2000 to 30 November 2018, which included 218 monthly observations for each stock index. The most representative descriptive statistics of the generic scenario, shown in Table 1, reveal a fundamental aspect: the huge level of variability of variables "price" and "trading volume" when both are measured in per se terms (especially in the latter case).

Table 1. Descriptive statistics and dependence evaluation of DJIA price and volume per se (1928–2009).

(A) Descriptive Statistics							
Variable	**T. Count**	**Mean**	**SEM**	**T. Mean**	**St. Dev.**	**Variance**	**CV**
Price (DJIA)	241	2366	227	1973	3528	12,445,239	149.10
Volume (DJIA)	241	310,592,490	52,3001,976	1.61×10^8	8.1×10^8	6.57×10^{22}	260.92
Variable	**Sum**	**SS**	**Min**	**Q1**	**Median**	**Q3**	**Max**
Price (DJIA)	570,211	4,335,989,110	60	218	827	2448	13,502
Volume (DJIA)	7.49×10^{10}	1.80865×10^{25}	210,000	1,970,000	10,710,000	1.68×10^8	5,531,290,000
Variable	**Range**	**IQR**	**Mode**	**Skewness**	**Kurtosis**	**MSSD**	
Price (DJIA)	13,441	2.3030	240,96	1.77	1.69	55,250	
Volume (DJIA) *	5.53×10^9	166,350,000	770,000; 880,000; 990,000; 1,440,000	3.99	18.10	1.44×10^{21}	

(B). Dependence Evaluation			
Correlation Price (DJIA)-Volume (DJIA)			
Correlation type	**Correlation Coefficient**	*p*-value	**Significant at 5%?**
Kendall rank	0.8279	0	Yes
Spearman's rank-order	0.9559	0	Yes
Pearson product-moment	0.7365	0	Yes

Subtable (A): (*) The analyzed data contain at least five mode values. Only the smallest four have been selected. T. Count: Total Count; SEM: Standard Error of the Mean; T. Mean: Trimmed Mean; CV: Coefficient of Variation; SS: Sum of Squares; IQR: Interquartile Range; MSSD: Mean of the Squared Successive Differences. Subtable (B): Source: Own elaboration.

In the same way, the values per se of the variables "price" and "trading volume" denote a relatively high degree of correlation in terms of the Pearson, Kendall, and Spearman correlation coefficients (0.7365, 0.8279, and 0.9559, respectively), which a priori could be considered significant measures of dependence. However, as underlined by Frey et al. [101], a high degree of correlation does not necessarily imply real dependence between the involved variables.

Figure 1 shows the huge level of dispersion and variability of both variables. The first two subfigures, elaborated according to Patton [29], exhibit a normalized time series plot of price (DJIA)–volume (DJIA) as well as a scatter plot of log-increments, both series normalized in base 100, according to the equality $100 \times \exp\left\{\sum_{i=1}^{n} \frac{\ln X_i}{\ln X_{i-1}}\right\}$. The third subfigure represents the Pearson regression coefficient of per se prices and volumes of the DJIA over the analyzed time horizon, showing a quasicyclical relationship between prices and transactional volume within this index, which a priori do not appear to be connected with the evolution of the economic cycle. Several phases or trends can be distinguished: relative decline (1934–1957, 1979–1984, and 2000 onwards), stabilization (1967–1977), and increase (1929–1933, 1958–1966, and 1985–1999) in the relationship between the variables in terms of Pearson's linear correlation coefficient (ρ).

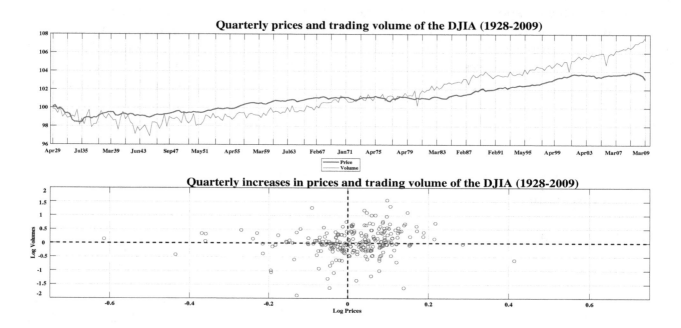

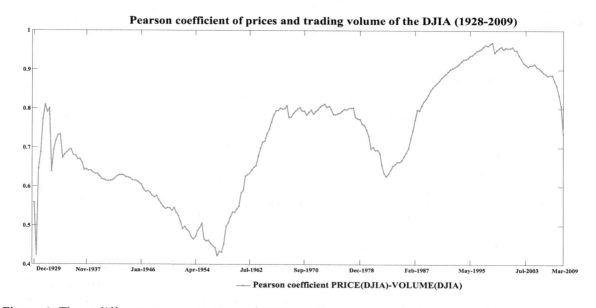

Figure 1. Three different representations of DJIA price-volume evolution and variability during the period 1928–2009. Source: Own elaboration.

Considering per se magnitudes, Figure 2 presents a three-dimensional scatter plot of the DJIA index that links variables X (volume) and Y (price) to the Pearson linear correlation coefficient ($Z = \rho$). Simply, it can be observed that this chart mostly associates the highest correlation levels of P and V to high per se values of P. Low trading volume per se usually fluctuates within a range from 5.00×10^9 to 15.00×10^9, although sometimes a relatively high degree of correlation between price and low trading volume can be detected (close to 5.00×10^9).

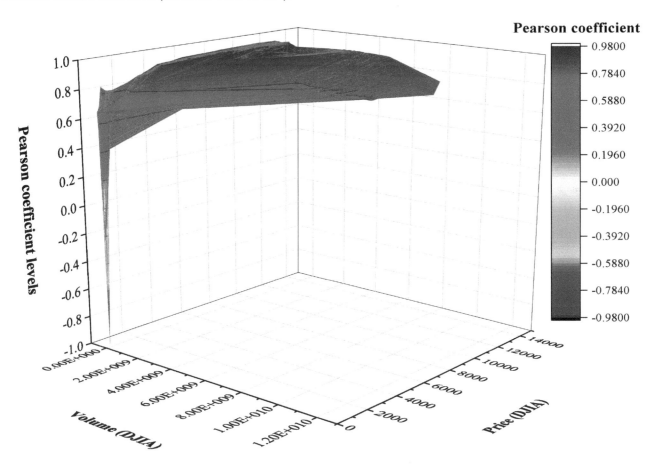

Figure 2. Scatter plot of ρ vs. Price (DJIA)-Volume (DJIA). Source: Own elaboration.

The aim of this paper is to highlight the key aspects of the SRA as an optimal methodological approach for the analysis of the PVR from an empirical perspective that is completely different from the rest of the predominant lines of research. In summary, this methodology can be characterized by: (1) the use of a high number of bivariate copulas (26, see Table 2), especially recommended to simultaneously represent different dependence structures and to conduct prospective inferences based on the chosen variables (not necessarily related to hydrology), such as the variables price and trading volume of a given financial asset or stock index. Notably, to the best of our knowledge, the large number of copulas jointly implemented in the SRA was employed for the first time in the investigation of the PVR. (2) This methodology is based on a unitary reference framework (Bayesian analysis, see Appendix A) in which the hybrid evolution algorithm of the Monte Carlo Markov Chain simulation (MCMCS) was introduced, focusing on the numerical estimation of the subsequent distribution of copula parameters within a context of uncertainty that is relatively similar to the uncertainty observable in financial markets, especially when the different volatility ranges can be conveniently delimited.

Table 2. Families of copulas used in this analysis, specifying their corresponding most common mathematical specifications.

Denomination	Mathematical Representation A	Parametric Range	Reference
Gaussian	$\int_{-\infty}^{\phi^{-1}(u)} \int_{-\infty}^{\phi^{-1}(v)} \frac{1}{2\pi\sqrt{1-\theta^2}} \exp\left(\frac{2\theta xy - x^2 - y^2}{2(1-\theta^2)}\right) dxdy$ B	$\theta \in [-1,1]$	[102]
t	$\int_{-\infty}^{t_{\theta_2}^{-1}(u)} \int_{-\infty}^{t_{\theta_2}^{-1}(v)} \frac{\Gamma(\frac{\theta_2+2}{2})}{\Gamma(\frac{\theta_2}{2})\pi\theta_2\sqrt{1-\theta_1^2}} \left(1 + \frac{x^2 - 2\theta_1 xy + y^2}{\theta_2}\right)^{\left(\frac{\theta_2+2}{2}\right)} dxdy$ C	$\theta_1 \in [-1,1]$ and $\theta_2 \in (0,\infty)$	[102]
Clayton	$\max(u^{-\theta} + y^{-\theta} - 1, 0)^{-\frac{1}{\theta}}$	$\theta \in [-1,\infty)\backslash 0$	[103]
Frank	$-\frac{1}{\theta}\ln\left[1 + \frac{(\exp(-\theta u)-1)(\exp(-\theta v)-1)}{\exp(-\theta)-1}\right]$	$\theta \in \mathbb{R}\backslash 0$	[102]
Gumbel	$\exp\{-[(-\ln(u))^\theta + (-\ln(v))^\theta]^{\frac{1}{\theta}}\}$	$\theta \in [1,\infty)$	[102]
Independence	uv		[104]
Ali-Mikhail-Haq (AMH)	$\frac{uv}{1 - \theta(1-u)(1-v)}$	$\theta \in [-1,1]$	[105]
Joe	$1 - [(1-u)^\theta + (1-v)^\theta - (1-u)^\theta(1-v)^\theta]^{\frac{1}{\theta}}$	$\theta \in [1,\infty)$	[102]
Farlie-Gumbel-Morgenstern (FGM)	$uv + [\theta(1-u)(1-v)]$	$\theta \in [-1,1]$	[18]
Gumbel-Barnett	$u + v - 1 + (1-u)(1-v)\exp[-\theta\ln(1-u)\ln(1-v)]$	$\theta \in [0,1]$	[55,106]
Plackett	$\frac{1 + (\theta-1)(u+v) - \sqrt{[1+(\theta-1)(u+v)]^2 - 4\theta(\theta-1)uv}}{2(\theta-1)}$	$\theta \in (0,\infty)$	[107]
Cuadras-Augé	$[\min(u,v)]^\theta [uv]^{(1-\theta)}$	$\theta \in [0,1]$	[108]
Raftery	$\begin{cases} u - \frac{1-\theta}{1+\theta}u^{\frac{1}{1-\theta}}\left(v^{-\frac{\theta}{1-\theta}} - v^{\frac{1}{1-\theta}}\right) & \text{if } u \leq v \\[2ex] v - \frac{1-\theta}{1+\theta}v^{\frac{1}{1-\theta}}\left(u^{-\frac{\theta}{1-\theta}} - u^{\frac{1}{1-\theta}}\right) & \text{if } v \leq u \end{cases}$	$\theta \in [0,1]$	[18]
Shih-Louis	$\begin{cases}(1-\theta)uv + \theta\min(u,v), & \text{if } \theta \in (\theta,\infty) \\ (1+\theta)uv + \theta(1+\theta)\Psi[u]\Psi^{-1}[-a^{-1}], & \text{if } \theta \in (-\infty,\theta] \end{cases}$ $\Psi(a) = 1$, if $a \geq 0$ $\Psi(a) = 0$, if $a < 0$		[109]

Table 2. *Cont.*

Denomination	Mathematical Representation[A]	Parametric Range	Reference
Linear-Spearman	$$\begin{cases} [u+\theta(1-u)]v, & \text{if } v \leq u \text{ and } \theta \in [0,1] \\[4pt] [v+\theta(1-v)]u, & \text{if } u < v \text{ and } \theta \in [0,1] \\[4pt] (1+\theta)uv, \text{ if } (u+v) < 1 \text{ and } \theta \in [-1,0] \\[4pt] (uv+\theta(1-u)(1-v), \text{ if } (u+v) \geq 1 \text{ and } \theta \in [-1,0] \end{cases}$$	$\theta \in [-1,1]$	[110]
Cubic	$uv[1+\theta(u-1)(v-1)(2u-1)(2v-1)]$	$\theta \in [-1,2]$	[111]
Burr	$u+v-1+[(1-u)^{-\frac{1}{\theta}}+(1-v)^{-\frac{1}{\theta}}-1]^{-\theta}$	$\theta \in (0,\infty)$	[50]
Nelse n	$-\dfrac{1}{\theta}\log\left\{1+\dfrac{[\exp(-\theta u)-1][\exp(-\theta v)-1]}{\exp(-\theta)-1}\right\}$	$\theta \in (0,\infty)$	[18]
Galambos	$uv\exp\{(-\ln(u))^{-\theta}+(-\ln(v))^{-\theta}\}^{-\frac{1}{\theta}}$	$\theta \in (0,\infty)$	[12]
Marshall-Olkin	$\min[u^{(1-\theta_1)}v, uv^{(1-\theta_2)}]$	$\theta_1, \theta_2 \in (0,\infty)$	[12]
Fischer-Hinzmann	$\{\theta_1[\min(u,v)]^{\theta_2}+(1-\theta_1)[uv]^{\theta_2}\}^{\frac{1}{\theta_2}}$	$\theta_1 \in [0,1], \theta_2 \in \mathbb{R}$	[112]
Roch-Alegre	$\exp\{1-[(((1-\ln(u))^{\theta_1}-1)^{\theta_2}+((1-\ln(v))^{\theta_1}-1)^{\theta_2})^{\frac{1}{\theta_2}}+1]^{\frac{1}{\theta_1}}\}$	$\theta_1 \in (0,\infty), \theta_2 \in [1,\infty)$	[113]
Fischer-Kock	$uv[1+\theta_2(1-u^{\frac{1}{\theta_1}})(1-v^{\frac{1}{\theta_2}})]^{\theta_1}$	$\theta_1 \in [1,\infty), \theta_2 \in [-1,1]$	
BB1	$\{1+[(u^{-\theta_1}-1)^{\theta_2}+(v^{-\theta_1}-1)^{\theta_2}]^{\frac{1}{\theta_2}}\}^{-\frac{1}{\theta_1}}$	$\theta_1 \in (0,\infty), \theta_2 \in (1,\infty)$	[4]
BB5	$\exp\{-[(-\ln(u))^{\theta_1}+(-\ln(v))^{\theta_1}-((-\ln(u))^{-\theta_1\theta_2}+(-\ln(v))^{-\theta_1\theta_2})^{-\frac{1}{\theta_2}}]^{\frac{1}{\theta_1}}\}$	$\theta_1 \in [1,\infty), \theta_2 \in (0,\infty)$	[4]
Taun	$\exp\{\ln(u^{(1-\theta_1)})+\ln(v^{(1-\theta_2)})-[(-\theta_1\ln(u))^{\theta_3}+(-\theta_2\ln(v))^{\theta_3}]^{\frac{1}{\theta_3}}\}$	$\theta_1, \theta_2 \in [0,1], \theta_3 \in [1,\infty)$	[12]

A. The different formulations of this table do not necessarily have to be unique. B. ϕ represents the distribution *Gaussian* or standard normal. C. t_{θ_2} denotes the *t student* distribution with θ_2 degrees of freedom. Source: Specifically readapted to this study from [8].

As stated by Johannes and Polson [114], the key aspect of the MCMCS is its ability to easily characterize the complete conditional distributions, $p(\theta|X, Y)$ and $p(X|\theta, Y)$, instead of analyzing the higher-dimensional joint distribution $p(\theta, X|Y)$. The SRA belongs to the class of econometric methods usually applied to the sampling of high-dimensional complex distributions, which implement a hybrid-evolution MCMCS algorithm to infer posterior parameter regions within a Bayesian context. This algorithm is considered a hybrid since it includes a combination of Gibbs steps and Metropolis–Hastings steps [114].

The hybrid-evolution MCMCS algorithm starts with an intelligent starting point selection, structured according to the use of adaptive metropolis (AM), differential evolution (DE), and snooker update. Table 3 summarizes, in descending order, the working schema implemented in the algorithm developed by Sadegh et al. [8]. For the sake of brevity, intermediate iterative conditions (i.e., end do, end if, etc.) have been omitted from the table.

Table 3. Description of the basis scheme of the hybrid MCMCS algorithm implemented in the SRA approach.

Intelligent prior sampling.
Draw $LN(\geq N)$ samples from prior $(p(\theta))$ using Latin Hypercube Sampling (LHS).
Randomly assign the LHS samples to N complexes.
Selecting the best sample in each complex as the starting point of a Markov chain (CH).
Snooker update (with a 10% of probability).
Drawing 3 samples, r_{1-3}, from parameter space $\{1:D\}\backslash\{i\}$.
Finding the update direction $Z = CH_j - CH_{r_1}$.
Projecting CH_{r2} and CH_{r3} onto Z, to get Z_{p_1} and Z_{p_2}.
Creating a proposal $CH^* = CH_j + \gamma_1(Z_{p_2} - Z_{p_1})$.
Computing the Metropolis ratio (1) $MR = \dfrac{\mathcal{L}(CH^*)||CH^* - CH_{r_1}||^{D-1}}{\mathcal{L}(CH_i)||CH_i - CH_{r_1}||^{D-1}}.$
Adaptive Metropolis and differential evolution updating (with a 90% of probability).
Randomly select d dimensions from D-dimensional parameter space to update (within Gibbs sampling). Creating a proposal sample (1) $CH^*(d) = CH_i(d) + (1-\beta)N(0_d, \gamma_2^2\Sigma_d) + \beta N(0_d, \gamma_3^2 I_d).$
Creating a proposal sample (2) $CH^*(d) = CH_i(d) + \gamma_4(CH_{r_2}(d) - CH_{r_1}(d)) + e.$
Computing the Metropolis ratio (2) $MR = \dfrac{\mathcal{L}CH^*}{\mathcal{L}CH_i}.$
Accepting proposal CH, with probability $\max(MR, 1)$, and update current chain, CH_i.
Checking for Gelman-Rubin $\hat{R}$ convergence diagnostic.

LN = number of samples drawn from the prior distribution $[p(\theta)]$, using Latin Hypercube Sampling (LHS) and N = number of Markov chains (CH). D = the dimension of the entire parameter space, d = the dimension of the subspace of the parameters randomly selected for update (Metropolis within Gibbs sampling), T = the total number of iterations, and N_{AM} = the number of chains selected for the Adaptive Metropolis algorithm. $\gamma_1 - \gamma_4$ = "jump factors", where γ_1 is randomly selected, $\gamma_2 = 2.38/\sqrt{d}$, $\gamma_3 = 0.1/\sqrt{d}$ and $\gamma_4 = 2.38/\sqrt{2d}$. Σ_d = adaptive covariance matrix, based on the last 50% samples of the Markov chains. Source: Specifically readapted to this study from [8].

4. Results

Despite the SRA employing a good number of new generation copulas, with some of them complex in mathematical terms (i.e., Plackett or Shih-Louis), Table 4 shows that two copulas with a not very analytically complex, Li et al. [102] and Frees and Valdez [50] best fit the price–volume time series of the DJIA during the considered period (1928–2009), emphasizing that, in all cases, the specified selection criteria coincide except for three copulas: Galambos, BB1, and BB5.

Complementarily, Table 5 provides estimations of the parameters of each copula (Par) by fixing a range of 95% of uncertainty in their estimation (Unc-Range) through the application of local optimization and MCMCS. The copulas with best performance (Rank) are defined in terms of the root mean square error (RMSE) and the Nash–Sutcliff Efficiency (NSE) criteria. At this point, the existing literature usually employs local optimization algorithms when estimating the parameters of copulas with the consequent risk of being trapped in local optima, thus often obtaining unbiased and nonsignificant results [8]. Conversely, the hybrid-evolution MCMCS algorithm used in the SRA overcomes this initial limitation by determining an efficient estimator of the global optimum as well as an accurate approximation of uncertainties in the content of a Bayesian conceptual framework in the form of isolines, which is another of the improvements provided by this methodology to PVR analysis.

Table 4. Selection of copulas fitted to the DJIA index (1928–2009) based on three different criteria. Performance-criterion ranking amongst the implemented copulas.

Rank	Max-Likelihood	AIC	BIC	Criteria Coincidence
1	*Joe*	*Joe*	*Joe*	YES
2	*Burr*	*Burr*	*Burr*	YES
3	*Fischer-Hinzmann*	*Fischer-Hinzmann*	*Fischer-Hinzmann*	YES
4	*Roch-Alegre*	*Roch-Alegre*	*Roch-Alegre*	YES
5	*Tawn*	*Tawn*	*Tawn*	YES
6	*Gumbel*	*Gumbel*	*Gumbel*	YES
7	*BB5*	*Galambos*	*Galambos*	NO
8	*BB1*	*BB5*	*BB5*	NO
9	*Galambos*	*BB1*	*BB1*	NO
10	*Marshal-Olkin*	*Marshal-Olkin*	*Marshal-Olkin*	YES
11	*Cuadras-Auge*	*Cuadras-Auge*	*Cuadras-Auge*	YES
12	*Nelsen*	*Nelsen*	*Nelsen*	YES
13	*Frank*	*Frank*	*Frank*	YES
14	*Linear-Spearman*	*Linear-Spearman*	*Linear-Spearman*	YES
15	*Shih-Louis*	*Shih-Louis*	*Shih-Louis*	YES
16	*t*	*t*	*t*	YES
17	*Gaussian*	*Gaussian*	*Gaussian*	YES
18	*Raftery*	*Raftery*	*Raftery*	YES
19	*Clayton*	*Clayton*	*Clayton*	YES
20	*Plackett*	*Plackett*	*Plackett*	YES
21	*AMH*	*AMH*	*AMH*	YES
22	*FGM*	*FGM*	*FGM*	YES
23	*Fischer-Kock*	*Fischer-Kock*	*Fischer-Kock*	YES
24	*Cubic*	*Cubic*	*Cubic*	YES
25	*Independence*	*Independence*	*Independence*	YES
26	*Gumbel-Barnet*	*Gumbel-Barnet*	*Gumbel-Barnet*	YES

Souce: Own elaboration.

The analysis of the SRA applied to the NIKKEI225, FTSE100, and IBEX35 indices using the Tawn's copula is summarized in Table 6, similarly to Table 5. The price–volume dependence structure of the per se NIKKEI225 index is optimal in accordance with the NSE criterion, as it is very close to unity (0.9914), indicating an almost perfect model fitting. The per se IBEX35 adjustment is relatively optimal (0.9737), being lower for the FTSE100 (0.8235). The range of uncertainty of the parameters defining the Tawn's copula (θ_1, θ_2, and θ_3, Table 2) is considerably lower in the Nippon index than in the other two stock market indices.

Figure 3 shows that each stock exchange index corresponds to a certain typology of its probability isolines. Rows 1 to 3 refer to the analyzed indices, whereas columns correspond to the following specifications: (A) fitted empirical copulas probabilities, (B) fitted empirical copulas, and (C) return period copulas, calculated according to [115] by considering the joint return $\left(\frac{1}{1-C(u,v)}\right)$ as a measure of the dependence structure between the observed price peaks and trading volumes.

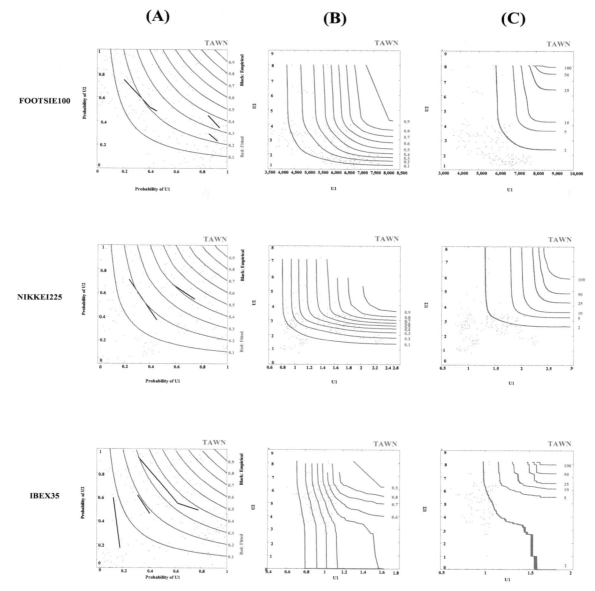

Figure 3. Probability isolines of Tawn's copula for FOOTSIE100, NIKKEI225, and IBEX35 indices. Source: Own elaboration.

The isolines derived from the application of Tawn's copula are ostensibly biased toward the upper left corner, which seems to indicate a low probability of occurrence of the price (U_1) synchronously linked to a high probability of occurrence of the trading volume (U_2) (both measured in magnitudes per se). Likewise, given the joint representation of the probability isolines and the empirical estimates of the joint probability distributions, the trends of the FOOTSIE100 and NIKKEI225 indices are fairly similar, although in the former index, high prices use to be related to trading volumes lower than those shown in the Japanese stock market. The P—V relationship in the IBEX35, although following a similar pattern, differs to some extent from the analysis of the other two indices, as low prices seem to be more related to high trading volumes quotas. This type of asymmetric and skewed dependence structure can be considered a common pattern of the three indices analyzed, equally extrapolated to the analysis of the fitted empirical copulas and return period copulas.

Table 5. Copula parameters estimation: DJIA (1928–2009).

Copula Name	Rank	RMSE [A]	NSE [B]	Par#1-Local	Par#2-Local	Par#3-Local	Par#1-MCMC	95%-Par#1-Unc-Range	Par#2-MCMC	95%-Par#2-Unc-Range	Par#3-MCMC	95%-Par#3-Unc-Range
AMH	21	1.4462	0.9051	1,0000	NaN	NaN	1.0000	[0.9793;0.9998]	NaN	[NaN;NaN]	NaN	[NaN;NaN]
BB1	8	0.1864	0.9984	0.0001	6.8711	NaN	0.0012	[0.0007;0.0890]	6.8738	[6.3355;7.4168]	NaN	[NaN;NaN]
BB5	7	0.1864	0.9984	1.0075	6.1177	NaN	6.8666	[1.0085;7.2476]	0.0434	[0.0260;6.3875]	NaN	[NaN;NaN]
Burr	2	0.1564	0.9989	0.0884	NaN	NaN	0.0884	[0.0832;0.0948]	NaN	[NaN;NaN]	NaN	[NaN;NaN]
Clayton	19	0.2617	0.9969	2.6215	NaN	NaN	27.7501	[22.3225;34.3061]	NaN	[NaN;NaN]	NaN	[NaN;NaN]
Cuadras-Auge	11	0.1919	0.9983	0.9401	NaN	NaN	0.9401	[0.9327;0.9474]	NaN	[NaN;NaN]	NaN	[NaN;NaN]
Cubic	24	2.1634	0.7877	2.0000	NaN	NaN	1.9998	[1.3902;1.9954]	NaN	[NaN;NaN]	NaN	[NaN;NaN]
FGM	22	1.6844	0.8713	1.0000	NaN	NaN	1.0000	[0.9550;0.9999]	NaN	[NaN;NaN]	NaN	[NaN;NaN]
Fischer-Hinzmann	3	0.1653	0.9988	0.9745	-1.7302	NaN	0.9738	[0.9622;0.9814]	-1.7073	[-2.0944;-1.2435]	NaN	[NaN;NaN]
Fischer-Kock	23	1.6846	0.8713	1.0000	1.0000	NaN	1.0005	[1.0015;1.1530]	0.9996	[0.9498;0.9996]	NaN	[NaN;NaN]
Frank	13	0.2041	0.9981	20.1073	NaN	NaN	25.7416	[23.5320;28.7390]	NaN	[NaN;NaN]	NaN	[NaN;NaN]
Galambos	9	0.1865	0.9984	6.1687	NaN	NaN	6.1688	[5.6654;6.7940]	NaN	[NaN;NaN]	NaN	[NaN;NaN]
Gaussian	17	0.2131	0.9979	0.9140	NaN	NaN	0.9785	[0.9735;0.9827]	NaN	[NaN;NaN]	NaN	[NaN;NaN]
Gumbel	6	0.1864	0.9984	4.3567	NaN	NaN	6.8717	[6.3810;7.5823]	NaN	[NaN;NaN]	NaN	[NaN;NaN]
Gumbel-Barnet	26	2.2788	0.7645	0.0000	NaN	NaN	0.0000	[0.0003;0.0321]	NaN	[NaN;NaN]	NaN	[NaN;NaN]
Independence	25	2.2788	0.7645	NaN	NaN	NaN	NaN	[NaN;NaN]	NaN	[NaN;NaN]	NaN	[NaN;NaN]
Joe	1	0.1563	0.9989	12.0596	NaN	NaN	12.0583	[11.3142;12.9402]	NaN	[NaN;NaN]	NaN	[NaN;NaN]
Linear-Spearman	14	0.2079	0.9980	0.9238	NaN	NaN	0.9238	[0.9113;0.9340]	NaN	[NaN;NaN]	NaN	[NaN;NaN]
Marshal-Olkin	10	0.1893	0.9984	8.6736	0.1012	NaN	0.9484	[0.9382;0.9714]	0.9298	[0.9019;0.9410]	NaN	[NaN;NaN]
Nelsen	12	0.2041	0.9981	24.0724	NaN	NaN	25.7465	[23.6645;28.8592]	NaN	[NaN;NaN]	NaN	[NaN;NaN]
Plackett	20	0.4651	0.9902	35.0000	NaN	NaN	34.9994	[34.0284;34.9944]	NaN	[NaN;NaN]	NaN	[NaN;NaN]
Raftery	18	0.2602	0.9969	0.9522	NaN	NaN	0.9522	[0.6394;0.9791]	NaN	[NaN;NaN]	NaN	[NaN;NaN]
Roch-Alegre	4	0.1707	0.9987	0.0001	9.0334	NaN	0.0007	[0.0029;0.1435]	9.0521	[8.3601;9.7642]	NaN	[NaN;NaN]
Shih-Louis	15	0.2079	0.9980	0.9238	NaN	NaN	0.9237	[0.9128;0.9348]	NaN	[NaN;NaN]	NaN	[NaN;NaN]
t	16	0.2085	0.9980	0.9363	3.9764	NaN	0.9809	[0.9745;0.9849]	0.5611	[0.2827;30.9390]	NaN	[NaN;NaN]
Tawn	5	0.1793	0.9985	0.9787	0.9466	11.5247	0.9786	[0.9580;0.9957]	0.9457	[0.9233;0.9662]	11.6332	[8.4142;23.0476]

A. Root Mean Square Error. B. Nash-Sutcliff Efficiency. Source: Own elaboration.

Table 6. Tawn copula parameters estimation: NIKKEI225, IBEX35, and FTSE100 (2000–2018).

Index	RMSE	NSE	Par#1-Local	Par#2-Local	Par#3-Local	Par#1-MCMC	95%-Par#1-Unc-Range	Par#2-MCMC	95%-Par#2-Unc-Range	Par#3-MCMC	95%-Par#3-Unc-Range
NIKKEI 225	0.2621	0.9914	0.0744	0.2153	34.9816	0.0738	[0.0551–0.1248]	0.219	[0.0977–0.4725]	25.9197	[2.2342–34.4984]
IBEX 35	0.3901	0.9737	0.005	0.8691	11.1339	0.0049	[0.0000–0.9876]	0.9969	[0.0000–0.9969]	22.6851	[1.0000–34.4965]
FTSE 100	0.9005	0.8235	0.3857	0	13.1732	0.0097	[0.0000–0.9896]	0.5024	[0.0000–0.9881]	1	[1.0000–35.0000]

Source: Own elaboration.

Figure 4 shows the degree of uncertainty associated with the three parameters defining the Tawn's copula. Figure 4 exhibits the specification of the copula parameters generated by the MCMCS through a Bayesian framework. Blue bins represent the MCMC-obtained parameters, blue crosses (bottom of each plot) denote the maximum likelihood estimation parameters, and red asterisks (top of each plot) indicate the copula parameter value obtained by local optimization.

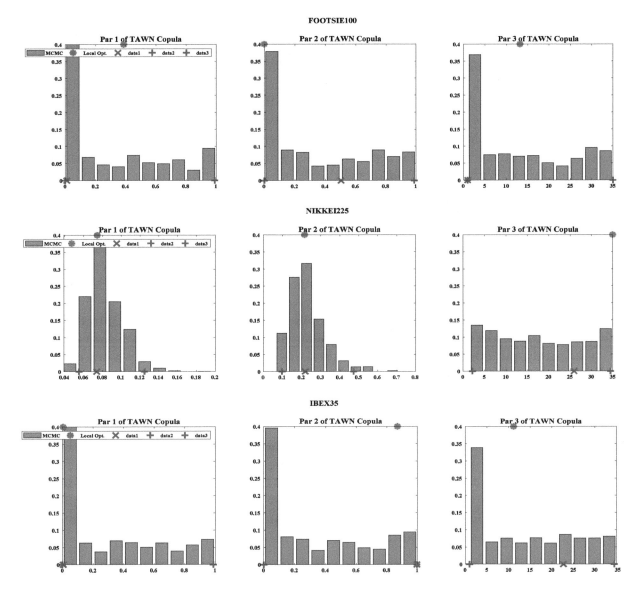

Figure 4. Posterior distribution of fitted Tawn's copula on FOOTSIE100, NIKKEI225, and IBEX35 indices obtained by the MCMCS. Source: Own elaboration.

In a context characterized by minimal uncertainty when specifying the parameters of the copula in each market, the parameters obtained by the local optimization algorithm should coincide with the mode of the distribution calculated through the MCMCS. However, this was only observed in the NIKKEI225 (parameters 1 and 2) and IBEX35 (parameter 1) and was not contrastable for any of the three parameters obtained from the Tawn's copula to the FOOTSIE100 index. These results are consistent with the previously calculated uncertainty ranges and with the delimitation of the degree of goodness of the adjustment performed by the NSE criteria (Table 6), according to which the NIKKEI225 index represented a quasiperfect fitting to this copula, followed by the IBEX35, and, to a lesser extent, the FOOTSIE100. This can be justified by the different range of variation of the parameters obtained for each index, where the FOOTSIE100 index is associated with a higher level of uncertainty compared with NIKKEI225 and IBEX35.

5. Discussion

The application of the SRA provides an alternative and innovative approach to PVR based on the simultaneous application of 26 copulas, which facilitated the analysis of their dependence structures and implicit morphology according with their probability isolines. Many of these copulas are dissimilar in form, although quite similar in performance. This also allowed us to model the relationship between prices and trading volumes from different points of view, quantifying the uncertainty underlying to the specification of the parameters defining each copula. The PVR, usually characterized by a markedly asymmetric relationship [13], is reinforced by the application of the SRA, since several of the copulas used in this methodology (e.g., Galambos, Bernstein, Tawn, etheory of copulas.) are especially effective in the study of phenomena with underlaying asymmetric skewed dependence structures.

From an empirical point of view, the joint implementation of the 26 copulas in the DJIA (generic scenario) confirmed that Joe's copula is able to more efficiently model the dependence structures of this index. Framing our findings with the existing literature, the use of Tawn's copula in the FOOTSIE100, NIKKEI225, and IBEX35 indices (specific scenario) confirms Ying [68]'s findings in their seminal analysis of the S&P 500 index. Similarly, our results confirm the analysis of the NIKKEI225 completed by Bremer and Kato [116], according to which an asymmetric relationship could be observed (negative correlation between past prices and current trading volume). This relationship was explained in the FOOTSIE100 by Huang and Masulis [117] based on the existence of a minority of informed-trading investors who simply sought immediate liquidity. The asymmetric PVR detected in the IBEX35 aligns with that already reported in the literature (see, for example, [118]). Its differentiated nature with respect to the other two indices is probably due to, according to [119] in the Spanish financial markets (Mercado Continuo), a strong linear causal relationship from returns to trading volume. Specifically, periods with high returns are usually followed by periods with particularly high trading volume. Such guidelines are comparable to those detected in other works [95,97], which explicitly used copulas in the study of PVR in the Asian financial markets, repeatedly verifying the existence of an inverse relationship between prices and volumes traded, in both cases foreseeably increased by the effects of the 1997 Asian financial crisis.

One of the improvements associated with the application of the SAR approach to the PVR is facilitating the analysis of both variables from a large number of copulas by defining the relationship based on ranges of uncertainty applying the RMSE and NSE criteria (see Tables 5 and 6), independent of the degree or sign of the linear correlation exhibited by the Pearson correlation coefficient (ρ), which, to the best of our knowledge, is an entirely new application in the field of quantitative finance of future utility for researchers and investors.

6. Conclusions

The main contribution of this research is the analysis of the existing relationship between prices and trading volume from multiple copulas, which allowed us to comparatively abstract the underlying dependency structures of both variables to establish possible analogies or differences. One of the most important limitations related to the empirical application of copulas is solved, which is employing a limited number of standard copulas when, in reality, there are multiple copulas not yet well extended in the literature [11]. Through the empirical methodology introduced in this article, the versatility of copulas increases when they are simultaneously combined with the polyvalence of the Bayesian analysis and with the hybrid-evolution MCMCS algorithm proposed by Sadegh et al. [8]. We are the first to implement the SRA, not just in PVR analysis, but in the ambit of quantitative finance. More specifically, for practical purposes, PVR analysis is decisive for both academics and practitioners, since, following the scheme constructed by Karpoff [13], it has the following implications: (1) it generates additional information regarding the structure of financial markets; (2) from an empirical point of view, it is fundamental in the generation of case studies that jointly use prices and trading volume, facilitating the implementation of analyses and inferences; (3) it is a crucial element in the study of the empirical distribution of speculative prices; and (4) its research would be particularly indicated in the futures markets where, a priori, the variability of prices used to affect the trading volume.

Additionally, we tried to answer and reconcile three questions linked to the theory of copulas: which copula is the "right one" [120], which copula should be used [20], and why copulas have been successful in many practical applications [44]? Versatility is the key term that best defines a copula; therefore, the most appropriate copula for analyzing a particular issue is the one that best summarizes its implicit dependence structures. Hence, copulas have been so successful in different fields of study.

A first conclusion to be drawn from this work is that the potential of the theory of copulas could be significantly reduced if certain copulas-type are systematically used in the analysis of bivariate time series. Precisely, this was the factor that caused a certain reluctance toward the use of copulas when the Gaussian copula [10] was employed massively in almost any scientific field, without considering either the intrinsic nature of the phenomena analyzed or that the use of a large number of copulas can substantially improve the knowledge of the different relations of dependence observable in a given dataset [50]. Thus, the SRA is not simply limited to the task of choosing and fitting the copula [121], but following the transdisciplinary perspective of econophysics, it supposes a new framework in the analysis of the PVR, extrapolated from the field of hydrology, which is directly applicable to many other areas such as quantitative finance.

Since Karpoff [13], the PVR has been practically subsumed to the generalization of the significance of Pearson's linear correlation coefficient of the price and trading volume variables. However, an alternative is provided in this methodology since the classical optimization methods applied to copulas often get trapped in local minima. The SRA is able to conveniently overcome this limitation by accurately describing the dependence structure of variables P and V and, importantly, by allowing the analysis of uncertainties given a determined time horizon (or length of record, see [8]). Another contribution of this work that may be important for future lines of research is the incorporation in the methodology of copula probability isolines in the analysis of PVR, which approximates this research to the multifractal models of Mandelbrot [22].

In our opinion, other future lines of research related to this work include, for example, the analysis of the role played by floating capital (outstanding shares vs. restricted shares) in the context of PVR, an aspect which has been often overlooked in the literature, or the rigorous enunciation and detailed compilation of those empirical stylized facts defining the price–volume time series, as well as the definitive consolidation of the works that have analyzed PVR from the perspective of the market microstructure of Garman [122]. This research could be gradually applied to the area of behavioral finance following the path of works such as Gomes [123], in which the analysis of PVR is directly connected to the prospective theory of Kahneman and Tversky [124].

Author Contributions: Conceptualization, methodology, software, writing—original draft preparation, P.A.M.C.; resources, writing—review and editing, funding acquisition, S.C.R.; investigation, data curation, supervision, M.d.C.V.M. All authors have read and agreed to the published version of the manuscript.

Acknowledgments: The authors would like to thank P. Embrechts (ETH, Zürich) for making us aware of some limitations derived from the misuse of copulas in certain specific assets, as well as E. Ragno (University of California at Irvine) and M. Sadegh (Boise State University, Idaho), two coauthors of the SRA, who advised and encouraged us in the use of this methodology given its first implementation in the area of quantitative finance.

Abbreviations

The following abbreviations are used in this manuscript:

PVR   price–volume relationship.
SRA   SRA approach.
MCMS   Markov Chain Monte Carlo simulation.
MDH   Mixture of Distribution Hypothesis.
SIAH   Sequential Information Arrival Hypothesis.
DBH   Dispersion of Beliefs Hypothesis.
NTH   Noise Trader Hypothesis.

Appendix A. The Bayesian Perspective of the SRA Approach

The Bayesian methodology constitutes one of the most recurrent approaches in economic and financial research, considered as an alternative third way to traditional perspectives. In previous studies [125,126], we can find an extensive introduction to Bayesian methods applied to finance, which created an important field of implementation in those contexts characterized by a high uncertainty, such as stress testing study cases [121,127] and the risk management optimization or the estimation of GARCH models in environments of extreme volatility [128,129]. Shemyakin [130] is essential for studying the Bayesian estimate of copulas based on the simplicity of Bayes' theorem (A1), that is, univocally assigning the corresponding uncertainties representatives of each parameter to the model and estimating its posterior distribution, the starting point of the SRA:

$$p(\theta|\tilde{Y}) = \frac{p(\theta)p(\tilde{Y}|\theta)}{p(\tilde{Y})}, \tag{A1}$$

where $p(\theta)$, $p(\theta|\tilde{Y})$, $p(\tilde{Y}|\theta) \cong \mathcal{L}(\theta|\tilde{Y})$, and $p(\tilde{Y}) = \int_\theta p(\tilde{Y}|\theta)\mathrm{d}\theta$ denote prior and posterior distribution (of parameters), likelihood function and coined (or real) evidence, respectively. Under the hypothesis that error residuals are Gaussian-distributed with mean zero, uncorrelated, and homoscedastic, the likelihood function can be reformulated as:

$$\mathcal{L}(\theta|\tilde{Y}) = \prod_{i=1}^{n} \frac{1}{\sqrt{2\pi\tilde{\sigma}^2}} \exp\left\{ -\frac{1}{2}\tilde{\sigma}^{-2}[\tilde{y}_i - y_i(\theta)]^2 \right\}, \tag{A2}$$

and logarithmically transformed into the formula [8]:

$$\ell(\theta|\tilde{Y}) = -\frac{n}{2}\ln(2\pi) - \frac{n}{2}\ln\tilde{\sigma}^2 - \frac{1}{2}\tilde{\sigma}^{-2}\sum_{i=1}^{n}[\tilde{y}_i - y_i(\theta)]^2, \tag{A3}$$

where $\tilde{\sigma}$ is an estimate of the standard deviation of the measurement error given by:

$$\tilde{\sigma}^2 = \frac{\sum_{i=1}^{n}[\tilde{y}_i - y_i(\theta)]^2}{n}, \tag{A4}$$

which allows us to simplify (A2) into:

$$\ell(\theta|\tilde{Y}) = -\frac{n}{2}\ln(2\pi) - \frac{n}{2} - \frac{n}{2}\ln\frac{\sum_{i=1}^{n}[\tilde{y}_i - y_i(\theta)]^2}{n} \tag{A5}$$

Finally, eliminating the constant terms of (A5), we would obtain a simplified equivalent log-likelihood function as:

$$\ell(\theta|\tilde{Y}) \approx -\frac{n}{2}\ln\frac{\sum_{i=1}^{n}[\tilde{y}_i - y_i(\theta)]^2}{n}. \tag{A6}$$

Once the data have been modeled according to any of the available copulas (Table 2), the SRA evaluates the goodness of fit using three different criteria: max-likelihood [131], Akaike information criterion (AIC) [132,133], and Bayesian information criterion (BIC) [134], taking the primary error residuals function as a reference under the assumption that, given a set of parameters, its maximum likelihood level completely minimizes the residuals between the model simulations and their linked observations. Notably, these assumptions are explicitly referred to the distribution of residual error that is applied to construct the likelihood function that summarizes the distance between the given observations and the prospective model simulations.

Appendix B. Brief Insight into the Theory of Copulas

The background of the theory of copulas can be traced to the works of Fréchet, Hoeffding, Menger, Féron, Gumbel, and Dell'Aglio, most of them analyzing the relationships between bivariate and trivariate distributions with their corresponding univariate marginal distributions. According to Sempi [135], the basis of the theory of copulas was established by Fréchet [136] and can be synthesized schematically according to the dimensions of Fréchet [136] and Hoeffding [137].

An n-dimensional *copula C* is a multivariate distribution function on the n-dimensional hypercube $[0,1]^n$ with uniformly distributed marginals.

The Sklar's theorem [15] is the starting point for the construction, development, and modeling of a new class of functions (or dependence functions, according to Galambos [138]), which have been generically denominated copulas since Sklar [15], who nominalized them using the Latin term *copulæ* ("couples") [4].

In short, this theorem [139] states that given a n-dimensional random vector $X = (X_1, X_2, \ldots, X_n)$ with joint distribution function F and marginal distribution functions $F_1, F_2, \ldots, F_n$, there exists an n-dimensional copula C, such that for every $(x_1, x_2, \ldots, x_n) \in \mathbb{R}^n$, Equation (A7) is satisfied. For absolutely continuous distributions, the copula C is unique.

Conversely, if C is the n-dimensional copula corresponding to a multivariate distribution function F with marginal distribution functions $F_1, F_2, \ldots, F_n$, then C can be expressed as:

$$C(u_1, \ldots, u_n) = F(F_1^{-1}(u_1), \ldots, F_n^{-1}(u_n)) \tag{A7}$$

and its copula density or probability function is given by:

$$c(u_1, \ldots, u_n) = \frac{f(F_1^{-1}(u_1), \ldots, F_n^{-1}(u_n))}{f_1(F_1^{-1}(u_1)) \cdots f_n(F_n^{-1}(u_n))}. \tag{A8}$$

If the joint distribution function is n times differentiable, the partial derivatives of order n can be calculated in (A7), by obtaining:

$$f(x) \equiv \frac{\partial^n}{\partial x_1 \partial x_2 \cdots \partial x_n} F(x) = \prod_{i=1}^{n} f_i(x_i) \times \frac{\partial^n}{\partial u_1 \partial u_2 \cdots \partial u_n} C(F_1(x_1), F_2(x_2), \ldots, F_n(x_n))$$

$$\equiv \prod_{i=1}^{n} f_i(x_i) \times c(F_1(x_1), F_2(x_2), \ldots, F_n(x_n)), \tag{A9}$$

from where:

$$\log f(x) = \sum_{i=1}^{n} \log f_i(x_i) + \log c(F_1(x_1), F_2(x_2), \ldots, F_n(x_n)). \tag{A10}$$

That is, the joint density function is equal to the product of the marginal densities and the density of the copula (represented by c [27]), from which it follows that the joint logarithmic probability is equal to the sum of the univariate logarithmic likelihoods and the copula logarithmic likelihood, which is a feature of extreme utility for the parametric estimation of multivariate model. Therefore, according to the Sklar's theorem (A7) and considering the equivalence relation (A9), given any couple of variables X and Y with respective marginal distributions $u = F(x_t)$ and $v = G(y_t)$ and joint distribution function $J(x_t, y_t)$, there is a copula C for all (x_t, y_t) in $\mathbb{R}^2$, which relates them according to the equation:

$$J(x_t, y_t) = C(F(x_t), G(y_t)). \tag{A11}$$

Again, calculating the partial derivatives in both terms of Equation (A11), we obtain:

$$\frac{\partial^2 J(x_t, y_t)}{\partial x_t \partial y_t} = \frac{\partial^2 C(F(x_t), G(y_t))}{\partial F \partial G} f(x_t) g(y_t)), \tag{A12}$$

which allows us to model the marginal distributions and the dependence structure between the variables separately from a certain copula [95].

Thus, the Sklar's theorem implies that the dependence relation between different variables can be completely subsumed to the construction of a copula, a process that can be summarized in two consecutive steps [51,139]: (1) identification of associated marginal distributions, and (2) election of a certain copula that appropriately represents the interrelations between the variables, so that the dependence between n random variables $X_1, X_2, \ldots, X_n$ is theoretically explained in its entirety from its joint distribution function $F(x_1, \ldots, x_n) = \mathbb{P}[X_1 \leq x_1, \ldots, X_n \leq x_n]$ [56].

References

1. Jovanovic, F.; Schinckus, C. The History of Econophysics' Emergence: A New Approach in Modern Financial Theory. *Hist. Political Econ.* **2013**, *45*, 443–474. [CrossRef]
2. Schinckus, C.; Jovanovic, F. Towards a transdisciplinary econophysics. *J. Econ. Methodol.* **2013**, *20*, 164–183. [CrossRef]
3. Hurst, H.E. Long Term Storage Capacity of Reservoirs. *Trans. Am. Soc. Civ. Eng.* **1951**, *116*, 770–799.
4. Genest, C.; Favre, A.C. Everything You Always Wanted to Know about Copula Modeling but Were Afraid to Ask. *J. Hydrol. Eng.* **2007**, *12*, 347–368. [CrossRef]
5. Reiß, R.D.; Thomas, M. *Statistical Analysis of Extreme Values: With Applications to Insurance, Finance, Hydrology and Other Fields*; Birkhäuser: Basel, Switzerland, 2007.
6. Schweizer, B. Introduction to Copulas. *J. Hydrol. Eng.* **2007**, *12*, 346. [CrossRef]
7. Genest, C. Everything You Always Wanted to Know about Copula Modeling but Were Afraid to Ask. In Proceedings of the NIPS 2011 Workshop on Copulas in Machine Learning, Sierra Nevada, Spain, 16 December 2011; Technical Report; American Society of Civil Engineers: Reston, VA, USA, 2011.
8. Sadegh, M.; Ragno, E.; AghaKouchak, A. Multivariate Copula Analysis Toolbox (MvCAT): Describing dependence and underlying uncertainty using a Bayesian framework. *Water Resour. Res.* **2017**, *53*. [CrossRef]
9. Genest, C.; Gendron, M.; Bourdeau-Brien, M. The Advent of Copulas in Finance. *Eur. J. Financ.* **2009**, *15*, 609–618. [CrossRef]
10. Li, D.X. On Default Correlation: A Copula Function Approach. *J. Fixed Income* **2000**, *9*, 4. [CrossRef]
11. Nadarajah, S.; Afuecheta, E.; Chan, S. A Compendium of Copulas. In *Probability and Statistics Group School of Mathematics, Research Reports*; Technical Report 10; The University of Manchester: Manchester, UK, 2016.
12. Huynh, V.N.; Inuiguchi, M.; Denoeux, T. (Eds.) *Integrated Uncertainty in Knowledge Modelling and Decision Making: Proceedings of the 4th International Symposium, IUKM 2015, Nha Trang, Vietnam, 15–17 October 2015*; Lecture Notes in Artificial Intelligence; Springer International Publishing: Cham, Switzerland, 2015; Volume 9376.

13. Karpoff, J.M. The Relation between Price Changes and Trading Volume: A Survey. *J. Financ. Quant. Anal.* **1987**, *22*, 109–126. [CrossRef]
14. Martín Cervantes, P.A. Hacia un Modelo Estocástico Eficiente Para la Valoración de Activos Financieros Basado en el Volumen de Negociación: Fundamentos Teóricos e Implementación Práctica. Ph.D. Thesis, Universidad de Almería, Almería, Spain, 2017.
15. Sklar, A. Fonctions de répartition à n dimensions et leurs marges. *Publ. L'Institut Stat. L'Université Paris* **1959**, *8*, 229–231.
16. Quesada, J.J.; Rodríguez, J.A.; Úbeda, M. What are copulas? In *Monografías del Seminario Matemático García de Galdeano*; Universidad de Zaragoza: Zaragoza, Spain, 2003; pp. 499–506.
17. Joe, H. *Multivariate Models and Multivariate Dependence Concepts*; Chapman & Hall/CRC Monographs on Statistics & Applied Probability; Springer Science & Business Media: Berlin/Heidelberg, Germany, 1997; Volume 73.
18. Nelsen, R.B. *An Introduction to Copulas*, 1st ed.; Lecture Notes in Statistics; Springer: New York, NY, USA, 1999; Volume 139.
19. Durante, F.; Sempi, C. *Principles of Copula Theory*; CRC Press: Boca Raton, FL, USA, 2015.
20. Embrechts, P. Copulas: A Personal View. *J. Risk Insur.* **2009**, *76*, 639–650. [CrossRef]
21. Daníelsson, J. *Financial Risk Forecasting: The Theory and Practice of Forecasting Market Risk with Implementation in R and Matlab*; The Wiley Finance Series; John Wiley & Sons: Chichester, UK, 2011.
22. Mandelbrot, B.B. Heavy Tails in Finance for Independent or Multifractal Price Increments. In *Handbook of Heavy Tailed Distributions in Finance*; Rachev, S.T., Ed.; North-Holland: Amsterdam, The Netherlands, 2003; Volume 1, Chapter 1, pp. 1–34.
23. Rachev, S.T.; Menn, C.; Fabozzi, F.J. Copulas. In *Fat-Tailed & Skewed Asset Return Distributions: Implications for Risk Management, Portfolio Selection, and Option Pricing*; Chapter 6; John Wiley & Sons: Hoboken, NJ, USA, 2005; pp. 71–80.
24. Junker, M.; Szimayer, A.; Wagner, N. Nonlinear term structure dependence: Copula functions, empirics, and risk implications. *J. Bank. Financ.* **2006**, *30*, 1171–1199. [CrossRef]
25. Ning, C.; Xu, D.; Wirjanto, T.S. *Modeling Asymmetric Volatility Clusters Using Copulas and High Frequency Data*; Technical Report 6, Working Papers; Ryerson University, Department of Economics: Toronto, ON, Canada, 2009.
26. Ibragimov, R.; Mo, J.; Prokhorov, A. *Fat Tails and Copulas: Limits of Diversification Revisited*; Technical Report 2015-06, Working Papers; University of Sydney Business School, Discipline of Business Analytics: Sydney, Australia, 2015.
27. Patton, A.J. Copula-Based Models for Financial Time Series. In *Handbook of Financial Time Series*; Andersen, T.G., Davis, R.A., Kreiß, J.P., Mikosch, T.V., Eds.; Mathematics and Statistics; Springer Science & Business Media: Berlin/Heidelberg, Germany, 2009; pp. 767–786.
28. Patton, A.J. A review of copula models for economic time series. *J. Multivar. Anal.* **2012**, *110*, 4–18. [CrossRef]
29. Patton, A.J. Copula Methods for Forecasting Multivariate Time Series. In *Handbook of Economic Forecasting*; Elliott, G., Timmermann, A., Eds.; Elsevier/North Holland: Amsterdam, The Netherlands, 2013; Volume 2, Chapter 16, pp. 899–960.
30. Giacomini, E.; Härdle, W.; Spokoiny, V. Inhomogeneous Dependence Modeling with Time-Varying Copulae. *J. Bus. Econ. Stat.* **2009**, *27*, 224–234. [CrossRef]
31. Manner, H.; Reznikova, O. A Survey on Time-Varying Copulas: Specification, Simulations, and Application. *Econom. Rev.* **2012**, *31*, 654–687. [CrossRef]
32. Patton, A.J. Modelling asymmetric exchange rate dependence. *Int. Econ. Rev.* **2006**, *47*, 527–556. [CrossRef]
33. Patton, A.J. On the out-of-sample importance of skewness and asymmetric dependence for asset allocation. *J. Financ. Econom.* **2004**, *2*, 130–168. [CrossRef]
34. Embrechts, P.; Höing, A.; Juri, A. Using copulae to bound the Value-at-Risk for functions of dependent risks. *Financ. Stochastics* **2003**, *7*, 145–167. [CrossRef]
35. Cherubini, U.; Luciano, E. Bivariate option pricing with copulas. *Appl. Math. Financ.* **2002**, *9*, 69–85. [CrossRef]
36. Van den Goorbergh, R.W.; Genest, C.; Werker, B.J. Bivariate option pricing using dynamic copula models. *Insur. Math. Econ.* **2005**, *37*, 101–114. [CrossRef]

37. Chiou, S.C.; Tsay, R.S. A copula-based approach to option pricing and risk assessment. *J. Data Sci.* **2008**, *6*, 273–301.

38. Morillas, P.M. A method to obtain new copulas from a given one. *Metrika* **2005**, *61*, 169–184. [CrossRef]

39. Chen, X.; Fan, Y. Estimation and model selection of semiparametric copula-based multivariate dynamic models under copula misspecification. *J. Econom.* **2006**, *135*, 125–154. [CrossRef]

40. García, C.; Herrerías, J.M.; Trinidad, J.E. Making Copulas Under Uncertainty. In *Distribution Models Theory*; Herrerías, R., Callejón, J., Herrerías, J.M., Eds.; World Scientific Publishing: Singapore, 2006; Chapter 2, pp. 27–53.

41. Genest, C.; Remillard, B.; Beaudoin, D. Goodness-of-fit tests for copulas: A review and a power study. *Insur. Math. Econ.* **2009**, *44*, 199–213. [CrossRef]

42. Joe, H.; Kurowicka, D. *Dependence Modeling: Vine Copula Handbook*; World Scientific Publishing: Singapore, 2011.

43. Kiatmanaroch, T.; Sriboonchitta, S. Relationship between Exchange Rates, Palm Oil Prices, and Crude Oil Prices: A Vine Copula Based GARCH Approach. In *Modeling Dependence in Econometrics: Selected Papers of the 7th International Conference of the Thailand Econometric Society, Faculty of Economics, Chiang Mai University, Thailand, 8–10 January 2014*; Huynh, V.N., Kreinovich, V., Sriboonchitta, S., Eds.; Advances in Intelligent Systems and Computing; Springer International Publishing: Cham, Switzerland, 2014; Volume 251, pp. 399–413.

44. Kreinovich, V.; Nguyen, H.T.; Sriboonchitta, S.; Kosheleva, O. Why Copulas Have Been Successful in Many Practical Applications: A Theoretical Explanation Based on Computational Efficiency. In *Integrated Uncertainty in Knowledge Modelling and Decision Making: Proceedings of the 4th International Symposium, IUKM 2015, Nha Trang, Vietnam, 15–17 October 2015*; Huynh, V.N., Inuiguchi, M., Denoeux, T., Eds.; Lecture Notes in Artificial Intelligence; Springer International Publishing: Cham, Switzerland, 2015; Volume 9376, pp. 112–126.

45. Embrechts, P.; Mcneil, A.J.; Straumann, D. Correlation and dependence in risk management. In Proceedings of the ASTIN Colloquium, Tokyo, Japan, 22–25 August 1999; Cambridge University Press: Cambridge, UK, 1999; pp. 176–223.

46. McNeil, A.J.; Frey, R.; Embrechts, P. *Quantitative Risk Management: Concepts, Techniques, and Tools: Concepts, Techniques, and Tools*; Princeton Series in Finance; Princeton University Press: Princeton, NJ, USA, 2005.

47. Schweizer, B.; Sklar, A. *Probabilistic Metric Spaces*; North Holland Series in Probability and Applied Mathematics; North Holland: Amsterdam, The Netherlands, 1983.

48. Genest, C.; Nešlehová, J. A Primer on Copulas for Count Data. *Astin Bull.* **2007**, *37*, 475–515. [CrossRef]

49. Mayor, G.; Suñer, J.; Torrens, J. Sklar's Theorem in Finite Settings. *IEEE Trans. Fuzzy Syst.* **2007**, *15*, 410–416. [CrossRef]

50. Frees, E.; Valdez, E. Understanding Relationships Using Copulas. *N. Am. Actuar. J.* **1998**, *2*, 1–25. [CrossRef]

51. Bouyé, E.; Durrleman, V.; Nikeghbali, A.; Riboulet, G.; Roncalli, T. *Copulas for Finance—A Reading Guide and Some Applications*; Technical Report; Crédit Lyonnais, Groupe de Recherche Opérationnelle: Paris, France, 2000.

52. Mikosch, T. Copulas: Tales and facts. *Extremes* **2006**, *9*, 3–20. [CrossRef]

53. Shiller, R.J. *Irrational Exuberance*; New York Times Bestseller, Broadway Books: New York, NY, USA, 2001.

54. Donnelly, C.; Embrechts, P. The Devil is in the Tails: Actuarial Mathematics and the Subprime Mortgage Crisis. *Astin Bull. J. Int. Actuar. Assoc.* **2010**, *40*, 1–33. [CrossRef]

55. Gumbel, E.J. Bivariate Exponential Distributions. *J. Am. Stat. Assoc.* **1960**, *55*, 698–707. [CrossRef]

56. Embrechts, P.; Mcneil, A.J.; Straumann, D. Correlation and dependence in risk management: Properties and pitfalls. In *RISK Management: Value at Risk and Beyond*; Cambridge University Press: Cambridge, UK, 2002; pp. 176–223.

57. Schachermayer, W. Mathematics and Finance. In Proceedings of the 7th European Congress of Mathematics (7ECM), Berlin, Germany, 18–22 July 2016. Technical report, The German Mathematical Society (DMV), the International Association of Applied Mathematics and Mechanics (GAMM), the Research Center Matheon, the Einstein Center ECMath and the Berlin Mathematical School (BMS).

58. Daníelsson, J. The emperor has no clothes: Limits to risk modelling. *J. Bank. Financ.* **2002**, *26*, 1273–1296. [CrossRef]

59. Zimmer, D.M. The Role of Copulas in the Housing Crisis. *Rev. Econ. Stat.* **2012**, *94*, 607–620. [CrossRef]

60. Salmon, F. The formula that killed Wall Street. *Significance* **2012**, *9*, 16–20. [CrossRef]
61. Rogers, L.C.G. Document in response to questions posed by Lord Drayson, UK Science and Innovation Minister. *Financ. Math. Credit. Crisis* **2009**.
62. Osborne, M.F.M. Brownian Motion in the Stock Market. *Oper. Res.* **1959**, *7*, 145–173. [CrossRef]
63. Samuelson, P.A. Rational Theory of Warrant Pricing. *Ind. Manag. Rev.* **1965**, *6*, 13–39.
64. Granger, C.W.J.; Morgenstern, O. Spectral analysis of New York stock market prices. *Kyklos* **1963**, *16*, 1–27. [CrossRef]
65. Godfrey, M.D.; Granger, C.W.J.; Morgenstern, O. The Random Walk Hypothesis of Stock Market Behavior. *Kyklos* **1964**, *17*, 1–30. [CrossRef]
66. Morgenstern, O. Demand Theory Reconsidered. *Q. J. Econ.* **1948**, *62*, 165–201. [CrossRef]
67. Granger, C.W.J. Investigating Causal Relations by Econometric Models and Cross-Spectral Methods. *Econometrica* **1969**, *37*, 424–438. [CrossRef]
68. Ying, C.C. Stock Market Prices and Volumes of Sales. *Econometrica* **1966**, *34*, 676–685. [CrossRef]
69. Clark, P.K. A Subordinated Stochastic Process Model with Finite Variance for Speculative Prices. *Econometrica* **1973**, *41*, 135–155. [CrossRef]
70. Epps, T.W. Security Price Changes and Transaction Volumes: Theory and Evidence. *Am. Econ. Rev.* **1975**, *65*, 586–597.
71. Epps, T.W.; Epps, M.L. The Stochastic Dependence of Security Price Changes and Transaction Volumes: Implications for the Mixture-of-Distributions Hypothesis. *Econometrica* **1976**, *44*, 305–321. [CrossRef]
72. Tauchen, G.E.; Pitts, M. The Price Variability-Volume Relationship on Speculative Markets. *Econometrica* **1983**, *51*, 485–505. [CrossRef]
73. Andersen, T.G. Return volatility and trading volume: An information flow interpretation of stochastic volatility. *J. Financ.* **1996**, *51*, 169–204. [CrossRef]
74. García, J. Volumen y volatilidad en mercados financieros: El caso del mercado de futuros español. *Rev. Espa NOla Financ. Contab.* **1998**, *XXVII*, 367–393.
75. Lamoureux, C.G.; Lastrapes, W.D. Heteroskedasticity in Stock Return Data: Volume versus GARCH Effects. *J. Financ.* **1990**, *45*, 221–229. [CrossRef]
76. Lamoureux, C.G.; Lastrapes, W.D. Endogenous Trading Volume and Momentum in Stock-Return Volatility. *J. Bus. Econ. Stat.* **1994**, *12*, 253–260.
77. Bollerslev, T. Generalized Autoregressive Conditional Heteroskedasticity. *J. Econom.* **1986**, *31*, 307–327. [CrossRef]
78. Copeland, T.E. A Model of Asset Trading under the Assumption of Sequential Information Arrival. *J. Financ.* **1976**, *31*, 1149–1168. [CrossRef]
79. Copeland, T.E. A Probability Model of Asset Trading. *J. Financ. Quant. Anal.* **1977**, *12*, 563–578. [CrossRef]
80. Darrat, A.F.; Zhong, M.; Cheng, L.T. Intraday volume and volatility relations with and without public news. *J. Bank. Financ.* **2007**, *31*, 2711–2729. [CrossRef]
81. Chen, Z.; Daigler, R.T. An Examination of the Complementary Volume-volatility Information Theories. *J. Futur. Mark.* **2008**, *28*, 963–992. [CrossRef]
82. DeLong, J.B.; Shleifer, A.; Summers, L.H.; Waldmann, R.J. Positive Feedback Investment Strategies and Destabilizing Rational Speculation. *J. Financ.* **1990**, *45*, 379–395. [CrossRef]
83. Black, F. Noise. Papers and Proceedings of the Forty-Fourth Annual Meeting of the America Finance Association. *J. Financ.* **1986**, *41*, 529–543.
84. Harris, M.; Raviv, A. Differences of Opinion Make a Horse Race. *Rev. Financ. Stud.* **1993**, *6*, 473–506. [CrossRef]
85. Shalen, C.T. Volume, Volatility, and the Dispersion of Beliefs. *Rev. Financ. Stud.* **1993**, *6*, 405–434. [CrossRef]
86. Gurgul, H.; Syrek, R. Archimedean copulas for price-volume dependencies of DAX companies. *Syst. Sci.* **2006**, *32*, 63–90.
87. Gurgul, H.; Mestel, R.; Syrek, R. Polish stock market and some foreign markets—Dependence analysis by copulas. *Oper. Res. Decis.* **2008**, *2*, 17–35.
88. Gurgul, H.; Mester, R.; Syrek, R. The testing of causal Stock returns-trading Volume Dependencies with the Aid of copulas. *Manag. Econ.* **2013**, *13*, 21–44. [CrossRef]
89. Bouezmarni, T.; Rombouts, J.V.; Taamouti, A. Nonparametric Copula-Based Test for Conditional Independence with Applications to Granger Causality. *J. Bus. Econ. Stat.* **2012**, *30*, 275–287. [CrossRef]

90. Gurgul, P.; Syrek, R. Testing of Dependencies between Stock Returns and Trading Volume by High Frequency Data. *Manag. Glob. Transit.* **2013**, *11*, 353–373.

91. Gurgul, H.; Syrek, R. The structure of contemporaneous price-volume relationships in financial markets. *Manag. Econ.* **2013**, *14*, 39–60. [CrossRef]

92. Rossi, E.; de Magistris, P.S. Long memory and tail dependence in trading volume and volatility. *J. Empir. Financ.* **2013**, *22*, 94–112. [CrossRef]

93. Gurgul, H.; Syrek, R.; Mitterer, C. Price duration versus trading volume in high-frequency data for selected DAX companies. *Manag. Econ.* **2016**, *17*, 241–260. [CrossRef]

94. Joe, H.; Xu, J.J. *The Estimation Method of Inference Functions for Margins for Multivariate Models*; Technical Report #166; University of British Columbia, Department of Statistics: Vancouver, BC, Canada, 1996.

95. Ning, C.; Wirjanto, T.S. Extreme Return-Volume Dependence in East-Asian Stock Markets: A Copula Approach. *Financ. Res. Lett.* **2009**, *6*, 202–209. [CrossRef]

96. Gallant, A.R.; Rossi, P.E.; Tauchen, G.E. Stock Prices and Volume. *Rev. Financ. Stud.* **1992**, *5*, 199–242. [CrossRef]

97. Naeem, M.; Hao, J.; Brunero, L. Negative return-volume relationship in Asian stock markets: FIGARCH-Copula Approach. *Eurasian J. Econ. Financ.* **2014**, *2*, 1–20. [CrossRef]

98. Larkin, M.; Shaw, R.; Flowers, P. Multiperspectival designs and processes in interpretative phenomenological analysis research. *Qual. Res. Psychol.* **2019**, *16*, 182–198. [CrossRef]

99. McKee, T.B.; Doesken, N.J.; Kliest, J. The relationship of drought frequency and duration to time scales. In Proceedings of the Eighth Conference on Applied Climatology, Anaheim, CA, USA, 17–22 January 1993; pp. 179–184.

100. Khoudraji, A. Contributions à L'etude des Copules et à la Modélisation de Valeurs Extrêmes Bivariées. Ph.D. Thesis, Université de Laval, Laval, QC, Canada, 1995.

101. Frey, R.; McNeil, A.J.; Nyfeler, M. *Modelling Dependent Defaults: Asset Correlations Are Not Enough!* Technical Report, Working Papers; ETH Zürich, Department of Mathematics: Zürich, Switzerland, 2001.

102. Li, C.; Singh, V.P.; Mishra, A.K. A bivariate mixed distribution with a heavy-tailed component and its application to single-site daily rainfall simulation. *Water Resour. Res.* **2013**, *49*, 767–789. [CrossRef]

103. Clayton, D.G. A Model for Association in Bivariate Life Tables and Its Application in Epidemiological Studies of Familial Tendency in Chronic Disease Incidence. *Biometrika* **1978**, *65*, 141–151. [CrossRef]

104. Nelsen, R.B. Properties and applications of copulas: A brief survey. In Proceedings of the First Brazilian Conference on Statistical Modeling in Insurance and Finance, Maresias, Brazil, 25–30 March 2003; Dhaene, J., Kolev, N., Morettin, P.A., Eds.; University of Sao Paulo: Sao Paulo, Brazil, 2003; pp. 10–28.

105. Ali, M.M.; Mikhail, N.N.; Haq, M.S. A class of bivariate distributions including the bivariate logistic. *J. Multivar. Anal.* **1978**, *8*, 405–412. [CrossRef]

106. Barnett, V. Some bivariate uniform distributions. *Commun. Stat. Theory Methods* **1980**, *9*, 453–461. [CrossRef]

107. Plackett, R.L. A Class of Bivariate Distributions. *J. Am. Stat. Assoc.* **1965**, *60*, 516–522. [CrossRef]

108. Cuadras, C.M.; Augé, J. A Continuous General Multivariate Distribution and its Properties. *Commun. Stat. Theory Methods* **1981**, *10*, 339–353. [CrossRef]

109. Shih, J.H.; Louis, T.A. Inferences on the Association Parameter in Copula Models for Bivariate Survival Data. *Biometrics* **1995**, *51*, 1384–1399. [CrossRef]

110. Joe, H. *Dependence Modeling with Copulas*; CRC Press: Boca Raton, FL, USA, 2014.

111. Durrleman, V.; Nikeghbali, A.; Roncalli, T. *A Note about the Conjecture about Spearman's rho and Kendall's Tau*; Technical Report; Crédit Lyonnais, Groupe de Recherche Opérationnelle: Paris, France, 2000.

112. Fischer, M.J.; Hinzmann, G. *A New Class of Copulas With Tail Dependence and a Generalized Tail Dependence Estimator*; Discussion Papers; Friedrich-Alexander University Erlangen-Nuremberg: Nuremberg, Germany, 2006.

113. Roch, O.; Alegre, A. Testing the bivariate distribution of daily equity returns using copulas. An application to the Spanish stock market. *Comput. Stat. Data Anal.* **2006**, *51*, 1312–1329. [CrossRef]

114. Johannes, M.; Polson, N. MCMC Methods for Continuous-Time Financial Econometrics. In *Handbook of Financial Econometrics: Applications*; Aït-Sahalia, Y., Hansen, L.P., Eds.; Handbooks in Finance; Elsevier: Amsterdam, The Netherlands, 2010; Volume 2, Chapter 13, pp. 1–72.

115. AghaKouchak, A. Water Resources Research. *J. Hydrometeorol.* **2014**, *15*, 1944–1973.

116. Bremer, M.; Kato, H.K. Trading Volume for Winners and Losers on the Tokyo Stock Exchange. *J. Financ. Quant. Anal.* **1996**, *31*, 127–142. [CrossRef]

117. Huang, R.D.; Masulis, R. Trading activity and stock price volatility: Evidence from the London Stock Exchange. *J. Empir. Financ.* **2003**, *10*, 249–269. [CrossRef]

118. Quiroga García, R.; Sánchez Álvarez, I. Intraday volatility and information arrival in the IBEX-35 futures markets. *Span. J. Financ. Account. Rev. EspañOla Financ. Contab.* **2006**, *35*, 523–540.

119. Zárraga Alonso, A. Análisis de causalidad entre rendimiento y volumen. *Investig. EconÓmicas* **1998**, *XXII*, 45–67.

120. Durrleman, V.; Nikeghbali, A.; Roncalli, T. *Which Copula Is the Right One?* Technical Report; Crédit Lyonnais, Groupe de Recherche Opérationnelle: Paris, France, 2000.

121. Rebonato, R.; Denev, A. Choosing and fitting the copula. In *Portfolio Management under Stress: A Bayesian-Net Approach to Coherent Asset Allocation*; Cambridge University Press: Cambridge, UK, 2014; Chapter 19, pp. 278–290.

122. Garman, M.B. Market microstructure. *J. Financ. Econ.* **1976**, *3*, 257–275. [CrossRef]

123. Gomes, F. Portfolio Choice and Trading Volume with Loss-Averse Investors. *J. Bus.* **2005**, *78*, 675–706. [CrossRef]

124. Kahneman, D.; Tversky, A. Prospect Theory: An Analysis of Decision under Risk. *Econometrica* **1979**, *47*, 263–291. [CrossRef]

125. Rachev, S.T.; Hsu, J.S.J.; Bagasheva, B.S.; Fabozzi, F.J. *Bayesian Methods in Finance*; The Frank J. Fabozzi Series; John Wiley & Sons: Hoboken, FL, USA, 2008; Volume 163.

126. Jacquier, E.; Polson, N. Bayesian Methods in Finance. In *The Oxford Handbook of Bayesian Econometrics*; Geweke, J., Koop, G., van Dijk, H., Eds.; Oxford Handbooks in Economics, Oxford University Press: Oxford, UK, 2011.

127. Rebonato, R. *Coherent Stress Testing: A Bayesian Approach to the Analysis of Financial Stress*; The Wiley Finance Series; John Wiley & Sons: Chichester, UK, 2010.

128. Ardia, D. *Financial Risk Management with Bayesian Estimation of GARCH Models: Theory and Applications*; Lecture Notes in Economics and Mathematical Systems; Springer: Berlin/Heidelberg, Germany, 2008; Volume 612.

129. Sekerke, M. *Bayesian Risk Management: A Guide to Model Risk and Sequential Learning in Financial Markets*; Wiley Finance, John Wiley & Sons: Hoboken, NJ, USA, 2015.

130. Shemyakin, A.; Kniazev, A. *Introduction to Bayesian Estimation and Copula Models of Dependence*; John Wiley & Sons: Hoboken, NJ, USA, 2017.

131. Barnard, G.A.; Jenkins, G.M.; Winsten, C.B. Likelihood Inference and Time Series. *J. R. Stat. Soc. Ser.* **1962**, *125*, 321–372. [CrossRef]

132. Akaike, H. A new look at the statistical model identification. *IEEE Trans. Autom. Control* **1974**, *19*, 716–723. [CrossRef]

133. Akaike, H. Information theory and an extension of the maximum likelihood principle. In *Selected Papers of Hirotugu Akaike*; Parzen, E., Tanabe, K., Kitagawa, G., Eds.; Springer Series in Statistics; Springer Science+Business Media: New York, NY, USA, 1998; Chapter 4, pp. 199–213.

134. Schwarz, G. Estimating the dimension of a model. *Ann. Stat.* **1978**, *6*, 416–464. [CrossRef]

135. Sempi, C. An introduction to Copulas. Technical report. In Proceedings of the 33rd Finnish Summer School on Probability Theory and Statistics, Tampere, Finland, 6–10 June 2011.

136. Fréchet, M.R. *Sur les Tableaux de Corrélation Dont les Marges Sont Données*; Annales de l'Université de Lyon, Sciences: Lyon, France, 1951; pp. 13–84.

137. Hoeffding, W. Schriften des Mathematischen Instituts und des Instituts für Angewandte Mathematik der Universität Berlin (Reprinted in english as "Scale-invariant correlation theory" in The Collected Works of Wassily Hoeffding, pp. 57–108, 1994). In *Maszstabinvariante Korrelationstheorie*; Fisher, N.I., Sen, P.K., Eds.; Springer Series in Statistics. Perspectives in Statistics; Springer: Berlin/Heidelberg, Germany, 1940; Volume 5, pp. 179–233.

138. Galambos, J. *The Asymptotic Theory of Extreme Order Statistics*; John Wiley & Sons: New York, NY, USA, 1978.

139. Molanes, E.M.; Romera, R. *Copulas in Finance and Insurance*; Technical Report ws086321, Universidad Carlos III. UC3M Working Papers, Statistics and Econometrics 08-21; Universidad Carlos III de Madrid, Departamento de Estadística: Madrid, Spain, 2008.

11

An Extension of the Concept of Derivative: Its Application to Intertemporal Choice

Salvador Cruz Rambaud [1,*] **and Blas Torrecillas Jover** [2]

[1] Departamento de Economía y Empresa, Universidad de Almería, La Cañada de San Urbano, s/n, 04120 Almería, Spain
[2] Departamento de Matemáticas, Universidad de Almería, La Cañada de San Urbano, s/n, 04120 Almería, Spain; btorreci@ual.es
* Correspondence: scruz@ual.es

Abstract: The framework of this paper is the concept of derivative from the point of view of abstract algebra and differential calculus. The objective of this paper is to introduce a novel concept of derivative which arises in certain economic problems, specifically in intertemporal choice when trying to characterize moderately and strongly decreasing impatience. To do this, we have employed the usual tools and magnitudes of financial mathematics with an algebraic nomenclature. The main contribution of this paper is twofold. On the one hand, we have proposed a novel framework and a different approach to the concept of relative derivation which satisfies the so-called generalized Leibniz's rule. On the other hand, in spite of the fact that this peculiar approach can be applied to other disciplines, we have presented the mathematical characterization of the two main types of decreasing impatience in the ambit of behavioral finance, based on a previous characterization involving the proportional increasing of the variable "time". Finally, this paper points out other patterns of variation which could be applied in economics and other scientific disciplines.

Keywords: derivation; intertemporal choice; decreasing impatience; elasticity

1. Introduction and Preliminaries

In most social and experimental sciences, such as economics, psychology, sociology, biology, chemistry, physics, epidemiology, etc., researchers are interested in finding, *ceteris paribus*, the relationship between the explained variable and one or more explaining variables. This relationship has not to be linear, that is to say, linear increments in the value of an independent variable does not necessarily lead to linear variations of the dependent variable. This is logical by taking into account the non-linearity of most physical or chemical laws. These circumstances motivate the necessity of introducing a new concept of derivative which, of course, generalizes the concepts of classical and directional derivatives. Consequently, the frequent search for new patterns of variations in the aforementioned disciplines justifies a new framework and a different approach to the concept of derivative, able to help in modelling the decision-making process. Let us start with some general concepts.

Let A be an arbitrary K-algebra (non necessarily commutative or associative), where K is a field. A *derivation* over A is a K-linear map $D : A \to A$ satisfying Leibniz's identity:

$$D(ab) = D(a)b + aD(b).$$

It can be easily demonstrated that the sum, difference, scalar product and composition of derivations are derivations. In general, the product is not a derivation, but the so-called *commutator*, defined as $[D_1, D_2] = D_1 D_2 - D_2 D_1$, is a derivation. We are going to denote by $\mathrm{Der}_K(A)$ the set of all derivations on A. This set has the structure of a K-module and, with the commutator operation, becomes a Lie Algebra. This algebraic notion includes the classical partial derivations of real functions of several variables and the Lie derivative with respect to a vector field in differential geometry. Derivations and differentials are important tools in algebraic geometry and commutative algebra (see [1–3]).

The notion of derivation was extended to the so-called (σ, τ)-derivation [4] for an associative $\mathbb{C}$-algebra A, where σ and τ are two different algebra endomorphisms of A ($\sigma, \tau \in \mathrm{End}_{\mathrm{Alg}}(A)$), as a $\mathbb{C}$-linear map $D : A \rightarrow A$ satisfying:

$$D(ab) = D(a)\tau(b) + \sigma(a)D(b).$$

If $\tau = \mathrm{id}_A$, we obtain $D(ab) = D(a)b + \sigma(a)D(b)$. In this case, we will say that D is a σ-derivation. There are many interesting examples of these generalized derivations. The q-derivation, as a q-differential operator, was introduced by Jackson [5]. In effect, let A be a $\mathbb{C}$-algebra (which could be $\mathbb{C}[z, z^{-1}]$ or various functions spaces). The two important generalizations of derivation are D_q and $M_q : A \rightarrow A$, defined as:

$$(D_q(f))(z) = \frac{f(qz) - f(z)}{qz - z} = \frac{f(qz) - f(z)}{(q - 1)z}$$

and

$$M_q(f)(z) = \frac{f(qz) - f(z)}{q - 1}.$$

These operations satisfy the q-deformed Leibniz's rule, $D(fg) = D(f)g + \sigma_q(f)g$, where $\sigma_q(f)(z) = f(qz)$, i.e., the q-derivation is a σ-derivation. Observe that this formula is not symmetric as the usual one.

Now, we can compare this q-derivation with the classical h-derivation, defined by:

$$(D_h(f))(z) = \frac{f(z + h) - f(z)}{h}.$$

In effect,

$$\lim_{q \to 1} D_q(f(z)) = \lim_{h \to 0} D_h(f(z)) = \frac{\mathrm{d}f(x)}{\mathrm{d}x},$$

provided that f is differentiable.

The q-derivation is the key notion of the quantum calculus which allows us to study those functions which are not differentiable. This theory has been developed by many authors and has found several applications in quantum groups, orthogonal polynomials, basic hypergeometric functions, combinatorics, calculus of variations and arithmetics [6,7].

In general, the q-derivation is more difficult to be computed. For instance, there is not a chain formula for this kind of derivation. We refer the interested reader to the books by Kac and Cheung [8], Ernst [9], and Annaby and Mansour [10] for more information about the q-derivations and q-integrals.

The q-derivation has been generalized in many directions within the existing literature. Recently, the β-derivative was introduced by Auch in his thesis [11], where $\beta(z) = az + b$, with $a \geq 1$, $b \geq 0$ and $a + b > 1$, the general case being considered in [12] and continued by several scholars [13]:

$$D_\beta(f)(z) = \frac{f(\beta(z)) - f(z)}{\beta(z) - z},$$

where $\beta \neq z$ and $\beta : I \to I$ is a strictly increasing continuous function, $I \subseteq \mathbb{R}$. Thus, q-derivation is a particular case of this new concept. Moreover, the operator by Hahn [14,15], defined as:

$$D_{q,\omega}(f)(z) = \frac{f(qz + \omega) - f(z)}{(q-1)z + \omega},$$

introduced to study orthogonal polynomials, is also a particular case. Another generalization of q-calculus is the so-called (p, q)-derivative which is a (σ, τ)-derivation [16].

Figure 1 summarizes the different types of derivations presented in this section and shows the relationships between them.

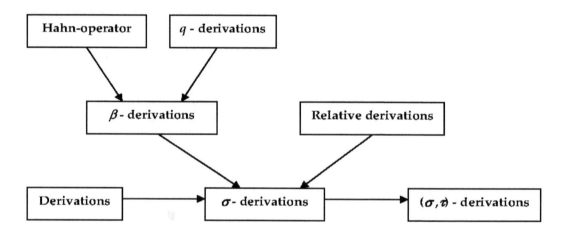

Figure 1. Chart of the different revised derivations.

This paper has been organized as follows. After this Introduction, Section 2 presents the novel concept of derivation relative to a given function f. It is shown that this derivative can be embodied in the ambit of relative derivations and satisfies Leibniz's rule. In Section 3, this new algebraic tool is used to characterize those discount functions exhibiting moderately and strongly decreasing impatience. In Section 4, the obtained results are discussed in the context of other variation patterns (quadratic, logarithmic, etc.) present in economics, finance and other scientific fields. Finally, Section 5 summarizes and concludes.

2. An Extension of the Concept of Derivative

2.1. General Concepts

Let A be a K-algebra and M be an A-module, where K is a field. Let $\sigma : A \to A$ an endomorphism of A. A σ-derivation D on M is an K-linear map

$$D : A \longrightarrow M,$$

such that

$$D(ab) = D(a)b + \sigma(a)D(b),$$

for every a and $b \in A$. From a structural point of view, let us denote by $\mathrm{Der}^{\sigma}_K(A, M)$ the set of all K-derivations on M. Obviously, $\mathrm{Der}^{\sigma}_K(A, M)$ is an A-module. In effect, if $D, D_1, D_2 \in \mathrm{Der}^{\sigma}_K(A, M)$ and $a \in A$, then $D_1 + D_2 \in \mathrm{Der}^{\sigma}_K(A, M)$ and $aD \in \mathrm{Der}^{\sigma}_K(A, M)$.

In the particular case where $M = A$, D will be called a *K-derivation on A*, and

$$\mathrm{Der}^{\sigma}_K(A, A) := \mathrm{Der}^{\sigma}_K(A)$$

will be called the *module of σ-derivations on A*.

2.2. Relative Derivation

Let us consider the module of K-derivations on the algebra A, $\text{Der}_K^\sigma(A)$. For every D_0 and $D \in \text{Der}_K^\sigma(A)$ and $a \in A$, we can define the *derivation relative to D_0 and a* as

$$D_a(\cdot) := D_0(a)D(\cdot).$$

Lemma 1. *If A is commutative, then D_a is a σ-derivation.*

Proof. In effect, clearly D is K-linear and, moreover, satisfies the generalized Leibniz's condition:

$$
\begin{aligned}
D_a(xy) &= D_0(a)D(xy) \\
&= D_0(a)[D(x)y + \sigma(x)D(y)] \\
&= D_0(a)D(x)y + \sigma(x)D_0(a)D(y) \\
&= D_a(x)y + \sigma(x)D_a(y).
\end{aligned}
$$

This completes the proof. $\square$

Given two σ-derivations, D_0 and $D \in \text{Der}_K^\sigma(A)$, we can define a map

$$\mathcal{D} : A \to \text{Der}_K^\sigma(A)$$

such that

$$\mathcal{D}(a) = D_a := D_0(a)D.$$

Example 1. *Consider the polynomial ring $A := K[x_1, x_2, \ldots, x_n, y_1, y_2, \ldots, y_n]$, $D_0 = \partial_{x_1} + \cdots + \partial_{x_n}$ and $D = \partial_{y_1} + \cdots + \partial_{y_n}$. Then, for $a = x_1 y_1 + \cdots + x_n y_n$ and every $f \in \mathcal{D}$, one has:*

$$
\begin{aligned}
D_a(f) &= D_0(a)D(f) \\
&= D_0(x_1 y_1 + \cdots + x_n y_n)D(f) \\
&= (y_1 + \cdots + y_n)[\partial_{y_1}(f) + \cdots + \partial_{y_n}(f))].
\end{aligned}
$$

Proposition 1. *For a commutative ring A, $\mathcal{D}$ is a σ-derivation.*

Proof. Firstly, let us see that $\mathcal{D}$ is K-linear. In effect, for every $a, b \in A$ and $k \in K$, one has:

$$
\begin{aligned}
\mathcal{D}(a+b) &= D_{a+b} = D_0(a+b)D \\
&= D_0(a)D + D_0(b)D = D_a + D_b = \mathcal{D}(a) + \mathcal{D}(b)
\end{aligned}
$$

and

$$
\begin{aligned}
\mathcal{D}(ka) &= D_{ka} = D_0(ka)D \\
&= kD_0(a)D = kD_a = k\mathcal{D}(a).
\end{aligned}
$$

Secondly, we are going to show that $\mathcal{D}$ satisfies the generalized Leibniz condition. In effect, for every $a, b \in A$, one has:

$$
\begin{aligned}
\mathcal{D}(ab) &= D_{ab} = D_0(ab)D = [D_0(a)b + \sigma(a)D_0(b)]D \\
&= [D_0(a)D]b + \sigma(a)[D_0(b)D] = D_a b + \sigma(a)D_b = \mathcal{D}_a b + \sigma(a)\mathcal{D}(b).
\end{aligned}
$$

Therefore, $\mathcal{D}$ is a σ-derivation. $\square$

Now, we can compute the bracket of two relative σ-derivations D_a and D_b, for every $a, b \in A$:

$$
\begin{aligned}
[D_a, D_b] &= D_a \circ D_b - D_b \circ D_a \\
&= D_a[D_0(b)D] - D_b[D_0(a)D] \\
&= D_0(a)D(D_0(b)D) - D_0(b)D(D_0(a)D) \\
&= D_0(a)[DD_0(b)D + \sigma(D_0(b))D^2] - D_0(b)[DD_0(a)D + \sigma(D_0(a))D^2] \\
&= [D_0(a)DD_0(b) - D_0(b)DD_0(a)]D + [D_0(a)\sigma(D_0(b)) - D_0(b)\sigma(D_0(a))]D^2.
\end{aligned}
$$

Observe that, although the bracket of two derivations is a derivation, in general it is not a relative derivation. However, if A is commutative and σ is the identity, then the former bracket could be simplified as follows:

$$
\begin{aligned}
[D_a, D_b] &= [D_0(a)DD_0(b) - D_0(b)DD_0(a)]D + [D_0(a), D_0(b)]D^2 \\
&= [D_0(a)DD_0(b) - D_0(b)DD_0(a)]D.
\end{aligned}
$$

Moreover, if A is commutative and σ is the identity, the double bracket of three derivations D_a, D_b and D_c, for every $a, b, c \in A$, is:

$$
\begin{aligned}
[[D_a, D_b], D_c] &= [D_0(a)DD_0(b) - D_0(b)DD_0(a)]DD_c - D_c[D_0(a)DD_0(b) - D_0(b)DD_0(a)]D \\
&= [D_0(a)DD_0(b) - D_0(b)DD_0(a)]DD_0(c)D - D_0(c)D[D_0(a)DD_0(b) - D_0(b)DD_0(a)]D \\
&= [D_0(a)DD_0(b) - D_0(b)DD_0(a)]DD_0(c)D + [D_0(a)DD_0(b) - D_0(b)DD_0(a))]D_0(c)D^2 \\
&= D_0(c)\{D[D_0(a)DD_0(b) - D_0(b)DD_0(a)]\}D - D_0(c)\{D[D_0(a)DD_0(b) - D_0(b)DD_0(a)
\end{aligned}
$$

Since the relative derivations are true derivations, they satisfy Jacobi's identity, i.e., for every $a, b, c \in A$, the following identity holds:

$$
[D_a, [D_b, D_c]] + [D_b, [D_c, D_a]] + [D_b, [D_a, D_b]] = 0.
$$

For σ derivation one could modify the definition of the bracket as in [17] and then a Jacobi-like identity is obtained [17, Theorem 5]. We left the details to the reader.

Given another derivation D_1, we can define a new relative σ-derivation $D'_a := D_1(a)D$. In this case, the new bracket is:

$$
\begin{aligned}
[D_a, D'_a] &= D_a D'_a - D'_a D_a \\
&= D_0(a)D(D_1(a)D) - D_1(a)D(D_0(a)D) \\
&= D_0(a)[DD_1(a)D - \sigma(D_1(a))D^2] - D_1(a)[DD_0(a)D - \sigma(D_0(a))D^2] \\
&= [D_0(a)DD_1(a) - D_1(a)DD_0(a)]D + [D_1(a)\sigma(D_0(a)) - D_0(a)\sigma(D_1(a))]D^2.
\end{aligned}
$$

If A is commutative and σ is the identity, then:

$$
[D_a, D'_a] = [D_0(a)DD_1(a) - D_1(a)DD_0(a)]D.
$$

The chain rule is also satisfied for relative derivations when A is commutative. In effect, assume that, for every $f, g \in A$, the composition, $f \circ g$, is defined. Then

$$
\begin{aligned}
D_a(f \circ g) &= D_0(f \circ g)D(f \circ g) \\
&= [D_0(f) \circ g]D_0(g)[D(f) \circ g]D(g) \\
&= [D_0(f) \circ g][D(f) \circ g]D_0(g)D(g) \\
&= [D_0(f)D(f) \circ g]D_0(g)D(g) \\
&= [D_a(f) \circ g]D_a(g).
\end{aligned}
$$

2.3. Derivation Relative to a Function

Let $f(x, \Delta)$ be a real function of two variables x and Δ such that, for every a:

$$\lim_{\Delta \to 0} f(a, \Delta) = a. \tag{1}$$

Let $F(x)$ be a real function differentiable at $x = a$. The *derivative of F relative to f*, at $x = a$, denoted by $D_f(F)(a)$, is defined as the following limit:

$$D_f(F)(a) := \lim_{\Delta \to 0} \frac{F[f(a, \Delta)] - F(a)}{\Delta}. \tag{2}$$

In this setting, we can define $g(x, \Delta)$ as the new function, also of two variables x and Δ, satisfying the following identity:

$$f(x, \Delta) := x + g(x, \Delta). \tag{3}$$

Observe that $g(x, \Delta) = f(x, \Delta) - x$ and, consequently,

$$\lim_{\Delta \to 0} g(a, \Delta) = 0.$$

The set of functions $g(x, \Delta)$, denoted by $\mathcal{S}$, is a subalgebra of the algebra of real-valued functions of two variables x and Δ, represented by $\mathcal{A}$. In effect, it is obvious to check that, if $g, g_1, g_2 \in \mathcal{S}$ and $\lambda \in \mathbb{R}$, then $g_1 + g_2$, $g_1 \cdot g_2$, and λg belong to $\mathcal{S}$. Therefore, if $\mathcal{F}$ denotes the set of the so-defined functions $f(x, \Delta)$, we can write:

$$\mathcal{F} = \mathrm{id} + \mathcal{S}, \tag{4}$$

where $\mathrm{id}(x) = x$ is the identity function of one variable. In $\mathcal{S}$, we can define the following binary relation:

$$g_1 \sim g_2 \text{ if, and only if, } \lim_{\Delta \to 0} \frac{g_1(x, \Delta)}{\Delta} = \lim_{\Delta \to 0} \frac{g_2(x, \Delta)}{\Delta}. \tag{5}$$

Obviously, $\sim$ is an equivalence relation. Now, we can define $h(x, \Delta)$ as the new function also of two variables x and Δ, satisfying the following identity:

$$g(x, \Delta) := h(x, \Delta)\Delta. \tag{6}$$

Thus,

$$h(x, \Delta) = \frac{f(x, \Delta) - x}{\Delta}. \tag{7}$$

Therefore,

$$D_f(F)(a) = \lim_{\Delta \to 0} \frac{F[a + h(a, \Delta)\Delta] - F(a)}{h(a, \Delta)\Delta} \lim_{\Delta \to 0} h(a, \Delta). \tag{8}$$

Observe that now $\lim_{\Delta \to 0} h(a, \Delta)$ only depends on a, whereby it can be simply denoted as $h(a)$:

$$h(a) := \lim_{\Delta \to 0} h(a, \Delta). \tag{9}$$

Thus, Equation (8) results in:

$$D_f(F)(a) = D(F)(a) \cdot h(a). \tag{10}$$

If $f(x, \Delta)$ is derivable at $\Delta = 0$, then $f(x, \Delta)$ is continuous at $\Delta = 0$, whereby

$$f(a, 0) = \lim_{\Delta \to 0} f(a, \Delta) = a \tag{11}$$

and, consequently,

$$h(a) = \lim_{\Delta \to 0} h(a, \Delta) = \lim_{\Delta \to 0} \frac{f(a, \Delta) - f(a, 0)}{\Delta} = \frac{\partial f(a, \Delta)}{\partial \Delta}\bigg|_{\Delta = 0}. \tag{12}$$

Therefore,

$$D_f(F)(a) = \frac{\partial f(a, \Delta)}{\partial \Delta}\bigg|_{\Delta = 0} D(F)(a). \tag{13}$$

Observe that we are representing by $D : \mathcal{C}^1(\mathbb{R}) \to \mathcal{C}^1(\mathbb{R})$ the operator $D = \frac{\mathrm{d}}{\mathrm{d}x}$. If, additionally, the partial derivative $\frac{\partial f(a, \Delta)}{\partial \Delta}\big|_{\Delta = 0}$ is simply denoted by $\partial_{y=0}(f)(a)$, expression (13) remains as:

$$D_f(F)(a) = \partial_{y=0}(f)(a)D(F)(a) = \partial_{y=0}(g)(a)D(F)(a)$$

or, globally,

$$D_f(F) = \partial_{y=0}(f)D(F) = \partial_{y=0}(g)D(F).$$

Thus, $D_f : \mathcal{C}^1(\mathbb{R}) \to \mathcal{C}^1(\mathbb{R})$ is really a derivation:

$$\begin{aligned}
D_f(FG) &= \partial_{y=0}(f)D(FG) \\
&= \partial_{y=0}(f)[D(F)G + FD(G)] \\
&= [\partial_{y=0}(f)D(F)]G + F[\partial_{y=0}(f)D(G)] \\
&= D_f(F)G + FD_f(G).
\end{aligned}$$

Observe that $h(a)$ or $\partial_{y=0}(f)(a)$ represents the equivalence class including the function $g(a, \Delta)$. Moreover, the set of all suitable values of $D_f(F)(a)$ is restricted to the set

$$D(F)(a)(\mathcal{S}/\sim),$$

where $\mathcal{S}/\sim$ is the quotient set derived from the equivalence relation $\sim$.

The name assigned to this derivative can be justified as follows. Observe that the graphic representation of $g(a, \Delta)$ is a surface which describes a kind of "valley" over the a-axis (that is to say, $\Delta = 0$) (see Figure 2). Therefore, for every value of a, a path can be obtained by intersecting the surface with the vertical plane crossing the point $(a, 0)$, giving rise to the function $g(a, \Delta)$, which represents the increment of a. As previously indicated, $g(a, \Delta)$ tend to zero as Δ approaches to zero (represented by the red arrow).

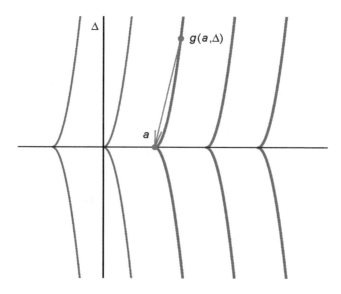

Figure 2. Plotting function $g(a, \Delta)$.

In the particular case in which

$$f(x, \Delta) = x + \Delta, \tag{14}$$

obviously, one has:

$$D_f(F)(a) = D(F)(a), \tag{15}$$

that is to say, the derivative relative to the function $f(x, \Delta) = x + \Delta$ (absolute increments) coincides with the usual derivative.

Example 2. *Assume that (percentage increments of the variable):*

$$f(x, \Delta) = x + \frac{\Delta}{x}.$$

In this case,

$$D_f(F)(a) = \frac{1}{a}D(F)(a).$$

In the context of certain scientific problems, it is interesting to characterize the variation (increase or decrease) of the so-defined derivative relative to a given function. In this case, the sign of the usual derivative of this relative derivative will be useful:

$$D[D_f(F)] = D[\partial_{y=0}(f)D(F)] = D[\partial_{y=0}(f)]D(F) + \partial_{y=0}(f)D^2(F). \tag{16}$$

Thus, if $D_f(F)$ must be increasing (resp. decreasing), then

$$D^2(F) > -\frac{D[\partial_{y=0}(f)]D(F)}{\partial_{y=0}(f)} \tag{17}$$

(resp. $D^2(F) < -\frac{D[\partial_{y=0}(f)]D(F)}{\partial_{y=0}(f)}$).

Example 3. *Assume that $f(x, \Delta) = \ln(\exp\{a\} + \Delta)$. In this case,*

$$D_f(F)(a) = \frac{1}{\exp\{a\}}D(F)(a).$$

The condition of increase of $D_f(F)$ leads to

$$D^2(F) > D(F).$$

3. An Application to Intertemporal Choice: Proportional Increments

This section is going to apply this new methodology to a well-known economic problem, more specifically to intertemporal choice. In effect, we are going to describe a noteworthy particular case of our derivative when the change in the variable is due to proportional instead to absolute increments. To do this, let us start with the description of the setting in which the new derivative will be applied (see [18,19]).

Let X be set $\mathbb{R}^+$ of non-negative real numbers and T a non-degenerate closed interval of $[0, +\infty)$. A *dated reward* is a couple $(x, t) \in X \times T$. In what follows, we will refer to x as the *amount* and t as the *time of availability* of the reward. Assume that a decision maker exhibits a continuous weak order on $X \times T$, denoted by $\preceq$, satisfying the following conditions (the relations $\prec, \succeq, \succ$ and $\sim$ can be defined as usual):

1. For every $s \in T$ and $t \in T$, $(0, s) \sim (0, t)$ holds.
2. Monotonicity: For every $t \in T$, $x \in X$ and $y \in X$, such that $x < y$, then $(x, t) \prec (y, t)$.
3. Impatience: For every $s \in T$ and $t \in T$, such that $s < t$, and $x \in X$ then $(x, s) \succ (x, t)$.

The most famous representation theorem of preferences is due to Fishburn and Rubinstein [20]: If order, monotonicity, continuity, impatience, and separability hold, and the set of rewards X is an interval, then there are continuous real-valued functions u on X and F on the time interval T such that

$$(x, s) \preceq (y, t) \text{ if, and only if, } u(x)F(s) \leq u(y)F(t).$$

Additionally, function u, called the *utility*, is increasing and satisfies $u(0) = 0$. On the other hand, function F, called the *discount function*, is decreasing, positive and satisfies $F(0) = 1$.

Assume that, for the decision maker, the rewards (x, s) and (y, t), with $s < t$, are indifferent, that is to say, $(x, s) \sim (y, t)$. Observe that, necessarily, $u(x) < u(y)$. The *impatience* in the interval $[s, t]$, denoted by $I(s, t)$, can be defined as the difference $u(y) - u(x)$ which is the amount that the agent is willing to loss in exchange for an earlier receipt of the reward. However, in economics the magnitudes should be defined in relative, better than absolute, terms. Thus, the impatience corresponding to the interval $[s, t]$, relatively to time and amount, should be:

$$I(s, t) := \frac{u(y) - u(x)}{(t - s)u(y)}.$$

According to [20], the following equation holds:

$$u(x)F(s) = u(y)F(t),$$

whereby

$$I(s, t) = \frac{F(s) - F(t)}{(t - s)F(s)}.$$

Observe that, in algebraic terms, $I(s, t)$ is the classical "logarithmic" derivative, with minus sign, of F at time s:

$$I(s, t) = -\left(\frac{D_{t-s}(F)}{F}\right)(s),$$

where D_{t-s} is the classical h-derivation, with $h = t - s$. However, in finance, the most employed measure of impatience is given by the limit of $I(s, t)$ when t tends to s, giving rise to the well-known concept of *instantaneous discount rate*, denoted by $\delta(s)$:

$$\delta(s) := -\lim_{t \to s}\left(\frac{D_{t-s}(F)}{F}\right)(s) = -D(\ln F)(s).$$

For a detailed information about the different concepts of impatience in intertemporal choice, see [21]. The following definition introduces a central concept to analyze the evolution of impatience with the passage of time.

Definition 1 ([19]). *A decision-maker exhibiting preferences $\preceq$ has decreasing impatience (DI) if, for every $s < t$, $k > 0$ and $0 < x < y$, $(x, s) \sim (y, t)$ implies $(x, s + k) \preceq (y, t + k)$.*

A consequence is that, under the conditions of Definition 1, given $\sigma > 0$, there exists $\tau = \tau(\sigma) > \sigma$ such that

$$(x, s + \sigma) \sim (y, t + \tau).$$

The existence of τ is guaranteed when, as usual, the discount function is regular, i.e., satisfies $\lim_{t \to \infty} F(t) = 0$. A specific case of DI is given by the following definition.

Definition 2 ([19]). *A decision-maker exhibiting decreasing impatience has strongly decreasing impatience if $s\tau \geq t\sigma$.*

The following proposition provides a nice characterization of strongly decreasing impatience.

Proposition 2 ([22]). *A decision-maker exhibiting preferences $\preceq$ has strongly decreasing impatience if, and only if, for every $s < t$, $\lambda > 1$ and $0 < x < y$, $(x,s) \sim (y,t)$ implies $(x, \lambda s) \prec (y, \lambda t)$.*

Definition 3. *Let $F(t)$ be a discount function differentiable in its domain. The elasticity of $F(t)$ is defined as:*

$$\epsilon_F(t) := t\frac{D(F)(t)}{F(t)} = tD(\ln F)(t) = -t\delta(t).$$

Theorem 1. *A decision-maker exhibiting preferences $\preceq$ has strongly decreasing impatience if, and only if, $D^2(F) > -\frac{D(F)}{id}$.*

Proof. In effect, for every $s < t$, $\lambda > 1$ and $0 < x < y$, by Proposition 1, $(x,s) \sim (y,t)$ implies $(x, \lambda s) \prec (y, \lambda t)$. Consequently,

$$u(x)F(s) = u(y)F(t)$$

and

$$u(x)F(\lambda s) < u(y)F(\lambda t).$$

By dividing the left-hand sides and the right-hand sides of the former inequality and equality, one has:

$$\frac{F(\lambda s)}{F(s)} < \frac{F(\lambda t)}{F(t)},$$

from where:

$$\ln F(\lambda s) - \ln F(s) < \ln F(\lambda t) - \ln F(t).$$

As $\lambda > 1$, we can write $\lambda := 1 + \Delta$, with $\Delta > 0$, and so:

$$\ln F((1+\Delta)s) - \ln F(s) < \ln F((1+\Delta)t) - \ln F(t).$$

By dividing both member of the former inequality by Δ and letting $\Delta \to 0$, one has:

$$D_f(F)(s) \leq D_f(F)(t),$$

where $f(x, \Delta) := (1 + \Delta)x$. Therefore, the function $D_f(F)$ is increasing, whereby:

$$D[D_f(F)] \geq 0.$$

In order to calculate $D_f(F)$, take into account that now there is a proportional increment of the variable, that is to say:

$$f(x, \Delta) = (1 + \Delta)x.$$

Thus,

$$D_f(F)(a) = aD(F)(a)$$

or, globally,

$$D_f(F) = idD(F).$$

Consequently, $idD(F)$ is increasing, whereby:

$$D[ID(F)] = D(F) + idD^2(F) > 0,$$

from where:

$$D^2(F) > -\frac{D(F)}{id}.$$

The proof of the converse implication is obvious. □

Example 4. *The discount function* $F(t) = \exp\{-\arctan(t)\}$ *exhibits strongly decreasing impatience. In effect, simple calculation shows that:*

- $D(F)(a) = -\frac{1}{1+a^2}\exp\{-\arctan(t)\}.$
- $D^2(F)(a) = \frac{1+2a}{1+a^2}\exp\{-\arctan(t)\}.$

In this case, the inequality $D^2(F) > -\frac{D(F)}{id}$ *results in* $a^2 + a - 1 > 0$ *which holds for* $a > \frac{-1+\sqrt{5}}{2}.$

The following result can be derived from Theorem 1 [22].

Corollary 1. *A decision-maker exhibiting preferences* $\preceq$ *has strongly decreasing impatience if, and only if,* ϵ_F *is decreasing.*

Proof. It is immediate, taking into account that $\mathrm{id}D(F)$ is increasing. As F is decreasing, then $\mathrm{id}\frac{D(F)}{F}$ is increasing and

$$\epsilon = -\mathrm{id}\delta$$

is decreasing. The proof of the converse implication is obvious. □

Another specific case of DI is given by the following definition.

Definition 4 ([19]). *A decision-maker exhibiting decreasing impatience has moderately decreasing impatience if* $s\tau < t\sigma.$

The following corollary provides a characterization of moderately decreasing impatience.

Corollary 2 ([22]). *A decision-maker exhibiting preferences* $\preceq$ *has moderately decreasing impatience if, and only if, for every* $s < t, k > 0, \lambda > 1$ *and* $0 < x < y$, $(x,s) \sim (y,t)$ *implies* $(x,s+k) \preceq (y,t+k)$ *but* $(x,\lambda s) \succeq (y,\lambda t).$

Corollary 3. *A decision-maker exhibiting preferences* $\preceq$ *has moderately decreasing impatience if, and only if,* $\frac{[D(F)]^2}{F} < D^2(F) \leq -\frac{D(F)}{id}.$

Proof. It is an immediate consequence of Theorem 1 and of the fact that, in this case, $\delta = -\frac{D(F)}{F}$ is decreasing. □

The following result can be derived from Corollary 3 [22].

Corollary 4. *A decision-maker exhibiting preferences* $\preceq$ *has moderately decreasing impatience f, and only if,* ϵ_F *is increasing but* δ *is decreasing.*

4. Discussion

In this paper, we have introduced a new modality of relative derivation, specifically the so-called derivation of $F(x)$ relative to a function $f(x,\Delta) := x + g(x,\Delta)$, where $g(x,\Delta)$ represents the increments in the variable x. Obviously, this novel concept generalizes the two most important derivatives used in differential calculus:

- The classical derivative, whose increments are defined as $g(x,\Delta) = \Delta.$
- The directional derivative, characterized by linear increments: $g(x,\Delta) = k\Delta, k \in \mathbb{R}.$

It is easy to show that, in the former cases, Equation (13) leads to the well-known expressions of these two derivatives. In this paper, we have gone a step further and have considered proportional variations of the independent variable. These increments appear in the so-called *sensitivity analysis* which is a financial methodology which determines how changes of a variable can affect variations of another variable. This method, also called simulation analysis, is usually employed in financial problems under uncertainty contexts and also in econometric regressions.

In effect, in some economic contexts, percentage variations of the independent variable are analyzed. For example, the *elasticity* is the ratio of the percentage variations of two economic magnitudes. In linear regression, if the explanatory and the explained variables are affected by the natural logarithm, it is noteworthy to analyze the percentage variation of the dependent variable compared to percentage changes in the value of an independent variable. In this case, we would be interested in analyzing the ratio:

$$\frac{f(x + \Delta x) - f(x)}{f(x)},$$

when $\frac{\Delta x}{x} = \lambda$, for a given λ. Thus, the former ratio remains as:

$$\frac{f(x + \lambda x) - f(x)}{f(x)}.$$

In another economic context, Karpoff [23], when searching the relationship between the price and the volume of transactions of an asset in a stock market, suggests quadratic and logarithmic increments:

- Quadratic increments aim to determine the variation of the volume when quadratic changes in the price of an asset have been considered. In this case,

$$g(x, \Delta) = (x + \Delta)^2 - x^2$$

and so

$$\partial_{y=0}(f)(a) = 2a.$$

- Logarithmic increments aim to find the variation of the volume when considering quadratic changes in the price of an asset. In this case,

$$g(x, \Delta) = \ln(x + \Delta) - \ln x$$

and so

$$\partial_{y=0}(f)(a) = \frac{1}{a}.$$

Figure 3 summarizes the different types of increments discussed in this section.

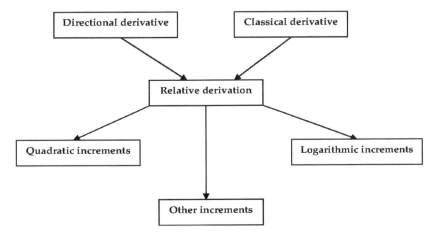

Figure 3. Chart of the different types of increments.

Indeed, some other variation models could be mentioned here. Take into account that some disciplines, such as biology, physics or economics, might be interested in explaining the increments in the dependent variable by using alternative patterns of variation. For example, think about a particle which is moving by following a given trajectory. In this context, researchers may be interested in knowing the behavior of the explained variable when the particle is continuously changing its position according to a given function.

5. Conclusions

This paper has introduced the novel concept of derivative of a function relative to another given function. The manuscript has been divided into two parts. The first part is devoted to the algebraic treatment of this concept and its basic properties in the framework of other relative derivatives. Moreover, this new derivative has been put in relation with the main variants of derivation in the field of abstract algebra. Given two σ-derivations over a K-algebra A, where K is a field, a relative σ-derivation has been associated to any function. This construction is, in fact, a derivation from A to the A-module of σ-derivations. Specifically, if σ is the identity of the algebra, these derivations can be applied to the theory of intertemporal choice.

The second part deals with the mathematical characterization of the so-called "strongly" and "moderately decreasing impatience" based on previous characterizations involving the proportional increasing of the variable "time". In effect, a specific situation, the case of proportional increments, plays a noteworthy role in economics, namely in intertemporal choice, where the analysis of decreasing impatience is a topic of fundamental relevance. In effect, the proportional increment of time is linked to the concept of strongly and moderately decreasing impatience. Therefore, the calculation of derivatives relatively to this class of increments will allow us to characterize these important modalities of decreasing impatience.

Moreover, after providing a geometric interpretation of this concept, this derivative has been calculated relatively to certain functions which represent different patterns of variability of the main variable involved in the problem.

Observe that, according to Fishburn and Rubinstein [20], the continuity of the order relation implies that functions F and u are continuous but not necessarily derivable. Indeed, this is a limitation of the approach presented in this paper which affects both function F and the variation pattern g. A further research could be to analyze the case of functions which are differentiable except at possibly a finite number of points in its domain.

Finally, apart from this financial application, another future research line is the characterization of other financial problems with specific models of variability. In this way, we can point out the proportional variability of reward amounts [24].

Author Contributions: Conceptualization, S.C.R. and B.T.J.; Formal analysis, S.C.R. and B.T.J.; Funding acquisition, S.C.R. and B.T.J.; Supervision, S.C.R. and B.T.J.; Writing – original draft, S.C.R. and B.T.J. All authors have read and agreed to the published version of the manuscript.

Acknowledgments: We are very grateful for the valuable comments and suggestions offered by three anonymous referees.

Abbreviations

The following abbreviations are used in this manuscript:

DI   Decreasing Impatience

References

1.   Kunz, E. *Kähler Differential*; Springer: Berlin, Germany, 1986.

2.   Eisenbud, D. *Commutative Algebra with a View toward Algebraic Geometry*, 3rd ed.; Springer: Berlin, Germany, 1999.

3.   Matsumura, H. *Commutative Algebra*; Mathematics Lecture Note Series; W. A. Benjamin: New York, NY, USA, 1970.

4.   Jacobson, N. *Structure of Rings*; Am. Math. Soc. Coll. Pub. 37; Amer. Math. Soc: Providence, RI, USA, 1956.

5.   Jackson, F.H. q-difference equations. *Amer. J. Math* **1910**, *32*, 305–314. [CrossRef]

6.   Chakrabarti, R.; Jagannathan, R.;Vasudevan, R. A new look at the *q*-deformed calculus. *Mod. Phys. Lett. A* **1993**, *8*, 2695–2701. [CrossRef]

7.   Haven, E. Itô's lemma with quantum calculus (*q*-calculus): Some implications. *Found. Phys.* **2011**, *41*, 529–537. [CrossRef]

8.   Kac, V.; Cheung, P. *Quantum Calculus*; Springer: Berlin, Germany, 2002.

9.   Ernst, T. *A Comprehensive Treatment of q-Calculus*; Birkhäuser: New York, NY, USA, 2012.

10.   Annaby, M.; Mansour, Z.S. *q-Fractional Calculus and Equations*; Lecture Notes in Mathematics, 2056.; Springer: New York, NY, USA, 2012.

11.   Auch, T. Development and Application of Difference and Fractional Calculus on Discrete Time Scales. Ph.D. Thesis, University of Nebraska-Lincoln, Lincoln, NE, USA, 2013.

12.   Hamza, A.; Sarhan, A.; Shehata, E.; Aldwoah, K.A. General quantum difference calculus. *Adv. Differ. Equ.* **2015**, *2015*, 1–19. [CrossRef]

13.   Faried, N.; Shehata, E.M.; El Zafarani, R.M. On homogeneous second order linear general quantum difference equations. *J. Inequalities Appl.* **2017**, *2017*, 198. [CrossRef] [PubMed]

14.   Hahn, W. On orthogonal polynomials satisfying a *q*-difference equation. *Math. Nachr.* **1949**, *2*, 4–34. [CrossRef]

15.   Hahn, W. Ein Beitrag zur Theorie der Orthogonalpolynome. *Monatshefte Math.* **1983**, *95*, 19–24. [CrossRef]

16.   Gupta, V.; Rassias T.M.; Agrawal, P.N.; Acu, A.M. Basics of Post-Quantum Calculus. In *Recent Advances in Constructive Approximation Theory. Springer Optimization and Its Applications*; Springer: Berlin, Germany, 2018; Volume 138.

17.   Hartwig, J.T.; Larsson, D.; Silvestrov, S.D. Deformations of Lie algebras using σ-derivations. *J. Algebra* **2006**, *295*, 314–361. [CrossRef]

18.   Baucells, M.; Heukamp, F.H. Probability and time trade-off. *Manag. Sci.* **2012**, *58*, 831–842. [CrossRef]

19.   Rohde, K.I.M. Measuring decreasing and increasing impatience. *Manag. Sci.* **2018**, *65*, 1455–1947. [CrossRef]

20.   Fishburn, P.C.; Rubinstein, A. Time preference. *Int. Econ. Rev.* **1982**, *23*, 677–694. [CrossRef]

21.   Cruz Rambaud, S.; Muñoz Torrecillas, M.J. Measuring impatience in intertemporal choice. *PLoS ONE* **2016**, *11*, e0149256. [CrossRef] [PubMed]

22.   Cruz Rambaud, S.; González Fernández, I. A measure of inconsistencies in intertemporal choice. *PLoS ONE* **2019**, *14*, e0224242. [CrossRef] [PubMed]

23.   Karpoff, J.M. The relation between price changes and trading volume: A survey. *J. Financ. Quant. Anal.* **1987**, *22*, 109–126. [CrossRef]

24.   Anchugina, N.; Matthew, R.; Slinko, A. *Aggregating Time Preference with Decreasing Impatience*; Working Paper; University of Auckland: Auckland, Australia, 2016.

12

Non-Parametric Analysis of Efficiency:
An Application to the Pharmaceutical Industry

Ricardo F. Díaz and Blanca Sanchez-Robles *

Department of Economic Analysis, Facultad CC Económicas y Empresariales, UNED, Senda del Rey 11, 28040 Madrid, Spain; rr_dos@hotmail.com
* Correspondence: bsanchez-robles@cee.uned.es

Abstract: Increases in the cost of research, specialization and reductions in public expenditure in health are changing the economic environment for the pharmaceutical industry. Gains in productivity and efficiency are increasingly important in order for firms to succeed in this environment. We analyze empirically the performance of efficiency in the pharmaceutical industry over the period 2010–2018. We work with microdata from a large sample of European firms of different characteristics regarding size, main activity, country of origin and other idiosyncratic features. We compute efficiency scores for the firms in the sample on a yearly basis by means of non-parametric data envelopment analysis (DEA) techniques. Basic results show a moderate average level of efficiency for the firms which encompass the sample. Efficiency is higher for companies which engage in manufacturing and distribution than for firms focusing on research and development (R&D) activities. Large firms display higher levels of efficiency than medium-size and small firms. Our estimates point to a decreasing pattern of average efficiency over the years 2010–2018. Furthermore, we explore the potential correlation of efficiency with particular aspects of the firms' performance. Profit margins and financial solvency are positively correlated with efficiency, whereas employee costs display a negative correlation. Institutional aspects of the countries of origin also influence efficiency levels.

Keywords: pharmaceutical industry; scale economies; profitability; biotechnological firms; non-parametric efficiency; productivity; DEA

---

1. Introduction

Pharmaceutical companies contribute crucially to the health and welfare of individuals. This issue is particularly relevant nowadays: as the Covid-19 pandemic has shown, no country is immune to the emergence of new diseases. Furthermore, the population in many countries is experiencing deep demographic transformations which increase life expectancy and raise new challenges for policymakers. Not surprisingly, the performance of the industry directly affects some of the Sustainable Development Goals of the 2030 Agenda for Sustainable Development.

The economic importance of the industry is also paramount. The pharmaceutical sector employs highly skilled labor and exhibits one of the largest figures of research and development (R&D) intensity (defined as expenditure in R&D as a share of sales). As recent contributions in the field of macroeconomics have shown, human capital and R&D are key drivers of economic growth, productivity and prosperity [1–3].

The pharmaceutical industry is facing new challenges because of several factors. New diseases as the Covid-19 demand quick, pathbreaking solutions. R&D costs grow because conditions become chronic and more complicated. Paradoxically, the progress in molecular biology which increases the range of potential innovations also raises the complexity of decisions related to the R&D strategy.

New investments seek increasingly *high risk/high premium* drugs [4]. Official agencies accumulate requirements for drug approvals. Firms must cope with the expiration of patents and with reductions in public expenditure in healthcare due to stability measures and fiscal adjustments.

Meanwhile the business model in the industry has experienced deep transformations over the last decades. Some firms have specialized in particular steps of the value chain, as R&D in the biotechnological sphere or clinical research, this last in the case of contract research organizations (CROs). Reductions in R&D productivity have brought about mergers and acquisitions, partly to profit from the expertise in research and the pipeline of other companies. Reference [5] argue that Japanese firms engaged in mergers and acquisitions over 1980–1997 to handle the declining productivity of R&D. Other firms outsource activities or engage in technological alliances [6,7]. In this context, firms must strive to increase their levels of productivity and efficiency, which may become a strategic asset [8].

In parallel, empirical research on productivity and efficiency (defined as output per unit of inputs) has grown over the last decades. Mathematical techniques such as data envelopment analysis (DEA) have facilitated the empirical assessment of efficiency at the country, entity or firm level. The literature has explored the levels and trends of efficiency in many activities and areas such as banking [9], farming [10], food [11], universities [12], airlines [13], shipping [14], oil [15], electricity distribution [16,17] and energy consumption [18,19], to quote just a few examples.

Recent meta-analyses and compilations of DEA exercises can be found in [20] for the public sector, [21] for energy and the environment, [22] for seaports, [23] for microfinance institutions and [24] for rail transport. [25] provide a thorough list of the main journal articles on DEA methodology and applications published between 1978 and 2016.

Researchers have also dealt with more theoretical aspects of the DEA model. Examples are [26], which describes a dynamic version of DEA that allows intertemporal links between inputs and outputs to be considered, and [27] which provides an alternative to the inverse DEA model. Furthermore, [28] explore the features of the model when the data are imprecise and [29] devise a DEA algorithm suitable to deal with Big Data.

The analysis of efficiency in the pharmaceutical industry has also been addressed in the recent past [8,30] although the number of contributions in this regard is comparatively sparse. Most of the studies in this area perform their analyses at the country level and/or focus on a (usually small) sample of companies. Examples are [31] for China; [32,33] for Japan; [6] for US; [34] for Jordan and [35] for India.

We intend to complement this literature with a two-stages analysis of efficiency within a relatively large sample of European firms. In the first stage we compute efficiency levels for the firms in our sample. In the second stage we explore by statistical modelling the connection between the efficiency scores obtained in the first stage and a set of variables potentially correlated with efficiency.

We are especially interested in the assessment of efficiency by type of activity and firm size. More specifically, we want to explore whether large firms exhibit higher levels of efficiency, which would be consistent with the potential presence of scale economies in the industry. Furthermore, it is feasible that firms which primarily operate in the R&D niche enjoy a different level of efficiency, on average, than companies with activities along the entire value chain. Finally, we want to explore the data to find common patterns and detect possible features of the economic and institutional framework and firm management strategy which can be correlated with efficiency.

In parallel, our empirical exercise may prove useful to illustrate how to apply modern mathematical, non-parametric techniques in order to get insights about the performance of firms in a particular industry, and how these tools are related to more traditional, parametric approaches.

Our paper is closely related to three DEA explorations of the pharmaceutical industry: [6,8,35].

Reference [8] analyze efficiency in a sample of 37 large firms from different countries over 2008–2013. They report an average level of efficiency in their sample of 0.9345 and find that firms with higher level of efficiency carry out more financial transactions with other companies.

We complement this exploration in several dimensions. First, our sample is different, broader and more heterogeneous, since it encompasses a large group of European firms, of different sizes and profiles. Second, we report an average efficiency score of 0.34. We think that this figure is a more accurate reflection of the mean efficiency for the whole industry, at least for the European case.

Third, we carry out a two-stage exploration of efficiency whereby in the second stage we look at variables potentially correlated with the efficiency levels obtained in the first stage. Reference [8] omit the second stage because it is somehow controversial. It is true that the literature has not reached a consensus yet on the right specification for the second stage; nonetheless, we think that this analysis can still provide some valid insights about efficiency.

Fourth, we work with a more recent time horizon, 2010–2018, and examine the dynamic performance of efficiency over time; they look at data from 2008–2013 but perform their analysis on average terms, so they do not uncover the pattern of efficiency over time.

Another related investigation is [6]. They employ proprietary data from a sample encompassed by 700 US pharmaceutical firms over the period 2001–2016. They assess the connection between open innovation methods and efficiency.

Reference [35] utilize data from a financial database to examine the performance of a group of Indian firms over the years 1991–2005. They perform a two-stage analysis. In the second stage they examine the determinants of efficiency in their sample by regression tools.

In contrast to [6,35], we work with a sample made up of European firms and explore the potential impact of alternative aspects of firm management and country characteristics. While [35] employ only a Tobit specification in the second stage of their analysis, we utilize also a pure random-effects and a Simar–Wilson procedure, and perform a comparison of the three methods.

We contribute to the literature in several ways. To the best of our knowledge, we are the first to perform a DEA analysis for a relatively large sample of European pharmaceutical firms, of different sizes and main activities, fully exploiting the time dimension of the data.

The inclusion of biotechnological companies in our sample and the exploration of their specific performance are also novel features of our investigation.

We introduce in the second stage of our empirical work a set of variables potentially correlated with efficiency, capturing different aspects of firm management and the macroeconomic environment where companies operate. Employing these variables is original as well in these kinds of analysis.

Finally, we compare the results for the second stage of three different estimation procedures (Tobit, pure random-effects, Simar–Wilson [36]). While the estimates yielded by the Tobit and the pure random-effects specifications are rather close, the Simar–Wilson tool provides larger point estimates. Nonetheless, the quantification of the marginal effects of the main covariates are more similar, and therefore the Simar–Wilson method may also be useful in applied research.

Our investigation suggests that the level of efficiency in the European pharmaceutical industry is moderate and has displayed a decreasing trend over the period 2010–2018. We find a connection between size and efficiency for the firms in our sample, where larger and very small firms tend to perform better as far as efficiency is concerned. Instead, efficiency is smaller for medium and small firms.

In terms of activity, companies operating over the complete value chain register higher levels of efficiency than firms that specialize in the R&D area. Moreover, the geographical market where firms operate seems to matter for their efficiency. Higher margins, sound financial management and lower levels of employee cost are also positively correlated with efficiency according to our results.

The structure of this paper is the following: Section 2 describes the theoretical background of our investigation. Section 3 describes the data and empirical strategy pursued. Sections 4 and 5 discuss the main results of our analysis and Section 6 concludes.

2. Theoretical Background

Conventional microeconomic theory assumes that firms optimize by producing the maximum possible quantity of output for a given input endowment or, equivalently, by producing a given amount of output with the minimum feasible inputs; this is tantamount to presupposing that they are efficient.

Empirical evidence and casual observation suggest that this is not necessarily the case. Inefficiencies exist and may arise due to managerial practices [37] or cultural beliefs [38]. Moreover, some features of the macroeconomic environment where companies operate, as information asymmetries or market rigidities, may also be detrimental for firms' productivity, as some important breakthroughs in macroeconomics in the last decades have pointed out.

Modern applied research pursues productivity analyses through two main avenues: stochastic frontier analysis (SFA) and DEA. While the intuition of both approaches is similar, the procedures are different.

In both cases the starting point is the idea of an efficient combination of inputs and outputs which encompasses a production function or *frontier*. The units of analysis are the so-called *decision-making units* or DMUs, i.e., the firms, organizations, institutions etc. whose efficiency is explored. The main difference between SFA and DEA lies in their methodology. SFA estimates the (continuous) production function by statistical techniques; DEA fits a piecewise hull enveloping the data which is assumed to approximate the true frontier, without making any statistical assumption about the data-generating process.

SFA originated with the pathbreaking contributions of [39,40]. In this setting, deviations from the estimated production function can be decomposed in statistical noise and inefficiency. Therefore, the error term in these models is usually composite [41].

An SFA model may be described by Equation (1)

$$
\begin{aligned}
y_i &= m(x_i; \beta) + \epsilon_i \\
\epsilon_i &= v_i - u_i \\
v_i &\sim N\left(0, \sigma_v^2\right) \\
u_i &\sim \mathcal{F}
\end{aligned}
\tag{1}
$$

where y_i is (log) output for the ith decision-making unit or DMU, x_i is a vector of inputs for the ith DMU, ε_i the vector of parameters to be estimated, u_i captures the (one sided) inefficiency of the ith DMU and v_i represents stochastic shocks. $m(.)$ is the production function, usually assumed to be Cobb Douglas or Translog. The estimation is ordinarily implemented by maximum likelihood or other appropriate methodologies.

The stochastic shock is usually considered normal with zero mean and known variance, whereas different distributions have been advocated and estimated in the literature for the term capturing inefficiency (for a thorough review, see [41]).

The assumption about the error term may be too restrictive. Sometimes it may be preferable to work with a more flexible specification which involves fewer hypotheses. This is why non-parametric techniques, and in particular DEA, have been developed and used increasingly in recent years.

In the applied work, nonetheless, parametric and non-parametric tools sometimes intertwine: the non-parametric approach may be complemented by some statistical analyses, usually by regression procedures, which explore the output of DEA and employ inference to generalize its results to a non-deterministic setting.

Data Envelopment Analysis

The seminal paper for DEA is [42]. This technique computes efficiency by linear programming. The technique operates in two steps: first, it constructs the frontier from the data; second, it computes the distance of each unit to the frontier. It is assumed that the DMUs with the greatest efficiency determine the frontier and have efficiency of 1.

Not all efficient DMUs, however, need to be real: they can be fictitious, i.e., linear combinations of other units. This assumes, in turn, that inputs can be used continuously, i.e., they are divisible. Moreover, it presupposes that the efficiency frontier is a convex set, and hence the linear combination of two points belonging to the feasible set are also feasible. The efficient DMUs which generate a fictitious unit are called referees.

The ideas of frontier and distance encompass an intuitively appealing way to address the study of efficiency. Consider a simple example, firms from an industry which produce a single output y by means of an input x (Figure 1) (this example can be immediately generalized to the case of a vector of outputs and a vector of inputs). There are several firms or DMUs dubbed A, B, C, D, and E. The coordinates for each point in the x, y, space symbolize the input employed and the output produced by each firm. The frontier (solid line) represents *optimal* combinations of inputs and outputs. It is immediate to notice that B provides more output than A, $y_B > y_A$, while using the same amount of input since $x_A = x_B$. Alternatively, D and E produce the same output, $y_D = y_E$, but firm D consumes a smaller amount of input than E, $x_D < x_E$.

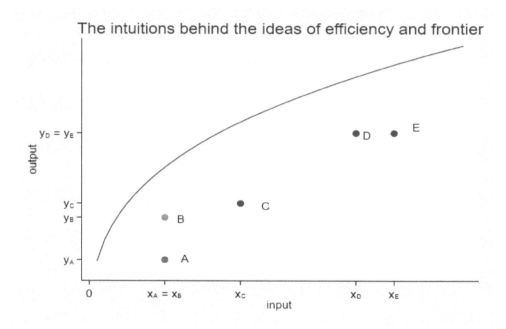

Figure 1. The intuitions behind the ideas of efficiency and frontier. Note: The figure portrays the ideas of efficiency and frontier. x is input and y is output. The concave solid line represents the technology or frontier of possibilities of production, the maximum attainable amount of output for each value of the input endowment. The dots A, B, C, D and E represent decision-making units or DMUs, i.e., firms, organizations, institutions, etc., whose efficiency is considered. Intuitively, B is more efficient than A because it produces more output than A ($y_B > Y_A$) with the same amount of input ($x_B = x_A$). Similarly, D is more efficient than E since D uses a smaller amount of input ($x_D < X_E$) to produce the same amount of output ($Y_D = Y_E$). The closer a DMU is to the frontier, the larger its level of efficiency. Source: own elaboration.

We say than B is more efficient than A and that D is more efficient than E. The closer a firm to the frontier, the larger its efficiency. Conversely, the deviations from the frontier can be understood as inefficiencies.

It is clear from Figure 1 that optimality can be defined in two alternative ways, maximum output per unit of input or minimal consumption of resources to attain a certain level of output. The first approach is named *output oriented* while the second is called *input oriented*.

Suppose there are N DMUs with a technology characterized by constant returns to scale. For the ith firm we can define the following ratio of outputs to inputs:

$$ratio\ i = \frac{\alpha' y_i}{\beta' x_i}$$

$$i = 1, \ldots, N$$

where y_i is a vector of M outputs and x_i a vector of K inputs.

The maximization of efficiency implies the following problem:

$$\max_{\alpha, \beta} \frac{\alpha' y_i}{\beta' x_i}$$

subject to the following constraints:

$$\frac{\alpha' y_s}{\beta' x_s} \leq 1, \quad s = 1, \ldots, N \tag{2}$$

$$\alpha_m \geq 0, \quad m = 1, \ldots, M \tag{3}$$

$$\beta_k \geq 0, \quad k = 1, \ldots, K \tag{4}$$

The restriction given by Equation (2) implies that the efficiencies of all firms have to be less or equal that 1. Restrictions given by (3) and (4) rule out negative weights of outputs and inputs.

Intuitively, the problem seeks the optimal weights such that the efficiency of the firm i is maximized, while operating within the feasible set implied by the constraints.

Imposing the restriction $\beta' x_i = 1$, this fractional programming problem can be linearized ([43]) and transformed into the following:

$$\max_{\alpha, \beta} \alpha' y_i$$

subject to:

$$\beta' x_i = 1$$

$$\alpha' y_s - \beta' x_s \leq 0, \qquad s = 1, \ldots, N$$

$$\alpha \geq 0$$

$$\beta \geq 0$$

which can be written in the envelopment form as:

$$\min_{\theta, \lambda} \theta_i$$

subject to:

$$\sum_{s=1}^{N} \lambda_s y_s - y_i \geq 0$$

$$\theta_i x_i - \sum_{s=1}^{N} \lambda_s x_s \geq 0$$

$$\lambda_s \geq 0$$

where θ_i is the input oriented *efficiency score* for the ith firm.

λ stands for the set of multipliers in the linear combinations of the DMUs' inputs and outputs, i.e., the weight of each DMU within the peer group of DMUs.

This set up can also be applied to a technology exhibiting variable returns to scale by adding the convexity condition:

$$\sum_{s=1}^{N} \lambda_s = 1$$

This is an optimization problem, with linear objective function and constraints, solvable by linear programming.

The value of θ_i, the input-oriented technical efficiency score for the ith firm, indicates to what extent the inputs can be reduced in percent while keeping the output constant. For example, if DMU i has an efficiency score of 90%, it can reduce all inputs by 10% while offering the same amount of output.

Notice the difference between this set up and the statistical approach of SFA as presented in Equation (1) above.

The empirical exercise described in this paper employs the non-parametric, DEA formulation of the optimization problem as the baseline for analysis.

3. Material and Method: Data and Empirical Strategy

Data have been gathered primarily from Amadeus [44] a rich database comprising disaggregated economic and financial information from a large number of European companies. [8,35] employ also financial information from similar databases for their analyses.

Within the pharmaceutical industry, we have selected two main categories of firms in Amadeus according to their main activity:

(i)   Manufacture of basic pharmaceutical products and pharmaceutical preparations;
(ii) Research and experimental development on biotechnology.

They will be labelled henceforth *manufacturers* and *R&D firms*, respectively. The two subgroups correspond to NACE (Nomenclature statistique des Activités Économiques dans la Communauté Européenne) codes 2110, 2120 (for manufacturers) and 7211 (for R&D firms). This is equivalent to NAICS (North American Industry Classification System) codes 541714 and 541715.

We work with yearly observations over the time horizon 2010–2018.

Following part of the literature on DEA, our research design has two stages (see Appendix A for an explanatory diagram of the design of our empirical exercise). The stages are detailed in Sections 4 and 5, respectively. In the first stage we compute the efficiency scores of the firms in our sample by DEA. In the second stage we design and estimate several statistical models to explore potential variables correlated with the efficiency scores; these models provide information regarding the sign of the correlation between the efficiency score and each variable, its statistical significance and its size.

Ordinarily, non-parametric techniques cannot be applied to data structured in panels because of tractability considerations, as is common, instead, with other methodologies which allow for an explicit time dimension and have been successfully employed with panels. We circumvent this problem computing measures of efficiency year by year. This feature may be regarded as a drawback on a priori grounds; nonetheless, the estimation of efficiency measures performed on a yearly basis has been useful to uncover interesting patterns in their evolution over time.

We have started to work with a sample encompassed by more than 4000 observations from 482 firms over the nine years in the period 2010–2018, evenly split among manufacturers and R&D firms.

For the computation of efficiency for a particular year, however, we have dismissed those observations corresponding to firms which do not report data of turnover, employees and/or assets for that same year. After discarding the firms with missing values, we end up with samples comprising around 200 companies for each year, of different sizes, geographical origins and performances over time. The samples, therefore, are quite representative of the industry.

In the case of multinationals, firms correspond to headquarters. In our selection of companies we have discarded local affiliates because internal accounting procedures of multinationals may reduce their degree of comparability.

Nominal variables have been deflated using the Harmonized European Index from Eurostat [45].

Our measure of output is turnover in real terms (in constant euros of 2015). The inputs labor and capital are proxied by the number of employees and total assets in real terms, respectively. Total assets in real terms are also measured in constant euros of 2015. The choice of these variables has been made in accordance with other contributions performing similar analyses, as [6,8,32].

Economic and financial conditions have been captured by cash flow over turnover, profit margin and average cost of employees, among others (see Appendix B).

We have constructed dummies for size, country of origin, main activity and years. The specific details will be provided in Sections 4 and 5 below.

Figure 2 conveys some information for selected variables, disaggregated in manufacturers and R&D firms. Real turnover is expressed in constant euros of 2015. It is apparent from the Figure that the firms encompassing the first category are considerably larger than those in the second, as shown by the average real turnover and average number of employees.

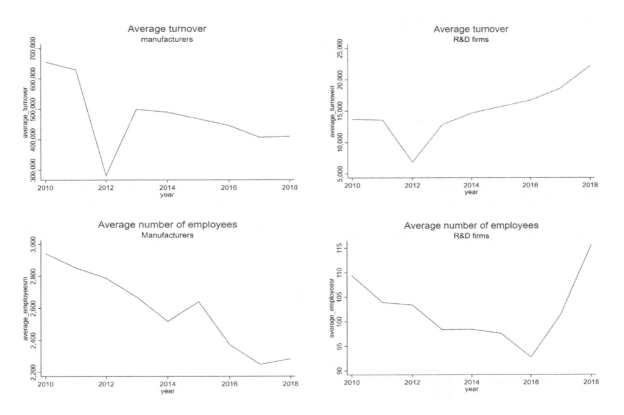

Figure 2. Average real turnover (in constant euros of 2015) and average number of employees over time by main activity. Notes: The figure displays the time pattern for average real turnover and average number of employees over 2010–2018, disaggregated by main activity of firms. Averages have been computed from the data year by year. Two main categories are considered: firms whose main activity is the manufacture of basic pharmaceutical products (manufacturers), and companies focused on research and experimental development on biotechnology (research and development (R&D) firms). Average turnover exhibits a decreasing trend over the period, with a big drop in 2012 for manufacturers, and an increasing trend for R&D firms since 2013. Average number of employees decreases over the period for the first category of firms and increases since 2016 for the second. Source: own elaboration with data from the Amadeus data basis).

It is also clear that both variables have experienced a decreasing pattern over time for manufacturers, with a very pronounced drop in 2012 in the case of real turnover. This is consistent with the increasingly difficult environment in which they operate. For R&D firms, the pattern is less straightforward.

Average real turnover has also plummeted in 2012 but has increased thereafter. Average number of employees falls until 2016 and rises in the last years of the period.

These trends may be associated to the progressive outsourcing of some stages of the value chain, which were traditionally performed by manufacturers and now are increasingly implemented by CROs and other biotechnological firms.

Two more considerations about our empirical strategy are in order. First, and as stated above, the DEA analysis can be implemented in an output oriented or input oriented setting. We have followed this second approach since it seems intuitively more appealing and conforming with firms' experience: their plans to increase efficiency are usually linked to reduction in costs, rather than to expansions in output.

Secondly, the relevant role played by R&D in this industry suggests that scale economies might be prevalent, but this is a controversial issue which the literature has not been able to settle yet. Reference [46] found evidence in favor of this hypothesis; Reference [47], however, did not, although they did suggest that economies of scope and accumulated knowhow were important for the firms in the sector. Reference [48] encountered knowledge spillovers among firms in Phase I of clinical research and diseconomies of scope in later phases. Reference [32] find that 60% of the firms in their sample of Japanese chemical and pharmaceutical companies operate with either increasing or decreasing returns to scale.

There is no consensus yet, therefore, on the degree of homogeneity of the production function in the industry. Anyhow, since the existence of increasing returns to scale cannot be ruled out, we have chosen to employ a variable returns to scale model as our theoretical framework, rather than a constant returns to scale. Reference [8] follow a similar approach.

4. Stage 1: Computation of Efficiency Scores

Pharmaceutical and biotechnological firms share some activities and hence compete with each other in certain stages of the value chain. We are interested in assessing whether the companies specialized in R&D activities are more or less efficient, being thus better or more poorly positioned to succeed and survive, than companies which are mainly producers and sellers. Hence, we analyze the firms in the industry jointly, i.e., with respect to an efficient frontier common for all of them (nonetheless, we have performed the analysis separately in each of the subgroups and basic results carry over).

Tables 1–5 and Figures 3 and 4 summarize some summary statistics about the efficiency of the firms that encompass our sample, as obtained employing DEA in our sample on a yearly basis.

Table 1. Efficiency in the pharma and biotechnological European industry by activity, 2010–2018.

	Efficiency Mean	Standard Deviation	Coefficient of Variation
Whole sample	0.341	0.265	0.777
Manufacturers	0.381	0.266	0.698
R&D firms	0.281	0.251	0.893

Note: the table summarizes selected statistics for efficiency levels, computed as described in the main text. We classify firms in two groups, manufacturers and R&D firms, according to their main activity. Source: Own elaboration.

The mean efficiency for the entire sample and over the period 2010–2018 is 0.341. Thus, firms in our sample could increase their efficiency on average in 0.659 points or 65.9%. It seems a reasonable figure. Reference [6] report values of efficiency between 0.42 and 0.58. Their sample is made up by US firms; it seems sensible to think that US firms are, by and large, more efficient than their European counterparts because the general level of efficiency of the US economy is larger and its regulatory burden is smaller. Furthermore, US pharmaceutical firms are larger, on average, than European firms and, as we shall argue below, our results suggest that larger firms are more efficient. The standard deviation is 0.265, which suggests a noticeable degree of dispersion in the sample.

The results are not very different from those obtained by [33]; they find that the average efficiency for a sample of Japanese firms is 0.68 for 1983–1987 and 0.47 for 1988–1993.

If we classify the firms according to their main activity, we find that the mean efficiency for the manufacturers is 0.381 whereas for the R&D firms the figure is smaller, 0.281. This is a somewhat surprising result: the common practice in the industry whereby manufacturers outsource some activities to R&D and biotechnological specialized companies like CROs would suggest on a priori grounds that the former be more efficient that the latter. Otherwise, the outsourcing could be questioned on economic grounds. This is not what we find, however.

One possible explanation for our results is that many manufacturers have been in the market longer, and their historical performance have endowed them with expertise, knowhow and managerial practices which have increased their productivity. This is related to the phenomenon called learning curve in engineering or learning by doing in economics. A classical example is provided by [49], who noticed that the number of hours necessary to produce an airframe was a decreasing function of the number of airframes already produced. Instead, many R&D firms are still relatively young; it is feasible, therefore, that there is still room for them to optimize their processes and value chains and improve their productivity and efficiency.

In addition, the R&D activity in order to develop new drugs is very risky. Success rates are low. Only a modest percentage of molecules are able to complete clinical phases successfully and enter the final market. Reference [50] report that only 10.4% of the drugs entering the clinical stage gain approval by the US Food and Drug Administration (FDA). Biotechnological firms displaying small sizes and relatively reduced pipelines may thus be very affected by failures in the R&D stage. These episodes, in turn, will entail lower levels of productivity.

Notice also that the standard deviation for R&D firms is comparatively high, 0.251. In fact the coefficient of variation, as measured by the ratio standard deviation to mean, is higher for this category. This implies that heterogeneity is more pronounced for this kind of firm.

In order to assess the connection between relative efficiency and size, we have created six categories of firms. Five of these categories (from very big to very small) are linked to the intervals delimited by the 95, 75, 50 and 25 percentiles of real turnover over the period. In particular, the classification is as follows:

- Huge: if the average real turnover over the period exceeds 2000 million euros.
- Very big: if the average real turnover is less or equal than 2000 million euros and higher than 426.92 million euros.
- Quite big: if the average real turnover is less or equal than 426.92 million euros and higher than 38.86 million euros.
- Medium: if the average real turnover is less or equal than 38.86 million euros and higher than 8.10 million euros.
- Small: if the average real turnover is less or equal than 8.10 million euros and higher than 2.10 million euros.
- Very small: if the average real turnover is less or equal than 2.10 million euros.

Table 2 displays summary statistics for relative efficiency classified according to these categories. The largest companies in the sample, those with turnover larger than 2000 million euros, have the highest level of efficiency in the sample, 0.98. In other words, most of them encompass the efficient frontier or are very close to it. There is very little dispersion within this category and the coefficient of variation is almost negligible.

For very big companies, with turnover roughly between 500 and 2000 million euros, efficiency is also remarkably high, 0.765 in average terms. The potential gains in efficiency for this category are only around 25% on average. Firms in the next turnover interval have a smaller record, 0.425. Medium-size firms register lower levels of efficiency on average, 0.312; this is slightly below the figure for the whole sample and period, 0.341.

Small firms, with turnover between 2.10 and 8.10 million euros, register the smallest value of average efficiency, only 0.267. Interestingly, their record is worse than that of the very small firms, with turnover below 2.10 million euros: this last category attains an indicator of 0.318, slightly above medium size firms. This result is consistent with [35], which find that small pharmaceutical firms display smaller levels of efficiency for the case of India.

Higher degrees of flexibility and capacity to adapt to the environment, more agile management and lower levels of conflicts among partners which characterize very small firms may be behind this result. The comparatives advantages provided by specialization may also play a role.

The performance within those categories, as reported by the coefficient of variation, is not uniform. Dispersion is maximum for the very small firms (0.9), whereas more limited for very big firms (0.267). Dispersion in the other categories is similar and quite high: between 0.6 and 0.71.

The implications of these results are interesting. There is not a monotonic, clear cut relationship between size, as captured by turnover, and relative efficiency. Our findings suggest that larger firms are more efficient but only beyond a certain threshold of income, located around 500 million euros. Companies above this figure are considerably more efficient, suggesting the possibility of scale economies for high levels of turnover. Firms with turnover between 38 and 500 thousand million euros also perform better than the whole sample, although their particular advantage amounts just to less than 10 points.

Intermediate and small firms do not profit from scale economies neither from the flexibility and specialization associated to very small firms, and therefore register the poorest results as far as efficiency is concerned.

Table 2. Relative efficiency in the pharma and biotechnological European industry by size, 2010–2018.

	Mean	Standard Deviation	Coefficient of Variation
Huge	0.98	0.039	0.039
Very big	0.765	0.205	0.267
Quite big	0.425	0.266	0.625
Medium	0.312	0.218	0.698
Small	0.267	0.19	0.71
Very Small	0.318	0.288	0.9

Note: the table summarizes selected statistics for efficiency levels, disaggregated by size of the firms (proxied by real turnover). The thresholds are described in the main text. Source: Own elaboration.

Table 3 and Figure 3 provide the dynamic context to these results by detailing the performance over the years 2010–2018. Average efficiency plummets from the beginning of the period until 2015, to recover thereafter. In year 2017, efficiency falls again, to increase in 2018, but it does not recover to the levels attained before 2010. Between 2010 and 2018 efficiency diminishes by almost 10 points. The decrease is especially acute for manufacturers, whereas R&D firms only lose 4 points on average.

These results are consistent with [6], who also document a decrease in efficiency for most of the firms in their sample for 2010–2015.

Table 3. Efficiency in the pharma and biotechnological European industry by activity, yearly results, 2010–2018.

	2010	2011	2012	2013	2014	2015	2016	2017	2018
Whole sample	0.428	0.392	0.348	0.308	0.304	0.292	0.383	0.311	0.334
Manufacturers	0.481	0.449	0.391	0.351	0.334	0.335	0.409	0.34	0.367
R&D firms	0.338	0.277	0.263	0.243	0.267	0.231	0.345	0.272	0.294

Note: the table details average levels of efficiency by year and main activity of firms. Efficiency is computed as described in the main text. Source: Own elaboration.

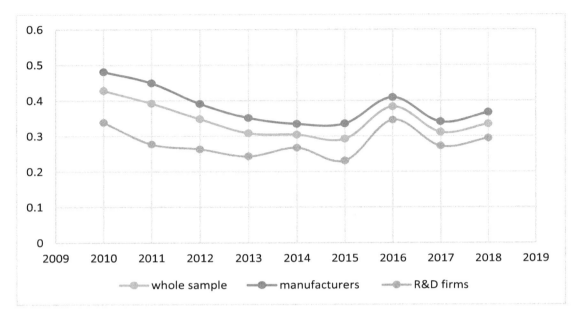

Figure 3. Efficiency in the pharma and biotechnological European industry by main activity, 2010–2018. Note: the figure summarizes the yearly trend of average efficiency, for the whole sample and disaggregated by categories corresponding to the main activity of firms. Efficiency decreases over the period, with a partial recovery in 2015–2016. Source: own elaboration.

Figure 4 portrays the behavior of firms over time classified according to their size. The largest companies exhibit a fairly consistent performance over time. Instead, for quite big companies the fall of efficiency between the beginning and end of the period is almost 20 points.

At the beginning of the period, in 2010, the efficiency of quite large firms was well above that of the entire sample, while this is not the case anymore in 2018. This category has been affected the most by the drop of efficiency over time.

Medium-sized and small firms exhibit a reduction of 10 points over time, whereas very small firms register a rather stable performance.

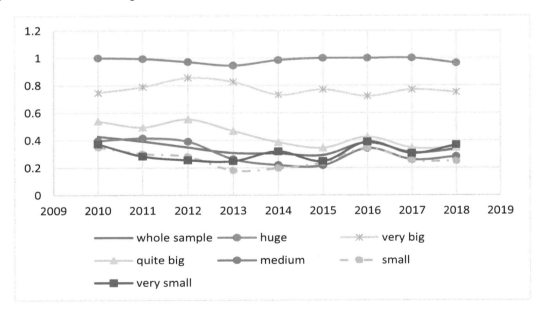

Figure 4. Average efficiency, pharma and biotechnological industry by size, 2010–2018. Note: the figure summarizes the yearly trend of average efficiency of the firms in our sample, disaggregated by size of firms. Size is proxied by real turnover. Efficiency decreases over the period for all categories except for the huge and very big firms. The thresholds are detailed in the main text. Source: own elaboration.

5. Stage 2: Variables Correlated with Efficiency

5.1. Overview

In the second stage of this research we have performed a regression analysis in order to explore several aspects of the firms' economic setting and management which may be correlated with efficiency. Efficiency is proxied by the efficiency scores obtained in the first stage, as detailed in Section 4.

The basic framework is a statistical model described in very general terms by Equation (5):

$$\theta = f(x; v) \tag{5}$$

where θ is a vector containing the efficiency scores, x is a matrix of covariates and v is the error term.

There are several statistical issues to be considered here.

First, the literature has not reached a consensus about the data generation process underlying Equation (5). Researchers have widely used the Tobit model and ordinary least squares (OLS) (see, for example, [35,51]).

Since the efficiency scores are censored at a maximum of 1 by construction, the Tobit specification seems especially appropriate for this analysis. In addition, References [52,53] argue that OLS provide consistent estimates which are quite similar to those obtained with Tobit and are, therefore, a convenient procedure. Reference [54] show, by means of Monte Carlo simulations, that OLS and Tobit outperform other procedures when employed in the second stage of DEA analyses.

Reference [36], however, have argued that the true data generation process for the efficiency scores is not a censored but a truncated distribution; they discard the analysis of the efficiency scores performed according to Tobit or ordinary least squares because this assessment would not rely on the *true* distribution of the data. With censored data, the *true* value of the variable is not known because of the measurement scale; in this particular case, since efficiency has an upper bound of 1. With truncated data, instead, the true value of the variable is unknown because of the sample limitations. The difference in practice between a censored and a truncation distribution may be unclear.

Furthermore, they claim that the efficiency scores are affected by serial correlation. Since the Tobit procedure does not correct for this problem, the estimates obtained from the Tobit model are, in their view, biased. This issue is also controversial, since [54] have argued that OLS and Tobit procedures are valid even if the X variables are correlated.

Reference [36] propose an alternative estimation technique which employs a truncated model, computes new standard errors by bootstrapping the data and corrects the biases in the estimates. There are downsides for this procedure. Reference [53] argues that the Simar–Wilson estimates lack robustness. Furthermore, the Simar–Wilson technique is convoluted and intensive in computing time. Furthermore, as we shall show below, the point estimates computed by the Simar–Wilson method are bigger than those obtained by Tobit or ordinary least squares, although the difference may not be very relevant in applied research.

The debate is still open. According to [53], the controversy about the correct statistical model underlying the data is ultimately methodological and exceeds the scope of our research. By and large, we agree with [53] and think that Tobit and ordinary least squares have helped obtain valid insights about the efficiency in numerous industries or activities, and thus can be employed in applied research.

Meanwhile, since the controversy has not been settled yet, we have decided to adopt a conservative strategy, employ the three methods and compare their results.

Second, the data we are going to use to estimate Equation (5) encompass a panel and hence comprises observations from firms at different points in time.

As is well known, panel data can be assessed by fixed effects or random effects models. [55] shows that Tobit models with fixed effects produce coefficients which are overestimated and asymptotic variances which are biased downwards. Moreover, our specification includes as regressors time-invariant characteristics of firms (such as country of origin, for example); these characteristics would be perfectly collinear with the terms capturing the idiosyncratic features of firms in a fixed effects model. In this case we cannot employ a Hausman test to compare the fixed effects and random effects models because our model cannot be specified within a fixed effects setting.

These considerations advise the utilization of random-effects models. This is the approach followed, for example, by [35].

Finally, at this point we are searching for correlations among efficiency and different aspects of firm idiosyncrasies and management. Looking for causality relationships exceeds the scope of this paper and is left for future research.

We shall start by discussing the main qualitative implications of this exercise, for reasons which will be apparent below.

5.2. Qualitative Implications

5.2.1. Tobit Estimation

Typically, a Tobit model distinguishes between the latent or unobservable dependent variable and the observable dependent variable, where the observed variable is a censored version of the unobserved.

Equation (6) represents a random-effects Tobit specification for the second stage of our analysis:

$$\theta_{it}^* = x_{it}\beta + u_i + \varepsilon_{it} \tag{6}$$

$$\theta_{it} = 1 \quad if \ \theta_{it}^* \geq 1$$

$$\theta_{it} = \theta_{it}^* \quad if \ 0 \leq \theta_{it}^* \leq 1$$

$$\theta_{it} = 0 \quad if \ \theta_{it}^* \leq 0$$

$$i = 1, 2, \ldots, n.$$

$$t = 2010, 2011, \ldots, 2018$$

wre θ_{it}^* is the latent or unobservable efficiency, θ_{it} is the observable efficiency, x_{it} is a matrix of covariates, β is a vector of coefficients, u_i is the time invariant component of the error term, ε_{it} is the time-varying component of the error term, i indexes firms and t time.

In the estimation of Equation (6) we have included several indicators as covariates in order to capture different dimensions of firms, such as main activity, size, margins, financial management and personnel costs. We have also included time dummies to capture the impact of the business cycle and country dummies to allow for idiosyncratic aspects related to the markets where firms operate. The data are structured in a panel over the period 2010–2018 in order to exploit both the cross section and time variations.

Table 4 shows a first set of results obtained from the estimation by maximum likelihood of the model described by Equation (6). In order to avoid multicollinearity among the regressors, we have not included all covariates simultaneously; instead, we have added them sequentially, conforming different specifications of the baseline Equation (6). In other words, Equation (6) describes Models 1–4, the differences among them being the variables considered in x_{it} in each case.

To correct for heteroskedasticity, estimations have been performed with the observed information matrix (OIM) corrected standard errors. In this particular case, the variance-covariance matrix of the estimators is the matrix of second derivatives of the likelihood function. This correction for heteroskedasticity is robust to the violation of normality if distribution is symmetrical.

The last lines of Table 4 include the results from a Lagrange multiplier Breusch–Pagan likelihood ratio test of whether the variance of the time invariant component of the error term is equal to zero. This test is can be regarded as an indirect text of the appropriateness of the random effect model. The null hypothesis of equality to 0 of the variance of the u_i component of the error term is rejected at the 99% significance level for the four models, hence supporting the utilization of the random-effects model.

Dummies for countries capture different aspects: on the one hand, cultural and institutional aspects and managerial practices ([38]). On the other, regulatory and microeconomic and macroeconomics conditions of the particular markets where the firms operate. Regulatory aspects and institutional and macroeconomic conditions in the host country have been shown to impact the performance of multinational firms ([56,57]).

Dummies for the United Kingdom (UK), Italy and Sweden are positive and highly significant in all specifications, implying that the institutional framework in these countries, the size of their markets and/or their macroeconomic and institutional conditions affect the efficiency of firms positively. The dummy for Germany is also positive and significant in two specifications (models 2 and 4), although in one of them at a smaller significance level (90% in model 4).

Instead, the dummies for Spain and France display positive and negative signs and are not significant.

UK pharmaceutical firms feature a swift decision-making process which facilitates a successful and fast adjustment to changing market conditions ([58]). Moreover, the level of distortions in the UK economy is low and factor markets are relatively flexible. In addition, the dynamic biotechnological landscape of the country has allowed the surge of alliances and collaborations. These facts may explain the positive sign of the UK dummy.

German firms typically work in less-flexible environments than their British counterparts; their access to bank funding, though, is comparatively easy. Since sound finance is one important determinant of firms' success, as will be detailed below, the availability of funding seems quite relevant for the performance of companies in the sector and help explain the positive sign of the dummy.

The Italian industry is populated by highly skilled, agile firms, with a large component of exports and close ties to US companies. These companies encompass an important hub for foreign investment in the industry, which in turn enhances the productivity of local firms through technology diffusion and *learning by watching*.

Swedish pharmaceutical and biotechnological firms benefit from a market with limited regulation where bureaucracy is kept at a minimum, government support and a highly skilled workforce. These aspects would explain the successful performance of the Swedish pharmaceutical industry.

The positive signs of the country dummies, therefore, are in accordance with particular features of their institutional frameworks and/or industries.

These features, however, are not present in the French and Spanish cases. The French pharmaceutical market has historically been very protected by an outdated industrial policy. Spanish companies have been damaged by a rigid labor market and a low level of interaction between universities, research centers and firms.

We have also captured the main activity of the firms by means of dummies variables. The dummy *manufacturers* is equal to 1 for those firms whose main activity corresponds to NACE codes 2110 and 2120, and 0 otherwise. Conversely, the dummy *biotech* is 1 for firms included under the 7211 NACE code and 0 otherwise.

The dummy manufacturers are positively and significantly correlated with efficiency (columns 1 and 3), while biotech displays a negative and significant correlation in one model (column 2) and is not significant in the other (column 4). Overall, these findings are in accordance with those reported in Section 4 above, which suggest consistently higher levels of efficiency for firms engaged in the production and commercialization of pharmaceutical articles.

Dummies for size have been assigned according to the thresholds detailed in Section 4 above. Again, the results for the estimations agree with the trends reported in the previous Section. Firms characterized by large sizes, as conveyed by their levels of turnover, are more efficient than their counterparts, since the dummies huge and very big are positively and significantly correlated with efficiency (Models 1 and 4). The dummy that is quite big is positive but not significant.

The positive correlation between size and efficiency, however, holds only for the first two categories we defined, i.e., for sales larger than 426.92 million euros or the 95 percentile in the distribution. For companies with real turnover between 38.86 and 426.92 million euros results are inconclusive.

Those companies whose level of sales is less or equal than 38.86 million and more than 2.10 million euros register smaller efficiency figures *ceteris paribus*, since the dummies medium and small are negative and significant (column 2). Finally, we do not find a significant correlation between the dummy capturing the *very small* level of sales and efficiency (column 2). This is not surprising since firms with sales lower than the 25% percentile register poor levels of efficiency in some years but are capable of surpassing the figure attained by medium and small others.

The results for the dummy variables reflecting size and activity are thus consistent with those reported in the previous section. They are also in accord with [35], who disclose a negative correlation between size and efficiency for a sample of Indian pharmaceutical firms.

Let us turn to the discussion of the variables capturing other aspects of firms in the industry.

As portrayed by column 1 of Table 4, the profit margin is positively and significantly correlated, at the 99% significance level, with efficiency. This means that more efficient firms operate with higher margins. This result makes sense because the industry we are scrutinizing provides goods and services characterized by high added value which can be reflected in large margins. In fact, Reference [59] argues that deviations from trend in profit margins are highly correlated with expenditure in R&D for pharmaceutical companies, thus confirming the links between efficiency, margins and R&D.

Interestingly, this finding suggests that successful firm strategies in this sector are featured by both high margins and high intensity of resource utilizations, at the same time. It is common to see that companies tend to choose to focus either on the achievement of high profits per unit or in the optimization of the installed capacity. This dichotomy, however, is not present in the companies in the pharmaceutical industry, according to our results.

Table 4. Variables correlated with efficiency, Tobit estimations. Dependent variable is efficiency.

	Model 1	Model 2	Model 3	Model 4
profit_margin	0.1539 *** (7.00)			
Germany	0.0799 (1.38)	0.1178 ** (2.02)	0.0818 (1.49)	0.1045 * (1.89)
Spain	−0.0232 (0.44)	−0.0614 (1.10)	0.0305 (0.54)	0.0435 (0.87)
France	0.0100 (0.17)	0.0544 (0.94)	−0.0117 (0.21)	0.0167 (0.31)
Sweden	0.2977 *** (3.93)	0.2615 *** (3.44)	0.2389 *** (3.45)	0.3008 *** (4.13)
Italy	0.1421 *** (2.62)	0.1549 *** (2.85)	0.1587 *** (2.85)	0.1374 *** (2.79)
UK	0.1389 *** (3.62)	0.1637 *** (4.16)	0.1128 *** (2.88)	0.1356 *** (3.64)
Manufacturers	0.0660 ** (2.00)		0.1599 *** (4.96)	
Huge	0.2054 ** (2.49)			0.2393 *** (3.02)
Verybig	0.1276 *** (3.61)			0.1163 *** (3.24)
Quitebig	0.0215 (1.39)			0.0179 (1.09)
year2014	−0.0795 *** (6.90)	−0.0744 *** (6.37)	−0.0633 *** (5.88)	−0.0738 *** (6.16)
year2015	−0.1733 *** (4.97)	−0.0758 *** (4.69)	−0.0556 *** (5.31)	−0.1537 *** (4.35)
year2016	0.0373 *** (3.32)	0.0465 *** (4.12)	0.0439 *** (4.34)	0.0441 *** (3.79)

Table 4. *Cont.*

	Model 1	Model 2	Model 3	Model 4
cash_flow		0.1650 ***		
		(6.86)		
Biotech		−0.1384 ***		−0.0494
		(4.21)		(1.59)
Medium		−0.0300 *		
		(1.81)		
Small		−0.0614 ***		
		(3.22)		
Verysmall		−0.0069		
		(0.29)		
collection_period			−0.0226 ***	
			(4.44)	
employee_cost				−0.3739 ***
				(10.22)
_cons	0.2808 ***	0.3788 ***	0.2245 ***	0.4390 ***
	(7.95)	(12.50)	(6.37)	(15.49)
Likelihood Ratio test of $\sigma^2_u = 0$: $X^2(1)$	928.17 ***	980.9 ***	1505.81 ***	771.79 ***
Likelihood Ratio test of $\sigma^2_u = 0$: p value	0	0	0	0
Number observations	1547	1344	1850	1353

Notes: The table summarizes the results from the Tobit estimation of Equation (6). Dependent variable is efficiency computed in Stage 1. Cons stands for the intercept. For the rest of variables, see main text. Data are organized in a panel varying across firms and time over 2010–2018. In order to circumvent heteroskedasticity, estimations have been performed with corrected standard errors; the variance-covariance matrix of the estimators is the matrix of second derivatives of the likelihood function. LR test of $\sigma^2_u = 0$ distributed as $X^2(1)$. * $p < 0.1$; ** $p < 0.05$; *** $p < 0.01$.

The literature has documented that cash flow influences R&D expenditure in the case of the industry we are considering ([60]). Reference [61] provide some additional evidence since they find that, for the Spanish firms, the proportion of expenditure in R&D financed with internal resources is 75% for pharmaceuticals and 40% for the rest of the industries. Again, we are confronted with another differential feature of this industry. Whereas it is commonly accepted that firms should heavily rely on external funding and increase their profitability through financial leverage, the empirical evidence for this industry suggests that successful companies enjoy comparatively low ratios of indebtedness. This prudent financial structure is consistent with the high risk and long maturing period associated with the R&D activity.

To test this idea in our sample, we have included in the analysis some variables which capture particular elements of financial management. Column 2 shows that cashflow (as a percentage of sales) is indeed positively and significantly correlated with efficiency. The level of significance is very high, 99%.

Column 3, in turn, displays the estimation results when the variable collection period is included as a regressor in the baseline specification. The point estimate is negative and significant at the 99% level. Higher collection periods increase the amount of working capital necessary to run the daily activity of the firm, while shorter spans imply a sounder financial management. Our findings, therefore, are consistent with the literature, and stress the importance of exhibiting solid, well-financed balance sheets in order to register high levels of productivity. In more detail, Reference [35] argue that the low efficiency scores achieved by some firms in their sample is associated to their inability to access financial resources.

Column 4 includes a variable capturing the cost of labor, average cost per employee, as a percentage of sales. It is highly significant and negatively correlated with efficiency.

In terms of the validations of Models 1–4, and as stated above, the literature has shown that the Tobit model provides consistent estimates ([52–54,62]).

Moreover, it has been argued that the severity of the problem implied by the presence of heteroskedasticity in Tobit models is a function of the degree of censoring. In our case, censoring is limited, and affects only to 6–7% of the data.

Since the estimations have been performed with OIM corrected standard errors, they are robust to the presence of heteroskedasticity. These standard errors are also robust to the violation of normality if the distribution is symmetric.

Finally, and as detailed below, results from Tobit are quite similar to those obtained by random-effects models. All these considerations lend countenance to the models described in this subsection.

5.2.2. Classical Estimation

In order to assess the robustness of these findings we have performed two complementary analyses. First, we have considered a pure random-effects model, as described by Equation (7).

$$\theta_{it} = x_{it}\beta + u_i + \varepsilon_{it} \tag{7}$$

where θ_{it} is efficiency, x_{it} is a matrix of covariates, β is a vector of coefficients, u_i is the time invariant component of the error term, ε_{it} is the time-varying component of the error term, i indexes firms and t time.

The estimation has been carried out with robust standard errors, in the spirit of [63–65], clustered at the firm level. This procedure is widely recommended in the literature in these types of estimations ([66]).

Table 5 summarizes the specification and results for Models 5–8, estimated according to (7). We see that the main conclusions obtained from the Tobit specification regarding the correlation of efficiency with selected variables carry over to the classical, pure random effects specification. The only remarkable differences are related to the dummy for Spain, which is now negative and significant at the 95% level (Model 6), and the dummy quite big, now significant at the 90% level.

Furthermore, the point estimates of the coefficients are very similar in the censored and the non-censored model. These results are reassuring and consistent with [52,53], who document this kind of similarity when Tobit and ordinary least squares are employed in the second stage analysis.

The last two lines of Table 5 display the results from the Lagrange multiplier Breusch–Pagan test for the presence of random effects. The null hypothesis of no random effects is rejected at conventional levels.

In terms of the validation of Models 5–8, we can invoke the result according to which OLS produces unbiased and consistent estimates because of the central limit theorem for large enough samples. In addition, the literature has also shown the consistency of OLS second-stage estimators for the particular case of DEA analyses. Moreover, cluster robust standard errors yield estimates that are robust to the presence of heteroskedasticity and correlation in the error term.

Table 5. Variables correlated with efficiency, random effects estimations. Dependent variable is efficiency.

	Model 5	Model 6	Model 7	Model 8
profit_margin	0.1531 ***			
	(5.33)			
Germany	0.0702	0.1064 *	0.0740	0.0908 *
	(1.23)	(1.85)	(1.41)	(1.70)
Spain	−0.0210	−0.0598 **	0.0304	0.0427
	(0.55)	(2.04)	(0.66)	(0.87)
France	0.0093	0.0504	−0.0150	0.0128
	(0.19)	(1.08)	(0.32)	(0.28)
Sweden	0.2779 ***	0.2420 ***	0.2280 ***	0.2922 ***
	(3.07)	(3.23)	(3.32)	(3.78)

Table 5. *Cont.*

	Model 5	Model 6	Model 7	Model 8
Italy	0.1375 **	0.1488 ***	0.1529 ***	0.1336 ***
	(2.52)	(2.74)	(2.86)	(2.78)
UK	0.1340 ***	0.1538 ***	0.1041 **	0.1295 ***
	(3.44)	(3.91)	(2.51)	(3.70)
Manufacturers	0.0619 *		0.1534 ***	
	(1.93)		(4.81)	
Huge	0.1189 ***			0.1649 ***
	(2.63)			(3.72)
Verybig	0.1277 ***			0.1247 ***
	(4.28)			(4.06)
Quitebig	0.0233 *			0.0218
	(1.71)			(1.56)
year2014	−0.0778 ***	−0.0736 ***	−0.0625 ***	−0.0728 ***
	(8.64)	(7.67)	(7.14)	(7.90)
year2015	−0.1712 ***	−0.0792 ***	−0.0558 ***	−0.1596 ***
	(6.11)	(6.84)	(7.03)	(5.51)
year2016	0.0366 ***	0.0450 ***	0.0430 ***	0.0430 ***
	(4.09)	(4.52)	(4.78)	(4.46)
cash_flow		0.1661 ***		
		(5.83)		
Biotech		−0.1298 ***		−0.0421
		(4.42)		(1.44)
Medium		−0.0349 **		
		(2.48)		
Small		−0.0648 ***		
		(3.62)		
Verysmall		−0.0092		
		(0.33)		
collection_period			−0.0226 ***	
			(3.97)	
employee_cost				−0.3701 ***
				(7.83)
_cons	0.2786 ***	0.3767 ***	0.2257 ***	0.4312 ***
	(7.92)	(15.55)	(6.51)	(19.16)
LR test of $\sigma^2_u = 0$: $X^2(1)$	1306.01 ***	1656.88 ***	2561.80 ***	1156.37 ***
LR test of $\sigma^2_u = 0$: p value	0	0	0	0
Number of observations	1547	1344	1850	1353

Notes: The table summarizes the results from a pure Random-effects estimation of Equation (5). Dependent variable is efficiency computed in Stage 1. Cons stands for the intercept. For the rest of variables, see main text. Data are organized in a panel varying across firms and time over 2010–2018. Robust standard errors clustered at the firm level. LR test of $\sigma^2_u = 0$ distributed as $X^2(1)$. * $p < 0.1$; ** $p < 0.05$; *** $p < 0.01$.

5.2.3. Simar–Wilson Estimation

We have employed the [36] methodology as a further robustness test. Accordingly, we have replicated the estimations described above, this time employing their technique. These are Models 9–12, whose detailed specifications and results are displayed in Table 6.

Once again, we see that the basic findings obtained by the Tobit and classical random effects estimations regarding the sign and significance of covariates carry over when the [36] procedure, based upon a truncated distribution for the data and bootstrapping, is employed.

As reported above, this tool aims to remove the alleged bias in the estimation due to correlation among residuals. It computes new standard errors and corrected parameters. In contrast to the Tobit and classical frameworks, the literature has not provided enough evidence yet to illustrate the properties of this estimator.

Table 6. Variables correlated with efficiency, Simar–Wilson estimations. Dependent variable is efficiency.

	Model 9	Model 10	Model 11	Model 12
profit_margin	0.3089 ***			
	(9.31)			
Germany	0.1287 ***	0.1562 ***	0.1405 ***	0.1204 ***
	(4.43)	(4.93)	(3.64)	(4.09)
Spain	−0.0356	−0.0971 ***	−0.0098	0.0053
	(1.36)	(3.25)	(0.24)	(0.20)
France	0.0342	0.0684 *	−0.1606 ***	−0.0364
	(0.92)	(1.72)	(3.06)	(0.97)
Sweden	0.2958 ***	0.2602 ***	0.3352 ***	0.3539 ***
	(8.04)	(6.04)	(7.06)	(8.41)
Italy	0.1548 ***	0.1539 ***	0.2307 ***	0.1506 ***
	(6.13)	(5.67)	(6.41)	(5.99)
UK	0.1439 ***	0.1596 ***	0.1370 ***	0.1396 ***
	(6.89)	(7.33)	(4.97)	(6.81)
Manufacturers	0.0859 ***		0.3157 ***	
	(4.54)		(10.51)	
Huge	0.7812 **			0.8741 **
	(2.06)			(2.45)
Verybig	0.4284 ***			0.3849 ***
	(9.48)			(8.47)
Quitebig	0.0552 ***			0.0678 ***
	(2.98)			(3.63)
year2014	−0.0994 ***	−0.1072 ***	−0.0982 ***	−0.0977 ***
	(4.20)	(4.16)	(2.80)	(3.77)
year2015	−0.4586 ***	−0.1540 ***	−0.1161 ***	−0.4179 ***
	(9.43)	(5.15)	(3.40)	(8.48)
year2016	0.0652 ***	0.0651 ***	0.0902 ***	0.0785 ***
	(3.04)	(2.76)	(3.07)	(3.66)
cash_flow		0.3351 ***		
		(8.31)		
Biotech		−0.1790 ***		−0.0229
		(8.07)		(1.15)
Medium		−0.1294 ***		
		(6.36)		
Small		−0.1091 ***		
		(4.63)		
Verysmall		0.0192		
		(0.60)		
collection_period			−0.0568 ***	
			(4.11)	
employee_cost				−0.6340 ***
				(10.95)
_cons	0.1328 ***	0.3237 ***	−0.0524	0.3822 ***
	(6.01)	(15.50)	(1.24)	(20.23)
Number of observations	1446	1257	1741	1264

Notes: The table summarizes the results from the Simar–Wilson estimation of Equation (5). Dependent variable in the estimations is efficiency. Data are set in a panel varying across firms and time. * $p < 0.1$; ** $p < 0.05$; *** $p < 0.01$.

5.3. Quantitative Implications

From the comparisons of Tables 4–6 we observe that Tobit and pure random-effects models yield point estimates which are rather similar. Instead, estimates obtained by the Simar–Wilson methodology are larger.

In contrast to what happens in the classical regression model, the marginal effect or impact of the individual regressor x_j on the dependent variable, defined as:

$$\frac{\partial \theta}{\partial x_j}$$

is not directly measured by the point estimates of regressions estimated by Tobit or Simar–Wilson methodologies, since they are non-linear models.

In order to extract more quantitative implications of the different estimations described in Section 5.2 above, we have computed the marginal effects of selected variables on efficiency implied by these two methods.

Basic results are displayed in Table 7. In order to facilitate comparisons, we have added the point estimates obtained by the pure random-effects estimation.

The variable exerting the highest impact on efficiency is employee cost. According to our results, an increase of one unit in the employee cost reduces efficiency in an amount which is comprised in the interval (0.368, 0.42).

If the profit margin rises in one unit, the correspondent increase in efficiency is around 0.15–0.2. The improvement of the financial position (as captured by cash flow/income) in one unit brings about a positive change in efficiency of 0.162–0.218. Finally, the increase of the collection period in one unit reduces efficiency around 0.02.

In our view, these findings have some interesting economic implications and may be useful for managers, owners and other stakeholders of firms in the industry. The efforts to contain personnel costs and increase margins translate directly into higher levels of productivity. Firms in the industry should also strive to achieve an adequate combination of external and internal finance, aligned with the risky and slow-paced nature of R&D activities.

There are implications for policymakers and policy analysts as well. Efficiency in the pharmaceutical sector, according to the empirical evidence presented here, hinges on the sound functioning of labor markets and financial markets. Measures to improve their behavior may have a noticeable impact on the performance of the firms in the industry.

It is apparent from Table 7 that the marginal effects obtained by the Tobit and the classical specifications are remarkably close, whereas those yielded by the Simar–Wilson procedure are slightly larger. It is important to notice that the difference among the Tobit/pure random effects results, on the one hand, and the Simar–Wilson, on the other, is smaller regarding the marginal effects (Table 7) that if we compare the point estimates (Tables 4–6).

This fact has several interesting implications:

- As far the particular goal of this subsection is concerned, the Simar–Wilson tool implies marginal effects slightly larger (about 15–35%) but of the same order of magnitude than those obtained from Tobit/pure random-effects model.
- In general terms, more research at the theoretical level and probably Monte Carlo simulations are necessary to know in more detail the properties of the Simar–Wilson estimator. This exceeds the scope of this paper.
- The Simar–Wilson procedure may be useful for applied research, especially in conjunction with other methodologies, although it has a higher cost in computing time if compared with Tobit or classical models.

Table 7. Comparison of marginal effects, Tobit, Simar–Wilson and random effects estimations.

Variable	Tobit	Simar–Wilson	Random Effects
Profit margin	0.1511	0.2053	0.1531
Cash flow/income	0.1628	0.2189	0.1661
Collection period	−0.0223	−0.026	−0.0226
Employee cost	−0.3683	−0.4215	−0.3701

Notes: The table details the marginal effects on efficiency levels of each one of the variables displayed in the first column. These marginal effects have been recovered from the Tobit (Models 1–4) and the Simar–Wilson (Models 9–12) estimations. The last column displays the marginal effects obtained in the pure random-effects models (Models 5–8) to facilitate the comparison; since this framework is linear, the marginal effects coincide with the point estimates of the variables as reported in Table 5.

6. Concluding Remarks

The pharmaceutical industry has experienced deep changes in the last few decades. The cost of R&D has soared while market conditions have become tougher. Companies have confronted these challenges by different strategies such as mergers, acquisitions, outsourcing and alliances. It remains an open question whether these transformations have brought about an increase in the efficiency of the firms that make up the industry.

We examine this issue employing disaggregated microdata from a large sample of European medium and large firms belonging to the pharmaceutical and biotechnological industry. In the first stage of our research, we perform a non-parametric DEA analysis of efficiency over the period 2010–2018. In the second stage we analyze which potential features of the environmental framework and management are correlated with efficiency by regression techniques.

The consideration of a large sample of European firms, disaggregating by main activity and isolating the performance of biotechnological firms is a novel feature of this paper. The comparison of the results provided by the Tobit, classical and Simar–Wilson frameworks for the second stage is also a contribution of the investigation presented here.

The main insights from our analysis are the following:

- The average level of efficiency in the industry is moderate, 0.341. This figure is not far from results obtained by other studies for alternative samples. Efficiency exhibits a decreasing trend over the years 2010–2018.
- Efficiency levels display a large level of heterogeneity when particular dimensions of companies are considered. Efficiency is higher for those companies whose main activity is manufacturing of pharmaceutical products than for firms focused on R&D activities. This result may be traced to the relative youth of R&D firms, which cannot fully exploit the learning curve yet. The specialization of this kind of firms in a few projects, characterized by low rates of success, may also be a relevant factor in this respect.
- We find a complex relationship between size and efficiency. By and large, bigger firms are more efficient, but only beyond the threshold of 426.92 million euros of turnover per year. Medium-size and small firms register the poorest levels of efficiency, whereas very small firms perform slightly better. This suggests that firms may benefit from either scale economies or high levels of specialization, while the middle ground does not yield good results.
- Our findings suggest that sound financial structures, lower employee costs and higher margins are correlated with higher levels of efficiency. Moreover, the idiosyncratic aspects of the country of origin of the firms may foster or jeopardize productivity.

Our results convey some messages for policymakers. The survival and buoyancy of companies in the pharmaceutical industry seems closely linked to the sound functioning of the labor and capital markets. The experience of selected countries, in particular the UK, suggests as well that the existence of agile, dynamic biotechnological firms is beneficial for the whole sector.

Finally, the higher levels of efficiency obtained for larger firms suggest that mergers and acquisitions may enhance the performance of pharmaceutical companies due to the influence of scale economies. These financial transactions should not be discouraged or jeopardized by policymakers on the basis of an allegedly anti-competitive strategy. It is important to keep in mind that the pharmaceutical and biotechnological industry relies heavily on R&D, and that R&D is only feasible for firms if their size is big enough.

We have also found that very small firms display a sounder behavior than medium size companies. The link between size and performance for the sector is thus nuanced. This suggests that industrial policies intending to enhance the sector should be horizontal rather than vertical: instead of featuring active interventions in favor of a particular firm size, it is better to adopt a less activist stance since it is hard to determine on an a priori basis which is the efficient scale of operations.

Our investigation has several limits. The time horizon is relatively short; it would be convenient to increase it whenever new data are available. We have computed efficiency scores in Stage 1 only by a non-parametric technique, DEA; another computation by means of parametric SFA would be useful to check whether efficiency scores are very sensible to the tool employed.

In stage 2 we have investigated the correlations among efficiency scores and other variables, but we have not explored the direction of causality among them. This last issue could be addressed by introducing lags and leads of the variables and/or employing other econometric techniques, such as general methods of moment or instrumental variables.

One of the techniques we have employed in Stage 2 is the Simar–Wilson estimation. It seems to be useful in applied work, especially in combination with other techniques. More evidence about its performance would be convenient, nonetheless.

Finally, and although country dummies have provided useful information about the potential impact of institutional and economic aspects on efficiency, they are ultimately dummies or *the measure of our ignorance*; it would be interesting to go one step further and characterize the specific features of the various countries which enhance or jeopardize efficiency. This could be done by introducing macroeconomic and institutional variables in the Stage 2 models.

These limitations suggest promising directions for new research.

Author Contributions: Conceptualization, R.F.D. and B.S.-R.; Methodology, B.S.-R.; Formal Analysis, R.F.D. and B.S.-R.; Data Curation, R.F.D. and B.S.-R.; Writing—Original Draft Preparation, R.F.D. and B.S.-R.; Writing-Review and Editing, R.F.D. and B.S.-R.; Supervision: B.S.-R. Both authors have read and agreed to the published version of the manuscript. All authors have read and agreed to the published version of the manuscript.

Acknowledgments: We are very grateful to José María Labeaga, Teresa Herrador and three anonymous referees for helpful suggestions and comments.

Appendix A

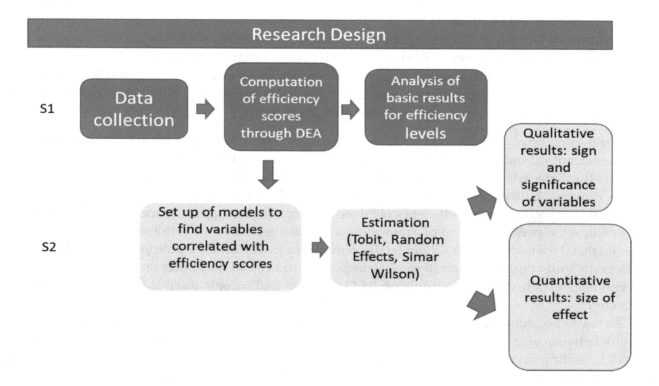

Figure A1. Explanatory diagram of our research design (S1 and S2 are Stage 1 and Stage 2).

Appendix B

Table A1. Variables definition and sources.

Variable	Description	Source
OPRE—Operating Revenue (Turnover)	Total Operating Revenues (Net Sales + Other Operating Revenues + Stock Variations)	Amadeus
TOAS—Total Assets	Total Assets (Fixed Assets + Current Assets)	Amadeus
PRMA—Profit Margin (%)	(Profit Before Tax/Operating Revenue) * 100	Amadeus
EMPL—Number of Employees	Total Number of Employees included in the Company's payroll	Amadeus
CFOP—Cash Flow/Operating Revenue (%)	(Cash Flow/Operating Revenue) * 100	Amadeus
SCT—Cost of Employees/Operating Revenue (%)	(Cost of Employees/Operating Revenue) * 100	Amadeus
COLL—Collection Period (days)	(Debtors/Operating Revenue) * 360	Amadeus
Yearly deflator	Computed from the Harmonized European Index	Eurostat

References

1. Lucas, R.E. On the mechanics of economic growth. *J. Monet. Econ.* **1988**, *22*, 3–42. [CrossRef]
2. Romer, P.M. Increasing Returns and Long-Run Growth. *J. Political Econ.* **1986**, *94*, 1002–1037. [CrossRef]
3. Romer, P.M. Endogenous Technological Change. *J. Political Econ.* **1990**, *98*, S71–S102. [CrossRef]
4. Pammolli, F.; Magazzini, L.; Riccaboni, M. The productivity crisis in pharmaceutical R&D. *Nat. Rev. Drug Discov.* **2011**, *10*, 428–438. [CrossRef] [PubMed]
5. Shimura, H.; Masuda, S.; Kimura, H. A lesson from Japan: Research and development efficiency is a key element of pharmaceutical industry consolidation process. *Drug Discov. Ther.* **2014**, *8*, 57–63. [CrossRef] [PubMed]
6. Shin, K.; Lee, D.; Shin, K.; Kim, E. Measuring the Efficiency of U.S. Pharmaceutical Companies Based on Open Innovation Types. *J. Open Innov. Technol. Mark. Complex.* **2018**, *4*, 34. [CrossRef]
7. Rafols, I.; Hoekman, J.; Siepel, J.; Nightingale, P.; Hopkins, M.M.; O'Hare, A.; Perianes-Rodriguez, A. Big Pharma, Little Science? A Bibliometric Perspective on Big Pharma's R&D Decline. *SSRN Electron. J.* **2012**, *81*, 22–38. [CrossRef]
8. Gascón, F.; Lozano, J.; Ponte, B.; De La Fuente, D. Measuring the efficiency of large pharmaceutical companies: An industry analysis. *Eur. J. Health Econ.* **2016**, *18*, 587–608. [CrossRef]
9. Jiang, H.; He, Y. Applying Data Envelopment Analysis in Measuring the Efficiency of Chinese Listed Banks in the Context of Macroprudential Framework. *Mathematics* **2018**, *6*, 184. [CrossRef]
10. Kumbhakar, S.C.; Lien, G.; Hardaker, J.B. Technical efficiency in competing panel data models: A study of Norwegian grain farming. *J. Prod. Anal.* **2012**, *41*, 321–337. [CrossRef]
11. Wang, C.-N.; Nguyen, M.N.; Le, A.L.; Tibo, H. A DEA Resampling Past-Present-Future Comparative Analysis of the Food and Beverage Industry: The Case Study on Thailand vs. Vietnam. *Mathematics* **2020**, *8*, 1140. [CrossRef]
12. Chen, C.F.; Soo, K.T. Some university students are more equal than others: Efficiency evidence from England. *Econ. Bull.* **2010**, *30*, 2697–2708.
13. Lozano, S.; Gutiérrez, E. A slacks-based network DEA efficiency analysis of European airlines. *Transp. Plan. Technol.* **2014**, *37*, 623–637. [CrossRef]

14. Lin, B.-H.; Lee, H.-S.; Chung, C.-C. The Construction and Implication of Group Scale Efficiency Evaluation Model for Bulk Shipping Corporations. *Mathematics* **2020**, *8*, 702. [CrossRef]

15. Zhou, Z.; Jin, Q.; Peng, J.; Xiao, H.; Wu, S. Further Study of the DEA-Based Framework for Performance Evaluation of Competing Crude Oil Prices' Volatility Forecasting Models. *Mathematics* **2019**, *7*, 827. [CrossRef]

16. Kuosmanen, T.; Saastamoinen, A.; Sipiläinen, T. What is the best practice for benchmark regulation of electricity distribution? Comparison of DEA, SFA and StoNED methods. *Energy Policy* **2013**, *61*, 740–750. [CrossRef]

17. Cherchye, L.; De Rock, B.; Walheer, B. Multi-output efficiency with good and bad outputs. *Eur. J. Oper. Res.* **2015**, *240*, 872–881. [CrossRef]

18. Orea, L.; Llorca, M.; Filippini, M. A new approach to measuring the rebound effect associated to energy efficiency improvements: An application to the US residential energy demand. *Energy Econ.* **2015**, *49*, 599–609. [CrossRef]

19. Alarenan, S.; Gasim, A.A.; Hunt, L.C.; Muhsen, A.R. Measuring underlying energy efficiency in the GCC countries using a newly constructed dataset. *Energy Transit.* **2019**, *3*, 31–44. [CrossRef]

20. Ahn, H.; Afsharian, M.; Emrouznejad, A.; Banker, R.D. Recent developments on the use of DEA in the public sector. *Socio-Econ. Plan. Sci.* **2018**, *61*, 1–3. [CrossRef]

21. Sueyoshi, T.; Yuan, Y.; Goto, M. A literature study for DEA applied to energy and environment. *Energy Econ.* **2017**, *62*, 104–124. [CrossRef]

22. Odeck, J.; Bråthen, S. A meta-analysis of DEA and SFA studies of the technical efficiency of seaports: A comparison of fixed and random-effects regression models. *Transp. Res. Part A Policy Pract.* **2012**, *46*, 1574–1585. [CrossRef]

23. Fall, F.; Akim, A.-M.; Wassongma, H. DEA and SFA research on the efficiency of microfinance institutions: A meta-analysis. *World Dev.* **2018**, *107*, 176–188. [CrossRef]

24. Marchetti, D.; Wanke, P.F. Efficiency in rail transport: Evaluation of the main drivers through meta-analysis with resampling. *Transp. Res. Part A Policy Pract.* **2019**, *120*, 83–100. [CrossRef]

25. Emrouznejad, A.; Yang, G.-L. A survey and analysis of the first 40 years of scholarly literature in DEA: 1978–2016. *Socio-Econ. Plan. Sci.* **2018**, *61*, 4–8. [CrossRef]

26. Emrouznejad, A.; Thanassoulis, E. A mathematical model for dynamic efficiency using data envelopment analysis. *Appl. Math. Comput.* **2005**, *160*, 363–378. [CrossRef]

27. Hu, X.-Y.; Li, J.; Li, X.; Cui, J. A Revised Inverse Data Envelopment Analysis Model Based on Radial Models. *Mathematics* **2020**, *8*, 803. [CrossRef]

28. Wei, G.-W.; Wang, J. A comparative study of robust efficiency analysis and Data Envelopment Analysis with imprecise data. *Expert Syst. Appl.* **2017**, *81*, 28–38. [CrossRef]

29. Khezrimotlagh, D.; Zhu, J.; Cook, W.D.; Toloo, M. Data envelopment analysis and big data. *Eur. J. Oper. Res.* **2019**, *274*, 1047–1054. [CrossRef]

30. You, T.; Chen, X.; Holder, M.E. Efficiency and its determinants in pharmaceutical industries: Ownership, R&D and scale economy. *Appl. Econ.* **2010**, *42*, 2217–2241. [CrossRef]

31. Mao, Y.; Li, J.; Liu, Y. Evaluating business performance of China's pharmaceutical companies based on data envelopment analysis. *Stud. Ethno-Med.* **2014**, *8*, 51–60. [CrossRef]

32. Sueyoshi, T.; Goto, M. DEA radial measurement for environmental assessment: A comparative study between Japanese chemical and pharmaceutical firms. *Appl. Energy* **2014**, *115*, 502–513. [CrossRef]

33. Hashimoto, A.; Haneda, S. Measuring the change in R&D efficiency of the Japanese pharmaceutical industry. *Res. Policy* **2008**, *37*, 1829–1836. [CrossRef]

34. Al-Refaie, A.; Wu, C.-W.; Sawalheh, M. DEA window analysis for assessing efficiency of blistering process in a pharmaceutical industry. *Neural Comput. Appl.* **2018**, *31*, 3703–3717. [CrossRef]

35. Mazumdar, M.; Rajeev, M.; Ray, S.C. *Output and Input Efficiency of Manufacturing Firms in India: A Case of the Indian Pharmaceutical Sector*; Institute for Social and Economic Change: Bangalore, India, 2009.

36. Simar, L.; Wilson, P.W. Estimation and inference in two-stage, semi-parametric models of production processes. *J. Econ.* **2007**, *136*, 31–64. [CrossRef]

37. Bloom, N.; Lemos, R.; Sadun, R.; Scur, D.; Van Reenen, J. International Data on Measuring Management Practices. *Am. Econ. Rev.* **2016**, *106*, 152–156. [CrossRef]

38. Bénabou, R.; Tirole, J. Mindful Economics: The Production, Consumption, and Value of Beliefs. *J. Econ. Perspect.* **2016**, *30*, 141–164. [CrossRef]

39. Aigner, D.; Lovell, C.; Schmidt, P. Formulation and estimation of stochastic frontier production function models. *J. Econ.* **1977**, *6*, 21–37. [CrossRef]

40. Meeusen, W.; Broeck, J.V.D. Efficiency Estimation from Cobb-Douglas Production Functions with Composed Error. *Int. Econ. Rev.* **1977**, *18*, 435. [CrossRef]

41. Kumbhakar, S.C.; Parmeter, C.F.; Zelenyuk, V. Stochastic frontier analysis: Foundations and advances. In *Handbook of Production Economics*; Springer: New York, NY, USA, 2017.

42. Charnes, A.; Cooper, W.; Rhodes, E. Measuring the efficiency of decision making units. *Eur. J. Oper. Res.* **1978**, *2*, 429–444. [CrossRef]

43. Banker, R.D.; Charnes, A.; Cooper, W.W. Some Models for Estimating Technical and Scale Inefficiencies in Data Envelopment Analysis. *Manag. Sci.* **1984**, *30*, 1078–1092. [CrossRef]

44. Van Dijk, B. *Amadeus Database*; Bureau van Dijk Electronic Publishing: Brussels, Belgium, 2020.

45. Eurostat. Available online: https://appsso.eurostat.ec.europa.eu/nui/show.do?dataset=prc_hicp_aind&lang=en (accessed on 5 May 2020).

46. Henderson, R.; Cockburn, I. Scale, Scope and Spillovers: The Determinants of Research Productivity in the Pharmaceutical Industry. *RAND J. Econ.* **1993**, *27*, 32–59. [CrossRef]

47. Cockburn, I.; Henderson, R.M. Scale and scope in drug development: Unpacking the advantages of size in pharmaceutical research. *J. Health Econ.* **2001**, *20*, 1033–1057. [CrossRef]

48. Danzon, P.M.; Nicholson, S.; Pereira, N.S. Productivity in pharmaceutical-biotechnology R&D: The role of experience and alliances. *J. Health Econ.* **2005**, *24*, 317–339. [CrossRef] [PubMed]

49. Arrow, K.J. The Economic Implications of Learning by Doing. *Rev. Econ. Stud.* **1962**, *29*, 155. [CrossRef]

50. Hay, M.; Thomas, D.W.; Craighead, J.L.; Economides, C.; Rosenthal, J. Clinical development success rates for investigational drugs. *Nat. Biotechnol.* **2014**, *32*, 40–51. [CrossRef]

51. Bravo-Ureta, B.E.; Solís, D.; López, V.H.M.; Maripani, J.F.; Thiam, A.; Rivas, T. Technical efficiency in farming: A meta-regression analysis. *J. Prod. Anal.* **2006**, *27*, 57–72. [CrossRef]

52. Hoff, A. Second stage DEA: Comparison of approaches for modelling the DEA score. *Eur. J. Oper. Res.* **2007**, *181*, 425–435. [CrossRef]

53. McDonald, J. Using least squares and tobit in second stage DEA efficiency analyses. *Eur. J. Oper. Res.* **2009**, *197*, 792–798. [CrossRef]

54. Banker, R.D.; Natarajan, R. Evaluating Contextual Variables Affecting Productivity Using Data Envelopment Analysis. *Oper. Res.* **2008**, *56*, 48–58. [CrossRef]

55. Greene, W. The behaviour of the maximum likelihood estimator of limited dependent variable models in the presence of fixed effects. *Econ. J.* **2004**, *7*, 98–119. [CrossRef]

56. Bengoa, M.; Sanchez-Robles, B. Policy shocks as a source of endogenous growth. *J. Policy Model.* **2005**, *27*, 249–261. [CrossRef]

57. Bengoa-Calvo, M.; Sanchez-Robles, B.; Shachmurove, Y. Back to BITs and Bites: Do Trade and Investment Agreements Promote Foreign Direct Investment within Latin America? *SSRN Electron. J.* **2017**, 3083980. [CrossRef]

58. Casper, S.; Matraves, C. Institutional frameworks and innovation in the German and UK pharmaceutical industry. *Res. Policy* **2003**, *32*, 1865–1879. [CrossRef]

59. Scherer, F.; Kleinke, J. The Link Between Gross Profitability and Pharmaceutical R&D Spending. *Health Aff.* **2001**, *20*, 216–220. [CrossRef]

60. Lakdawalla, D.N. Economics of the Pharmaceutical Industry. *J. Econ. Lit.* **2018**, *56*, 397–449. [CrossRef]

61. Mondrego, A.; Barge-Gil, A. La I+D en el sector farmacéutico español en el periodo 2003–2015. *Pap. Econ. Esp.* **2019**, *160*, 76–93.

62. Greene, W.H. *Econometric Analysis Fifth Edition*; Prentice Hall: New York, NY, USA, 2003.

63. Eicker, F. Limit theorems for regressions with unequal and dependent errors. In Proceedings of the Fifth Berkeley Symposium on Mathematical Statistics and Probability, Davis, CA, USA, 21 June–18 July 1965.

64. Huber, P.J. The behavior of maximum likelihood estimates under nonstandard conditions. In Proceedings of the Fifth Berkeley Symposium on Mathematical Statistics and Probability, Davis, CA, USA, 21 June–18 July 1965; pp. 221–233.

65. White, H. A Heteroskedasticity-Consistent Covariance Matrix Estimator and a Direct Test for Heteroskedasticity. *Econometrica* **1980**, *48*, 817. [CrossRef]
66. Stock, J.; Watson, M. Heteroskedasticity-Robust Standard Errors for Fixed Effects Panel Data Regression. *NBER Tech. Work. Pap.* **2006**, *323*. [CrossRef]

Permissions

The contributors of this book come from diverse backgrounds, making this book a truly international effort. This book will bring forth new frontiers with its revolutionizing research information and detailed analysis of the nascent developments around the world.

We would like to thank all the contributing authors for lending their expertise to make the book truly unique. They have played a crucial role in the development of this book. Without their invaluable contributions this book wouldn't have been possible. They have made vital efforts to compile up to date information on the varied aspects of this subject to make this book a valuable addition to the collection of many professionals and students.

This book was conceptualized with the vision of imparting up-to-date information and advanced data in this field. To ensure the same, a matchless editorial board was set up. Every individual on the board went through rigorous rounds of assessment to prove their worth. After which they invested a large part of their time researching and compiling the most relevant data for our readers.

The editorial board has been involved in producing this book since its inception. They have spent rigorous hours researching and exploring the diverse topics which have resulted in the successful publishing of this book. They have passed on their knowledge of decades through this book. To expedite this challenging task, the publisher supported the team at every step. A small team of assistant editors was also appointed to further simplify the editing procedure and attain best results for the readers.

Apart from the editorial board, the designing team has also invested a significant amount of their time in understanding the subject and creating the most relevant covers. They scrutinized every image to scout for the most suitable representation of the subject and create an appropriate cover for the book.

The publishing team has been an ardent support to the editorial, designing and production team. Their endless efforts to recruit the best for this project, has resulted in the accomplishment of this book. They are a veteran in the field of academics and their pool of knowledge is as vast as their experience in printing. Their expertise and guidance has proved useful at every step. Their uncompromising quality standards have made this book an exceptional effort. Their encouragement from time to time has been an inspiration for everyone.

The publisher and the editorial board hope that this book will prove to be a valuable piece of knowledge for researchers, students, practitioners and scholars across the globe.

List of Contributors

Kehinde Damilola Ilesanmi and Devi Datt Tewari
Department of Economics, Faculty of Commerce, Administration and Law, University of Zululand, Private Bag X1001, KwaDlangezwa 3886, South Africa

Van-Dai Ta, Chuan-Ming Liu and Direselign Addis Tadesse
Department of Computer Science and Information Engineering, National Taipei University of Technology, Taipei 106, Taiwan

Yu-Sheng Kao and Kazumitsu Nawata
Department of Technology Management for Innovation, The University of Tokyo, 7-3-1 Hongo, Bunkyo-ku, Tokyo 113-8656, Japan

Chi-Yo Huang
Department of Industrial Education, National Taiwan Normal University, Taipei 106, Taiwan

Dawen Yan
School of Mathematical Sciences, Dalian University of Technology, Dalian 116024, China

Guotai Chi
School of Economics and Management, Dalian University of Technology, Dalian 116024, China

Kin Keung Lai
College of Economics, Shenzhen University, Shenzhen 518060, China

Andrés García-Mirantes
IES Juan del Enzina, 24001 Leon, Spain

Beatriz Larraz
Statistics Department/Faculty of Law and Social Sciences, Universidad de Castilla-La Mancha, 45071 Toledo, Spain

Javier Población
Banco de España, 28014 Madrid, Spain

Ana María Sánchez Pérez
Departamento de Economía y Empresa, Universidad de Almería, La Cañada de San Urbano, s/n, 04120 Almería, Spain

Muhammad Asif Khan
Faculty of Management Sciences, University of Kotli, Azad Jammu and Kashmir, Kotli 11100, Pakistan

Masood Ahmed
Faculty of Management Sciences, University of Kotli, Azad Jammu and Kashmir, Kotli 11100, Pakistan
Lee Kuan Yew School of Public Policy, National University of Singapore, Kent Ridge, 469C Bukit Timah Road, Singapore 259772, Singapore

József Popp
Faculty of Economics and Social Sciences, Szent István University, 2100 Gödölő, Hungary
TRADE Research Entity, Faculty of Economic and Management Sciences, North-West University, Vanderbijlpark 1900, South Africa

Judit Oláh
TRADE Research Entity, Faculty of Economic and Management Sciences, North-West University, Vanderbijlpark 1900, South Africa
Faculty of Economics and Business, University of Debrecen, 4032 Debrecen, Hungary

Venelina Nikolova and Juan E. Trinidad Segovia
Department of Accounting and Finance, Faculty of Economics and Business, Universidad de Almería, 04120 Almería, Spain

Manuel Fernández-Martínez
University Centre of Defence at the Spanish Air Force Academy, MDE-UPCT, 30720 Santiago de la Ribera, Región de Murcia, Spain

Miguel Angel Sánchez-Granero
Department of Mathematics, Faculty of Science, Universidad de Almería, 04120 Almería, Spain

Elena Druică, Rodica Ianole-Călin and Răzvan Mihail-Papuc
Faculty of Business and Administration, University of Bucharest, 030018 Bucharest, Romania

Călin Vâlsan
Williams School of Business, Bishop's University, Sherbrooke, QC J1M1Z7, Canada

Irena Munteanu
Faculty of Economic Sciences, Ovidius University, 900470 Constanta, Romania

Pedro Antonio Martín Cervantes, Salvador Cruz Rambaud and María del Carmen Valls Martínez
Department of Economics and Business, University of Almería, La Cañada de San Urbano, 04120 Almería, Spain

Salvador Cruz Rambaud
Departamento de Economía y Empresa, Universidad de Almería, La Cañada de San Urbano, s/n, 04120 Almería, Spain

Blas Torrecillas Jover
Departamento de Matemáticas, Universidad de Almería, La Cañada de San Urbano, s/n, 04120 Almería, Spain

Ricardo F. Díaz and Blanca Sanchez-Robles
Department of Economic Analysis, Facultad CC Económicas y Empresariales, UNED, Senda del Rey 11, 28040 Madrid, Spain

Index

Printed in the USA
CPSIA information can be obtained
at www.ICGtesting.com
JSHW051403091023
49903JS00006B/251